THE AMERICAN INDIAN

Past and Present

THE AMERICAN INDIAN

Past and Present

FOURTH EDITION

Edited by
Roger L. Nichols
University of Arizona

McGraw-Hill, Inc.

New York   St. Louis   San Francisco   Auckland   Bogotá   Caracas
Lisbon   London   Madrid   Mexico   Milan   Montreal   New Delhi
Paris   San Juan   Singapore   Sydney   Tokyo   Toronto

The American Indian: Past and Present

Copyright © 1992, 1986 by McGraw-Hill, Inc. All rights reserved. Printed in the United States of America. Except as permitted under the United States Copyright Act of 1976, no part of this publication may be reproduced or distributed in any form or by any means, or stored in a data base or retrieval system, without the prior written permission of the publisher.

2 3 4 5 6 7 8 9 0 DOC DOC 9 0 9 8 7 6 5 4 3 2

ISBN 0-07-046499-5

This book was set in Plantin by Carlisle Communications, Ltd.
The editor was David Follmer;
the production supervisor was Richard A. Ausburn.
The cover was designed by Wanda Siedlecka.
Project supervision was done by Carlisle Publishers Services.
R. R. Donnelley & Sons Company was printer and binder.

Library of Congress Cataloging-in-Publication Data

The American Indian: past and present / edited by Roger L. Nichols. — 4th ed.
     p.   cm.
Includes bibliographical references and index.
ISBN 0-07-046499-5
1. Indians of North America.   I. Nichols, Roger L.
E77.2.A47   1992
973.04'97 — dc20   91-27133

ABOUT THE EDITOR

ROGER L. NICHOLS, a Wisconsin native, received his Ph.D. in American history from the University of Wisconsin. He has taught at Wisconsin State University, the University of Georgia, the University of Maryland, and, since 1969, at the University of Arizona. Currently a professor of history, he teaches courses in frontier America, Western America, and the Indians in American history. In addition to earlier editions of *The American Indian,* he has written or edited five other books: *General Henry Atkinson, The Missouri Expedition, Natives and Strangers, Stephen Long and American Frontier Exploration,* and *American Frontier and Western Issues.* He has written articles, chapters in multi-authored books, and essays on frontier towns, Western literature, transportation, the army, and Indian affairs. Nichols is married and has four children.

For Sarah E. Nichols

CONTENTS

ix

PREFACE

During the past fifteen years the American public has paid increasingly less attention to minority affairs. Throughout President Reagan's two terms the Republican administration set out to reshape the scope and operations of the federal government. They sought to reduce federal social actions, slowed civil rights enforcement, and brought fundamental alterations in governmental relations with the citizens, often through inaction. As a result, minority programs of many kinds shrank. This shift in emphasis resulted from the perception many people in and out of government held that the social and economic efforts of the 1960s and 1970s had failed. Opinion polls reflected that idea and indicated that the public felt that despite the billions of dollars being spent on a variety of federal activities, the results were disappointing. This meant that after a generation of turmoil and much reform activity, the voters seemed ready to accept the idea that less was better—at least as far as the government and minority groups were concerned.

Despite the lessening of interest in Native Americans and issues pertaining to them, their position in the general society and many of their basic social and economic problems continued. Often some of the government programs that aimed at improving living conditions, increasing job opportunities, or making educational benefits available still fail to consider tribal customs or ignore established community leadership. The notion that whites still know what is best for Indian people remains deeply entrenched. Nevertheless, studies by congressional committees, foundations, or independent scholars continue to report that the social and economic difficulties reservation dwellers face remain much as they have been for the past half century or more. Even overt discrimination, although illegal and perhaps declining, continues to disrupt Indian-white relations in many parts of the nation. Obviously the adage "the more things change, the more they remain the same" applies here.

While politicians and voters may have lost interest in developing programs to assist Native Americans, scholarly, student, and public fascination with things Indian continues. Books, articles, papers, newspaper feature stories, and college courses all have appeared to meet those concerns. At the same time, however, scholars have continued to shift their foci and now ask questions and consider issues that attracted little interest only a decade ago. For example, nearly half of the articles in the earlier editions of this anthology dealt with United States policy toward Indians. Only five or six of the articles in this version are limited to Indian-white relations or federal policy. That change reflects continuing scholarly efforts to place tribal people at the center of the discussion. This has brought about an increased use of ethnohistorical and environmental sources. A clear example of this approach is found in Richard White's discussion of how the Indians of the

Puget Sound area altered their local environment to increase yields of plants they used for food. In this and many other selections, policy considerations remain in the background or are only one part of a complex picture.

Clearly the approaches to Native American studies continue to refocus. Yet, while emphases change, basic issues that need attention do not. As the table of contents shows, the actions of invading Anglo-Americans and tribal responses to them remain central topics of discussion. However one studies tribal societies, there is no escaping the process through which Indian peoples went from a position of superiority to equality and then to some form of dependence on the European invaders and their descendants in both the United States and Canada. That growing dependence receives attention in articles that consider the forced acculturation of Native Americans through the actions of missionaries and teachers, legal and judicial actions, trade and economic efforts, acquisition of tribal lands and resources, forced relocation of tribes, modification of gender roles, and the destruction or alteration of aboriginal religious and political leadership. The articles in this edition illustrate the pattern of European and Anglo-American efforts to destroy Native American societies and cultures. Few wanted to destroy Indian people physically, but most hoped to blend them into the general population. Authors discussing these issues no longer ignore the tribal side of the story as some did twenty or thirty years ago. So the scholarship of the 1980s tends to give an improved look at how and why the events occurred.

Many of the articles in this anthology fall into another category. True, they may consider issues related to Indian-white relations in some ways, but more importantly they examine the internal workings of the tribes and the motivations of individuals and groups within the minority societies. These articles consider such things as tribal leadership; medical, health, and dietary practices; the significance of tradition, religion, and the family; the roles and significance of women in village life and decision-making; internal decision-making practices; and Indian experiences in multitribal organizations and in the cities. In examining these topics, the authors have not ignored white actions; they merely shifted the emphasis to tribal practices that heretofore received little attention. No scholar who studies Indian history can, in any honesty, ignore the impact of Anglo-American ideas, actions, and institutions on tribal people. However, a clear understanding of the issues demands an ethnohistorical approach that makes every effort to place the Native Americans at the center of the story.

Most of the essays included here are used for the first time. In fact, the field of Native American studies continues to change so rapidly that only one article from the second edition and six others from the third have been retained. Some of the sixteen new items are too recent to have been used earlier. Others represent the continuing movement of literature away from policy studies or from what whites thought about Indians. Older questions about the record of military defeat, American land-grabbing, broken treaties, and the dismal mismanagement of Indian affairs remain, but now scholars approach them from new or alternative perspectives. As a result, interested readers may benefit from having a broader range of personal and group motivations placed before them to explain how and why Native Americans acted as they did.

These readings should lay to rest popular stereotypes, such as the idea that Indians only reacted to white initiatives or that tribal people accepted Anglo-American economic benefits or knowledge with little discrimination, rather than choosing what to adopt and what to ignore or reject. Notions such as that all tribal people wore feathers in their hair, lived in tepees, or allowed themselves to be destroyed by the fur trade and alcohol now seem nonsensical. Rather, Indians appear as rational people choosing between often difficult or unpleasant alternatives, while frequently ignoring the desires of the invaders. At the same time, the articles show that whites were by no means always more able, better equipped, or even successful in direct competition with the tribes. Indian diplomats, religious leaders, warriors, and entire societies often held their own within American society for generations. What stands out most clearly from this collection is the complexity of even modest, almost everyday events and decisions. Both Indians and whites had mixed motives, objectives, and experiences, and to get anything like a reasonable understanding of the events, one must give each side equal and careful attention.

Readers having a variety of concerns should find this collection of articles interesting and useful. One basic goal of the readings is to offer material related to all parts of the country and the entire range of American history, at least from colonial Virginia to the present. Another goal is to include the most interesting articles on each of the topics being presented so that students and others will actually read this material. These essays can be used as a text or a supplement in a variety of courses in either the social sciences or the humanities. Classes in United States history, American Indian or Native American history, Native American studies, ethnic studies, and minority history will all benefit from the insights the readings offer. In compiling this anthology, every effort has been made to select items by the most competent scholars. Except for deleting the footnotes—and in one case making minor deletions in the prose with the publisher's permission—all of the articles appear in full, as their authors intended them. Brief headnotes introduce each chapter and provide background information or historical perspective for the reader. In response to student requests, this edition includes a chronology of important events and an index.

Many people helped with the planning and preparation of this anthology, and they all deserve thanks. Several scholars read my proposed outline or responded to my request for items to be considered for this edition. Even though at times I ignored their suggestions, the ideas they offered stimulated my thinking about the project and affected my choice of the items that do appear. My thanks to each of those people: R. David Edmunds, Indiana University; Kristina Foss, Santa Barbara City College; Michael Green, Dartmouth College; Fred A. Nicklason, University of Maryland, College Park; and Theda Perdue, University of Kentucky. Having the cooperation of the authors whose works are included and of the editors in whose journals the articles appeared was essential. Thanks are also due to David C. Follmer and the editorial and production staff at McGraw-Hill for their cooperation and support.

Roger L. Nichols

IMPORTANT EVENTS IN NATIVE AMERICAN HISTORY

1535	Jacques Cartier visits St. Lawrence Valley
1540	Coronado visits the New Mexico pueblos
	DeSoto visits the southeastern United States
1585	St. Augustine, Florida is founded by Spain
	English land at Roanoke Island, North Carolina
1598	Oñate brings settlers into New Mexico
1607	English found Jamestown, Virginia settlement
1608	French found Quebec settlement
1609–14	First Anglo-Powhatan War in Virginia
1616–19	Epidemics sweep through coastal tribes of New England
1620	Pilgrims found Plymouth Colony
1621	Massasoit and Pilgrims make a long-lasting treaty
1622	Opechancanough leads major Indian attack on Virginia
1637	English defeat the Pequots in New England
1642–43	Dutch defeat Hudson River Valley Tribes in New York
1644	Opechancanough is defeated and killed in last Powhatan resistance
1649	Iroquois begin destruction of Hurons
1661	Franciscans raid Pueblo kivas to destroy Indian religious items
1675–76	Metacom's (King Philip's) War is major defeat for New England tribes
1676	Bacon's Rebellion brings last major war to Virginia tribes
1680	Pueblo Revolt drives Spanish from Southwest
1691	Spanish reconquer New Mexico
1701	Iroquois Confederacy makes peace with France and Great Britain
1703–04	Slave raids against Apalachees in northern Florida
1711–12	Tuscarora War in Carolina
1715	Yamassee War in Carolina
1722	Abenaki War in Maine

1864	Sand Creek Massacre of Cheyennes by Colorado Volunteers
1866	Fetterman Massacre
1867	Board of Indian Commissioners is established
1868	Red Cloud leads Sioux to victory; Bozeman Trail is closed
	Fourteenth Amendment to the Constitution denies Indians the vote
1869	President Grant launches his Quaker Policy
1870	Congress appropriates first money specifically for Indian education
1871	Congress ends the treaty system
1872–73	Modoc War in Oregon
1874	Red River War in Texas
1875–77	Great Sioux War; Custer is defeated in 1876
1877	Nez Perce War
1878	Funds appropriated for Indian police forces on the reservations
1879	National Indian Association is founded
	Richard Pratt founds Carlisle Indian School
1881	Sun Dance is outlawed, and tribal medicine men are arrested
1882	Indian Rights Association is founded
1883	Lake Mohonk Conferences begin
	Courts of Indian Offenses are established
1884	Beginning of modern peyotism rites
1885	Helen Hunt Jackson publishes *A Century of Dishonor*
1886	Geronimo's surrender ends the Apache Wars
1887	Dawes Severalty Act (General Allotment Act) is passed
1889	Wovoka spreads his Ghost Dance teachings
1890	Massacre of Sioux at Wounded Knee, S. D.
1896	Office of Indian Affairs orders adult males to have hair cut
1903	*Lone Wolf* v. *Hitchcock* decision
1907	Burke Act amends the Dawes Act
1911	Society of American Indians is founded
1917–18	8,000 Indians serve in World War I
1918	Native American Church incorporated in Oklahoma
1923	Committee of One Hundred investigation of Indian affairs
1924	American Indian Citizenship Act
1926	National Council of American Indians is founded
1928	Meriam Report is published
1934	Indian Reorganization Act is passed
1935	Indian Arts and Crafts Board is established

1941–45   25,000 Indians serve in World War II
1944   National Congress of American Indians is founded
1946   Indian Claims Commission is established
1952   Public Law 280
1953   House Concurrent Resolution 108
          Congress revises liquor regulations for Indians
1957   Reservation industries program begins
1961   American Indian Chicago Conference demands self-
          determination
          National Indian Youth Council is founded
1964   Institute of American Indian Arts is founded at Santa Fe
1966   Navajo found Rough Rock Demonstration School
1968   Congress passes the Indian Bill of Rights
          American Indian Movement (AIM) is founded
1969   N. Scott Momaday (Kiowa) wins Pulitzer Prize for *House Made of Dawn*
          Indians occupy Alcatraz Island
1970   Taos Pueblo regains Blue Lake
1971   Congress settles the Alaska Native Claims issue
1972   Trail of Broken Treaties and occupation of BIA office in
          Washington, D.C.
1973   Sixty-seven day confrontation at Wounded Knee
1975   Indian Self-Determination and Educational Assistance Act
          United States v. *State of Washington*—Boldt decision
1978   American Indian Religious Freedom Act
          Tribally Controlled Community College Act is passed
          Federal Tribal Acknowledgement Program is established
1980   Penobscot/Passamaquoddy claims settled

COLONIAL AMERICA
WITHOUT THE INDIANS:
COUNTERFACTUAL REFLECTIONS

JAMES AXTELL

Many Americans have little knowledge of Indians beyond the TV or motion picture stereotypes, so this essay confronts that ignorance by asking the ahistorical question "What would colonial America have been like had there been no native people here when the invading Europeans arrived?" For some this may appear to be little more than a semantic game, but the author raises significant issues that are worth consideration. In particular he shows that Native Americans did more than resist the Europeans or become victims of their Anglo-American descendents. Rather, the narrative suggests that fundamental changes in the colonists' agriculture, transportation, and economic life all resulted from the presence of tribal people. To demonstrate the centrality of Indians in early American developments, the author depicts a continent without population when the Europeans arrived. He suggests that the vast wealth of Central and South America would not have been discovered for generations or perhaps centuries had not the Indians been mining gold and silver for eons. The fur trade that lured the French into the heart of North America could not have functioned without tribal hunters to gather the hides and pelts the traders sought so eagerly. American pioneers' lives would have differed widely without the Indians to oppose their advance or to play off the Americans, British, French, and Spanish against each other. While arguably not history, this discussion offers plenty of ideas for thought and chances for discussion.

James Axtell is a professor of history at the College of William and Mary.

It is taking us painfully long to realize that throughout most of American history the Indians were "one of the principal *determinants* of historical events." A growing number of scholars understand that fact, but the great majority of us still regard the

Source: Axtell, James, "Colonial America without the Indians: Counterfactual Reflections," *Journal of American History*, 73 (March 1987), 981–996. Text only. Copyright © 1987 by the Organization of American Historians. Published by permission of the author and the publisher.

native Americans—if we regard them at all—as exotic or pathetic footnotes to the main course of American history.

This is patently clear from American history textbooks. As Virgil Vogel, Alvin Josephy, and most recently Frederick Hoxie have shown in embarrassing detail, "Indians in textbooks either do nothing or they resist." In their colonial and nineteenth-century manifestations, they are either "obstacles to white settlement" or "victims of oppression." "As victims or obstacles, Indians have no textbook existence apart from their resistance." In short, the texts reflect our "deep-seated tendency to see whites and Indians as possessing two distinct species of historical experience" rather than a mutual history of continuous interaction and influence.

Attempts to redress the balance have suffered from serious flaws. Some observers have exaggerated and oversimplified the Indian impact. We certainly ought to avoid the fatuity of the argument that "what is distinctive about America is Indian, through and through" or that Americans are simply Europeans with "Indian souls." Historians have been more drawn to other, less sweeping, approaches. Robert Berkhofer described four well-meaning but unproductive remedial approaches to "minority" history, especially the history of American Indians. They are the "great man" or "heroes" approach (the "devious side of treaty making"), the "who-is-more-civilized" approach ("barbarities committed by whites against Indians" contrasted with the "civilized" contributions of Indians), the "crushed-personality" and "cultural-theft" approach ("change only destroys Indian cultures, never adds to them"), and—by far the most important—the "contributions" approach ("long lists of the contributions Native Americans made to the general American way of life"). The first two approaches offer variations on the theme of Indian heroism and resistance. The third presents Indians as victims. None of the three gives much help in analyzing processes in which both Indians and whites played varying and evolving roles. At best they alert us to the moral dimensions of Indian-white history.

The contributions approach, although flawed, is useful. We inevitably employ it when we seek to define the Indian role in American history, rather than the white role in Indian history. Since most scholars who refer to Indian history are primarily interested in the evolution of the dominant Anglo-American "core culture" and political nationhood, they will write in terms of Indian contributions. It is therefore essential to understand the pitfalls in the approach and to devise ways of avoiding them.

A relative disregard for chronology weakens the contributions approach. By focusing on the modern legacy of Indian culture, it usually ignores the specific timing of the various white adaptations and borrowings. Generic "Indian" contributions seem to have been made any time after 1492, it hardly matters when. Such cavalier chronology ought to offend historians not only because it is imprecise but also because it prevents us from determining causation with any accuracy. If we do not know *which* Indian group lent the word, trait, or object and *when*, we will be unable to measure the impact of the adaptive changes in Anglo-American culture at the time they occurred and as they reverberated.

An even more serious flaw is an almost exclusive focus on native material culture (and names of native or American objects and places) that neglects how those items were used, perceived, and adapted by their white borrowers. That focus and the neglect of chronology restrict discussion to a narrow range of additions to contemporary American life (i.e., material culture) rather than opening it up to the cultural and social fullness of American *history*. What the approach sadly ignores are the changes wrought in Anglo-American culture, not by borrowing and adapting native cultural traits, words, and objects, but by reacting negatively and perhaps unconsciously to the native presence, threat, and challenge. Without consideration of these deeply formative *reactive* changes, we can have no true measure of the Indians' impact on American history.

In seventeenth- and eighteenth-century Anglo-America, the adaptive changes whites made in response to their contacts with Indians significantly shaped agriculture, transport, and economic life. The more elusive reactive changes significantly shaped the identity of a new people and the nation they founded.

One striking way to register the sheer indispensability of the Indians for understanding America's past is to imagine what early American history might have looked like in the utter absence of Indians in the New World. The emphasis should be on historical control, not the free flight of fancy. If we posited an Indianless New World in 1492 and then tried to reconstruct the course of later history, we would end up in a speculative quagmire because each dependent variable could develop in many alternative ways, depending on the others. By the time we reached 1783, we might have a familiar historical product or, more likely, a virtually unrecognizable one. Whatever the outcome, its artificiality would make it heuristically useless. But by following the historical course of events in America and at selected points imaginatively removing the Indians from the picture, we reduce the artificiality of the exercise and the opportunity for conjectural mayhem. Such a controlled use of the counterfactual can invigorate the search for historical causation.

The following series of counterfactual reflections is offered as a heuristic exercise. "Had the European colonists found an utterly unpopulated continent," we ask, "would colonial American life have differed in any major respect from its actual pattern?"

To begin at the beginning, in the period of European discovery and exploration, we can say with confidence that if Christopher Columbus had not discovered the people whom he called *los Indios* (and they, him), the history of Spanish America would have been extremely short and uneventful. Since Columbus was looking for the Far East, not America or its native inhabitants, it would not have surprised him to find no Indians in the Caribbean—the new continent was surprise enough. But he would have been disappointed, not only because the islands of the Orient were known to be inhabited, but also because there would have been little reason to explore and settle an unpopulated New World instead of pursuing his larger goal. He would have regarded America as simply a huge impediment to his plan to mount an old-fashioned crusade to liberate Jerusalem with profits derived from his shortcut to Cathay.

If the Caribbean and Central and South America had been unpopulated, the placer mines of the islands and the deep mines of gold and silver on the mainland probably would not have been discovered; they certainly would not have been quickly exploited without Indian knowledge and labor. It is inconceivable that the Spanish would have stumbled on the silver deposits of Potosí or Zacatecas if the Incas and Aztecs had not set Spanish mouths to watering with their sumptuous gold jewelry and ornaments. Indeed, without the enormous wealth to be commandeered from the natives, it is likely that the Spanish would not have colonized New Spain at all except to establish a few supply bases from which to continue the search for the Southwest Passage.

It is equally possible that without the immediate booty of Indian gold and silver, the Spanish would have dismissed Columbus after one voyage as a crack-brained Italian and redirected their economic energies eastward in the wake of the Portuguese, toward the certifiable wealth of Africa, India, and the East Indies. Eventually, sugar cane might have induced the Iberians to colonize their American discoveries, as it induced them to colonize the Cape Verde, Madeira, and Canary islands, but they would have had to import black laborers. Without Indian labor and discovery, however, saltwater pearls and the bright red dye made from the cochineal beetle—the second largest export of the Spanish American empire in the colonial period—would not have contributed to Spain's bulging balance sheets and to the impact of that wealth on the political and economic history of Europe in the sixteenth and early seventeenth centuries.

Perhaps most important, without the millions of native Americans who inhabited New Spain, there would have been no Spanish conquest—no "Black Legend," no Cortés or Montezuma, no brown-robed friars baptizing thousands daily or ferreting out "idolatry" with whip and fagot, no legalized plunder under the encomienda system, no cruelty to those who extracted the mines' treasures and rebuilt Spanish cities on the rubble of their own, no mastiffs mangling runaways. And without the fabulous lure of Aztec gold and Inca silver carried to Seville in the annual bullion fleets, it is difficult to imagine Spain's European rivals racing to establish American colonies of their own as early as they did.

Take the French, for example. As they did early in the sixteenth century, the cod teeming on the Grand Banks off Newfoundland would have drawn and supported a small seasonal population of fishermen. But without the Indians, the French would have colonized no farther. Giovanni da Verrazzano's 1524 reconnaissance of the Atlantic seaboard would have been an even bigger bust than it was, and Jacques Cartier would probably have made two voyages instead of three, the second only to explore the St. Lawrence River far enough to learn that China did not lie at the western end of Montreal Island. He would have reported to Francis I that "the land God gave to Cain" had no redeeming features, such as the greasy furs of Indian fishermen and the promise of gold and diamonds in the fabled Kingdom of the Saguenay, of which the Indians spoke with such apparent conviction.

If by chance Samuel de Champlain had renewed the French search for the Northwest Passage in the seventeenth century, he would have lost his backers quickly without the lure of an established fur trade with the natives of Acadia and Canada, who hunted, processed, and transported the pelts in native canoes or on native snowshoes and toboggans. And without the "pagan" souls of the Indians as a goad and challenge, the French religious orders, male and female, would not have cast their lot with Champlain and the trading companies that governed and settled

New France before 1663. In short, without the Indian fur trade, no seigneuries would have been granted along the St. Lawrence, no *habitants, engagés* (indentured servants) or marriageable "King's girls" shipped out to Canada. Quebec and Montreal would not have been founded even as crude *comptoirs*, and no Jesuit missionaries would have craved martyrdom at an Iroquois stake. No "French and Indian" wars would mar our textbooks with their ethnocentric denomination. North America would have belonged solely to settlements of English farmers, for without the Indians and their fur trade, the Swedish and the Dutch would have imitated the French by staying home or turning to the Far East for economic inspiration.

Without the lure of American gold and the Elizabethan contest with Spain that it stimulated, the English, too, would probably have financed fewer ocean searches for the Northwest Passage. If no one thought that Indian chamber pots were made of gold, far fewer gentle-born investors and lowborn sailors would have risked their lives and fortunes on the coasts of America. Unless the Spanish had reaped fabulous riches from the natives and then subjected them to cruel and unnatural bondage, Sir Walter Raleigh would not have sponsored his voyages of liberation to Guiana and Virginia. If the Spanish bullion fleets had not sailed regularly through the Straits of Florida, English privateers would not have preyed on the West Indies nor captured the booty they used to launch permanent colonies in Ireland and North America. Arthur Barlowe's 1584 voyage to North Carolina would probably not have been followed up soon, if he had not discovered friendly natives able to secure a fledgling colony from Spanish incursions.

Sooner or later, the English would have established colonies in America as a safety valve for the felt pressures of population growth and economic reorganization and as a sanctuary for religious dissenters. Once English settlement was under way, the absence of native villages, tribes, and war parties would have drastically altered the chronology of American history. In general, events would have been accelerated because the Indian presence acted as a major check on colonial development. Without a native barrier (which in the colonial period was much more daunting than the Appalachians), the most significant drag on colonial enterprise would have been the lack of Indian labor in a few minor industries, such as the domestic economy of southern New England (supplied by Indians captured in the Pequot and King Philip's wars) and the whale fisheries of Cape Cod, Long Island, and Nantucket. Indians were not crucial to wheat farming, lumbering, or rice and tobacco culture and would not have been missed by the English entrepreneurs engaged in them.

Without Indians to contest the land, English colonists would have encountered opposition to their choice of prime locations for settlement only from English competitors. They would not have had to challenge Indian farmers for the fertile river valleys and coastal plains the natives had cultivated for centuries. Without potential Indian or European enemies, sites could be located for economic rather than military considerations, thus removing Jamestown, Plymouth, and St. Mary's City from the litany of American place-names. Boston, New York, Philadelphia, and Charleston would probably be where they are, either because Indian opposition did not much affect their founding or because they were situated for optimal access to inland markets and Atlantic shipping lanes.

In an empty land, English leaders would also have had fewer strategic and ideological reasons for communal settlements of the classic New England type. Without the military and moral threat of Indian war parties, on the one hand, and the puzzling seduction of native life, on the other, English colonists would have had to be persuaded by other arguments to cast their lots together. One predictable result is that New England "Puritans" would have become unbridled "Yankees" even faster than they did. Other colonies would have spread quickly across the American map. By 1776, Anglo-American farmers in large numbers would have spilled over the Appalachians, headed toward their "Manifest Destiny" in the West. Without Indians, Frenchmen, or Spaniards in the Mississippi Valley and beyond to stop them, only the technology of transportation, the supply of investment capital, and the organization of markets en route would have regulated the speed of their advance.

Another consequence of an Indian-less America would be that we could not speak with any accuracy of "the American frontier" because there would be no people on the other side; only where two peoples and cultures intersect do we have a bona fide frontier. The movement of one people into uninhabited land is merely exploration or settlement; it does not constitute a frontier situation. In fact, without viable Indian societies, colonial America would have more nearly resembled Frederick Jackson Turner's famous frontier in which Indians are treated more as geographical features than as sociological teachers. In Turner's scenario, the European dandy fresh from his railroad car is "Americanized" less by contact with palpably attractive human societies than by the "wilderness" or Nature itself. Moreover, the distinctively American character traits that Turner attributed to life on the edge of westering "civilization" would have been exaggerated by the existence of truly limitless cheap land and much less control from the Old World and the Eastern Establishment.

Not only would Turner's mythopoeic frontier really have existed in a non-Indian America, but three other common misunderstandings of colonial history would have been realities. First, America would indeed have been a virgin land, a barren wilderness, not home to perhaps four million native people north of Mexico. If those people had not existed, we would not have to explain their catastrophic decline, by as much as 90 percent, through warfare, injustice, forced migrations, and epidemics of imported diseases—the "widowing" of the once-virgin land, as Francis Jennings has so aptly called it.

Second, colonial history would be confined roughly to the eastern and midwestern parts of the future United States (which themselves would be different). Without Indians, we could ignore French Canada and Louisiana, the Spanish Southwest, the Russian Northwest (whose existence depended on the Indian-staffed seal trade), and the borderless histories of Indian-white contact that determined so much of the shape and texture of colonial life.

And third, we would not have to step up from the largely black-and-white pageant of American history we are offered in our textbooks and courses to a richer polychromatic treatment, if the Indians had no role in the past. We would not even have to pay lip service to the roll call of exclusively male Indian leaders who have been squeezed into the corners of our histories by Indian militance during the last twenty years. Still less would we have to try to integrate into our texts an understanding of the various native peoples who were here first, remained against staggering odds, and are still here to mold our collective past and future.

To get a sharper perspective on an Indian-free scenario of colonial history, we should increase our focal magnification and analyze briefly four distinguishable yet obviously related aspects of colonial life: economics, religion, politics, and acculturation. The economy of Anglo-America without the Indians would have resembled in general outline the historical economy, with several significant exceptions. Farming would certainly have been the mainstay of colonial life, whether for family subsistence or for capitalist marketing and accumulation. But the initial task of establishing farms would have required far more grubbing and clearing without the meadows and parklike woods produced by seasonal Indian burning and especially without the cleared expanses of Indian corn fields and village sites. Many colonists found that they could acquire cleared Indian lands with a few fathoms of trading cloth, some unfenced cows, or a well-aimed barrel of buckshot.

There would have been no maize, or Indian corn, the staple crop grown throughout the colonial period to feed people and sometimes to fatten livestock for export. If Indians had not adapted wild Mexican corn to the colder, moister climates of North America and developed the agricultural techniques of hilling, fertilizing by annual burning, and co-planting with nitrogen-fixing beans to reduce soil depletion, the colonists would have lacked a secure livelihood, particularly in the early years before traditional European cereal crops had been adapted to the American climate and soils. Even if traditional crops could have been transplanted with ease, colonial productivity would not have benefitted from the efficiency and labor savings of native techniques, which were often taught by Indian prisoners (as at Jamestown) or by allies like Squanto at Plymouth. So central was maize to the colonial economy that its absence might have acted as a severe brake on westward settlement, thereby somewhat counteracting the magnetic pull of free land.

The colonial economy would also have been affected by the lack of Indian trade, whose profits fueled the nascent economies of several colonies, including Massachusetts, Rhode Island, New York, Pennsylvania, Virginia, and South Carolina. Without fortunes made from furs, some of the "first families" of America— the Byrds, Penns, Logans, Winthrops, Schuylers—would not have begun to accumulate wealth so soon in the form of ships, slaves, rice, tobacco, or real estate. Nor would the mature economies of a few major colonies have rested on the fur trade well into the eighteenth century. New York's and Pennsylvania's balance of payments with the mother country would have been badly skewed if furs supplied by Indians had not accounted for 30 to 50 percent of their annual exports between 1700 and 1750. A substantial portion of English exports to the colonies would not have been sent to colonial traders for Indian customers, whose desire for English cloth and appetite for West Indian rum were appreciated even though throughout the colonial period furs accounted for only 0.5 percent of England's colonial imports, far less than either tobacco or sugar.

The lack of Indians and Indian property rights in America would have narrowed another classic American road to wealth. If the new land had been so close to inexhaustible and "dirt cheap," the range of legal and extralegal means to

acquire relatively scarce land for hoarding and speculation would have been markedly reduced. Within the unknown confines of the royal response to a huge, open
continent, every man, great and small, would have been for himself. If the law
condoned or fostered the selective aggrandizement of colonial elites, as it tended to
do historically, unfavored farmers and entrepreneurs could simply move out of the
government's effective jurisdiction or find leaders more willing to do their bidding.
The proliferation of new colonies seeking economic and political independence
from the felt tyranny of an Eastern Establishment would have been one certain
result, as would a flattening of social hierarchy in all the mainland colonies.

Finally, in an America without Indians the history of black slavery would
have been different. It is likely that, in the absence of Indians, the colonial demand
for and use of African slaves would have begun earlier and accelerated faster. For
although the historical natives were found to be poor workers and poorer slaves, the
discovery took some time. Not only would the rapid westward spread of settlements have called for black labor, perhaps more of it indentured, but the rice and
tobacco plantations of the Southeast probably would have been larger than they
were historically, if scarce land and high prices had not restricted them. In a
virgin-land economy, agriculture entrepreneurs who wanted to increase their acre-
age could easily buy out their smaller neighbors, who lacked no access to new lands
in the West. Greater numbers of black laborers would have been needed because
white indentured servants would have been extremely hard to get when so much
land and opportunity beckoned. The slaves themselves would have been harder to
keep to the task without surrounding tribes of Indians who could be taught to fear
and hate the African strangers and to serve the English planters as slave catchers.
The number of maroon enclaves in the interior would have increased considerably.

While most colonists came to the New World to better their own material
condition, not a few came to ameliorate the spiritual condition of the "godless"
natives. Without the challenge of native "paganism" in America, the charters of
most English colonies would have been frankly materialistic documents with pride
of motive going to the extension of His (or Her) Majesty's Eminent Domain. Thus,
American history would have lost much of its distinctively evangelical tone, though
few of its millenarian, utopian strains. Without the long, frustrated history of
Christian missions to the Indians, there would have been one less source of de-
nominational competition in the eighteenth century. And we would lack a sensitive
barometer of the cultural values that the European colonists sought to transplant in
the New World.

Without Indian targets and foils, even the New England colonists might not
have retained their Chosen People conceit so long or so obdurately. On the other
hand, without the steady native reminder of their evangelical mission in America,
their early descent into ecclesiastical tribalism and spiritual exclusiveness might
have been swifter. The jeremiads of New England would certainly have been less
shrill in the absence of the Pequot War and King Philip's War, when the hostile
natives seemed to be scourges sent by God to punish a sinful people. Without the
military and psychological threat of Indians within and without New England's
borders, the colonial fear of limitless and unpredictable social behavior would have
been reduced, thereby diminishing the harsh treatment of religious deviants such

as Roger Williams, Anne Hutchinson, the Quakers, and the Salem witches. Finally, the French "Catholic menace" to the north would have been no threat to English Protestant sensibilities without hundreds of Indian converts, led by "deviously" effective Jesuit missionaries, ringing New England's borders. The French secular clergy who would have ministered to the handful of fishermen and farmers in Canada would have had no interest in converting Protestant "heretics" hundreds of miles away and no extra manpower to attempt it.

Colonial politics, too, would have had a different complexion in the absence of American natives. Even if the French had settled the St. Lawrence Valley without a sustaining Indian fur trade, the proliferating English population and European power politics would have made short work of the tiny Canadian population, now bereft of Indian allies and converts in the thousands. In all likelihood, we would write about only one short intercolonial war, beginning much earlier than 1689. Perhaps the English privateers David and Jarvis Kirke, who captured New France in 1629, would not have given it back to the French in 1632. Without the Catholic Indian *reserves* (praying towns) of Lorette, Caughnawaga, and St. François to serve as military buffers around French settlements, Canada would quickly have become English, at least as far north as arable land and lumber-rich forests extended.

Without a formidable French and Indian threat, early Americans would not have developed—in conjunction with their conceit as God's Chosen People—such a pronounced garrison mentality, picturing themselves as innocent and holy victims threatened by heavily armed satanic forces. If the English had not been virtually surrounded by Indian nations allied with the French and an arc of French trading forts and villages from Louisiana to Maine, the Anglo-American tendencies toward persecuted isolationism would have been greatly reduced.

As the colonies matured, the absence of an Indian military threat would have lightened the taxpayers' burden for colonial defense, lessening the strains in the political relations between governors and representative assemblies. Indeed, the assemblies would not have risen to political parity with the royal administrators without the financial crises generated by war debts and defense needs. Intercolonial cooperation would have been even rarer than it was. Royal forces would not have arrived during the eighteenth century to bolster sagging colonial defenses and to pile up imperial debts that the colonies would be asked to help amortize. Consequently, the colonies would have had few grievances against the mother country serious enough to ignite an American Revolution, at least not in 1776. On the other hand, without the concentration of Indian allies on the British side, the colonists might have achieved independence sooner than they did.

Indeed, without the steady impress of Indian culture, the colonists would probably not have been ready for revolution in 1776, because they would not have been or felt sufficiently Americanized to stand before the world as an independent nation. The Indian presence precipitated the formation of an American identity.

Without Indian societies to form our colonial frontiers, Anglo-American culture would have been transformed only by internal developments, the evolving influence of the mother country, and the influence of the black and other ethnic groups who shared the New World with the English. Black culture probably would have done the most to change the shape and texture of colonial life, especially in the South. But English masters saw little reason to emulate their black slaves, to make adaptive changes in their own cultural practices or attitudes in order to accommodate perceived superiorities in black culture. English colonial culture changed in response to the imported Africans largely in reaction to their oppositional being, and pervasive and often virulent racism was the primary result. Other changes, of course, followed from the adoption of staple economies largely but not necessarily dependent on black labor.

English reactions to the Indians, on the other hand, were far more mixed; the "savages" were noble as well as ignoble, depending on English needs and circumstances. Particularly on the frontier, colonists were not afraid or loath to borrow and adapt pieces of native culture if they found them advantageous or necessary for beating the American environment or besting the Indians in the contest for the continent. Contrary to metropolitan colonial opinion, this cultural exchange did not turn the frontiersmen into Indians. Indian means were simply borrowed and adapted to English ends. The frontiersmen did not regard themselves as Indians, nor did they appreciably alter their basic attitudes toward the native means they employed. But they also knew that their American encounters with the Indians made them very different from their English cousins at home.

While the colonists borrowed consciously and directly from Indian culture only on the frontier, English colonial culture as a whole received a substantial but indirect impress from the Indians by being forced to confront the novel otherness of native culture and to cope with its unpredictability, pride, and retaliatory violence. Having the Indians as adversaries sometimes and contraries at all times not only reinforced the continuity of vital English traits and institutions but also Americanized all levels of colonial society more fully than the material adaptations of the frontiersmen. The colonial experience of trying to solve a series of "Indian problems" did much to give the colonists an identity indissolubly linked to America and their apprenticeship in political and military cooperation. In large measure, it was the *reactive* changes that transformed colonial Englishmen into native Americans in feeling, allegiance, and identity, a transformation without which, John Adams said, the American Revolution would have been impossible.

What identity-forming changes would *not* have taken place in colonial culture had the continent been devoid of Indians? The adaptive changes are the easiest to describe. Without native precedent, the names of twenty-eight states and myriad other place-names would carry a greater load of Anglophonic freight. The euphonious Shenandoah and Monongahela might well be known as the St. George and the Dudley rivers. We might still be searching for suitable names for the *moose*, *skunk*, and *raccoon*, the *muskellunge* and *quahog*, the *hickory* tree and marshy *muskeg*. It would be impossible, no doubt, to find *moccasins* in an L. L. Bean catalog or canned *succotash* in the supermarket. We would never refer to our children playfully as *papooses* or to political bigshots as *mugwumps*. Southerners could not start their day with *hominy* grits.

Without Indian guides to the New World, the newly arrived English colonists could not have housed themselves in bark-covered wigwams and longhouses. Not only would their diet have depended largely on imported foods, but even their techniques for hunting American game and fowl and coping in the woods would have been meager. Without native medicines, many colonists would have perished and the *U.S. Pharmacopeia* would lack most of the 170 entries attributable to Indian discovery and use. Without Indian snowshoes and toboggans, winter hunting and travel would have been sharply curtailed. Without the lightweight bark canoe, northern colonists would have penetrated the country on foot. English hunters probably would have careered around the woods in gaudy colors and torn English garments much longer, unaware that the unsmoked glint of their musket barrels frightened the game. And what would Virginia's patriotic rifle companies have worn in 1775 as an alternative to moccasins, leggings, fringed hunting shirts, scalping knives, and tomahawks?

Without native opponents and instructors in the art of guerilla warfare, the colonists would have fought their American wars—primarily with the British—in traditional military style. In fact, without the constant need to suppress hostile natives and aggressive Europeans, they might have lost most of their martial spirit and prowess, making their victory in the now postponed Revolution less than certain. Beating the British regulars at their own game without stratagems and equipment gained from the Indians would have been nearly impossible, particularly after the British gained experience in counterinsurgent warfare in Scotland and on the continent.

The absence of such adaptive changes would have done much to maintain the Anglicized tone and texture of colonial life; the absence of Indians would have preserved more fundamental cultural values that were altered historically. The generalized European fear of barbarism that colonial planners and leaders manifested would have dissipated without the Indian embodiment of a "heathenism" that seemed contagious to English frontiersmen or the danger of Englishmen converting to an Indian way of life in captivity or, worse still, voluntarily as "apostates" and "renegades." Without the seduction of an alternative lifestyle within easy reach, hundreds of colonists would not have become white Indians.

More generally, the Anglo-Americans' definition of themselves would have lacked a crucial point of reference because the Indians would no longer symbolize the "savage" baseness that would dominate human nature if man did not "reduce" it to "civility" through government, religion, and the capitalist work ethic. Only imported Africans, not American natives, would then have shown "civilized men [what] they were not and must not be." Because the settlers were "especially inclined to discover attributes in savages which they found first but could not speak of in themselves," they defined themselves "less by the vitality of their affirmations than by the violence of their abjurations." All peoples define themselves partly by contrast with other peoples, but the English colonists forged their particular American identity on an Indian anvil more than on a (non-English) European or African one.

The Indians were so crucial to the formation of the Anglo-American character because of the strong contrasts between their culture and that of the intruders, which the English interpreted largely as native deficiencies. While English technology had reached the Age of Iron, Indian technology was of the Stone Age, without wheels, clocks, compasses, cloth, iron, glass, paper, or gunpowder. While the English participated in a capitalist economy of currency and credit, the natives bartered in kind from hand to hand. While the English were governed by statutes, sheriffs, parliaments, and kings, the Indians' suasive politics of chiefs and councils seemed to be no government at all. While the English worshipped the "true God" in churches with prayer books and scripture, native shamans resembled "conjurers" who preyed on the "superstitious" natures of their dream-ridden, "devil-worshipping" supplicants. While the English enjoyed the benefits of printing and alphabetic literacy, the Indians were locked in an oral culture of impermanence and "hearsay." While the English sought to master nature as their religion taught them, the natives saw themselves as part of nature, whose other "spirits" deserved respect and thanks. While English men worked in the fields and women in the house, Indian women farmed and their menfolk "played" at hunting and fishing. While English time shot straight ahead into a progressive future, Indian time looped and circled upon itself, blurring the boundaries between a hazy past, a spacious present, and an attenuated future. While the English lived in permanent towns and cities, the Indians' annual subsistence cycle of movement seemed aimlessly "nomadic." While the English waged wars of state for land, crowns, wealth, or faith, Indian warriors struck personally for revenge, honor, and captives. While English society was divided into "divinely sanctioned" strata of wealth, power, and prestige, Indian society fostered an "unnatural" sense of democratic individualism in the people. And while English ethnocentrism was based on a new religion, technology, social evolution, and ultimately race, the Indians' own strong sense of superiority, color-blind and religiously tolerant, could not be undermined except by inexplicable European diseases.

For the whole spectrum of colonial society, urban and rural, the Indians as cultural contraries were not so frustrating, alarming, or influential as the Indian enemy. As masters of an unconventional warfare of terror, they seared the collective memories, imaginations, and even subconscious of the colonists, leaving a deep but blurred intaglio of fear and envy, hatred and respect. Having the American natives as frequent and deadly adversaries—and even as allies—did more to "Americanize" the English colonists than any other human factor and had two contradictory results. When native warfare frustrated and humbled the English military machine, its successes cast into serious doubt the colonists' sense of superiority, especially when the only recourse seemed to be the hiring of mercenaries from other tribes. At the same time, victorious Indians seemed so insufferably insolent—a projection of the Christians' original sin—that the colonists redoubled their efforts to claim divine grace and achieve spiritual and social regeneration through violence. One of the pathetic ironies of early America is that in attempting to exterminate the wounding pride of their Indian enemies, the colonists inflated their own pride to sinful proportions.

The Indians' brand of guerilla warfare, which involved the "indiscriminate slaughter of all ranks, ages and sexes," torture, and captivity for adoption, gave rise to several colonial reactions. The first reaction was a well-founded increase in fear and paranoia. The second reaction was the development of a defensive garrison mentality, which in turn reinforced the colonists' sense of being a chosen if momentarily abandoned people. And the colonists' third response was a sense of being torn from their own "civilized" moorings and swept into the kind of "savage" conduct they deplored in their enemies, motivated by cold-blooded vengeance. Without Indian enemies, it is doubtful if the colonist would have slaughtered and tortured military prisoners, including women and children, taken scalps from friends and enemies to collect government bounties, encouraged the Spanish-style use of dogs, or made boot tops and tobacco pouches from the skin of fallen foes. It is a certainty that non-Indian enemies would not have been the target of frequent if unrealized campaigns of genocide; it is difficult to imagine English settlers coining an aphorism to the effect that "the only good Dutchman is a dead one."

It is both fitting and ironic that the symbol chosen by Revolutionary cartoonists to represent the American colonies was the Indian, whose love of liberty and fierce independence had done so much to Americanize the shape and content of English colonial culture. It is fitting because the Indians by their long and determined opposition helped to meld thirteen disparate colonies into one (albeit fragile) nation, different from England largely by virtue of having shared that common history of conflict on and over Indian soil. It is ironic because after nearly two centuries of trying to take the Indians' lives and lands, the colonists appropriated not only the native identity but the very characteristics that thwarted the colonists' arrogations.

2

VIRGIN-SOIL EPIDEMICS AS A FACTOR IN THE ABORIGINAL DEPOPULATION IN AMERICA

ALFRED W. CROSBY, JR.

During the late 1960s the idea that the aboriginal population of North America stood at about one million people came under sharp attack. Medical historians and demographers examined population estimates for the entire Western Hemisphere, and during the debates that followed some claimed a population of from nine to twelve million people for pre-Columbian North America. Today few accept those figures, but generally historians and ethnologists agree that earlier estimates of only a million people living here were too low. Those same scholars found that the Indian population of the Americas suffered drastic reductions once the Europeans arrived. Epidemic diseases struck down millions of Native American people during the centuries following the interracial contacts. In explaining this vast depopulation, some researchers suggested that a genetic weakness made the Indians uniquely susceptible to the major diseases the Europeans introduced here. This author rejects that view. While he uses the term "virgin-soil epidemics" to describe the situations where Native Americans encountered illnesses to which they had no acquired immunity, he demonstrates how and why the diseases struck with such devastating effect. Although he lacks substantial historical and demographic data for North America, the author examines recent incidents in South America and in the Arctic to illustrate and develop his ideas. His discussion of how tens of thousands of Indians died because of epidemic disease adds another dimension to the story of early Indian-white relations. It also demonstrates the complexities that need attention in order to achieve an understanding of the historical processes at work in colonial America.

Alfred W. Crosby, Jr., is a professor of American Studies at the University of Texas.

Source: Alfred W. Crosby, Jr., "Virgin-Soil Epidemics as a Factor in the Aboriginal Depopulation in America," *William and Mary Quarterly*, 3 ser. 33 (April 1976), pp. 289–299. Published with permission of *William & Mary Quarterly* and Alfred W. Crosby.

During the last few decades, historians have demonstrated increasing concern with the influence of disease in history, particularly the history of the New World. For example, the latest generation of Americanists chiefly blames diseases imported from the Old World for the disparity between the number of American aborigines in 1492—new estimates of which soar as high as one hundred million or approximately one-sixth of the human race at that time—and the few million pure Indians and Eskimos alive at the end of the nineteenth century. There is no doubt that chronic disease was an important factor in the precipitous decline, and it is highly probable that the greatest killer was epidemic disease, especially as manifested in virgin-soil epidemics.

Virgin-soil epidemics are those in which the populations at risk have had no previous contact with the diseases that strike them and are therefore immunologically almost defenseless. The importance of virgin-soil epidemics in American history is strongly indicated by evidence that a number of dangerous maladies—smallpox, measles, malaria, yellow fever, and undoubtedly several more—were unknown in the pre-Columbian New World. In theory, the initial appearance of these diseases is as certain to have set off deadly epidemics as dropping lighted matches into tinder is certain to cause fires.

The thesis that epidemics have been chiefly responsible for the awesome diminution in the number of Native Americans is based on more than theory. The early chronicles of America are full of reports of horrendous epidemics and steep population declines, confirmed in many cases by recent quantitative analyses of Spanish tribute records and other sources. The evidence provided by the documents of British and French America is not as definitely supportive of the thesis because the conquerors of those areas did not establish permanent settlements and begin to keep continuous records until the seventeenth century, by which time at least some of the worst epidemics of imported diseases had probably already taken place. Furthermore, the British tended to drive the Indians away, rather than ensnaring them as slaves and peons, as the Spaniards did, with the result that many of the most important events of aboriginal history in British America occurred beyond the range of direct observation by literate witnesses.

Even so, the surviving records for North America do contain references—brief, vague, but plentiful—to deadly epidemics among the Indians, of which we shall cite a few of the allegedly worst. In 1616–1619 an epidemic, possibly of bubonic or pneumonic plague, swept coastal New England from Cape Cod to Maine, killing as many as nine out of every ten it touched. During the 1630s and into the next decade, smallpox, the most fatal of all the recurrent Indian killers, whipsawed back and forth through the St. Lawrence–Great Lakes region, eliminating half the people of the Huron and Iroquois confederations. In 1738 smallpox destroyed half the Cherokees, and in 1759, nearly half the Catawbas. During the American Revolution it attacked the Piegan tribe and killed half its members. It ravaged the plains tribes shortly before they were taken under United States jurisdiction by the Louisiana Purchase, killing two thirds of the Omahas and perhaps half the population between the Missouri River and New Mexico. In the 1820s fever devastated the people of the Columbia River area, erasing perhaps four fifths of them. In 1837 smallpox returned to the plains and destroyed about half of the aborigines there.

Unfortunately, the documentation of these epidemics, as of the many others of the period, is slight, usually hearsay, sometimes dated years after the events described, and often colored by emotion. Skepticism is eminently justified and is unlikely to be dispelled by the discovery of great quantities of first-hand reports on epidemics among the North American Indians. We must depend on analysis of what little we now know, and we must supplement that little by examination of recent epidemics among Native Americans.

Let us begin by asking why the American aborigines offered so little resistance to imported epidemic diseases. Their susceptibility has long been attributed to special weakness on their part, an explanation that dates from the period of colonization, received the stamp of authority from such natural historians as the Comte de Buffon, and today acquires the color of authenticity from the science of genetics. In its latest version the hypothesis of genetic weakness holds that during the pre-Columbian millennia the New World Indians had no occasion to build up immunities to such diseases as smallpox and measles. Those aborigines who were especially lacking in defenses against these maladies were not winnowed out before they passed on their vulnerabilities to their offspring. Although there is no way to test this hypothesis for pre-Columbian times, medical data on living American aborigines do not sustain it, and the scientific community inclines toward the view that Native Americans have no special susceptibility to Old World diseases that cannot be attributed to environmental influences and probably never did have.

The genetic-weakness hypothesis may have some validity, but it is unproven and probably unprovable and is therefore a weak reed to lean upon. What is more, we have no need of it. The death rate among white United States soldiers in the Civil War who contracted smallpox, a disease to which their ancestors had been exposed for many generations, was 38.5 percent, probably about the percentage of Aztecs who died of that disease in 1520. The difference between the Union troops and the Aztec population is, of course, that most of the former had been vaccinated or Exposed to the disease as children, while the latter was a completely virgin-soil population.

It should also be asked why the decline in numbers of the American aborigines went on as long as it did, 400 years or so, in contrast to the decline caused by Europe's most famous virgin-soil epidemic, the Black Death, which lasted no more than 100 to 200 years. The answer is that the Indians and Eskimos did not experience the onslaught of Old World diseases all at the same time and that other factors were also responsible for depressing their population levels. As far as we can say now, Old World diseases were the chief determinants in the demographic histories of particular tribes for 100 to 150 years after each tribe's first full exposure to them. In addition, the newcomers, whose dire influence on Native Americans must not be underestimated just because it has been overestimated, reduced the aboriginal populations by warfare, murder, dispossession, and interbreeding. Thereafter the Indians began a slow, at first nearly imperceptible, recovery. The greatest exceptions were the peoples of the tropical lowlands and islands who, under the extra heavy burden of insect-borne fevers, mostly of African provenance, held the downward course to oblivion.

The Indians of Mexico's central highlands perfectly fit this pattern of sharp decline for four to six generations followed by gradual recovery. Appalling depopulation began with the nearly simultaneous arrival of Cortés and smallpox; the nadir occurred sometime in the seventeenth century; and then Indian numbers slowly rose. The pattern of European population history was approximately the same in the two centuries following the Black Death. The recovery in numbers of the Indians of the United States in the twentieth century is probably part of a similar phenomenon.

But why did Europeans lose one third or so to the Black Death, imported from Asia, while the American aborigines lost perhaps as much as 90 percent to the diseases imported from the Old World? The answers are probably related to the factors that have caused many fatalities in recent virgin-soil epidemics among Native Americans, not of such deadly diseases as smallpox and plague, which are tightly controlled in our era, but of such relatively mild maladies as measles and influenza. In 1952 the Indians and Eskimos of Ungava Bay, in Northern Quebec, had an epidemic of measles: 99 percent became sick and about 7 percent died, even though some had the benefit of modern medicine. In 1954 an epidemic of measles broke out among the aborigines of Brazil's remote Xingu National Park: the death rate was 9.6 percent for those of the afflicted who had modern medical treatment and 26.8 percent for those who did not. In 1968 when the Yanomamas of the Brazilian-Venezuelan borderlands were struck by measles, 8 or 9 percent died despite the availability of some modern medicines and treatment. The Kreen-Akorores of the Amazon Basin, recently contacted for the first time by outsiders, lost at least 15 percent of their people in a single brush with common influenza.

The reasons for the massive losses to epidemics in the last four hundred years and the considerable losses to the epidemics just cited can be grouped conveniently in two categories, the first relating to the nature of the disease or diseases, and the second having to do with how individuals and societies react to the threat of epidemic death.

First, we must recognize that the reputations of measles and influenza as mild diseases are not entirely justified. Contemporary Native Americans who contract them are not cured by "miracle drugs," even when modern medical treatment is available, because there are no such drugs. Modern physicians do not *cure* measles, influenza, and such other viral maladies as smallpox, chicken pox, and mumps, but try, usually successfully, to keep off other infections until the normal functioning of undistracted immune systems kills off the invading viruses. If doctors fail in this task or are not available, the death rate will be "abnormally high." Measles killed more than 6 percent of all the white Union soldiers and almost 11 percent of all the black Union soldiers it infected during the Civil War, even though the waves of this disease that swept the army were not virgin-soil epidemics.

Virgin-soil epidemics are different from others in the age incidence of those they kill, as well as in the quantity of their victims. Evidence from around the world suggests that such epidemics of a number of diseases with reputations as Indian killers—smallpox, measles, influenza, tuberculosis, and others—carry off disproportionately large percentages of people aged about fifteen to forty—men and women of the prime years of life who are largely responsible for the vital functions of food procurement, defense, and procreation. Unfortunately, little evidence exists to support or deny the hypothesis that Native American virgin-soil epidemics have been especially lethal to young adults. There is no doubt, however, that they have been extremely deadly for the very young. Infants are normally protected against infectious diseases common in the area of their births by antibodies passed on to them before birth by their immunologically experienced mothers, antibodies that remain strong enough to fend off disease during the first precarious months of life. This first line of defense does not exist in virgin-soil epidemics. The threat to young children is more than just bacteriological: They are often neglected by ailing adults during such epidemics and often die when their ailing mother's milk fails. Infants in traditional aboriginal American societies are commonly two years of age or even older before weaning, so the failure of mothers' milk can boost the death rate during epidemics to a greater extent than modern urbanites would estimate on the basis of their own child-care practices.

Mortality rates rise sharply when several virgin-soil epidemics strike simultaneously. When the advance of the Alaska Highway in 1943 exposed the Indians of Teslin Lake to fuller contact with the outside world than they had ever had before, they underwent in one year waves of measles, German measles, dysentery, catarrhal jaundice, whooping cough, mumps, tonsillitis, and meningococcic meningitis. This pulverizing experience must have been common among aborigines in the early post-Columbian generations, although the chroniclers, we may guess, often put the blame on only the most spectacular of the diseases, usually smallpox. A report from Española in 1520 attributed the depopulation there to smallpox, measles, respiratory infection, and other diseases unnamed. Simultaneous epidemics of diseases, including smallpox and at least one other, possibly influenza, occurred in Meso-America in the early 1520s. The action of other diseases than the one most apparently in epidemic stage will often cause dangerous complications, even if they have been long in common circulation among the victims. In the Ungava Bay and Yanomama epidemics the final executioner was usually bronchopneumonia, which advanced when measles leveled the defenses of aborigines weakened by diseases already present: malaria and pneumonia among the South Americans and tuberculosis and influenza among the North Americans.

Successive epidemics may take longer to dismantle societies than simultaneous attacks by several diseases, but they can be as thorough. The documentation of American Indians' experience of successive epidemics is slim and not expressed as statistics, but the records are nonetheless suggestive. The Dakotas kept annual chronicles on leather or cloth showing by a single picture the most important event of each year. These records indicate that all or part of this people suffered significantly in the epidemics listed below, at least one of which, cholera, and possibly several others were virgin-soil. It should be noted that the considerable lapses of time between the smallpox epidemics meant that whole new generations of susceptibles were subject to infection upon the return of the disease and that the repeated ordeals must have had much of the deadliness of virgin-soil epidemics.

Epidemics among the Dakota Indians, 1780–1851

1780–1781	Smallpox.
1801–1802	Smallpox ("all sick winter").
1810	Smallpox.
1813–1814	Whooping cough.
1818–1819	Measles ("little smallpox winter").
1837	Smallpox.
1845–1846	Disease or diseases not identified ("many sick winter").
1849–1850	Cholera ("many people had the cramps winter").
1850–1851	Smallpox ("all the time sick with the big smallpox winter").

Virgin-soil epidemics tend to be especially deadly because no one is immune in the afflicted population and so nearly everyone gets sick at once. During a period of only a few days in the 1960s every member of the Tchikao tribe of Xingu Park fell ill with influenza, and only the presence of outside medical personnel prevented a general disaster. Witnesses to the Ungava Bay and Yanomama epidemics noted the murderous effect of nearly universal illness, however brief in duration. The scientists with the Yanomamas found that when both parents and children became sick, "there was a drastic breakdown of both the will and the means for necessary nursing." The observers saw several families in which grandparents, parents, and their children were simultaneously ill.

The fire goes out and the cold creeps in; the sick, whom a bit of food and a cup of water might save, die of hunger and the dehydration of fever; the seed remains above the ground as the best season for planting passes, or there is no one well enough to harvest the crop before the frost. In the 1630s smallpox swept through New England, and William Bradford wrote of a group of Indians who lived near a Plymouth colony trading post that "they fell down so generally of this disease as they were in the end not able to help one another, no not to make a fire nor to fetch a little water to drink, nor any to bury the dead. But would strive as long as they could, and when they could procure no other means to make fire, they would burn the wooden trays and dishes they ate their meat in, and their very bows and arrows. And some would crawl out on all fours to get a little water, and sometimes die by the way and not to be able to get in again."

The second category of factors—those which pertain to the ways Native Americans reacted to epidemic diseases—often had as decisive an influence on the death rate as did the virulency of the disease. American aborigines were subjected to an immense barrage of disease, and their customs and religions provided little to help them through the ordeal. Traditional treatments, though perhaps effective against pre-Columbian diseases, were rarely so against acute infections from abroad, and they were often dangerous, as in the swift transfer of a patient from broiling sweathouse to frigid lake. Thus, to take a modern example, when smallpox broke out among the Moqui Indians in Arizona in 1898, 632 fell ill but only 412 accepted treatment from a physician trained in modern medical practice. Although he had no medicines to cure smallpox or even to prevent secondary bacterial infections, only 24 of his patients died. By contrast, 163 of the 220 who refused his help and, presumably, put their faith in traditional Indian therapy died.

Native Americans had no conception of contagion and did not practice quarantine of the sick in pre-Columbian times, nor did they accept the new theory or practice until taught to do so by successive disasters. The Relation of 1640 of the Jesuit missionaries in New France contains the complaint that during epidemics of the most contagious and deadly maladies the Hurons continued to live among the sick "in the same indifference, and community of all things, as if they were in perfect health." The result, of course, was that nearly everyone contracted the infections, "the evil spread from house to house, from village to village, and finally became scattered throughout the country."

Such ignorance of the danger of infection can be fatal, but so can knowledge when it creates terror, leading to fatalism or to frenzied, destructive behavior. A large proportion of those who fall acutely ill in an epidemic will die, even if the disease is a usually mild one, like influenza or whooping cough, unless they are provided with drink, food, shelter, and competent nursing. These will be provided if their kin and friends fulfill the obligations of kinship and friendship, but will they do so? Will the sense of these obligations be stronger than fear, which can kill by paralyzing all action to help the sick or by galvanizing the healthy into flight?

If we may rely on negative evidence, we may say that aboriginal kin and tribal loyalties remained stronger than the fear of disease for a remarkably long time after the coming of the micro-organisms from the Old World. We will never be able to pinpoint chronologically any change as subtle as the failure of these ties, but whenever it happened for a given group in a given epidemic, the death rate almost certainly rose. In most epidemics contagious disease operating in crowded wigwams and long houses would spread so fast before terror took hold that panicky flight would serve more to spread the infection than to rob it of fresh victims, and any decline in the number of new cases, and consequently of deaths that might result from flight, would at the very least be cancelled by the rise in the number of sick who died of neglect. Observers of the Ungava Bay epidemic reported that a fatalistic attitude toward the disease caused the loss of several entire families, whose members would not help each other or themselves. Scientists with the Yanomamas during their battle with measles recorded that fatalism killed some and panic killed more: The healthy abandoned the sick and fled to other villages, carrying the disease with them.

When a killing epidemic strikes a society that accepts violence as a way of reacting to crises and believes in life after death—characteristics of many Christian and many Indian societies—the results can be truly hideous. Many fourteenth-century Europeans reacted to the Black Death by joining the Flagellants or by killing Jews. Some Indians similarly turned on the whites whom they blamed for the epidemics, but most were obliged by their circumstances to direct their fear and rage against themselves. During the epidemic of 1738 many Cherokees killed themselves in horror of permanent disfigurement, according to their contemporary James Adair. Members of the Lewis and Clark expedition were told that in the 1802 smallpox epidemic the Omahas "carried their franzey to verry extrodinary length, not only burning their Village, but they put their *wives* and children to *Death* with a view of their all going to some better Countrey." In 1837 smallpox killed so many of the Blackfeet and so terrified those left alive after the first days of the epidemic that many committed suicide when they saw the initial signs of the disease in themselves. It is estimated that about 6,000, two thirds of all the Blackfeet, died during the epidemic.

The story of that same epidemic among the Mandans, as George Catlin received it, cannot be exceeded in its horror:

> It seems that the Mandans were surrounded by several war-parties of their most powerful enemies the Sioux, at that unlucky time, and they could not therefore disperse upon the plains, by which many of them could have been saved; and they were necessarily inclosed within the piquets of their village, where the disease in a few days became so very malignant that death ensued in a few hours after its attacks; and so slight were their hopes when they were attacked, that nearly half of them destroyed themselves with their knives, with their guns, and by dashing their brains out by leaping head-foremost from a thirty foot ledge of rocks in front of their village. The first symptoms of the disease was a rapid swelling of the body, and so very virulent had it become, that very many died in two or three hours after their attack, and in many cases without the appearance of disease upon their skin. Utter dismay seemed to possess all classes and ages and they gave themselves up in despair, as entirely lost. There was but one continual crying and howling and praying to the Great Spirit for his protection during the nights and days; and there being but few living, and those in too appalling despair, nobody thought of burying the dead, whose bodies, whole families together, were left in horrid and loathsome piles in their own wigwams, with a few buffalo robes, etc. thrown over them, there to decay, and be devoured by their own dogs.

During that epidemic the number of Mandans shrank from about 1,600 to between 125 and 145.

Whether the Europeans and Africans came to the Native Americans in war or peace, they always brought death with them, and the final comment may be left to the Superior of the Jesuit Missions to the Indians of New France, who wrote in confusion and dejection in the 1640s, that "since the Faith has come to dwell among these people, all things that make men die have been found in these countries."

3

OPECHANCANOUGH: INDIAN RESISTANCE LEADER

J. FREDERICK FAUSZ

As the field of Native American history continues to mature, scholars have begun to analyze individual leaders for insights into the motivations of tribal peoples. A biographic focus allows some writers to dispel at least a few of the ethnocentric ideas that remain current about Indians. For example, many people still seem to think that Native Americans treated the Europeans who stumbled ashore near their villages as gods or magical creatures with immense power. Although the invaders did possess firearms, the wheel, and domesticated animals, frequently the native peoples dealt with the local situation in more effective ways. This reading shows that the Virginia tribal leaders Powhatan and his brother Opechancanough recognized clearly both the dangers and the opportunities the English colonists presented. After Powhatan's death, Opechancanough strove to keep the colonists from taking tribal lands for tobacco production. Throughout his several decades of leadership the forceful chief showed his skill as a diplomat, an inspirational leader, and a military planner. The author demonstrates Opechancanough's efforts to use Indian religious beliefs and traditions to generate a backlash against English incursions. In analyzing the Indian's motivations and actions, this essay shows how much can be learned about the internal workings of a tribal society. Biography can not answer all of the questions historians want to raise, but in this case it shows how both the English and the native people tried to manipulate the local situation to their own advantage. It also presents the depth of Indian cultural pride and the ethnocentrism of both whites and Indians alike.

J. Frederick Fausz is a professor of history at St. Mary's College in Maryland.

In May 1607, as the loblolly pines swayed in the spring breeze and the sturgeon were beginning their spawning runs up the broad tidal rivers, a determined band

Source: J. Frederick Fausz, "Opechancanough: Indian Resistence Leader," in David Sweet; Gary Nash. *Struggle and Survival in Colonial America*, pages 21–37 (text only). Copyright © 1981 The Regents of the University of California.

of 105 Englishmen established an invasion beachhead among the fertile meadows and marshy lowlands of Indian Virginia. Only four decades later, with their once-meager numbers now swelled to some fifteen thousand persons, the invaders had made themselves the masters of tidewater Virginia.

The possessors of this rich land—the people the English defeated, displaced, and nearly annihilated in creating the first successful colony in British America—were Algonquian Indians, known collectively as the Powhatans. Because they lost and because historians of the United States have been the political descendants of the victorious English invaders, there have been few attempts to comprehend the personalities or motivations of the Virginia Indians. The legends and tales that abound about the romantic Pocahontas and her father, the "Emperor" Powhatan, have remained popular primarily because they symbolize the so-called superiority and strength of the English conquerors. Pocahontas was a "good Indian" because she renounced her culture and became a converted Englishwoman, while Powhatan confirmed the myths of Indian weakness by capitulating to the whites within a few years after 1607.

While it is true that Pocahontas and Powhatan dealt with the English presence as they saw fit, there was a more characteristic manner of responding to invaders in the context of Powhatan cultural traditions. This was the way represented by Opechancanough (O-puh-can'-can-ō), kinsman of Pocahontas and Powhatan and the much-vilified architect of the bloody Indian uprisings of 1622 and 1644.

Who was this man who has been referred to as the cruel leader of the "perfidious and inhumane" Powhatans, the "unflinching enemy . . . of the Saxon race," and a chieftain "of large Stature, noble Presence, and extraordinary Parts" who "was perfectly skill'd in the Art of Governing"? Although few details are known about his early life or background, Opechancanough—or Mangopeesomon, as he was later called by his people—was trained from boyhood to be a leader of the Powhatans in war and in peace.

When the English arrived in Virginia, they reported that Opechancanough was linked by blood and alliance to Powhatan, the supreme chieftain (*Mamanatowick*), who had constructed a proud and strong tidewater Indian empire in the last quarter of the sixteenth century. By 1607 Powhatan ruled the largest, most politically complex and culturally unified chiefdom in Virginia. Called Tsenacommacah (Sen-ah-com'-ma-cah)—meaning "densely inhabited land"—this Indian chiefdom had a total population of some twelve thousand persons. Forged by conquest, based on efficient administration and common defense, and maintained by force of arms, tribute, religious beliefs, and the authoritarian personality of a determined ruler, Tsenacommacah was a sovereign and extensive political domain. Powhatan was regarded as the great lord of an integrated kinship society administered by carefully selected local chiefs, or governors, of much power and wealth. These tribal leaders were called *werowances* ("he who is rich"), and among them there was none stronger than Opechancanough.

From a cluster of villages located near the present West Point, Virginia, where tributaries form the York River, Opechancanough ruled over the important Pamunkey tribe. The largest single tribe in Powhatan's domain, the Pamunkeys around 1607 had a population of some twelve hundred, including over three hundred warriors. Their territory—called Opechancheno, after their leader—abounded in fresh water, deer-filled forests, large villages, and acres of planted corn, tobacco, beans, and squash. The Pamunkeys' homeland was also rich in copper and in pearls from freshwater mussels, and Opechancanough's influence derived at least partially from his monopoly of the latter commodity.

The most important source of Opechancanough's power, and a significant factor in explaining many of his later actions, was undoubtedly his role as chief of the most fearsome band of Powhatan warriors. The English often spoke of how disciplined and fierce the Pamunkeys were and reported that Opechancanough was able to mobilize a thousand bowmen in two days' time. His warriors joined battle armed with skillfully made longbows, four-foot arrows, and wooden clubs; their faces and shoulders were smeared with scarlet pigment, and they were adorned with mussel shells, beads, copper medallions, feathers, bird talons, and fox fur.

Despite his considerable power and influence, in 1607 Opechancanough was still subordinate to Powhatan. Although second to his kinsman, Opitchapam, in the line of succession to the title of *Mamanatowick*, he was forced to do the great chief's bidding, just as was any other tribesman less endowed with talent and status. Powhatan had no rivals in tidewater Virginia. As long as he lived, all the *werowances*, including Opechancanough, owed him deference and paid him tribute from the tribes under their control.

In May 1607, only two weeks after the English landed at Jamestown, the *Mamanatowick* mobilized his *werowances* and decided to test the white men by force of arms. It was Opechancanough's duty to keep the more important English leaders distracted some miles upriver from the settlement while other *werowances* attacked James Fort. This assault by several hundred warriors failed to dislodge the English garrison, however, and within days Powhatan altered his strategy. He now decided to offer hospitality to the invaders, and again Opechancanough followed his lead by sending presents of food and overtures of peace to Jamestown.

Similarly, when in December 1607 the *Mamanatowick* desired his first audience with an Englishman, Opechancanough was dispatched to capture Captain John Smith, the most conspicuous leader at Jamestown, and to conduct him safely to Werowocomoco, Powhatan's capital. This Opechancanough did, although some of his own Pamunkey tribesmen called for the death of the white captain.

Opechancanough's inferior position was further emphasized in the February–March 1608 negotiations for a joint Anglo-Powhatan expedition against the Monacan Indians to the west. It was decided that Powhatan and Captain Christopher Newport, "being great Werowances," would not personally lead their forces into battle but would leave the military details to lesser war chiefs: John Smith and Opechancanough.

Although there is no evidence that Opechancanough was ever disloyal to Powhatan in these years, he was an ambitious man who doubtless resented his subordinate status under the *Mamanatowick*. His position became increasingly undesirable after 1608, since while trying to preserve the tenuous peace advocated by Powhatan, he was forced to endure insufferable aggressions by the English. After September 1608 John Smith initiated a purposeful campaign of intimidation, using both threats and force to put Powhatan's people on the defensive. On one occasion Smith captured and imprisoned two Indian warriors, and Opechancanough was obliged to humble himself and negotiate for their release. He sent his own shooting glove and wrist guard to Smith as a token of goodwill and entreated the captain to free the hostages "for his sake." The prisoners were eventually released, but the fact that Opechancanough had been forced to beg meant that the cost in pride had been high.

It was only a matter of time before the brash Smith took still further advantage of his reputed ability to intimidate Indian leaders. In January 1609 he brazenly led a contingent of armed Englishmen into Opechancanough's Pamunkey enclave in search of food. When the warriors refused to supply corn to the English, an enraged Smith grabbed Opechancanough by the hair and held a loaded pistol to his chest. He threatened the frightened *werowance* in front of the Pamunkeys and forced the tribesmen "to cast downe their armes, little dreaming anie durst in that manner have used their king." Smith demanded pledges of good behavior and a regular corn tribute from Opechancanough's people and vowed to load his ship with their "dead carkasses" if they ever again crossed him. In addition, soon after this incident Smith physically assaulted a son of Opechancanough and "spurned [him] like a dogge."

Such harsh and shockingly disrespectful treatment of a Pamunkey leader was unprecedented, and Opechancanough's credibility as a war chief and status as a "royal" *werowance* were jeopardized by such incidents. Perhaps as a result of this, sometime between 1608 and 1612 Opechancanough was humiliated by a fellow *werowance* named Pipsco. Pipsco brazenly stole away one of Opechancanough's favorite wives and flaunted his relationship with the woman for years afterward. In the light of such events, how was the Pamunkey chieftain to cope with his own declining status as well as with the larger threat that the increasingly aggressive English invaders posed to all of Indian Virginia?

Matters soon got worse for the Powhatans in general, although Opechancanough's particular position gradually improved after 1609. John Smith's policy of intimidation with limited bloodshed was succeeded in 1609 by a chaotic period during which short-sighted Englishmen senselessly robbed and murdered Indians. Violent retaliation by the Powhatans quickly escalated into full-scale warfare between 1609 and 1614. Although many Englishmen were killed at first, their overall position was eventually strengthened by increased financial and moral support from London, by large supplies of arms, and by the arrival in Virginia of several dozen fighting men under experienced military commanders.

This First Anglo-Powhatan War proved disastrous for the Powhatans. In a series of sharp and brutal engagements, armored English musketeers attacked tribe after tribe until they gained control of the James River from Chesapeake Bay to the fall line. Powhatan, the aging chief, was unable to halt the English advance, but Opechancanough and his Pamunkeys fared better. In November 1609 they decimated an English force that had come to steal corn, and the result was that the leaders of the colony cautiously waited until 1613 before they felt confident enough to invade the Pamunkeys' territory again. Because of their strength in arms and the placement of their villages at some distance from the area of most active fighting along the James River, the Pamunkeys were spared the worst ravages of the war. Relative to Powhatan's declining power and the losses sustained by other area tribes, the Pamunkeys under Opechancanough became ever stronger.

Powhatan, the once-awesome ruler of tidewater Virginia, spent the war years largely in seclusion. The repeated English onslaughts had taken their toll on the energy and abilities of the *Mamanatowick,* already in his late sixties. By this time Powhatan "delighted in security, and pleasure, and . . . peace" and desired to be "quietly settled amongst his owne." He had tired of conflict. "I am old," he told the English, "and ere long must die. . . . I knowe it is better to eat good meat, lie well, and sleep with my women and children, laugh and be merrie . . . then [to] bee forced to flie . . . and be hunted." Powhatan's favorite daughter, Pocahontas, was captured by the English in 1613. In the next year she renounced her heritage, accepted the Anglican faith, and prepared to marry an English planter, John Rolfe. But Powhatan stubbornly refused to capitulate to the English until the Pamunkeys under Opechancanough were attacked by a large force of armed musketeers. Now a broken man, Powhatan meekly accepted a humiliating peace treaty in the spring of 1614. He who might have crushed the English in 1607 found himself, only seven years later, pathetically entreating his enemies for a shaving knife, bone combs, fishhooks, a dog, and cat.

While Powhatan contented himself with making ceremonial tours throughout his domain after 1614, Opechancanough boldly stepped into the power vacuum created by the war. In the year of the peace, Indian informants told colony leaders that whatever Opechancanough "agreed upon and did, the great King [Powhatan] would confirme." The English noted that Opechancanough was the Powhatans' "chief Captaine, and one that can as soone (if not sooner) as Powhatan commande the men." And in 1615 it was reported that Opechancanough "hath already the commawnd of all the people." Finally, in the summer of 1617, Powhatan, grief-stricken upon learning of Pocahontas's death in England, allegedly "left the Government of his Kingdom to Opachanko [Opechancanough] and his other brother [Opitchapam]" and sought refuge among the Patawomeke tribe along the Potomac River.

Powhatan's abdication in 1617 revealed a power struggle among the tidewater Indian *werowances.* At the center of this contest was Opechancanough, who deftly used the English to increase his authority over the area tribes. In 1616 he convinced the proud and quick-tempered governor of the colony, George Yeardley, that the independent Chickahominy tribe had been killing English livestock. This carefully planted information resulted in an English attack during which some forty Chickahominies were treacherously murdered. It was no coincidence that Opechancanough was nearby to witness the slaughter and that he quickly stepped forward to comfort the bloodied and frightened Chickahominies. That tribe then declared Opechancanough their king, gave him their allegiance, and agreed to pay him tribute. As John Smith later explained these events, Opechancanough had succeeded in his plan "for the subjecting of those people, that neither hee nor Powhatan could ever [before] bring to their obedience."

Such maneuvers clearly demonstrated Opechancanough's ambition, and upon Powhatan's death in April 1618 the wily Pamunkey *werowance* became the effective overlord of the tidewater tribes. Opechancanough was finally the "great Kinge," and as "a great Captaine" who "did always fight," he was called upon to use his talents and status in an active, dangerous struggle against the English. But his lust for political control was not only a personal one; it was also an unselfish and desperate attempt to prevent the total collapse of a weakened and threatened Tsenacommacah. Between 1618 and 1622 Opechancanough's priorities were clearly focused on strengthening and revitalizing his people.

The challenges he faced were immense. In the years immediately following the First Anglo-Powhatan War, the English had dispossessed the Indians of much of their best land. This was especially true after 1618, when a boom in tobacco prices sharpened English land appetites, and famine and disease wracked the once-strong Powhatans. Poor harvests made the Indians dependent on their hated enemies for food, while epidemics devastated the Powhatans and even the deer in their forests between 1617 and 1619. Although disease attacked all the tidewater tribes, Opechancanough's Pamunkeys may have suffered proportionately less than other Powhatans because their territory lay at some distance from the English settlements.

In the wake of these tragedies the Powhatans were pitiable but not pitied. Their English enemies regarded the debilitated, depopulated, and seemingly unthreatening Indians more as defeated and downtrodden pawns than as proud and fierce warriors. Complacent in the peace of 1614 and temporarily less dependent on the Indians for food, the English considered the Powhatans merely impotent and troublesome obstacles to the exploitation of Virginia's lands and resources. It was in these exceedingly adverse circumstances that Opechancanough began his methodical consolidation of the remnants of Powhatan's once-united chiefdom, along with the recruitment of tribes like the Chickahominies who had never been a part of Tsenacommacah. It was ironic that although Opechancanough had often displayed his potential for leadership, it was only the harsh presence of the English that brought him to the fore.

Opechancanough's plan depended on manipulating two intertwined social pressures: the desire of the Indians to procure the colonists' muskets and the attempts of the English to convert and "civilize" the Powhatans. The Virginia Company of London, the joint-stock corporation in charge of colony affairs, was sincerely interested in Christianizing and educating Indian youths, and colonial officials approached Opechancanough many times in an effort to borrow or even buy Powhatan children for this purpose. But the chief refused to allow any Indians to live among the English unless they were permitted the use of muskets. Ever since 1607 the Powhatans had been attempting to obtain firearms from the English. Recognizing that this single technological advantage was the key to English domination, Opechancanough was determined somehow to alter the colonists' monopoly of muskets. Faced with his refusal to provide children for Christianization and under unceasing pressure from missionary idealists among the company's investors in London, the Virginia leaders finally allowed some Powhatans to be trained in the use of firearms.

Thus, while the colonists were preoccupied with growing tobacco and were complacent about the Indians' reputed powerlessness, Opechancanough's men

were becoming competent marksmen. By 1618 Englishmen were occasionally being killed by Indians using muskets, and it was reported that the Powhatans would
be "boulde . . . to assault" white settlements whenever they concluded that English firearms were "sicke and not to be used" against them.

By 1622 Opechancanough's leadership had made the tidewater tribes stronger than at any other time since 1607. The English judged the chief's own stronghold so defensible that three hundred musketeers—more men than had been drawn
together in a single force during the First Anglo-Powhatan War—would be required to launch an attack against the Pamunkeys. This was a far cry from the
English assessment of a decade before that the Indians were incapable of inflicting
harm.

Opechancanough had succeeded in engineering this military renaissance and
the psychological revitalization of his people in large part through the efforts of
Nemattanew (Ne-mat'-ten-ū), a mysterious prophet, war captain, and advisor, who
was himself one of the first Powhatans to become an able marksman with English
muskets. Called "Jack of the Feathers" by the colonists, Nemattanew always went
about attired in elaborate and unique feather garments, "as thowghe he meant to
flye." He was respected by the Powhatans, and by Opechancanough especially, as
a charismatic and talented policymaker, while the English called him a "very
cunning fellow" who "took great Pride in preserving and increasing . . . [the
Indians'] Superstition concerning him, affecting every thing that was odd and
prodigious to work upon their Admiration." Significantly, Nemattanew told his
people that he was immortal, that he was therefore invulnerable to English bullets,
and that he possessed "an Ointment" and special powers "that could secure them"
from bullets as well.

By the spring of 1621, as Nemattanew's revitalizing influence grew among
the Powhatans, Opechancanough made plans to annihilate the hated English. His
first step was to conclude a firm peace with the colony so that the whites would
confidently put aside their muskets for plows and allow the Powhatans to move
freely among their plantations. Then, further to lure the English into complacency,
Opechancanough decided to tell his adversaries what they wanted to hear concerning the religious and cultural conversion of his people.

He was able to accomplish his goals because in 1620–21 the Virginia Company had sent two naive and optimistic reformers to the colony to implement its
program for the "civilization" of the Indians. These men were Sir Francis Wyatt,
Jamestown's new governor, and George Thorpe, an idealistic proselytizer. They
tried to win over Opechancanough's people with lavish gifts, English clothes, and
kind words. Wyatt and especially Thorpe set out to undermine Powhatan religion
and traditions and to alienate Indian youths from their elders by promoting English
customs and Christianity among them. This energetic new campaign seemed especially dangerous to Opechancanough, but he acted coolly and resourcefully in
the face of it.

Late in 1621 Opechancanough met with the zealous Thorpe, who had been
trying to convert him for months, and to the astonishment of everyone renounced
the major teachings of Powhatan religion. He promised to allow English families to
live among the Pamunkeys and gave his permission for the colonists to take any

lands not actually occupied by the Powhatans! These startling announcements would have amounted to heresy had they been made sincerely, but Opechancanough was purposefully deceptive in initiating the final chapter in his consolidation of power. By lulling Thorpe, Wyatt, and the other Englishmen into complacency, Opechancanough was forging a strategy more subtle in its execution, more ethnocentric in its foundation, and more revolutionary in its potential impact than Thorpe's.

Thanks to the efforts of Opechancanough and Nemattanew, the Powhatans were by this time more strongly committed to their own culture than ever. Opechancanough saw clearly that there could be no Anglo-Powhatan relations based on peace. Every tragedy that could have befallen the Indians had occurred, and the English had brought destruction to the tribes as readily in times of peace as in times of war. A prolonged peace could only result in more seizures of Indian corn and territory and in further attempts to destroy his people's culture. What did the Powhatans have to gain by keeping the peace? What could they lose by breaking it?

From Opechancanough's personal standpoint, everything the English had done before 1621 had served to increase his power and leverage in Powhatan politics; anything they might do from that time forward was likely to weaken his position. The chief's bold strategy with Thorpe nevertheless revealed confidence in the Indians' future rather than despair. Opechancanough had no intention of leading the Powhatans into physical or cultural suicide; his statements and actions reflected strength and pride, not weakness or desperation.

Opechancanough's plans were suddenly put in jeopardy when in early March 1622 some Englishmen "accidentally" murdered the "immortal" Nemattanew under suspicious circumstances. But Powhatan resiliency and Opechancanough's resolve were confirmed only two weeks later when, as spring breezes once again replaced winter's chill among the pines, an impressive Indian alliance suddenly attacked the English settlements along the entire length of the James River. In this famous uprising of March 22, 1622, Opechancanough's warriors infiltrated white homesteads without arousing suspicion and managed to kill some 330 people before the colony mobilized its forces. Shocked and frightened by this bold and bloody stroke, the English grudgingly recognized Opechancanough's skill as the "Great generall of the Salvages."

The 1622 uprising touched off a ten-year war, and for a brief time Powhatan warriors outdid their enemies, using muskets made in England. Distraught whites reported that the Indians became "verie bold, and can use peeces [muskets] . . . as well or better than an Englishman." With the Powhatans well armed with captured weapons, the colonists feared that they would "brave our countrymen at their verie doors."

This Second Anglo-Powhatan War reached its peak in autumn 1624, when an intertribal force of eight hundred warriors, dominated by Pamunkeys, fought English musketeers in a fierce, two-day battle in open field. In this unusual engagement waged in Pamunkey territory, Opechancanough's warriors fought to defend their homeland and to preserve their excellent reputation among other area tribes. Although the Pamunkeys were eventually forced to retreat, never before had the

Indians demonstrated such tenacity under fire. Even Governor Wyatt had to admit that this battle "shewed what the Indyans could doe."

Recognizing Opechancanough's importance to the Indians' courage and persistence, Jamestown officials placed a bounty on his head. The English came close to killing him in 1623 by means of an elaborate plot to ambush and poison several parleying chiefs. Opechancanough was almost certainly present at the meeting, where many Indian leaders died, but somehow he managed to escape the English trap.

The war continued, but by 1625 both sides had come to the realization that the annihilation of their enemies was impossible. For almost three years Governor Wyatt and his commanders had "used their uttermost and Christian endeavours in prosequtinge revenge against the bloody Salvadges" without making Opechancanough or his people submit. The Pamunkey *werowance* had proved a better "generall" than Powhatan, and in 1625 the fatigued English soldiers decided to suspend their twice-yearly campaigns against him. Choosing to plant tobacco rather than to pursue the utter destruction of the Powhatans, the colonists had, in Governor Wyatt's words, "worne owt the Skarrs of the Massacre."

Although the Second Anglo-Powhatan War did not end officially until 1632, the early years of the conflict were the most significant in demonstrating that the Indians' pride had not been extinguished by a decade and a half of disruptive and frequently brutal contact with the Englishmen. By war's end it might be said that Opechancanough had won a qualified victory. If he had not succeeded in annihilating the colonists, he had at least ended the threat of enforced culture change. His people had willingly risked death rather than adopt the Christian religion and English manners. Although many Powhatans did die, their traditions were for the time being preserved.

After peace was agreed to in 1632, there followed a decade of tenuous coexistence between the Powhatans and the English. The Indians had been weakened by the war, and they welcomed an opportunity to tend their fields in peace. In the long run, however, the period after 1632 proved more damaging to the Powhatans than the war years. The Virginia colony developed so rapidly that the Indians' territorial and cultural foundations were quickly and irrevocably eroded. After a dozen years, with nowhere to go and with a smaller and smaller amount of land on which to preserve their traditions and to raise their children, the Powhatans once again chose the desperate option of war.

In the spring of 1644, as the sturgeon and the meadows again experienced nature's season of renewal, the tireless Opechancanough mobilized a new generation of warriors for an even more desperate rebellion. As in 1622, the Powhatans struck at the English plantations without warning and killed some five hundred of the land-hungry colonists. But this uprising proved futile, for by this time the odds against success were overwhelming. In 1646, after almost two years of brutal warfare, the by now infirm but indefatigable Pamunkey chief, who had seen some eighty winters, was captured and murdered by the English.

Opechancanough's death ended a talented and tempestuous career of leadership that spanned four eventful decades. He had known and warred with an entire generation of Englishmen, long since dead. The Virginia governor who captured him in 1646 had been a mere babe in the cradle when Jamestown was founded.

The last of the "true" Powhatans, Opechancanough had symbolized the precontact glory of Tsenacommacah, while adapting to the postcontact exigencies of cultural survival. He had demonstrated resiliency and political resolve in his magnificent effort to save the Powhatan way of life, and he had in fact succeeded in the difficult task of rebuilding and enlarging Powhatan's domain after the first peace with the English in 1614. The Pamunkeys' resort to arms in two bloody wars between 1622 and 1646 reveal that Opechancanough had managed to reinstill pride and purpose in his people.

Opechancanough coped as best he knew how with the strange and aggressive forces of European colonization. Although his indomitable courage and unyielding fight against foreign domination failed to prevent the eventual subjugation of the Powhatans, Opechancanough's refusal to submit was a reassertion of the proud warrior traditions of his culture. He led his people in a struggle for survival while trying to preserve their self-respect. When the Powhatans had to choose between cultural survival and individual sacrifice, they proudly chose death over enslavement. Victory or defeat mattered less to them than the act of resistance.

In this the "Great generall" set a strong personal example. Even as a captive in 1646, the exhausted Opechancanough displayed pride and dignity until the end. Just before he was treacherously shot in the back by an English guard, the aged Pamunkey *werowance*—"so decrepit that he was not able to walk alone," with "Eye-lids . . . so heavy that he could not see"—was protesting the fact that he had been placed on public exhibition like a caged animal. For such a man and such a culture in such an era, the ability to cope was the ability to fight bravely against overwhelming odds and to die with dignity and purpose.

4

RED-WHITE POWER RELATIONS AND JUSTICE IN THE COURTS OF SEVENTEENTH-CENTURY NEW ENGLAND

LYLE KOEHLER

While some ethnohistorians have moved away from studies of Indian-European relations, that issue remains a significant one. Native Americans tended to see their own culture as superior to that of the invading whites, but during the first generation of contact they learned that they could not avoid their new neighbors. At first Indian leaders dealt with the English from a position of numerical strength and superior environmental knowledge. Yet during the first half-century of colonial settlement in New England the relations between the tribes and the intruders shifted dramatically. The author traces the changes by examining the varied approaches that colonial legal and governmental authorities used in dealing with Indians. Through examples from each of the New England colonies he discusses how and why the courts came to deal with individuals rather than with tribes as a whole. During the early decades of contact tribal leaders disciplined their own people and white authorities frequently accepted customary Indian practices of punishment and repayment. As the colonial settlements grew, this changed: The courts began to deal more harshly with the tribal people than with the settlers. The author notes that each colony treated its tribal neighbors differently and that even within any one colony the treatment of Indians by the white courts varied depending on the local circumstances. This essay shows how the changes in the relationships between the races came about in New England and explains why events took the course they did at the time.

Lyle Koehler is Director of Tutorial and Referral Services at the University of Cincinnati.

Source: Lyle Koehler, "Red-White Power Relations and Justice in the Courts of Seventeenth-Century New England," *American Indian Culture and Research Journal,* vol. 3, no. 4 (1979), pp. 1–31. Reprinted by permission of the author.

Recently there has been considerable disagreement over how well or badly Puritan magistrates treated Native Americans who appeared before them. No one has, however, systematically compared, colony by colony, the penalties assessed red and white offenders who committed similar seventeenth-century crimes. Nor do most observers recognize that European dealings with the Indians constituted a dynamic, changing reality that depended significantly on how secure the early whites considered themselves from any native threat. This essay will attempt to describe how Puritan legal policies toward and punishment of red offenders developed variously throughout southern New England, with particular reference to that issue. Although the New England colonies dealt with Indians in a far from uniform manner, we shall see that white men generally exhibited considerable fairness only when they believed that their safety was at stake. They demonstrated an ethnocentric and, by late century, even racist unfairness once they had achieved some dominion over the Native American peoples around them. When that point was reached, the sentences Calvinist justices handed down to red and white offenders reveal remarkable differences.

In the earliest years of white settlement it was expedient for the Pilgrim and Puritan newcomers to deal fairly with the Indians. Few in number, these transplanted Europeans could hardly afford to alienate nearby tribes. Although the Massachusetts, the Pennacook confederacy of what would become New Hampshire, the Abenaki of Maine, and the Cape Cod residents had been decimated by epidemics from 1616 to 1619, the Narragansetts to the south and Pequots to the west could still muster sizable contingents of warriors. Even the Massachusetts and Wampanoags, despite heavy losses, collectively outnumbered the early English.

Even before boarding the *Mayflower*, Pilgrims fretted about the "continual danger" posed by a "savage people" whom they stereotyped as "cruel, barbarous, and most treacherous." Despite a quick alliance with the Wampanoags, antipathy soon developed between the English and Native American groups such as the Nausets, Massachusetts, and Narragansetts. In fact, some Pilgrims, appalled at the ease with which the Indians acquired arms and ammunition, complained to the King's Council for New England, "We shall be forced to quit the country . . . ; for we shall be beaten with our own arms if we abide." Miles Standish acted in a singularly cocky manner toward red warriors, but his action scarcely covered up the Pilgrims' underlying general anxiety.

Puritans came to the new world in greater numbers, but with similar feelings of insecurity. Although an occasional leader might bluster that "40 of our musketeers will drive five hundred" Indians "out of the fields," he and his contemporaries soon discovered that Indians did not fight English-style, in the open. And while the first colonists at Salem in 1628 had a great quantity of guns, powder, and bullets, they were beset by illness and could spare almost no one to use the firearms at a time when reports of a Narragansett-led "conspiracy" were rife. One of the major concerns of the party of English settlers who landed at Charlestown in June 1630 was aptly expressed by Roger Clap. He wrote, concerning the Indians, "Alas, had they come upon us, how soon they might have destroyed us!"

The Calvinists carefully settled on lands depopulated by the 1616 to 1619 plague, where, they rejoiced, "there is none to hinder our possession; or lay claim to it." Soon after settlement, Pilgrims successfully established friendship with the Wampanoag sachem Massasoit. On a 1623 voyage to Plymouth Virginian John Pory marvelled to find that the Indians "generally do acknowledge" the English occupancy of that locale "and do themselves disclaim all title from it; so that the right of those planters to it is altogether unquestionable." Such a "favor," he related, "since the discovery of America, God hath not vouchsafed, so far as ever I could learn, upon any Christian nation within that continent."

The earliest Puritans to arrive in the Bay Colony received orders from the New England Company in 1629 to "make composition" with any local sachem who "pretended" ownership of land, in an effort to "avoid the least scruple of intrusion." The transplanted Puritan authorities respected the spirit of that injunction. English settlers at Dorchester acquired the occupancy right from Native Americans, then "for a valuable consideration" purchased some extra territory. Seeking both trade goods and allies against their Abenaki enemies, the three hundred Indians at Charlestown welcomed English residency. Sachem Wonohaquaham gave the English "liberty" to locate there. Other colonists secured the right to inhabit Saugus from the ruler of that area, while the first white Bostonians acquired the occupancy right there from the only two remaining Indian inhabitants, as well as from the Massachusetts chief sachem Chickataubot. Another local leader "sold" Nahant to Thomas Dexter for a suit of clothes.

Many sachems had little apparent objection to the English settling on the depopulated seacoast lands they governed. Unfortunately no record of the contracts early Indians made with the whites remains. It may be that the English, claiming ultimate title from the King anyway, had no pressing need to preserve an account of their dealings with the natives, who obviously could not read it. All that mattered, for purposes of white security, was that the Indians be reasonably satisfied. The gift of some trade goods could insure that, since red people did not conceive of nourishing Mother Earth as a merchantable commodity. Native Americans continued to hunt, fish, and plant on lands inhabited by the whites. Indeed, Indian-English land conveyances recorded between the late 1630s and early 1660s almost always guaranteed such privileges.

In an effort to enhance their own standing with red neighbors and thereby insure their security, the Bay Colony authorities acted in accordance with a New England Company directive to punish any Englishman who injured a native, if only "in the least kinde." When Puritan cattle destroyed Indian maize, adequate compensation was awarded. Red victims of other property destruction or theft received damages. One Massachusetts couple was "very well satisfied" when Puritans whipped a settler for soliciting the squaw's sexual favors. Similarly, if a red man shot an English pig or assaulted a white person, the authorities expected the appropriate sachem to penalize the offender, a practice consistent with Indian custom. Neither Puritan nor Pilgrim attempted to interfere with the internal affairs of any tribe.

Such fairness in English-Indian relations occurred at a time when New England Calvinists had considerable concern over their precarious position, not only vis-a-vis the Indians, but also with respect to the French in Acadia and the Anglicans at home in England. In 1632 the French looted the Plymouth trading house at Penobscot and a year later took another post at Machias. This, coupled with a Privy Council order to stay ships carrying Puritans out of England and the final revocation of the Puritan charter, made friendly relations with the Indians imperative. Calvinists could not hope to survive in the event of war with the French, English, *and* Native Americans.

In the mid-1630s the Calvinists became somewhat more confident of their position. The reason was that epidemic illness in 1633 again hit the Massachusetts and Pennacooks hard and claimed 700 victims among the powerful Narragansetts. In May 1634 John Winthrop declared, "For the natives, they are neere all dead of the small Poxe, so as the Lord hathe cleared our title to what we possess." In 1636 the Puritan Assistants felt secure enough to punish the Indian Chausop in a white court. That red man was sentenced to perpetual slavery for some unspecified offense. After the quick war in 1637 between the Pequots and the English with their numerous red allies, Calvinists had no compunction about making servants out of Pequot women and children and shipping many Pequot males off to slavery in Bermuda, practices rarely used in European wars. Pequot servants who rejected the subsequent English effort to force their attendance at Sabbath assemblies and reading classes by running away from their appointed masters were, upon apprehension, branded on the shoulder.

The Puritans assumed some jurisdiction over the weakened Narragansetts as well, even though that tribe had fought against the Pequots. In 1638 Bay Colony Assistants ordered one Narragansett who had killed a cow to supply satisfaction or directed that the same be taken from the tribe. Four years later the same court ordered the Narragansetts to send another of their people to Boston for allegedly attempting to rape a Dorchester woman.

Puffed up with pride after the defeat of the Pequots, Puritans no longer simply notified the appropriate sachem whenever any difficulty arose. Now, in some instances, they demanded that tribes hand over Indians who committed crimes against whites to Puritan magistrates, although they never relinquished any whites guilty of crimes against the Indians to an offended tribe for trial. The Bay Colony legislature went so far as to pass two laws specifically directed against Indians. In 1637 one ordered all towns to restrain Native Americans from profaning the Sabbath, and in 1641 another directed that Indian substitutes be taken from those peoples who refused to return runaway servants.

It appears, however, that the Calvinists' new-found confidence after the Pequot War had its limits. Massachusetts magistrates did not yet interfere much in intertribal affairs or punish Indians for crimes against other members of the same tribe. Nor did the Puritans actually summon any red Sabbath violators into court. Sometimes white leaders even extended considerable justice to their red contemporaries, albeit not necessarily from the purest motives. For example, when an ex–Pequot War soldier and three servant runaways from Plymouth Colony killed a Narragansett for his wampum, his tribesmen captured and brought them before the Rhode Island authorities. Bay Colony magistrates, when consulted, recommended that the killers either be sent to Plymouth or, since the murder occurred outside English jurisdiction, that the ringleader be turned over to the Narragansett sachem Miantonimo (though with the caution that the Indians should not torture him).

The Rhode Islanders ultimately delivered the murderers to Plymouth officials. Despite talk from "some of the rude and ignorant sort . . . that any English should [not] be put to death for the Indians," Plymouth hanged the offenders on September 4, 1638. Quick action, however, may have been forthcoming only because Roger Williams informed John Winthrop that the victim's "friends and kindred were ready to rise in arms and provoke the rest thereunto, some conceiving that they should now find the Pequots' words true, that the English would fall upon them." Only hesitantly did Native American witnesses to the crime show up in the Plymouth court, for they feared the English could more easily kill them there. Plymouth magistrates may have felt it particularly necessary to extend the Narragansetts justice because of the dispersion of the colony's small population; between 1632 and 1639 Plymouth colonists expanded into seven new communities.

In yet another instance, Connecticut officials considered the case of the Wongunk sachem Sequin, who had joined the Pequots after the colonists at Wethersfield drove him and his people away by force. Later, when Indians killed nine Wethersfield settlers, Sequin's accountability became a matter of concern. Ultimately, the Connecticut magistrates concluded that Sequin's war had been "just" and appointed commissioners to compose the differences between him and the colonists.

The extension of justice to Sequin and the Narragansetts may have been in part designed to woo potentially hostile Native Americans into accepting the white man's law. Connecticut's fairness to Sequin was a part of that colony's tentative approach toward the Indians. Located near the still powerful Narragansetts, Pocumtucks, and Connecticut River tribes, this most westerly of Puritan colonies had only about 800 white inhabitants in 1637. In 1638 the Connecticut General Court directed private citizens not to imprison, restrain, or whip Indians. Any menacing speeches by white persons were illegal unless hurled at Indians discovered assaulting a settler's person or property. No law required Native Americans to return runaway servants or to respect the Sabbath. In 1640 Connecticut deputies decided that Indians should merely supply double restitution for theft, although white thieves usually received that penalty plus a whipping. (From the Indian perspective, however, even that punishment was too severe, as Native American custom specified only that the value of the stolen goods be returned and, in intertribal relations, held the group, not the individual, responsible.)

Still, Connecticut practices were far from equitable overall. The General Court held sachems accountable for any English swine or cattle killed in their territories, even if the act were done by an Indian of another tribe (1638). Yet no English colony would ever hold a local magistrate accountable for a crime committed in his jurisdiction. Similarly, Connecticut magistrates bound all Indians who had received Pequot captives, in a postwar distribution, to pay tribute to the colony—a practice inconsistent with the postwar division of spoils among European allies. On occasion the white authorities could also threaten to use force against smaller tribes for the most unreasonable of reasons. In 1638, for example, the deputies sent six men to the Waranots to learn why those Indians "saide they are afraid of vs, and if they will not come to vs willingly then to compell them to come by violence."

Notwithstanding such actions, Connecticut could not afford to become overly belligerent. Relations between that colony and Massachusetts Bay had deteriorated after the Pequot War as a consequence of Connecticut's declaration of independence. Indeed, Connecticut made a separate treaty with the Narragansetts and told them their 1636 treaty with the Massachusetts Puritans was no longer binding. Furthermore, some of the River tribes disliked the English alliance with the Mohegan sachem Uncas. One River leader, Sequasson of the Waranots, went so far as to pay a Pocumtuck to assassinate three prominent Connecticut magistrates; the prospective killer was told that he should "give it out that Vncas had hired him for so much Wampum," so that the English would go to war against the Mohegans. The assassination plan was not successful; the authorities were also concerned because, whenever English constables did incarcerate an Indian for committing an offense against whites, the man usually escaped, an act which presumably increased Indian "insolence."

Worried over their vulnerability, Connecticut settlers took precautions against the possibility of Indian-English conflict. They levied a fine on any red man who handled English weapons. The deputies procured a type of armor for distribution at the major villages, required every plantation to keep a magazine of powder and shot, and directed every militiaman to keep a quantity of powder, bullets, and match at his home.

Connecticut was not alone in its apprehensiveness. Despite the assumption by Massachusetts and, after 1639, by Plymouth that white courts could try Indian offenders, Pilgrim and Puritan prudence forced the magistrates of every colony to leave Native Americans relatively free to govern their own intratribal relations and most of their intertribal affairs. Existing court records indicate that the only crimes Calvinists actually prosecuted Indians for were theft, murder, assault against whites, and, in one instance, adultery with a white woman.

Calvinist New Englanders had good reason to pursue a cautious course. There were fears that local tribes might join the anti-English alliance being forged by Miantonimo between 1639 and 1643. The Narragansett sachem's charges that the English had sent smallpox among Native Americans, depleted the game supply, spoiled Indian cornfields by allowing livestock to run free, and permitted their hogs to ravage the clam banks made too much sense to be taken lightly. The Narragansetts, in particular, also represented the fact that, on a 1632 journey to Boston, Governor Winthrop had "with some difficulty" persuaded Miantonimo "to make one of his sanapps [*i.e.*, minor officials]" beat three members of his party who "being pinched with hunger . . . broke into an English house in sermon time to get victuals."

Such punishment for "burglary" greatly upset the Narragansetts because it violated one of their most deeply held customs: the tradition that any traveler could enter an Indian residence and expect to be fed. If the wigwam's inhabitants were absent, the stranger then simply helped himself to the available food. The concept of theft had no meaning to the Indian in this context, unless the traveler carried off a large portion of the existing food supply or some of the occupants' personal possessions. Even then Native Americans simply reprimanded a thief for his first offense and beat him only when he repeated the crime. Miantonimo's reluctance to whip the alleged thieves is understandable. He may have done so only to appease the numerically superior Puritans at Boston. Once the Narragansetts had returned, however, many of that tribe hurled "divers insolent Speeches" at Englishmen and refused to frequent Puritan houses any more.

The English responded quickly to the threat posed by Miantonimo's plans for Indian union. Winthrop believed that if war should begin "we must then be forced to stand continually upon our guard, and the desert our farms and business abroad, and all our trade with the Indians, which things would bring us very low." The Massachusetts governor shuddered at the thought of a conflict in which Indians could flee into the wilderness after ambushing parties of English. White settlers in the four Calvinist colonies (Massachusetts, Connecticut, Plymouth, and New Haven) kept a constant watch, fortified English habitations, formed convoys to travel between plantations, secured heavy cotton wool coats for protection against arrows, and made every effort to increase their stock of easily transportable, efficient wheelocks and flintlocks over the supply of the less useful matchlocks. Finally, in May 1643 commissioners from these colonies formed a league for "offence and defence, mutuall advice, and succour upon all occasions."

Meanwhile, Miantonimo had difficulty getting his alliance off the ground. In 1639 and 1640 another smallpox epidemic destroyed numbers of his confederates among both the Abenaki in Maine and the Long Island Indians. The western Connecticut tribes and remaining Long Islanders became embroiled in war with the New Amsterdam Dutch, thereby decreasing the possibility that they could be mustered against the English. The Indians suffered approximately nine hundred casualties in that war. The Shawomets, tributary to the Narragansetts, caused Miantonimo problems at home by attaching themselves to the Bay Colony. Ultimately, the Narragansetts endured a serious loss when their Puritan-allied enemies, the Mohegans, captured and, with Puritan authorization, killed Miantonimo.

The Narragansett sachem's death brought Miantonimo's plans for Indian union to an untimely end, as smaller groups of Native Americans located between the Merrimack River and Taunton in Plymouth Colony now submitted to Calvinist rule. Finally, in 1645 the Commissioners of the United Colonies declared war on the Narragansetts and Niantics. Three hundred English troops forced the Indian leaders to attend the next Commissioners' meeting at Hartford. There the Indians signed an oppressive treaty.

After the intimidation of the largest Indian group in New England, the Calvinists had reason to feel more secure about bringing their brand of "civilization" to Native Americans. The small seacoast tribes could not have anticipated that Puritans would view submission as a legal justification for cultural dismemberment. White missionaries began bringing Calvinist ideas and values to red populations in eastern Massachusetts, Plymouth, Martha's Vineyard, and portions of Connecticut. In 1646 Massachusetts became the first colony to attempt regulation of virtually all aspects of Indian behavior. Bay Colony Indians were expected to cease powwowing and worshipping their own gods. The Massachusetts General Court agreed not to force any Native Americans to become Christians, but levied the death penalty on any red person who obstinately denied "the true God" or reproached Puritanism "as if it were but a politicke devise to keep ignorant men in awe." Within a year Puritan magistrates in that colony began keeping courts for the trial of small cases among the Indians. Soon, pro-Puritan Indian magistrates would also hold court in the several new praying villages.

The newly created Massachusetts Indian courts sought to use the power of Puritan law to transform Native American ethical standards. Local Indian ruling officials were expected to assess fines for idleness, lying, Sabbath profanation, eating lice, polygyny, and fornication, none of which were offenses before the Puritan intrusion. The strong cultural taboo calling for isolation of a menstruating woman collided with a new law penalizing that action. Native Americans who sought to release tensions or generate excitement through the gambling so common at Indian festivals now risked prosecution. Puritans particularly wanted to curb the expressiveness and sensuality of the Indian lifestyle. Men and women who greased themselves paid a five shilling fine, so that the traditional Indian measures of attractiveness and allure—the dark-stained cheeks and nose, the deep black eye hollows—might give way to the aesthetic wasteland Calvinism offered. The man who bore long locks and the woman who wore her hair loose about her shoulders, instead of "tied up," could also be fined. So could the Indian woman who exposed her breasts in public, even though that was common before the English arrival. The expressively mournful markings, called "disguises" by the Puritans, and the cathartic howls of anguish which accompanied Native American funerals gave way to the inexpressive solemnity of Calvinist graveside ritual. Obsessed with their belief in the essential sinfulness of the Indian's "degenerate" and "disordered" nature, Calvinists attempted to remove what joys and emotional outlets Indian society possessed, substituting for them a morbid introspection. By preaching self-blame, Calvinism helped to devitalize Indian response to the readily apparent erosion of their culture.

Massachusetts prosecutions for fornication, in particular, probably struck "pagan" Indians as incomprehensible. Young Native Americans of both sexes appear to have indulged freely in sex and even discussed their lovers with their parents. As early as 1637 one Pequot maidservant fled to Rhode Island, complaining of having been beaten with firesticks at Boston "because a fellow lay with her." Moreover, Indians did not feel they had to hide their sexual contacts from the prying eyes of neighbors or limit them to the cloaking darkness of night. Their spontaneity created an image that led William Bradford of neighboring Plymouth Colony to imagine lusty red bucks leading chaste English women astray; and when that did not happen, he attributed the result not to Indian disinterest but the "Gods great mercy."

In the 1640s and 1650s Massachusetts officials had a difficult time determining whether "the foul demon of lust" and other offensive Indian practices were being systematically beaten down by the praying village courts. The justices in county and colony courts did, however, begin to punish those red persons who lived in English households. Before 1665 one red man and two female Indian servants received minor whippings for fornication, penalties which were generally consistent with what English fornicators received. Another Indian man was sentenced to pay a fine for adulterous "lewdness." Bay Colony magistrates made no further effort, however, to bring all Indian offenders into white or praying village courts.

Plymouth officials, cognizant of their colony's small white population and of the proximity of sizable numbers of Wampanoags and Narragansetts, pursued a less zealous course than their Bay Colony contemporaries. Plymouth missionaries also established many praying villages, but the colony authorities did not try Indians for offenses committed against other Indians, even though they did expect native peoples to abide by colony law in their relations with the English. Between 1639 and 1665 Plymouth magistrates fined a few Indians for thievery—the only red thief lashed was not from Plymouth but Nantucket—and whipped one red man for adultery with a white woman. Pilgrim courts were also careful to uphold contracts made with Indians, to limit the number of Europeans who could legitimately purchase land from them, and to fine whites who assaulted Native Americans.

In Connecticut, where the Indian presence was strongest, Puritans were unable to intrude much upon Native American life. Many of the Native Americans there had not submitted themselves to rule by the English, nor could they be forced to do so. Those red peoples opposed the extension of Christianity into their villages, with the result that praying villages could not be established. The General Court began locating smaller tribes on reservations as early as 1659 and prohibited red men from hunting within the limits of Puritan towns on Sundays, but generally the authorities made no effort to impose Puritan law upon their red neighbors. Even though the deputies worried about the "immorality" attendant upon the frequent mixing of Indians and English laborers, those legislators took no action against Native Americans who entertained such laborers.

The relative freedom Native Americans enjoyed to govern their own affairs—at least outside of Massachusetts—was eroded sharply in the years following the mid-1660s. Calvinist security was insured by the recurrence of epidemic illness among the Indian populations of New England, including "an universal sickness" on Martha's Vineyard in 1645, a wide-ranging "Plague and the Pox" in 1650 and 1651, the "Bloody-Flux" in Massachusetts villages in 1652, and smallpox on Long Island in 1658, 1659, and 1662. As illness decimated and enervated Native Americans, the populations of Calvinist locales, particularly in Massachusetts, swelled from both natural increase and immigration. By 1665 the Bay Colony had fully 23,467 people. Connecticut could claim another eight or nine thousand and Plymouth about four thousand. Moreover, Massachusetts and Plymouth by that date had established enough praying villages to buffer the whites there against their potential enemies. By 1670 Plymouth magistrates no longer chose to consider Native American tribes as separate nations, adequately dealt with only at the highest levels of colonial government. Instead, the authorities attempted to bring all Indians under the purview of the selectmen who supervised town affairs.

As a consequence of these population changes, Calvinists began to bring more Native Americans before the county and colony courts and for a wider variety of offenses. No longer did Indians receive light penalties. They appeared in court for murder, manslaughter, assault, drunkenness, contemptuous remarks, theft, resisting the authority of the Indian court at Nantucket, fornication, rape, adultery, and bigamy. More often than not, the sentences levied on Indians were severe, when compared with those assigned to their white contemporaries for the same offense. When an Indian was the victim, the offender usually escaped with a lesser punishment. In Plymouth and Massachusetts, discrimination, rooted in Calvinist ethnocentrism and racism, became readily apparent.

Between 1665 and 1699 all of the Bay Colony's courts revealed such discrimination. Although fornicators, adulterers, rapists, and murderers received equal sentences, regardless of their race, at least once the Massachusetts General Court considered hanging a red adulteress, even though for thirty years the courts had not inflicted that penalty on an English offender. Red men who killed whites during war hanged, as did at least one red, one black and three white rapists. However, those English who maliciously killed nonhostile red persons during wartime could usually get away scot-free. Decisions in manslaughter cases were more directly inequitable. Between 1670 and 1690 the Massachusetts Court of Assistants tried sixteen men, including two Indians, for manslaughter. Eight white offenders paid fines of £5 to £20, but both Indians were ordered whipped. Magistrates directed nine of the offenders to pay the father or widow of the deceased a sizable sum. While white widows received £10 or £20, John Dyar paid just £6 to John Ahat-tawants' widow after that Englishman had "wickedly" shot the Indian in the back.

When an Indian thief came before the Massachusetts justices, he or she often received more severe treatment than whites convicted of the same offense. The Suffolk County justices between 1670 and 1692 sentenced only 3.5% (six of 170) of the white males convicted of stealing or receiving stolen goods to as many as thirty lashes, plus threefold restitution, while 28.5% (six of twenty-one) of Indian males were penalized that severely. This court ordered 5.8% (ten) of the whites and 14.3% (three) of the Indians to be branded on the forehead with a B, for burglary. The harshest punishment for theft was executed on Sam, an Indian who stole goods valued at but five shillings in 1685, and Thomas Carr, a white who committed burglaries on two consecutive Sundays in 1675, taking goods valued at £19.5s.7d. The magistrates forced both Sam and Carr to submit to a branding, the removal of one ear, and the usual threefold restitution. By contrast, two whites who stole goods valued at as little as five shillings had only to supply triple restitution. Additional examples of inequitable sentencing abound. Three white hog stealers paid triple damages, but two Indians received for the same offense that sentence *plus* thirty lashes each. Whites who broke into homes or warehouses but did not take anything paid fines; Indians were lashed twenty or thirty stripes. Red women also received more severe corporal punishment. Two of three such thieves, but just four of thirty-five pilfering white women, felt the sting of the constable's lash as many as twenty times. And when the victim was red, the white thief who stole some corn, wampum, or a canoe did not even have to pay triple restitution; replacement of the goods or their value was enough. Whites did not receive whippings for theft from Indians and they only occasionally paid a fine.

Distinctions are also readily apparent in the penalties assigned persons convicted of assault. In Suffolk County (1670–1692), thirty-two of ninety-six white assailants paid a fine of ten shillings or less (plus the usual cost of the physician's treatment of the victim). Only thirteen Englishmen received a sentence of corporal punishment, the maximum of thirty lashes being given to one man who wounded a prominent Hingham resident and to a servant who cut his master with a knife. By contrast, seven of the nine Indians convicted of assault suffered bodily punishment. Those who attacked whites got twenty or thirty lashes. Tom of Martha's Vineyard in 1685 became the only assaulter to face a branding. When the victim was red, penalties were considerably less. One Indian who assaulted another received a sentence of ten—instead of two or three times as many—lashes and the Suffolk magistrates allowed him to discharge that sentence by paying a fine. Essex County justices ordered Papaqueeste to pay Jackstrow only six fathoms of wampum for pulling that red man's hair out by the roots, although damages *and* fines were usual in cases of white assault. Similarly, the Superior Court of Judicature ordered Ephraim of Hingham to pay just the costs of the cure for wounding his wife. Whites who struck or wounded red men, once they had paid the costs of treatment, escaped without a fine or whipping.

Indians convicted of drunkenness also experienced more harsh courtroom treatment in Massachusetts than did white inebriates. The Suffolk County Court corporally penalized only six of the thirty-nine white males but all four of the Indians guilty of immoderate drinking. In Essex County three Native Americans were given ten strokes each for drunkenness, while the 382 white offenders almost always paid a ten-shilling fine. Judge Pynchon's magistrates' court in western Massachusetts directed that two of seven white drunkards be wellwhipped, both of whom were convicted of several other offenses as well; he also ordered two of three Native American offenders to be lashed, although neither of them was charged with any other crime.

A similar pattern of discrimination emerged in the Plymouth Colony courts between 1667 and 1699. Before 1667 Plymouth officials ordered none of three recorded Indian thieves to be whipped or sold into slavery; but after that date sixteen of twenty-one offenders were so punished, including one man for merely "lurking about" a house from which £8 turned up missing. The few Englishmen guilty of theft had the option of paying a fine or being whipped. Five red thieves, on the other hand, were sold as slaves, while seven were lashed, two banished, one branded, and the remainder less severely punished. Only one Indian was given the option of buying his way out of a lashing. The same inequities existed with respect to assault punishments. Whites who physically abused or fought with other persons usually paid 3s.4d. fines, irrespective of the victim's race, but Indians who assaulted whites paid 5s. or more. One red man, Sampson, was severely whipped and branded on the shoulder for threatening and abusive carriage toward three women, a punishment far beyond anything any white assailant received.

Historians have made much of the fact that one Indian rapist received a whipping in Plymouth because he was "in an incapacity to know the horibleness of the wickedness of this abominable act," instead of the hanging specified by law. Such treatment, however, reveals no leniency on the part of the Plymouth officials because white rapists were not hanged either. The authorities ordered offenders of both races lashed. It is therefore noteworthy that capital punishment was even considered and then only in the case of the Indian.

Clearcut distinctions existed in the prosecution of Indian and European offenders in Massachusetts and Plymouth, but in the remaining Calvinist colony, conditions were different. Connecticut, even after its incorporation of New Haven Colony, had about one third the population of Massachusetts in nearly the same area, with 10,000 potentially hostile Indians residing in or near the colony. Connecticut courts directed 26.2% (eleven of forty-two) of red thieves and 27.5% (twenty-eight of 102) of whites to be punished corporally. Two Indians and eight Europeans were allowed to discharge their sentence by paying a fine. All assaulters received equal treatment. So did drunkards. Just two of twenty inebriated Indians were sentenced to a lashing, compared to five of 110 whites, and the Indians were permitted to discharge the corporal punishment by paying small fines.

Even in Connecticut, however, instances of discrimination existed. When one white man sexually assaulted a red woman, he became the only rapist in all of New England to escape with merely a fine. The colony Assistants threatened either to hang or banish three Indians who burglarized a white man's house if they fell into such miscarriages again, but no white thief of record was ever frightened with capital punishment. Moreover, only 11.8% of Indians but 31.4% of white offenders were allowed to pay a fine in lieu of a whipping. Out of court, examples of unfair treatment were even more blatant. Connecticut officials usually favored their Mohegan allies in any intertribal difficulties. Like their associates in Massachusetts and Plymouth, those persons designated to purchase land from the Indians, especially after King Philip's War, often no longer made any provision for protecting Indian hunting and fishing rights. Sometimes Englishmen paid drunken, often impoverished Indians for land with wampum or English money, instead of trade goods. Despite many Indian protests about land sales, Massachusetts and Connecticut speculators purchased thousands of acres in Nipmuck, Pennacook, and Mohegan territory after 1676 or just appropriated land without purchasing it.

In all fairness to the Calvinists, it should be mentioned that they did not assume Indians had no rights before the law. The Massachusetts, Plymouth, and Connecticut authorities directed white settlers to fence Indian lands, as well as their own, so that stray livestock would not ruin Native American maize fields; made some effort to determine contested land claims to the satisfaction of all parties; and compensated injured red men. Notwithstanding this, the Suffolk County magistrates ordered just 5% of white but fully 40% of all red offenders to face a whipping of thirty lashes or worse. The Pynchon courts sentenced to a lashing or branding 37.5% of all Indians and 15.1% of all English appearing before those two justices. Plymouth authorities whipped, stocked, branded, or hanged 9.8% of the guilty English but 47.3% of the Indians brought before them. All the Calvinist colonies attempted to extend their legal authority over the many Indian tribes of New England. Connecticut and Plymouth waited until after King Philip's War before they began prosecuting Indian sexual offenders, but before that time they brought some Indians into court for crimes committed against other Indians.

In all of New England south of the Merrimack River just one colony made no effort to extend English law over neighboring Indians, to provide red people with English clothing to help civilize them, to regulate the moral behavior of Native Americans in intricate detail, or to interfere in intra- and intertribal relations. Between 1649 and 1699 white magistrates in Rhode Island and Providence Plantations prosecuted no red person for fornication, adultery, wearing long hair, eating lice, or drunkenness. The General Assembly, in fact, did not create a law against Indian drunkenness until 1673, and then only after consultation with the sachems of five different tribes. That law specified not a whipping but a minor fine of 6s. or a week's labor, and not one Indian was ever penalized under that enactment. The Rhode Island authorities apprehended Native Americans for only the most serious crimes committed against whites. They placed in custody thirteen Indians for theft, three for destruction of English property, two for murder, two for rape, and one for assault, although six of these escaped from the constable or jailor.

The Rhode Island courts did not penalize red offenders any more harshly than whites for the same offense. Murderers and rapists hanged, irrespective of race. Red and white thieves faced usual whippings of fifteen lashes, and only one Indian received as many as thirty lashes. In 1659 the General Assembly enacted a severe measure, one penalizing with sale out of the colony as slaves those Native Americans who stole over £1 worth of property and then refused to make restitution. Again, however, the authorities never actually implemented that law, only going so far as to threaten two thieves with it. Justices did sentence some *white* thieves to West Indian slavery, however, and in one case ordered that a white burglar be hanged, a verdict later suspended. In the land of religious "errors," then, it appears that Calvinist practice was turned on its head: white thieves sometimes fared worse than their red counterparts. Moreover, the white "heretics" sharply punished Englishmen who violated that which the Indians held in sacred trust. In a notable example, when four settlers dug open and robbed some Narragansett graves of what the whites considered a few worthless relics, the offenders were all whipped ten lashes, fined £1 each, and ordered to return everything to its proper place.

Rhode Island also became the first colony to utilize Indian jurors, and pagan ones at that. In 1673 the General Assembly asked two sachems to select six Indians to comprise a jury in one murder case involving members of different tribes. This was the only time of record that the Rhode Island authorities intervened in any intertribal criminal matter, and it was apparently done at the request of the respective Narragansett and Niantic sachems.

Perhaps because of their fairness, Rhode Island officials enjoyed good relationships with the Narragansetts and Niantics, even at such times as those Indians were antagonistic to the Calvinists. It was, of course, expedient for the few white settlers in that colony not to alienate their five thousand Indian neighbors. However, even after King Philip's War had dispersed and sharply decreased the numbers of Native Americans there, Rhode Island policymakers did not begin to intrude in Indian affairs or lifestyles, at least until the eighteenth century. Such Englishmen, believing in the radical religious notion of freedom of conscience, had less need to "civilize" their red contemporaries, even though they did appropriate ten thousand acres of land in Narragansett country after the defeat of that tribe in King Philip's War.

But were the Calvinists really so different from their Rhode Island counterparts? Were the Bay Colony and Plymouth officials motivated by more practical than racist or ethnocentric concerns after 1665? Did they not, in two instances after 1665, give red offenders lesser sentences because the Indians "know not our law"? Did they not merely whip Native Americans because Indians were poor with little maize to discharge a fine at a time when wampum no longer served as lawful currency? And did not Calvinists whip poor whites as well as poor Indians? These issues must be cleared up before the charge of discrimination can be conclusively proven.

Since, as Kai T. Erikson has pointed out, Calvinist justice was coldly righteous, the fact that two red offenders received lightened sentences appears suggestive. One of these, however, lived in Connecticut, where the Puritans pursued a more cautious course. The other, the Plymouth rapist, as previously mentioned, in actuality received no lessened punishment. Harsh treatment, instead of leniency, was the rule. Such harshness was not due to the Calvinist desire to punish red pagans as unregenerate sinners, since it "is the genius and nature of *all* men out of Christ, to be unrighteous." Red pagans could not be trusted, even though whites who had been excommunicated from the Puritan churches or were non–church members, also technically "out of Christ," did not receive harsher treatment in court than church members.

Indian poverty, coupled with the colonial rejection of wampum as legal tender, fails to explain the more severe treatment of red offenders, because almost *all* of the white offenders, at least in Boston and New Haven, were also poor. Three fourths (thirty-one of forty-one) of all criminals tried between 1675 and 1685 and who appear on the 1680 New Haven tax list were rated at £30 or less, while 56.1% of all family heads possessed more than that amount. An additional eleven offenders were propertyless servants or seamen. At Boston 82% of all offenders tried between 1680 and 1692 and appearing on the 1687 tax list held realty valued at £20 or less. This category comprised 65% of all rated persons. When two vagabonds, forty-eight servants or slaves, eighteen seamen, and one seaman's wife are added to the offender totals, fully 90.5% of all criminals owned less than £20 worth of real estate. As many as 26.9% of all New Haven and 43.6% of Boston offenders owned no ratable property at all. Therefore, the comparisons made between white and red criminals are, by and large—and especially when the type of crime is held constant—actually comparisons between Indians and poor whites. In fact, virtually every white person accused of theft was rated extremely low on the tax lists. Yet these offenders, unlike their red counterparts, were still often given the option of paying a fine, even though the fine plus threefold restitution of property usually totaled more than the rated value of their estates. Even propertyless offenders were allowed to pay a fine, thus enabling them to enlist the assistance of friends or relatives for the requisite amount. White servants or poor white offenders were sometimes allowed to work off a fine, but only Connecticut made such a provision for Indians, and then just for cases of drunkenness. All in all, the question of relative ability to pay a fine obscures the essential issue of discrimination, for it does not explain why Indians received more lashes for the same offense.

Nor does the argument wash that Calvinists punished Indians more severely to curb an Indian crime wave. Aboriginal society underwent considerable modification at late century, but no evidence can be found to substantiate an Indian crime wave. A much smaller percentage of the Indian population appeared in any English court than of the white population. Moreover, Puritans expressed no concern that red crime was on the upsurge, even though they complained about the increase of crime among servants, seamen, and adolescents. And these groups were not punished more severely than other English offenders, though it might be reasonably hypothesized—from the Puritan perspective—that such white offenders needed to be taught a lesson.

White Calvinists simply could not view red people as a tawny version of themselves, deserving of equitable treatment. They made little effort to help Indians with courtroom procedure, even though only one of every thirty Native Americans summoned into court had ever been there before in a criminal matter. Not until 1698 did Indians enlist the assistance of white attorneys, and then only at their own initiative. The use of praying Indian jurors after 1674 undoubtedly helped to iron out some difficulties concerning language and the credibility of Calvinist law, but their support for any offender was countermanded by their pro-Puritan sympathies. Hand-picked by the white authorities, these jurors never comprised more than half the members of any jury and never sat on a case in which an Englishman was tried for an alleged wrong done to an Indian. Believing from the earliest years in their own superiority to these people they called savages, rattlesnakes, lazy drones, hellish fiends, and the most sordid and contemptible part of the human species, Puritan and Pilgrim alike only reluctantly allowed Indians to testify against whites, and then only because Calvinists wished to combat the increased sale of spiritous liquors among Native Americans. Indeed, the Indian who in Plymouth Colony could not make good his charge that a white sold him or other red persons strong liquors was ordered whipped. Whites, of course, were not similarly penalized.

Even religious conversion could not erode Calvinist racism. Puritans and Pilgrims made no distinctions in punishments assigned red servants, the inhabitants of praying villages, or tribesmen. No praying Indian ever sat as a judge over Englishmen. No red Christian helped the Calvinists revise their laws. And no Indian, church member or not, was allowed to punish an Englishman. One Plymouth law directed constables to procure some person to lash offenders, "Provided, an Indian or Negro shall not Whip an Englishman."

In summation, then, neither the argument that Calvinists "respected the ability as well as the interests of the natives" nor the equally static view that the invading English ran roughshod over New England Indians from the earliest years of settlement makes good sense. Not being fools, Calvinists treated Indians fairly when red "savages" proved dangerous. As part of a policy to ease white fears of, as William Bradford put it, those "brutish men, which range up and down little otherwise than wild beasts," Calvinists initially made a considerable effort not to offend their red neighbors. Only later, in Massachusetts and Plymouth—areas depopulated of Indians—did Puritans and Pilgrims begin dragging Native Americans into white courts and sharply whipping them for violating Calvinist laws. Connecticut, less secure, pursued a more tentative course, but that colony too interfered by late century in intertribal and intratribal matters and often failed to respond positively to Indian charges of land fraud. Only the Rhode Islanders, those reputed "riff-raff" of New England, appeared to be much motivated by tolerance and fairmindedness, especially after King Philip's War. By 1700 it had become clear to the red peoples of southern New England that, with the exception of Rhode Island, white courts controlled Native American behavior in a most self-serving fashion.

5

THE SILLERY EXPERIMENT: A JESUIT-INDIAN VILLAGE IN NEW FRANCE, 1637–1663

JAMES P. RONDA

Throughout North America a host of missionaries sought to convert the tribal people to one or another variety of Christianity for many generations. Indians, at the same time, viewed their traditional beliefs and practices as serving their needs well. They often rejected the clerics' teachings when they had a chance to do so. In Florida and California the Spanish invaders cooperated fully with the missionaries in establishing strings of missions. Farther north, among the English colonists, religious imperialism moved less rapidly and certainly in a less organized manner as the Protestant denominations spent most of their time and energy among the European colonists or squabbling with each other rather than making any large-scale effort to bring Christianity to the Indians.

In New France, by contrast, the Jesuits moved quickly to found mission stations among the sedentary Hurons in present southern Ontario, as well as carrying on a generationlong effort to locate Christian villages among the nomadic peoples of the St. Lawrence Valley. In this selection the author discusses the serious obstacles the Jesuits faced among the Quebec tribes. These included the nomadic character of the Indians, divisions among the tribal people once some of them accepted and began acting on the Jesuits' teachings, and the continuing threat of attack by raiding Iroquois war parties. The narrative traces the various responses to the missionaries that the Montagnais tribe used during the middle of the seventeenth century. Of equal importance, it shows how the acceptance of Christianity brought division and dissension into Indian society and caused bitter fighting within the settlement. Questions of clan obligations, marriage practices, and Indian local government and leadership all receive some attention. As Ronda shows, the Canadian experience includes significant parallels with events in what is now the United States.

Source: James P. Ronda, "The Sillery Experiment: A Jesuit-Indian Village in New France, 1637-1663," *American Indian Culture and Research Journal*, vol. 3, no. 1 (1979), pp. 1-18. Text only. Reprinted by permission of the author.

The Age of Discovery brought to Western Christianity a missionary challenge of epic proportions. Medieval Christianity had always claimed to be universal, but it was the geographical discoveries of the fifteenth, sixteenth, and seventeenth centuries that moved the claim toward reality. By the seventeenth century the frontier of the Christian mission stretched from China to Paraguay and from Mexico City to Quebec. On that frontier the Society of Jesus was perhaps the best organized and most effective force for the spread of Christianity. Jesuit missions in the New World were a major institution on the frontier and a crucial arena for the confrontation of European and Native American cultures. It is that arena and the meeting of cultural values in one mission region that is the subject of this essay.

While historians of the Christian mission and of Indian-white relations have been quick to see the importance of Jesuit missionaries on the frontiers of the Americas, these same observers have done little to explore the theories and methods of the missionaries, and have been less than quick to examine the impact of the mission on Native Americans. This historiographical failure is nowhere more evident than in studies of the Jesuit missions in New France. From Francis Parkman to the most recent comprehensive history of the Christian mission, the treatment of the missionaries and the Indians has been remarkably similar. The Fathers, so goes this interpretation, brought the blessings of civilization and Christianity to the savage barbarians of the Canadian wilderness while themselves suffering terrible tortures at the hands of the pagans. A new and supposedly scholarly study of the Society of Jesus perpetuates this stereotype by depicting the mission in terms of "cultured and refined Black Robes squatting in a circle of filthy savages . . . or standing as an object of derision before jeering Indians." This is not history; this is hagiography, the lives of martyred saints. As such, it does justice neither to Jesuits nor Indians. The mission as a center of culture contact was far more complex than a simple struggle between civilization and barbarism, Christianity and paganism.

What is needed is the creation of an approach to mission history which blends the insights of history and anthropology in such a way as to analyze the mission as a major point of encounter between Europeans and Native Americans. The essential element in such an approach must be the realization that the mission was much more than simply an instrument for the spread of Christianity. Missionaries, whether in New France, New England, or New Spain, conceived of their task as going far beyond obtaining converts. The Christian mission was an attempt to effect massive culture change upon Native Americans by the introduction of European social and cultural values and institutions into Indian life. Christianization really meant Europeanization, whether at the hands of the Spanish, English, or French. Historians of the Spanish colonies, following the pioneer work of Herbert Eugene Bolton, have long viewed the mission in such a perspective. Bolton's influential 1917 essay "The Mission as a Frontier Institution in the Spanish American Colonies" indicated the methods used by missionaries to make Native Americans into European Indians. What must now be added to Bolton's approach is an understanding of how Native Americans accepted some things the mission had to offer, while often rejecting or modifying the ideological message of Christianity. The application of this perspective—the mission in culture contact—to New

France can suggest, in microcosm, many of the broader patterns of Indian-white relations in the New World.

In 1632 three French Jesuits, led by Superior Paul Le Jeune, arrived in Quebec to establish a mission field. The missionaries were immediately faced with a vast undertaking. Le Jeune soon discovered that the seminomadic Montagnais Indians of the St. Lawrence Valley were very difficult subjects for conversion. Their constant wandering in search of food forced the Jesuits to travel with them, placing severe strains on mission manpower and finances. During the winter of 1633–34 Le Jeune spent all his time with the Montagnais, learning their language and trying without success to convince them of the truths of Christianity and European values. The experience of that winter and its frustrations forced Le Jeune to rethink his whole approach to missionary work. He had never doubted that Indians were human beings with normal intellect. What Le Jeune did believe was that the social environment of the Montagnais was so unstable and so uncivilized that unless it was changed, Christianity would never grow in New France. What was required, so it seemed to the Superior, was the creation of European-styled agricultural communities where the Montagnais could become both Christianized and Europeanized.

It was in his *Relation* for 1634 that Father Le Jeune enunciated his master plan for conversion and culture change. Chapter Three of the *Relation*, significantly titled "On the Means of Converting the Savages," contained the basic elements of the scheme. Equating civilization and Christianity with stable village life, Le Jeune declared that methods had to be found to make such life attractive to the Montagnais. He suggested that hired workmen be sent to help the Montagnais clear farmland and build a small village. Le Jeune also felt that the presence of a few pious French families would serve as a good example to the Indians. He envisioned orderly and peaceful Indian communities founded on true religion and European ways. Le Jeune insisted that once Indians were Europeanized, they "could be more easily won and instructed." Within such Indian communities all the European institutions of church, home, school, and marriage could be brought to bear on the Native American personality. Le Jeune was certain the result would be beneficial both for the Indians and the French colony.

In 1635 Le Jeune began to make specific plans for the development of a Montagnais village. He was convinced that "it would be a great blessing for their bodies, for their souls, and for the traffic of these Gentlemen, [the Company of New France] if those tribes were stationary, and if they became docile to our direction, which they will do, I hope, in the course of time." Knowing that it would demand considerable money and labor to develop a village, Le Jeune turned for help to the colonizer and explorer Samuel de Champlain. Le Jeune suggested that if the Jesuits provided three hired workers and Champlain offered an additional two, this labor force could clear and plant land, thus encouraging at least one Montagnais family to become sedentary. Aware of Champlain's activities in the Three Rivers region below Quebec, the Superior believed that Three Rivers would be an ideal site for the future village. While the missionaries were convinced that their plan "would be the true way to gain the savages," both Champlain and the Montagnais were unimpressed. Champlain evidently felt that the whole effort was too expensive. Even more serious a blow for the project, no Montagnais families seemed at all interested in becoming Frenchified farmers. Far from abandoning the idea, Le Jeune renewed his drive to find adequate financial support for the undertaking.

It was not until 1637 that the Jesuits were able to make real progress with their village plans. On April 27 a Montagnais representative came to visit Le Jeune at Quebec. The Indian discussed with the Superior the possibility of obtaining French aid to build a village in the Three Rivers area. What is clear from the records of the discussion is that the change in the Montagnais position from 1635 was due in large part to their growing fear of the Iroquois and a rapidly declining food supply. Some Montagnais quite realistically saw a French-supported village as an answer to a very serious set of military and economic problems. However, when Le Jeune introduced the idea of Christianity and religious instruction into the meeting, Indian enthusiasm suddenly cooled. The Montagnais were especially unhappy about the prospect of having their children taken from them and educated at the Quebec seminary. All the elders favored French aid, but there was a nearly uniform rejection of any moves toward accepting Christianity. This opposition and the ever present problem of insufficient funds again forced the postponement of the venture. Le Jeune, deeply disappointed, bitterly declared, "it is a pitiable thing, I cannot repeat too often, that the spiritual welfare of these barbarians should be retarded by the lack of temporal resources."

Undaunted by two failures, Le Jeune was still convinced of the workability of his plan. The Superior was optimistic that Montagnais opposition would be easily overcome once sufficient funds were found to clear land and build at least one house. From internal evidence in Le Jeune's *Relations* for 1637 and 1638 it can be inferred that during 1637 he carried on an extensive correspondence with laymen of the French nobility who might provide funds for the village. Sometime during 1637, perhaps in the spring, Le Jeune's letter campaign bore fruit. News came to Quebec that Noël Brûlart de Sillery, Commander of the Order of Malta and formerly a minister and ambassador of the king, had decided to furnish funds to hire workers for the village project. Armed with this information, Le Jeune moved quickly to implement his plans. Having abandoned a Three Rivers site as being too open to Iroquois attack, Le Jeune selected a location at the foot of the cliff of Cape Diamond, about a league and a half from Quebec. The Jesuits hoped that Montagnais familiarity with the place—the Indians often used its sandy bay—would be an additional attraction for the settlement. Committing himself even further, the Superior ordered that in July work be commenced on a Jesuit residence house at the village site. Finally, Le Jeune made arrangements with François Derré de Gand, owner of the Cape Diamond property. De Gand agreed to give the Jesuits 10,584 arpents (8,820 acres) for a village and adjoining farmland. The remaining task, surely the most difficult one, was to find one or more Montagnais families willing to abandon their traditional ways to become Christian farmers.

Early in 1638 Paul Le Jeune began to search among his handful of Montagnais converts for prospective inhabitants of the village now named St. Joseph de Sillery. The Jesuit found two baptized family leaders interested in occupying the first house at Sillery. These men, Noël Negabamat and François Xavier Nenaskoumat, met with Le Jeune in the winter of 1638 to discuss settlement plans. The two Montagnais very cautiously approached the subject of living permanently in a village. Negabamat warned Le Jeune that if the promised house and lands were taken away from the Indians after a short time, the Jesuits would suffer a severe loss of prestige. Assured by the missionary that such an action would never be taken, the Montagnais then pursued the question of house occupancy after they died. Noël Negabamat asked pointedly, "we are already old, if we happen to die, will you not drive our children from this house, will you not refuse them the help that you will have given us?" Again Le Jeune offered assurances that their fears were unfounded. With these problems resolved, the two Indians agreed to bring their families to Sillery in the spring of 1638.

By the summer of 1638 about twenty Montagnais were living in rather close quarters in a one-room house at Sillery. In spite of such crowded conditions Le Jeune was proud to report that he had "yet to notice the least quarrel or the least dispute among them." The residents of the village of Sillery were not the only Indians living on Sillery land during the first summer. Other Montagnais, hearing about the project, came to the reserve and settled for the season in their bark cabins. Le Jeune was certain that this would mean more converts and more human material for his Sillery experiment. The Superior wrote, "notice, if you please, a great blessing in this matter; not one of them hopes to be lodged and assisted who does not resolve to be an honest man, and to become a Christian, so much so that it is the same thing in a savage to wish to become sedentary and to wish to believe in God." The possibilities for conversion and culture change now seemed limitless and Le Jeune lamented only a lack of funds and workers for his growing village.

The Jesuits of New France expected great results from the Sillery experiment. In an analysis of the major mission institutions in the colony, Le Jeune declared that everything depended upon the success of the village effort. "Let these barbarians always remain nomads," wrote the missionary, "then their sick will die in the woods and their children will never enter the seminary." Thus, as Sillery entered its first full year of life, Jesuit hopes were high. Those expectations were bolstered by two important events. First, the Jesuits convinced the Company of New France to extend special trading privileges normally reserved to French *habitants* to the Christian residents of Sillery. The missionaries assumed that such rights would be a powerful economic incentive for additional Montagnais to accept Christianity and village life. Second, and even more important for the physical development of Sillery, the great landowner de Gand promised Le Jeune funds to hire more French constructure workers. But suddenly in 1639 Le Jeune's dream was shattered by the ever present companion of European expansion, smallpox. Fearing that all the Indians of Sillery would sicken and die, Le Jeune ordered the village abandoned. Seeing the house and lands empty, Le Jeune described his mood as "disconsolate indeed." Yet he was convinced that this trial came from God and was a proper test for the faith of the new converts.

As the epidemic began to subside in 1640, the Jesuits worked to reestablish Sillery. Once the village was reoccupied, the missionaries urged those Indians who were to live at Sillery to create their own civil government and code of moral conduct. A careful analysis of those actions and their consequences will be offered later in this study. Suffice it to say that the Jesuits were highly pleased with the results, since Christian Indians dominated the civil administration and promptly enacted a very rigid moral code based on European social values. Once again all seemed promising at Sillery. For the first time the Montagnais began to be involved in agricultural labor, clearing land and planting crops. During the winter of 1640–41 the Sillery Christians met again and strengthened their hold on village administration. Finally Le Jeune saw his village blessed at the end of 1640 by an unexpected event. After a serious fire gutted their building at Quebec, the Hospital Nuns decided to rebuild at Sillery. Thus the village now had both a Jesuit residence and a hospital.

When Barthelemy Vimont, Le Jeune's successor as Superior, described the physical development of Sillery in his *Relation* for 1642–43, it was plain that the village had grown considerably since those first precarious years. Vimont reported a population of thirty-five to forty Christian families with a much larger number of non-Christians also living on the Sillery reserve. The Montagnais had now been joined by some Algonquians although Vimont suspected that the latter were more interested in free food and shelter than in religious instruction. Population growth was matched by an increased number of village dwellings. The Superior noted that Sillery now had four one-room houses "built on the French plan," with two more under construction, and an additional house planned for the following spring. Yet housing remained a major problem for the village. Vimont observed that most Sillery residents still lived in the traditional bark cabins, and, with a lack of funds and workmen, the Jesuit saw little hope that the situation would soon change. From Vimont's *Relation* it is possible to construct a fairly accurate picture of Sillery as it must have appeared in the early 1640s. The village was laid out in two loose wings. At the center of the wings were the Jesuit residence house and the hospital. The Montagnais, both those living in houses and cabins, lived together in the wing closest to the Jesuit residence. The Algonquians occupied the wing on the hospital side. The agricultural lands outside the village were not well developed, apparently due to danger from Iroquois attack and the Indian desire to maintain the traditional economic habits of the hunt.

Problems with farming aside, Sillery appeared to be moving in the direction Le Jeune and the Jesuits had hoped when the village was created. However, the people of Sillery, Christians and non-Christians alike, were not immune from the violent events of the 1640s and early 1650s. In those years the French colony and its allies, especially the Huron, were assaulted and battered by intermittent Iroquois attacks. Such warfare eventually decimated the Huron. Sillery also paid a high price. Throughout the 1640s the village lived under the constant threat of attack, which meant that village men frequently formed war parties, leaving for long periods of time and forcing those left behind to abandon the town for the safety of Quebec. During the war season of 1643–44, for example, Sillery was virtually abandoned as the men went to war, and the women, the old, and the sick sought shelter in Quebec. Superior Vimont wrote bitterly, "we have greater trouble in keeping our Christians than in acquiring them. Their wandering life is a great obstacle to virture, and still the difficulties that exist with respect to their becoming settled are almost insurmountable. The land that we clear, the houses that we build for them, and the other aid, spiritual and material, keep them stationary for a while, but not permanently." Disease joined war to thwart progress at Sillery, and when it was necessary to abandon the hospital in 1644 because of the Iroquois menace, Sillery lost much of its appeal for many Indians. Throughout the 1640s the story remained much the same. In times of war Sillery was a ghost town. During those brief moments of peace the village came back to life. December 1645 found 167 Christians living on Sillery land with a larger number of non-Christians also present. The following year Sillery was unoccupied from February to April. In April the missionaries were able to convince some Indians to begin farm work, and fifteen arpents of land were prepared for planting. When the Jesuits counted the population of the village in November 1646, they recorded 120 Christians and an uncounted number of non-Christians. Later in November, as food supplies ran low, the Indians left Sillery and once again it was empty.

During the last years of the 1640s, as war, hunger, and disease swept through Sillery, the missionaries continued their efforts to develop the village. In 1647 the Jesuits undertook a major building project: the construction of a village church. When completed, the church of St. Michael was viewed as a primary means to maintain piety and proper worship in the village. This building and so many others in Sillery were destroyed by three sudden crises. During the war season of 1649–50 many Sillery Christians went off to battle against the Iroquois and were killed. Their deaths deprived the village of its leadership elite. As the Iroquois war intensified, Sillery became more and more a French military outpost for the defense of Quebec. During 1649 masonry fortifications were built in the village. A few short years later Sillery itself was attacked. On May 29, 1655, Iroquois raiders attacked a work party of Indians who were preparing a site for a fort on Sillery land. In the fighting that followed, Jesuit brother Jean Liegeois was killed and several Sillery Indians wounded. The third crisis came to the village in the afternoon of June 13, 1656. A fire, started in the kitchen chimney of the Jesuit house and whipped by a high wind, raced through the village, destroying the mission residence, the church, and most of the small houses. The fire was a disaster from which the experimental village of Sillery would never recover.

In 1663 the Jesuits of New France prepared a report listing all lands under their control. The report reveals the final dissolution of Indian Sillery. Most of the Sillery land was now occupied by French farmers. The two Jesuits living at the Sillery site were primarily involved in caring for the needs of French settlers. The Indian village of St. Joseph de Sillery was dead.

What has been offered thus far has been a traditional picture of a mission idea—its genesis, growth, and decline. The analysis has been a physical one in terms of fund raising, building construction, and numbers of converts. While important, such an external examination cannot penetrate to the inner history of Sillery. The most important questions have yet to be posed. What effect did village life and European morality have upon the Montagnais and Algonquians? How successful were the Jesuits in remodeling Native American life and producing Europeanized Indians? How much resistance was there to such efforts, and what forms did the resistance take? Exploring these questions takes us beyond mission-centered history to the inner, Indian life of Sillery and to the essence of the mission as an arena for culture contact.

Paul Le Jeune and the Jesuits of New France dreamed of Indian villages populated by hard-working farmers whose lives were regulated by the wise decisions of Christian Indian magistrates and their missionary mentors. A village like Sillery could not prosper unless Christians dominated its civil life. As early as 1637 Le Jeune wrote "if some one could . . . give authority to one of them to rule the others, we would see them converted and civilized in a short time." What Le Jeune was asking for was the destruction of traditional Indian polity and the establishment of new civil-political relationships based on European models of authority and leadership. Consensus was to be replaced by coercion. The Jesuit did not realize that to begin such a process would unravel the bonds of Montagnais culture and introduce new conflicts into Indian life.

In 1640, after the smallpox epidemic of the previous year had abated, Montagnais Indians began to gather at the Sillery reserve. Le Jeune and Vimont were eager for the process of accepting village life and civil order to begin quickly. Thus they encouraged the Christian minority to hold mass meetings for the purpose of village organization. Even before the meetings were held, Sillery Christians had agreed on the exclusivistic course they planned to pursue. Reflecting the Jesuit position which demanded a total rejection of the Indian past, the Montagnais Christians declared "that if any one showed himself an open enemy to the faith, they resolved to drive him away from the village." When the first tribal meeting was held, Christians dominated much of the discussion. Estienne Pigarouik, a former traditional religious leader and now a zealous recent convert, demanded that all those who were not Christians be expelled from the village. Pigarouik leveled his harshest criticism at those who practiced the Montagnais tradition of polygamy. The message to the non-Christians was simple and blunt: Either believe or separate. Not all the Sillery Christians spoke with such harshness or made such rigid demands. At the same meeting Noël Negabamat urged a more moderate course. Steering clear of ideology and demands for immediate conversion, Negabamat argued that as all planned to live in one village, it would be most practical for all to accept one religion. Jean Baptiste Etinechkavat, a Montagnais leader by birth and another recent convert, rounded out the Christian position by maintaining that the acceptance of Christianity and French aid was the only means to halt the eventual destruction of the Montagnais people. The stance of the Sillery Christians was a blend of zealous coercion and pragmatic persuasion. What it amounted to was a broad attack on the traditions and values of Montagnais life.

Christian voices were not the only ones heard at the crucial gathering. The Christian challenge quickly produced a Traditionalist, or as the Jesuits styled it, a "pagan," faction of considerable size and power. Montagnais Traditionalists effectively countered the Christian minority by portraying the converts as petty, power-hungry men bent on dividing the Montagnais. Replying to the attack on polygamy, the Traditionalists observed that having several wives was a very ancient practice and they saw no reason to abandon it now. Finally, the Traditionalists charged that Christian doctrine was both too complex to understand and ill suited to Indian life. The meeting was deadlocked. The Montagnais were divided for the first time in their history into two rival and hostile ideological factions. The Christians were in the minority and as the assembly broke up, the new converts had to find ways to gain power and influence if their cause was to succeed.

In the days that followed the meeting, representatives of the Sillery Christians sought French support to enhance their position. First visiting Governor Montmagny, they asked him to appoint only Christians to the civil administration of Sillery. The governor replied with a general declaration of support, but hesitated to grant such large amounts of power to a minority, even a Christian minority. The Sillery Christians found the aid they were searching for when they went to the Jesuits. Le Jeune and Vimont wanted the Christians dominant in village government. For that reason the Jesuits apparently suggested that a large number of Montagnais men gather at the mission residence house to hold an election for village officers. Such an election had no precedent in traditional Montagnais culture. After the votes were counted by the missionaries, it was declared that four men—three Christians and one Traditionalist—had been elected village magistrates. To these posts were added two men—one Christian and one Traditionalist—who would enforce proper moral conduct among Montagnais young men. Finally, one man was selected as Captain of Prayers to act as a lay teacher in Sillery. These seven men were to serve for one year, after which a new election would be held. What emerged from all these events was a village government dominated by the Christian minority, supported by powerful outside allies and bent on imposing new values and beliefs on a reluctant and often hostile majority.

Sillery quickly became a divided and suspicious community. The suspicion and division was the product of the tactics used by the Jesuits and the Sillery Christians to remake Montagnais life. The most explosive points of confrontation proved to be questions of sexual behavior, polygamy, and the nature of the marriage institution. The Jesuits had always been highly critical of Montagnais sexual customs and marriage patterns. Missionary preaching repeatedly insisted that conversion and true Christianity demanded monogamous marriage and European courtship practices. One of the first acts of the new Sillery Christian officers was to round up all the women and young people and verbally assault them for their supposed transgressions. The Christian men charged that the women, most of whom were not Christians, had been the source of all Montagnais troubles. Demonstrating the means they would use to hold their power, the Christians declared "now know that you must obey your husbands, and you young people, you will obey your parents and our Captains, and, if any fail to do so, we have concluded to give them nothing to eat."

When the Christian officers attempted to enforce the European-based moral code, there was great uproar, confusion, and resistance. One young wife, after having an argument with her husband, fled into the forest for fear of punishment. Sillery officials hunted her down and then requested the Jesuits to supply a chain so that the woman could do four days of fasting chained to a post. Another incident further reveals the depth of division in Sillery. A Christian couple engaged in a fierce argument, eventually coming to blows. Their quarrel was so noisy that it soon attracted a large crowd of Sillery residents. The neighboring Christians complained that this couple was not honoring the marriage vows. More important as an indicator of village conflict, many opponents of Christianity used the event to attack the faithful and mock their convictions. When village officers tried to stop the courting of Christians by non-Christians, the results were less than satisfactory. All the conflict and divisiveness caused by the efforts of the missionaries and their converts can be best summed up in one last example. Two young boys, one a Christian and the other a Traditionalist, fell to fighting outside a Sillery house. The Jesuits present proudly reported that they were fighting "on account of their beliefs." Which lad emerged the victor from the theological scrap was not recorded.

It was clear by the winter of 1640–41 that the Jesuit expectations of a peaceful, united, and Christian Sillery were not coming to pass. The experiment was failing not only because of a lack of food or funds but because of the tensions and animosities produced by Christianization and culture change. The Jesuit answer to these failures was to encourage the Sillery Christians to double their efforts in compelling piety and virtue. During the winter of 1640–41 the Sillery Christian faction met to discuss their problems. They were confronted with a Traditionalist majority who wanted to enjoy some of the material advantages of village life while stoutly refusing to accept any real changes in cultural values. After considerable debate, the Christians decided to use prison sentences and even the threat of execution to force adherence to their orders. The Jesuits, concerned that talk of chains and prisons might drive away potential converts, cautioned moderation. Their advice was rejected as the Indian Christians accused the missionaries of cowardice and backsliding!

The Sillery Christians acted promptly to implement the new order. Their first targets were young Montagnais who courted each other in the traditional manner. Montagnais courting centered on evening meetings of a couple or small group of couples. These meetings sometimes involved sexual intercourse, but this was not always the case. Such liaisons shocked the newly found European sensibilities of Sillery Christians. They flooded the French governor with requests to accept violators in Quebec dungeons. When Governor Montmagny showed some reluctance to overpopulate his cells, the Christians obtained permission in 1642 to build their own prison in Sillery. Soon a number of young women found themselves incarcerated for short periods of time. There is no record of any young men being imprisoned. On this point at least, Jesuit and Indian attitudes coincided conveniently; both cultures decreed that women bear the burden of guilt in matters of sex. As old courting practices persisted, Sillery Christians moved to even harsher methods to force acceptance of their moral code. Public floggings of young women by village officers became a common sight. While such punishments served only to widen the gap between Traditionalists and Christians, one Jesuit later defended them as necessary in order to teach "savages" the principles of justice and government. Yet the intensified moral puritanism of the Christian minority, employing even the most extreme measures, failed to alter old habits and customs.

It was the purpose of Sillery to remold Montagnais lifestyle and religion. The Jesuits were convinced that such goals were both possible and desirable. Sillery was to be a proving ground for the future. Barthelemy Vimont once described Sillery as "the seed of Christianity amid this great barbarism." How successful were the missionaries and their convert allies? Was the Montagnais culture significantly transformed along the desired lines by the village experience? Did the Montagnais give up or even modify traditional religious beliefs and practices? Certainly the Christians of Sillery wanted outsiders to believe that they were living new lives. One Christian boasted that "we are no longer what we once were, we have given up our old customs to accept better ones." This claim was hardly borne out in fact. In something as basic as the economy, nearly all Montagnais remained firmly rooted in the indigenous past. There is no evidence to suggest that agriculture ever became an important part of Sillery life. The most farmland ever planted was fifteen arpents, or about twelve acres, and that was done in one year only. On the other hand, there is considerable evidence that most Montagnais simply viewed the village as a convenient base camp for their yearly hunts. The constant hunger at Sillery also indicates the failure of agriculture to take hold in Montagnais life.

While the purpose of Sillery was to effect massive social change, the Jesuits ultimately wanted to reap a harvest of converts. How successful were the missionaries in destroying Montagnais religion and replacing it with Christianity? The Jesuits were not foolish enough to think that the Montagnais had no religion. Early field experience had taught them that the Indian religious universe was populated with many spirits and gods, interpreted through Indian priests and prophets. Montagnais religious practice was distinctly Iroquoian in structure, emphasizing dream interpretation, communal rituals, and the supernatural value of small sacred objects. That the mission obtained a few dedicated converts is undeniable. However, the evidence suggests that most Montagnais clung tenaciously to their own beliefs and rituals. The Sillery Montagnais, both Christians and Traditionalists, occasionally participated in Christian pageants and processions, but even such public manifestations of piety were rare. What happened in Sillery, in a religious sense, can best be described as interior survival or the persistence of precontact religion. In Sillery the Traditionalists maintained an active religious underground. Le Jeune reported that "there are savages who come to inform us of superstitious rites which are performed secretly in the cabins." The continued presence of traditional ceremonies was both an embarrassment and a challenge to the authority of Sillery Christians. At the very time when Christian officers were using strong measures to enforce holy living, one Christian was forced to admit that "it is a matter of deep regret to see our relatives and friends so persistent in their slavery to Satan." Traditional religious leaders scored their greatest success in keeping alive a belief which had hindered mission growth from the beginning. Because the Jesuits frequently baptized those on the verge of death, a popular folk belief emerged that death was the sure consequence of that sacrament. Traditionalists effectively used this pervasive belief to challenge both the converts and the missionaries. Since baptism often meant contact with Europeans and their diseases, it was very difficult to counter the arguments offered by the shamans. With the Traditionalist religious underground flourishing, the Jesuits began to preach sermons urging converts to search Sillery cabins and destroy all non-Christian religious objects. In spite of these efforts, the old ways hung on. As one of the Sillery faithful put it, "there appear only too many among us who grow deaf and blind. They close their ears to the instructions which are given them. They put a vail [sic] before their eyes for fear of seeing what prayer and the faith command them."

Christianity in Sillery was always a minority belief rejected by most Indians as a strange, complicated, and potentially dangerous ideology.

The Jesuits attempted to create in Sillery a harmonious Christian community. What resulted instead was a Montagnais people sharply divided into two ideological factions. Jesuit reports about Sillery always contained references to the fundamental division between "our Christians" and the "pagans." Christian piety and European values were enforced by prison sentences and public beatings. The Jesuits and their converts demanded what was unthinkable to most Native Americans—that they cease being Indians. In the Indian mind, to become a Christian was to lose one's identity as a Montagnais. As one Traditionalist put it to a Christian, "go then thou Frenchman, that is right, go away into thine own country. Embark in the ships, since thou art a Frenchman. Cross the sea and go to thine own land." The missionaries never seemed to understand that most Montagnais were unwilling to give up their own traditions and beliefs, no matter what the promised rewards. The Sillery experiment failed not simply because of war, disease, and lack of funds but because it demanded cultural suicide.

6

THE INDIANS' NEW WORLD: THE CATAWBA EXPERIENCE

JAMES H. MERRELL

Many discussions of the European discovery and early settlement of the Western Hemisphere refer to North and South America as the New World. Certainly for the tens of thousands of Europeans and Africans who crossed the Atlantic, labeling this region as "new" was accurate. For the resident Native American peoples, however, the flood of invaders into their homeland soon changed their entire existence so drastically that the author claims that they also faced a New World. In making this assertion, he examines both place and process as important factors. Tracing the experiences of coastal groups from Virginia south through the Carolinas, he demonstrates how the spreading of European activities and settlement all affected the local tribes adversely. Not only did the invasion hurt the Native American societies, but it brought fundamental changes in the ways those peoples dealt with each other and with their physical environment. Social forms, demographic patterns, economic practices, technology, and even locations all changed because of the European intrusion. Gradually these changes altered tribal existence. The author's discussion shows how and why these trends occurred, while placing the Indian experiences in the Southeast within the broader context of European colonial actions in North America. This essay considers the story not just from the tribal side but from within the local villages and small groups whenever possible. Its analysis presents Indians as acting in their own interests, not merely as responding to the invading Europeans.

James H. Merrell is an associate professor of history at Vassar College.

In August 1608 John Smith and his band of explorers captured an Indian named Amoroleck during a skirmish along the Rappahannock River. Asked why his men—a hunting party from towns upstream—had attacked the English, Amoroleck replied that they had heard the strangers "were a people come from under the

Source: James H. Merrell, "The Indians' New World: The Catawba Experience," *William & Mary Quarterly*, 3 ser. 41 (October 1984), pp. 537-565. Reprinted by permission.

world, to take their world from them." Smith's prisoner grasped a simple yet important truth that students of colonial America have overlooked: After 1492 Native Americans lived in a world every bit as new as that confronting transplanted Africans or Europeans.

The failure to explore the Indians' new world helps explain why, despite many excellent studies of the Native American past, colonial history often remains, "a history of those men and women—English, European, and African—who transformed America from a geographical expression into a new nation." One reason Indians generally are left out may be the apparent inability to fit them into the new-world theme, a theme that exerts a powerful hold on our historical imagination and runs throughout our efforts to interpret American development. From Frederick Jackson Turner to David Grayson Allen, from Melville J. Herskovits to Daniel C. Littlefield, scholars have analyzed encounters between peoples from the Old World and conditions in the New, studying the complex interplay between Europeans or African cultural patterns and the American environment. Indians crossed no ocean, peopled no faraway land. It might seem logical to exclude them.

The natives' segregation persists, in no small degree, because historians still tend to think only of the new world as the New World, a geographic entity bounded by the Atlantic Ocean on the one side and the Pacific on the other. Recent research suggests that process was as important as place. Many settlers in New England re-created familiar forms with such success that they did not really face an alien environment until long after their arrival. Africans, on the other hand, were struck by the shock of the new at the moment of their enslavement well before they stepped on board ship or set foot on American soil. If the Atlantic was not a barrier between one world and another, if what happened to people was more a matter of subtle cultural processes than mere physical displacements, perhaps we should set aside the maps and think instead of a "world" as the physical and cultural milieu within which people live and a "new world" as a dramatically different milieu demanding basic changes in ways of life. Considered in these terms, the experience of natives was more closely akin to that of immigrants and slaves, and the idea of an encounter between worlds can—indeed, must—include the aboriginal inhabitants of America.

For American Indians a new order arrived in three distinct yet overlapping stages. First, alien microbes killed vast numbers of natives, sometimes before the victims had seen a white or black face. Next came traders who exchanged European technology for Indian products and brought natives into the developing world market. In time traders gave way to settlers eager to develop the land according to their own lights. These three intrusions combined to transform native existence, disrupting established cultural habits and requiring creative responses to drastically altered conditions. Like their new neighbors, then, Indians were forced to blend old and new in ways that would permit them to survive in the present without forsaking their past. By the close of the colonial era native Americans as well as whites and blacks had created new societies, each similar to, yet very different from, its parent culture.

The range of native societies produced by this mingling of ingredients probably exceeded the variety of social forms Europeans and Africans developed.

Rather than survey the broad spectrum of Indian adaptations, this article considers in some depth the response of natives in one area, the southern piedmont (see map). Avoiding extinction and eschewing retreat, the Indians of the piedmont have been in continuous contact with the invaders from across the sea almost since the beginning of the colonial period, thus permitting a thorough analysis of cultural intercourse. Moreover, a regional approach embracing groups from South Carolina to Virginia can transcend narrow (and still poorly understood) ethnic or "tribal" boundaries without sacrificing the richness of detail a focused study provides.

Indeed, piedmont peoples had so much in common that a regional perspective is almost imperative. No formal political ties bound them at the onset of European contact, but a similar environment shaped their lives, and their adjustment to this environment fostered cultural uniformity. Perhaps even more important, these groups shared a single history once Europeans and Africans arrived on the scene. Drawn together by their cultural affinities and their common plight, after 1700 they migrated to the Catawba Nation, a cluster of villages along the border between the Carolinas that became the focus of native life in the region. Tracing the experience of these upland communities both before and after they joined the Catawbas can illustrate the consequences of contact and illuminate the process by which natives learned to survive in their own new world.

For centuries ancestors of the Catawbas had lived astride important aboriginal trade routes and straddled the boundary between two cultural traditions, a position that involved them in a far-flung network of contacts and affected everything from potting techniques to burial practices. Nonetheless, Africans and Europeans were utterly unlike any earlier foreign visitors to the piedmont. Their arrival meant more than merely another encounter with outsiders; it marked an important turning point in Indian history. Once these newcomers disembarked and began to feel their way across the continent, they forever altered the course and pace of native development.

Bacteria brought the most profound disturbances to upcountry villages. When Hernando de Soto led the first Europeans into the area in 1540, he found large towns already "grown up in grass" because "there had been a pest in the land" two years before, a malady probably brought inland by natives who had visited distant Spanish posts. The sources are silent about other "pests" over the next century, but soon after the English began colonizing Carolina in 1670 the disease pattern became all too clear. Major epidemics struck the region at least once every generation—in 1698, 1718, 1738, and 1759—and a variety of less virulent illnesses almost never left native settlements.

Indians were not the only inhabitants of colonial America living—and dying—in a new disease environment. The swamps and lowlands of the Chesapeake were a deathtrap for Europeans, and sickness obliged colonists to discard or rearrange many of the social forms brought from England. Among native peoples long isolated from the rest of the world and therefore lacking immunity to pathogens introduced by the intruders, the devastation was even more severe. John Lawson, who visited the Carolina upcountry in 1701, when perhaps ten thousand Indians were still there, estimated that "there is not the sixth Savage living within two hundred Miles of all our Settlements, as there were fifty Years ago." The recent

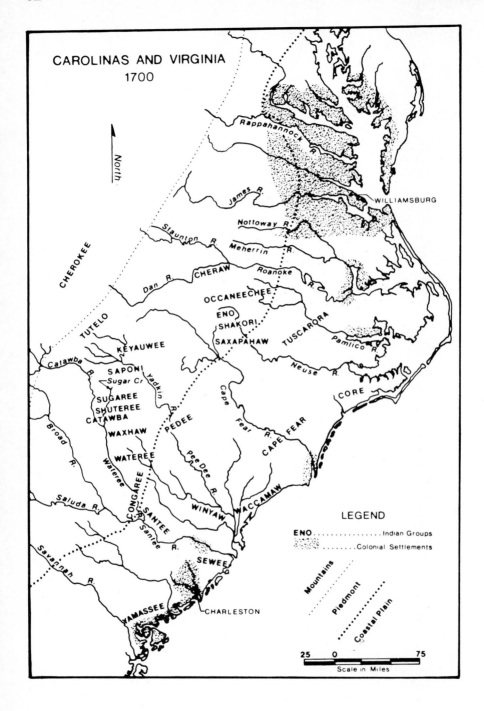

CAROLINAS AND VIRGINIA
1700

North

CHEROKEE

Rappahannock R.

James R.

WILLIAMSBURG

Nottoway R.

Staunton R.

Meherrin R.

CHERAW

Roanoke R.

Dan R.

OCCANEECHEE

ENO

SHAKORI

TUTELO

SAXAPAHAW

TUSCARORA

KEYAUWEE

Pamlico R.

Catawba R.

SAPONI

Neuse R.

Sugar Cr

Yadkin R.

CORE

SUGAREE

SHUTEREE

CATAWBA

Cape Fear R.

Broad R.

WAXHAW

PEDEE

CAPE FEAR

WATEREE

Pee Dee R.

Wateree R.

Saluda R.

CONGAREE

SANTEE

WINYAW

WACCAMAW

Savannah R.

Santee R.

SEWEE

LEGEND

ENO . . . . Indian Groups

. . . . Colonial Settlements

YAMASSEE

CHARLESTON

Mountains

Piedmont

Coastal Plain

25   0   75

Scale in Miles

smallpox epidemic "destroy'd whole Towns," he remarked, "without leaving one *Indian* alive in the Village." Resistance to disease developed with painful slowness; colonists reported that the outbreak of smallpox in 1759 wiped out 60 percent of the natives, and, according to one source, "the woods were offensive with the dead bodies of the Indians; and dogs, wolves, and vultures were . . . busy for months in banqueting on them."

Survivors of these horrors were thrust into a situation no less alien than what European immigrants and African slaves found. The collected wisdom of generations could vanish in a matter of days if sickness struck older members of a community who kept sacred traditions and taught special skills. When many of the elders succumbed at once, the deep pools of collective memory grew shallow and some dried up altogether. In 1710 Indians near Charleston told a settler that "they have forgot most of their traditions since the Establishment of this Colony, they keep their Festivals and can tell but little of the reasons: their Old Men are dead." Impoverishment of a rich cultural heritage followed the spread of disease. Nearly a century later a South Carolinian exaggerated but captured the general trend when he noted that Catawbas "have forgotten their ancient rites, ceremonies, and manufactures."

The same diseases that robbed a piedmont town of some of its most precious resources also stripped it of the population necessary to maintain an independent existence. In order to survive, groups were compelled to construct new societies from the splintered remnants of the old. The result was a kaleidoscopic array of migrations from ancient territories and mergers with nearby peoples. While such behavior was not unheard of in aboriginal times, population levels fell so precipitously after contact that survivors endured disruptions unlike anything previously known.

The dislocations of the Saponi Indians illustrate the common course of events. In 1670 they lived on the Staunton River in Virginia and were closely affiliated with a group called Nahyssans. A decade later Saponis moved toward the coast and built a town near the Occaneechees. When John Lawson came upon them along the Yadkin River in 1701, they were on the verge of banding together in a single village with Tutelos and Keyauwees. Soon thereafter Saponis applied to Virginia officials for permission to move to the Meherrin River, where Occaneechees, Tutelos, and others joined them. In 1714, at the urging of Virginia's Lt. Gov. Alexander Spotswood, these groups settled at Fort Christanna farther up the Meherrin. Their friendship with Virginia soured during the 1720s, and most of the "Christanna Indians" moved to the Catawba Nation. For some reason this arrangement did not satisfy them, and many returned to Virginia in 1732, remaining there for a decade before choosing to migrate north and accept the protection of the Iroquois.

Saponis were unusual only in their decision to leave the Catawbas. Enos, Occaneechees, Waterees, Keyauwees, Cheraws, and others have their own stories to tell, similar in outline if not in detail. With the exception of the towns near the confluence of Sugar Creek and the Catawba River that composed the heart of the Catawba Nation, piedmont communities decimated by disease lived through a common round of catastrophes, shifting from place to place and group to group in search of a safe haven. Most eventually ended up in the Nation, and during the opening decades of the eighteenth century the villages scattered across the southern upcountry were abandoned as people drifted into the Catawba orbit.

No mere catalog of migrations and mergers can begin to convey how profoundly unsettling this experience was for those swept up in it. While upcountry Indians did not sail away to some distant land, they, too, were among the uprooted, leaving their ancestral homes to try to make a new life elsewhere. The peripatetic existence of Saponis and others proved deeply disruptive. A village and its surrounding territory were important elements of personal and collective identity, physical links in a chain binding a group to its past and making a locality sacred. Colonists, convinced that Indians were by Nature "a shifting, wandring People," were oblivious to this, but Lawson offered a glimpse of the reasons for native attachment to a particular locale. "In our way," he wrote on leaving an Eno-Shakori town in 1701, "there stood a great Stone about the Size of a large Oven, and hollow; this the *Indians* took great Notice of, putting some Tobacco into the Concavity, and spitting after it. I ask'd them the Reason of their so doing, but they made me no Answer." Natives throughout the interior honored similar places—graves of ancestors, monuments of stones commemorating important events—that could not be left behind without some cost.

The toll could be physical as well as spiritual, for even the most uneventful of moves interrupted the established cycle of subsistence. Belongings had to be packed and unpacked, dwellings constructed, palisades raised. Once migrants had completed the business of settling in, the still more arduous task of exploiting new terrain awaited them. Living in one place year after year endowed a people with intimate knowledge of the area. The richest soils, the best hunting grounds, the choicest sites for gathering nuts or berries—none could be learned without years of experience, tested by time and passed down from one generation to the next. Small wonder that Carolina Indians worried about being "driven to some unknown Country, to live, hunt, and get our Bread in."

Some displaced groups tried to leave "unknown Country" behind and make their way back home. In 1716 Enos asked Virginia's permission to settle at "Enoe Town" on the North Carolina frontier, their location in Lawson's day. Seventeen years later William Byrd II came upon an abandoned Cheraw village on a tributary of the upper Roanoke River and remarked how "it must have been a great misfortune to them to be obliged to abandon so beautiful a dwelling." The Indians apparently agreed: In 1717 the Virginia Council received "Divers applications" from the Cheraws (now living along the Pee Dee River) "for Liberty to Seat themselves on the head of Roanoke River." Few natives managed to return permanently to their homelands. But their efforts to retrace their steps hint at a profound sense of loss and testify to the powerful hold of ancient sites.

Compounding the trauma of leaving familiar territories was the necessity of abandoning customary relationships. Casting their lot with others traditionally considered foreign compelled Indians to rearrange basic ways of ordering their existence. Despite frequent contacts among peoples, native life had always centered in kin and town. The consequences of this deep-seated localism were evident even to a newcomer like John Lawson, who in 1701 found striking differences in language, dress, and physical appearance among Carolina Indians living only a few miles apart. Rules governing behavior also drew sharp distinctions between outsiders and one's own "Country-Folks." Indians were "very kind, and charitable to one another," Lawson reported, "but more especially to those of their own Nation." A visitor desiring a liaison with a local woman was required to approach her relatives and the village headman. On the other hand, "if it be an *Indian* of their own Town or Neighbourhood, that wants a Mistress, he comes to none but the Girl." Lawson seemed unperturbed by this barrier until he discovered that a "Thief [is] held in Disgrace, that steals from any of his Country-Folks," "but to steal from the *English* [or any other foreigners] they reckon no Harm."

Communities unable to continue on their own had to revise these rules and reweave the social fabric into new designs. What language would be spoken? How would fields be laid out, hunting territories divided, houses built? How would decisions be reached, offenders punished, ceremonies performed? When Lawson remarked that "now adays" the Indians must seek mates "amongst Strangers," he unwittingly characterized life in native Carolina. Those who managed to withstand the ravages of disease had to redefine the meaning of the term *stranger* and transform outsiders into insiders.

The need to harmonize discordant peoples, an unpleasant fact of life for all Native Americans, was no less common among black and white inhabitants of America during these years. Africans from a host of different groups were thrown into slavery together and forced to seek some common cultural ground, to blend or set aside clashing habits and beliefs. Europeans who came to America also met unexpected and unwelcome ethnic, religious, and linguistic diversity. The roots of the problem were quite different; the problem itself was much the same. In each case people from different backgrounds had to forge a common culture and a common future.

Indians in the southern uplands customarily combined with others like themselves in an attempt to solve the dilemma. Following the "principle of least effort," shattered communities cushioned the blows inflicted by disease and depopulation by joining a kindred society known through generations of trade and alliances. Thus, Saponis coalesced with Occaneechees and Tutelos—nearby groups "speaking much the same language"—and Catawbas became a sanctuary for culturally related refugees from throughout the region. Even after moving in with friends and neighbors, however, natives tended to cling to ethnic boundaries in order to ease the transition. In 1715 Spotswood noticed that the Saponis and others gathered at Fort Christanna were "confederated together, tho' still preserving their different Rules." Indians entering the Catawba Nation were equally conservative. As late as 1743 a visitor could hear more than twenty dialects spoken by peoples living there, and some bands continued to reside in separate towns under their own leaders.

Time inevitably sapped the strength of ethnic feeling, allowing a more unified Nation to emerge from the collection of Indian communities that occupied the valleys of the Catawba River and its tributaries. By the mid-eighteenth century, the authority of village headmen was waning and leaders from the host population had begun to take responsibility for the actions of constituent groups. The babel of different tongues fell silent as "Kàtahba," the Nation's "standard, or court-dialect,"slowly drowned out all others. Eventually entire peoples followed their languages and their leaders into oblivion, leaving only personal names like Santee Jemmy, Cheraw George, Congaree Jamie, Saponey Johnny, and Eno Jemmy as reminders of the Nation's diverse heritage.

No European observer recorded the means by which nations became mere names and a congeries of groups forged itself into one people. No doubt the colonists' habit of ignoring ethnic distinctions and lumping confederated entities together under the Catawba rubric encouraged amalgamation. But Anglo-American efforts to create a society by proclamation were invariably unsuccessful; consolidation had to come from within. In the absence of evidence, it seems reasonable to conclude that years of contacts paved the way for a closer relationship. Once a group moved to the Nation, intermarriages blurred ancient kinship networks, joint war parties or hunting expeditions brought young men together, and elders met in a council that gave everyone some say by including "all the Indian Chiefs or Head Men of that [Catawba] Nation and the several Tribes amongst them together." The concentration of settlements within a day's walk of one another facilitated contact and communication. From their close proximity, common experience, and shared concerns, people developed ceremonies and myths that compensated for those lost to disease and gave the Nation a stronger collective consciousness. Associations evolved that balanced traditional narrow ethnic allegiance with a new, broader, "national" identity, a balance that tilted steadily toward the latter. Ethnic differences died hard, but the peoples of the Catawba Nation learned to speak with a single voice.

Muskets and kettles came to the piedmont more slowly than smallpox and measles. Spanish explorers distributed a few gifts to local headmen, but inhabitants of the interior did not enjoy their first real taste of the fruits of European technology until Englishmen began venturing inland after 1650. Indians these traders met in up-country towns were glad to barter for the more efficient tools, more lethal weapons, and more durable clothing that colonists offered. Spurred on by eager natives, men from Virginia and Carolina quickly flooded the region with the material trappings of European culture. In 1701 John Lawson considered the Wateree Chickanees "very poor in *English* Effects" because a few of them lacked muskets.

Slower to arrive, trade goods were also less obvious agents of change. The Indians' ability to absorb foreign artifacts into established modes of existence hid the revolutionary consequences of trade for some time. Natives leaped the technological gulf with ease in part because they were discriminating shoppers. If hoes were too small, beads too large, or cloth the wrong color, Indian traders refused them. Items they did select fit smoothly into existing ways. Waxhaws tied horse bells around their ankles at ceremonial dances, and some of the traditional stone pipes passed among the spectators at these dances had been shaped by metal files. Those who could not afford a European weapon fashioned arrows from broken glass. Those who could went to great lengths to "set [a new musket] streight, sometimes shooting away above 100 Loads of Ammunition, before they bring the Gun to shoot according to their Mind."

Not every piece of merchandise hauled into the upcountry on a trader's packhorse could be "set streight" so easily. Liquor, for example, proved both impossible to resist and extraordinarily destructive. Indians "have no Power to refrain this Enemy," Lawson observed, "though sensible how many of them (are by it) hurry'd into the other World before their Time." And yet even here, natives aware of the risks sought to control alcohol by incorporating it into their ceremonial life as a device for achieving a different level of consciousness. Consumption was usually restricted to men, who "go as solemnly about it, as if it were part of their Religion," preferring to drink only at night and only in quantities sufficient to stupefy them. When ritual could not confine liquor to safe channels, Indians went still further and excused the excesses of overindulgence by refusing to hold an intoxicated person responsible for his actions. "They never call any Man to account for what he did, when he was drunk," wrote Lawson, "but say, it was the Drink that caused his Misbehaviour, therefore he ought to be forgiven."

Working to absorb even the most dangerous commodities acquired from their new neighbors, aboriginal inhabitants of the uplands, like African slaves in the lowlands, made themselves at home in a different technological environment. Indians became convinced that "Guns, and Ammunition, besides a great many other Necessaries, . . . are helpful to Man" and eagerly searched for the key that would unlock the secret of their production. At first many were confident that the "*Quera*, or good Spirit," would teach them to make these commodities "when that good Spirit sees fit." Later they decided to help their deity along by approaching the colonists. In 1757 Catawbas asked Gov. Arthur Dobbs of North Carolina "to send us Smiths and other Tradesmen to teach our Children."

It was not the new products themselves but the Indians' failure to learn the mysteries of manufacture from either Dobbs or the *Quera* that marked the real revolution wrought by trade. During the seventeenth and eighteenth centuries everyone in eastern North America—masters and slaves, farmers near the coast and Indians near the mountains—became producers of raw materials for foreign markets and found themselves caught up in an international economic network. Piedmont natives were part of this larger process, but their adjustment was more difficult because the contrast with previous ways was so pronounced. Before European contact, the localism characteristic of life in the uplands had been sustained by a remarkable degree of self-sufficiency. Trade among peoples, while common, was conducted primarily in commodities such as copper, mica, and shells, items that, exchanged with the appropriate ceremony, initiated or confirmed friendships among groups. Few, if any, villages relied on outsiders for goods essential to daily life.

Intercultural exchange eroded this traditional independence and entangled natives in a web of commercial relations few of them understood and none controlled. In 1670 the explorer John Lederer observed a striking disparity in the trading habits of Indians living near Virginia and those deep in the interior. The "remoter Indians," still operating within a precontact framework, were content with ornamental items such as mirrors, beads, "and all manner of gaudy toys and knacks for children." "Neighbour-Indians," on the other hand, habitually traded with colonists for cloth, metal tools, and weapons. Before long, towns near and far were demanding the entire range of European wares and were growing accustomed—even addicted—to them. "They say we English are fools for . . . not always going with a gun," one Virginia colonist familiar with piedmont Indians wrote in the early 1690s, "for they think themselves undrest and not fit to walk abroad, unless they have their gun on their shoulder, and their shot-bag by their side." Such an enthusiastic conversion to the new technology eroded ancient craft skills and hastened complete dependence on substitutes only colonists could supply.

By forcing Indians to look beyond their own territories for certain indispensable products, Anglo-American traders inserted new variables into the aboriginal equation of exchange. Colonists sought two commodities from Indians—human beings and deerskins—and both undermined established relationships among native groups. While the demand for slaves encouraged piedmont peoples to expand their traditional warfare, the demand for peltry may have fostered conflicts over hunting territories. Those who did not fight each other for slaves or deerskins fought each other for the European products these could bring. As firearms, cloth, and other items became increasingly important to native existence, competition replaced comity at the foundation of trade encounters as villages scrambled for the cargoes of merchandise. Some were in a better position to profit than others. In the early 1670s Occaneechees living on an island in the Roanoke River enjoyed power out of all proportion to their numbers because they controlled an important ford on the trading path from Virginia to the interior, and they resorted to threats, and even to force, to retain their advantage. In Lawson's day Tuscaroras did the same, "hating that any of these Westward *Indians* should have any Commerce with the *English,* which would prove a Hinderance to their Gains."

Competition among native groups was only the beginning of the transformation brought about by new forms of exchange. Inhabitants of the piedmont might bypass the native middleman, but they could not break free from a perilous dependence on colonial sources of supply. The danger may not have been immediately apparent to Indians caught up in the excitement of acquiring new and wonderful things. For years they managed to dictate the terms of trade, compelling visitors from Carolina and Virginia to abide by aboriginal codes of conduct and playing one colony's traders against the other to ensure an abundance of goods at favorable rates. But the natives' influence over the protocol of exchange combined with their skill at incorporating alien products to mask a loss of control over their own destiny. The mask came off when, in 1715, the traders—and the trade goods—suddenly disappeared during the Yamassee War.

The conflict's origins lay in a growing colonial awareness of the Indians' need for regular supplies of European merchandise. In 1701 Lawson pronounced the Santees "very tractable" because of their close connections with South Carolina. Eight years later he was convinced that the colonial officials in Charleston "are absolute Masters over the *Indians* . . . within the Circle of their Trade." Carolina traders who shared this conviction quite naturally felt less and less constrained to obey native rules governing proper behavior. Abuses against Indians mounted until some men were literally getting away with murder. When repeated appeals to colonial officials failed, natives throughout Carolina began to consider war. Persuaded by Yamassee ambassadors that the conspiracy was widespread and convinced by years of ruthless commercial competition between Virginia and Carolina that an attack on one colony would not affect relations with the other, in the spring of 1715 Catawbas and their neighbors joined the invasion of South Carolina.

The decision to fight was disastrous. Colonists everywhere shut off the flow of goods to the interior, and after some initial successes Carolina's native enemies soon plumbed the depths of their dependence. In a matter of months refugees holed up in Charleston noticed that "the Indians want ammunition and are not able to mend their Arms." The peace negotiations that ensued revealed a desperate thirst for fresh supplies of European wares. Ambassadors from piedmont towns invariably spoke in a single breath of restoring "a Peace and a free Trade," and one delegation even admitted that its people "cannot live without the assistance of the English."

Natives unable to live without the English henceforth tried to live with them. No upcountry group mounted a direct challenge to Anglo-America after 1715. Trade quickly resumed, and the piedmont Indians, now concentrated almost exclusively in the Catawba valley, briefly enjoyed a regular supply of necessary products sold by men willing once again to deal according to the old rules. By mid-century, however, deer were scarce and fresh sources of slaves almost impossible to find. Anglo-American traders took their business elsewhere, leaving inhabitants of the Nation with another material crisis of different but equally dangerous dimensions.

Indians casting about for an alternative means of procuring the commodities they craved looked to imperial officials. During the 1740s and 1750s native dependence shifted from colonial traders to colonial authorities as Catawba leaders repeatedly visited provincial capitals to request goods. These delegations came not to beg but to bargain. Catawbas were still of enormous value to the English as allies and frontier guards, especially at a time when Anglo-America felt threatened by the French and their Indian auxiliaries. The Nation's position within reach of Virginia and both Carolinas enhanced its value by enabling headmen to approach all three colonies and offer their people's services to the highest bidder.

The strategy yielded Indians an arsenal of ammunition and a variety of other merchandise that helped offset the declining trade. Crown officials were especially generous when the Nation managed to play one colony off against another. In 1746 a rumor that the Catawbas were about to move to Virginia was enough to garner them a large shipment of powder and lead from officials in Charleston concerned about losing this "valuable people." A decade later, while the two Carolinas fought for the honor of constructing a fort in the Nation, the Indians encouraged (and received) gifts symbolizing good will from both colonies without reaching an agreement with either. Surveying the tangled thicket of promises and presents, the Crown's superintendent of Indian affairs, Edmond Atkin, ruefully admitted that "the People of both Provinces . . . have I beleive [sic] tampered too much on both sides with those Indians, who seem to understand well how to make their Advantage of it."

By the end of the colonial period delicate negotiations across cultural boundaries were as familiar to Catawbas as the strouds they wore and the muskets they carried. But no matter how shrewdly the headmen loosened provincial purse strings to extract vital merchandise, they could not escape the simple fact that they no longer held the purse containing everything needed for their daily existence. In the space of a century the Indians had become thoroughly embedded in an alien economy, denizens of a new material world. The ancient self-sufficiency was only a dim memory in the minds of the Nation's elders.

The Catawba peoples were veterans of countless campaigns against disease and masters of the arts of trade long before the third major element of their new world, white planters, became an integral part of their life. Settlement of the Carolina uplands did not begin until the 1730s, but once underway it spread with frightening speed. In November 1752 concerned Catawbas reminded South Carolina governor James Glen how they had "complained already . . . that the white People were settled too near us." Two years later five hundred families lived within thirty miles of the Nation and surveyors were running their lines into the middle of native towns. "[T]hose Indians are now in a fair way to be surrounded by White People," one observer concluded.

Settlers' attitudes were as alarming as their numbers. Unlike traders who profited from them or colonial officials who deployed them as allies, ordinary colonists had little use for Indians. Natives made poor servants and worse slaves; they obstructed settlement; they attracted enemy warriors to the area. Even men who respected Indians and earned a living by trading with them admitted that they made unpleasant neighbors. "We may observe of them as of the fire," wrote the South Carolina trader James Adair after considering the Catawbas' situation on the eve of the American Revolution, " 'it is safe and useful, cherished at proper distance; but if too near us, it becomes dangerous, and will scorch if not consume us.' "

A common fondness for alcohol increased the likelihood of intercultural hostilities. Catawba leaders acknowledged that the Indians "get very Drunk with [liquor] this is the Very Cause that they oftentimes Commit those Crimes that is offencive to You and us." Colonists were equally prone to bouts of drunkenness. In the 1760s the itinerant Anglican minister, Charles Woodmason, was shocked to find the citizens of one South Carolina upcountry community "continually drunk." More appalling still, after attending church services "one half of them got drunk before they went home." Indians sometimes suffered at the hands of intoxicated farmers. In 1760 a Catawba woman was murdered when she happened by a tavern shortly after four of its patrons "swore they would kill the first Indian they should meet with."

Even when sober, natives and newcomers found many reasons to quarrel. Catawbas were outraged if colonists built farms on the Indians' doorstep or tramped across ancient burial grounds. Planters, ignorant of (or indifferent to) native rules of hospitality, considered Indians who requested food nothing more than beggars and angrily drove them away. Other disputes arose when the Nation's young men went looking for trouble. As hunting, warfare, and other traditional avenues for achieving status narrowed, Catawba youths transferred older patterns of behavior into a new arena by raiding nearby farms and hunting cattle or horses.

Contrasting images of the piedmont landscape quite unintentionally generated still more friction. Colonists determined to tame what they considered a wilderness were in fact erasing a native signature on the land and scrawling their own. Bridges, buildings, fences, roads, crops, and other "improvements" made the area comfortable and familiar to colonists but uncomfortable and unfamiliar to Indians. "The Country side wear[s] a New face," proclaimed Woodmason proudly; to the original inhabitants, it was a grim face indeed. "His Land was spoiled," one Catawba headman told British officials in 1763. "They have spoiled him 100 Miles every way." Under these circumstances, even a settler with no wish to fight Indians met opposition to his fences, his outbuildings, his very presence. Similarly, a Catawba on a routine foray into traditional hunting territories had his weapon destroyed, his goods confiscated, his life threatened by men with different notions of the proper use of the land.

To make matters worse, the importance both cultures attached to personal independence hampered efforts by authorities on either side to resolve conflicts. Piedmont settlers along the border between the Carolinas were "people of desperate fortune," a frightened North Carolina official reported after visiting the area. "[N]o officer of Justice from either Province dare meddle with them." Woodmason, who spent even more time in the region, came to the same conclusion. "We are without any Law, or Order," he complained; the inhabitants' "Impudence is so very high, as to be past bearing." Catawba leaders could have sympathized. Headmen informed colonists that the Nation's people "are oftentimes Cautioned from . . . ill Doings altho' to no purpose for we Cannot be present at all times to Look after them." "What they have done I could not prevent," one chief explained.

Unruly, angry, intoxicated—Catawbas and Carolinians were constantly at odds during the middle decades of the eighteenth century. Planters who considered Indians "proud and deveilish" were themselves accused by natives of being "very bad and quarrelsome." Warriors made a habit of "going into the Settlements, robbing and stealing where ever they get an Oppertunity." Complaints generally brought no satisfaction—"they laugh and makes their Game of it, and says it is what they will"—leading some settlers to "whip [Indians] about the head, beat and abuse them." "The white People . . . and the Cuttahbaws, are Continually at varience," a visitor to the Nation fretted in June 1759, "and Dayly New Animositys Doth a rise Between them which In my Humble oppion will be of Bad Consequence In a Short time, Both Partys Being obstinate."

The litany of intercultural crimes committed by each side disguised a fundamental shift in the balance of physical and cultural power. In the early years of colonization of the interior the least disturbance by Indians sent scattered planters into a panic. Soon, however, Catawbas were few, colonists many, and it was the natives who now lived in fear. "[T]he white men [who] Lives Near the Neation is Contenuely asembleing and goes In the [Indian] towns In Bodys . . . ," worried another observer during the tense summer of 1759. "[T]he[y] tretton the[y] will Kill all the Cattabues."

The Indians would have to find some way to get along with these unpleasant neighbors if the Nation was to survive. As Catawba population fell below five hundred after the smallpox epidemic of 1759 and the number of colonists continued to climb, natives gradually came to recognize the futility of violent resistance. During the last decades of the eighteenth century they drew on years of experience in dealing with Europeans at a distance and sought to overturn the common conviction that Indian neighbors were frightening and useless.

This process was not the result of some clever plan; Catawbas had no strategy for survival. A headman could warn them that "the White people were now seated all round them and by that means had them entirely in their power." He could not command them to submit peacefully to the invasion of their homeland. The Nation's continued existence required countless individual decisions, made in a host of diverse circumstances, to complain rather than retaliate, to accept a subordinate place in a land that once was theirs. Few of the choices made survive in the record. But it is clear that, like the response to disease and to technology, the adaptation to white settlement was both painful and prolonged.

Catawbas took one of the first steps along the road to accommodation in the early 1760s, when they used their influence with colonial officials to acquire a reservation encompassing the heart of their ancient territories. This grant gave the Indians a land base, grounded in Anglo-American law, that prevented farmers from shouldering them aside. Equally important, Catawbas now had a commodity to exchange with nearby settlers. These men wanted land, the natives had plenty, and shortly before the Revolution the Nation was renting tracts to planters for cash, livestock, and manufactured goods.

Important as it was, land was not the only item Catawbas began trading to their neighbors. Some Indians put their skills as hunters and woodsmen to a different use, picking up stray horses and escaped slaves for a reward. Others bartered their pottery, baskets, and table mats. Still others traveled through the upcountry, demonstrating their prowess with the bow and arrow before appreciative audiences. The exchange of these goods and services for European merchandise marked an important adjustment to the settlers' arrival. In the past, natives had acquired essential items by trading peltry and slaves or requesting gifts from representatives of the Crown. But piedmont planters frowned on hunting and warfare, while provincial authorities—finding Catawbas less useful as the Nation's population declined and the French threat disappeared—discouraged formal visits and handed out fewer presents. Hence the Indians had to develop new avenues of exchange that would enable them to obtain goods in ways less objectionable to their neighbors. Pots, baskets, and acres proved harmless substitutes for earlier methods of earning an income.

Quite apart from its economic benefits, trade had a profound impact on the character of Catawba-settler relations. Through countless repetitions of the same simple procedure at homesteads scattered across the Carolinas, a new form of intercourse arose, based not on suspicion and an expectation of conflict but on trust and a measure of friendship. When a farmer looked out his window and saw Indians approaching, his reaction more commonly became to pick up money or a jug of whiskey rather than a musket or an axe. The natives now appeared, the settler knew, not to plunder or kill, but to peddle their wares or collect their rents.

The development of new trade forms could not bury all of the differences between Catawba and colonist overnight. But in the latter half of the eighteenth century the beleaguered Indians learned to rely on peaceful means of resolving intercultural conflicts that did arise. Drawing a sharp distinction between "the good men that have rented Lands from us" and "the bad People [who] has frequently imposed upon us," Catawbas called on the former to protect the Nation from the latter. In 1771 they met with the prominent Camden storekeeper, Joseph Kershaw, to request that he "represent us when [we are] a grieved." After the Revolution the position became more formal. Catawbas informed the South Carolina government that, being "destitute of a man to take care of, and assist us in our affairs," they had chosen one Robert Patten "to take charge of our affairs, and to act and do for us."

Neither Patten nor any other intermediary could have protected the Nation had it not joined the patriot side during the Revolutionary War. Though one scholar has termed the Indians' contribution to the cause "rather negligible," they fought in battles throughout the southeast and supplied rebel forces with food from time to time. These actions made the Catawbas heroes and laid a foundation for their popular renown as staunch patriots. In 1781 their old friend Kershaw told Catawba leaders how he welcomed the end of "this Long and Bloody War, in which You have taken so Noble a part and have fought and Bled with your white Brothers of America." Grateful Carolinians would not soon forget the Nation's service. Shortly after the Civil War an elderly settler whose father had served with the Indians in the Revolution echoed Kershaw's sentiments, recalling that "his father never communicated much to him [about the Catawbas], except that all the tribe . . . served the entire war . . . and fought most heroically."

Catawbas rose even higher in their neighbors' esteem when they began calling their chiefs "General" instead of "King" and stressed that these men were elected by the people. The change reflected little if any real shift in the Nation's political forms, but it delighted the victorious Revolutionaries. In 1794 the Charleston *City Gazette* reported that during the war "King" Frow had abdicated and the Indians chose "General" New River in his stead. "What a pity," the paper concluded, "certain people on a certain island have not as good optics as the Catawbas!" In the same year, the citizens of Camden celebrated the anniversary of the fall of the Bastille by raising their glasses to toast "King Prow [*sic*]—may all kings who will not follow his example follow that of Louis XVI." Like tales of Indian patriots, the story proved durable. Nearly a century after the Revolution one nearby planter wrote that "the Catawbas, emulating the examples of their white brethren, threw off regal government."

The Indians' new image as republicans and patriots, added to their trade with whites and their willingness to resolve conflicts peacefully, brought settlers to view Catawbas in a different light. By 1800 the natives were no longer violent and dangerous strangers but what one visitor termed an "inoffensive" people and one group of planters called "harmless and friendly" neighbors. They had become traders of pottery but not deerskins, experts with a bow and arrow but not hunters, ferocious warriors against runaway slaves or tories but not against settlers. In these ways Catawbas could be distinctively Indian yet reassuringly harmless at the same time.

The Nation's separate identity rested on such obvious aboriginal traits. But its survival ultimately depended on a more general conformity with the surrounding society. During the nineteenth century both settlers and Indians owned or

rented land. Both spoke proudly of their Revolutionary heritage and their republican forms of government. Both drank to excess. Even the fact that Catawbas
were not Christians failed to differentiate them sharply from nearby white settlements, where, one visitor noted in 1822, "little attention is paid to the sabbath, or
religeon."

In retrospect it is clear that these similarities were as superficial as they were
essential. For all the changes generated by contacts with vital Euro-American and
Afro-American cultures, the Nation was never torn loose from its cultural moorings. Well after the Revolution Indians maintained a distinctive way of life rich in
tradition and meaningful to those it embraced. Ceremonies conducted by headmen
and folk tales told by relatives continued to transmit traditional values and skills
from one generation to the next. Catawba children grew up speaking the native
language, making bows and arrows or pottery, and otherwise following patterns of
belief and behavior derived from the past. The Indians' physical appearance and
the meandering paths that set Catawba settlements off from neighboring communities served to reinforce this cultural isolation.

The natives' utter indifference to missionary efforts after 1800 testified to the
enduring power of established ways. Several clergymen stopped at the reservation
in the first years of the nineteenth century; some stayed a year or two; none enjoyed
any success. As one white South Carolinian noted in 1826, Catawbas were "Indians
still." Outward conformity made it easier for them to blend into the changed
landscape. Beneath the surface lay a more complex story.

Those few outsiders who tried to piece together that story generally found it
difficult to learn much from the Indians. A people shrewd enough to discard the
title of "King" was shrewd enough to understand that some things were better left
unsaid and unseen. Catawbas kept their Indian names, and sometimes their language, a secret from prying visitors. They echoed the racist attitudes of their white
neighbors and even owned a few slaves, all the time trading with blacks and hiring
them to work in the Nation, where the laborers "enjoyed considerable freedom"
among the natives. Like Afro-Americans on the plantation who adopted a happy,
childlike demeanor to placate suspicious whites, Indians on the reservation learned
that a "harmless and friendly" posture revealing little of life in the Nation was best
suited to conditions in post-Revolutionary South Carolina.

Success in clinging to their cultural identity and at least a fraction of their
ancient lands cannot obscure the cost Catawba peoples paid. From the time the first
European arrived, the deck was stacked against them. They played the hand dealt
them well enough to survive, but they could never win. An incident that took place
at the end of the eighteenth century helps shed light on the consequences of
compromise. When the Catawba headman, General New River, accidentally injured the horse he had borrowed from a nearby planter named Thomas Spratt,
Spratt responded by "banging old New River with a pole all over the yard." This
episode provided the settler with a colorful tale for his grandchildren; its effect on
New River and his descendants can only be imagined. Catawbas did succeed in the
sense that they adjusted to a hostile and different world, becoming trusted friends
instead of feared enemies. Had they been any less successful, they would not have
survived the eighteenth century. But poverty and oppression have plagued the

Nation from New River's day to our own. For a people who had once been proprietors of the piedmont, the pain of learning new rules was very great, the price of success very high.

On that August day in 1608 when Amoroleck feared the loss of his world, John Smith assured him that the English "came to them in peace, and to seeke their loves." Events soon proved Amoroleck right and his captor wrong. Over the course of the next three centuries not only Amoroleck and other piedmont Indians but natives throughout North America had their world stolen and another put in its place. Though this occurred at different times and in different ways, no Indians escaped the explosive mixture of deadly bacteria, material riches, and alien peoples that was the invasion of America. Those in the southern piedmont who survived the onslaught were ensconced in their new world by the end of the eighteenth century. Population levels stabilized as the Catawba peoples developed immunities to once-lethal diseases. Rents, sales of pottery, and other economic activities proved adequate to support the Nation at a stable (if low) level of material life. Finally, the Indians' image as "inoffensive" neighbors gave them a place in South Carolina society and continues to sustain them today.

Vast differences separated Catawbas and other natives from their colonial contemporaries. Europeans were the colonizers, Africans the enslaved, Indians the dispossessed: From these distinct positions came distinct histories. Yet once we acknowledge the differences, instructive similarities remain that help to integrate natives more thoroughly into the story of early America. By carving a niche for themselves in response to drastically different conditions, the peoples who composed the Catawba Nation shared in the most fundamental of American experiences. Like Afro-Americans, these Indians were compelled to accept a subordinate position in American life yet did not altogether lose their cultural integrity. Like settlers of the Chesapeake, aboriginal inhabitants of the uplands adjusted to appalling mortality rates and wrestled with the difficult task of "living with death." Like inhabitants of the Middle Colonies, piedmont groups learned to cope with unprecedented ethnic diversity by balancing the pull of traditional loyalties with the demands of a new social order. Like Puritans in New England, Catawbas found that a new world did not arrive all at once and that localism, self-sufficiency, and the power of old ways were only gradually eroded by conditions in colonial America. More hints of a comparable heritage could be added to this list, but by now it should be clear that Indians belong on the colonial stage as important actors in the unfolding American drama rather than bit players, props, or spectators. For they, too, lived in a new world.

7

"POOR RICHARD" MEETS THE NATIVE AMERICAN: SCHOOLING FOR YOUNG INDIAN WOMEN IN EIGHTEENTH-CENTURY CONNECTICUT

MARGARET CONNELL SZASZ

Throughout the centuries of Indian-white encounters the intruding Europeans and their descendants sought to eradicate the cultures of the Native Americans. The church, the school, and the farm stood at the center of this cultural onslaught. During the generations since early colonial settlement a long line of teachers and clergy have worked diligently to persuade young tribal people that their own language, society, economy, and beliefs needed to be replaced. In this selection the author traces the experiences of several young women, members of New England tribes, as they experienced the full force of the whites' acculturative efforts at Moor's Indian Charity School. Eleazar Wheelock hoped to prepare young tribesmen at the school to become Protestant ministers and to return to their home villages to introduce Christianity there. He accepted Indian girls as students in order to train them to become proper spouses for the young Indian missionaries. Education for the young women included basic literacy, household skills, and family management tactics. Only a small number of Indian girls attended the missionary school, and for most of them the experience proved anything but beneficial. They spent most of their time working as domestic servants in local homes while getting only a single day of training at the school each week. This selection discusses the difficulties the young women encountered and explains why Wheelock's efforts seemed to fail.

Margaret Connell Szasz is an associate professor of history at the University of New Mexico.

Source: Margaret Connell Szasz, "'Poor Richard' Meets the Native American: Schooling for Young Indian Women in Eighteenth Century Connecticut," *Pacific Historical Review*, vol. 49, no. 2 (May 1980), pp. 215-35. © 1980 by the Pacific Coast Branch, American Historical Association. Reprinted by permission.

In a small, hand-sewn memo booklet, a colonial schoolmaster, the Reverend Eleazar Wheelock, carefully jotted down the record of one of his female pupils: "One pair of shoes, . . . 5 yards and ½ of corse [osnaberg] . . . 9 yards and ¼ of salt sacking . . . . " He listed several more items and concluded with a measure of muslin for an apron. Schoolmasters in this period seldom trained Indian boys in their classrooms; instruction for Indian girls was almost unheard of. Hence, this memo—a clothing ration for an Indian girl who attended a charity boarding school in eighteenth-century Connecticut—is a unique colonial document. The experience shared by this girl and her companions was unusual for the 1760s, but in the ensuing generations it would be repeated by thousands of young Indians and white educators. At the core of their experience lay the failure of externally imposed education.

This failure is best understood from the perspective of ethnohistory—a method which seeks to understand the complexity of change and continuity when two cultures interact. Several prominent ethnohistorians, including Francis Jennings, Neal Salisbury, James P. Ronda, and James Axtell, have significantly altered our understanding of seventeenth-century missionary efforts to educate Indians by emphasizing the "reciprocal relationships between two cultures in contact." As yet, however, historians of eighteenth-century Indian education have failed to make use of these insights. No major study about Wheelock, or about his contemporaries in Indian education, has appeared since James Dow McCallum and Harold Blodgett wrote monographs for the Dartmouth College series in the 1930s. Ethnohistorical considerations shed new light on Wheelock's experiment in educating Indian boys and girls.

The developing body of ethnohistorical studies suggests that three overlapping forces led to the failure of externally imposed efforts by whites to educate Indians. Probably the most powerful force was the persistence of native culture. But in the context of Indian education, this meant that externally imposed schooling forced students to face conflicting cultural values. The artificial environment of the school only compounded the dilemma for Indians and whites, for the confined atmosphere of the classroom, an unnatural situation at best, stood in sharp contrast to the influences of family and community that traditionally molded the attitudes and behavior of Indian children. A third force shaping the dimensions of Indian education was racial prejudice. Whether overt or subtle, a pervasive prejudice existed in and out of the classroom. Under its hostile influence, the student remained an outsider and was further encouraged to return to his or her own people, where there was some assurance of belonging. Each of these factors played a significant role in the paradox and conflict comprising the history of American Indian education. Nowhere was the interplay of native culture, the classroom, and prejudice more clearly illustrated than in Wheelock's eighteenth-century experiment in education for Indian girls.

Eleazar Wheelock was a Congregational minister who lived in Lebanon, Connecticut, a small community southeast of Hartford. In 1754 he founded Moor's School, one of the few institutions to accept girls. He supervised its sixteen-year life span in Lebanon and engineered its metamorphosis and relocation to Hanover, New Hampshire, where it formed the nucleus for the newly founded Dartmouth College.

A descendant of a nonconformist minister who had emigrated to New England in the seventeenth century, Wheelock graduated from Yale College in 1733. He accepted his first call to the ministry just as the Great Awakening was transforming the religious convictions of many New Englanders. The revival motivated Wheelock's contemporaries to take up the task initiated by their Puritan forebears: spreading the gospel to the Indians. As a leading figure among these men, Wheelock turned to Indian schooling as an outlet for the tremendous energy generated by the current religious enthusiasm.

Encouraged by the scholarly successes of Samson Occom, a young Mohegan whom he had taken under his wing, Wheelock determined to begin a charity boarding school for Indian and white youth. Six years after Occom left the Wheelock home, the minister's dream took shape. In December 1754 the first two Algonquian pupils—John Pumshire, a fourteen-year-old Delaware, and Jacob Woolley, an eleven-year-old Delaware—enrolled in Moor's Indian Charity School. By the end of the decade Wheelock determined to add Indian girls to his all-male school, and his first female pupils—Amy Johnson, a Mohegan, and Miriam Storrs, an eleven-year-old Delaware—arrived in 1761.

Launching Moor's School had not been an easy task. In the early stage, before Wheelock had considered the advantages of coeducation, the school remained small. In 1755 Wheelock had received "about 2 Acres of Pasturing, a small House and Shop" from Colonel Joshua Moor, a farmer of nearby Mansfield, for whom the school was named, but the minister-schoolmaster still enrolled fewer than ten pupils and all of them were recruited from nearby Algonquian communities. Over the years, the institution increased its enrollment, adding not only female Algonquian but also both male and female Iroquois pupils because of Wheelock's skills as director and promoter. He assessed his needs in a practical fashion and then set about to meet them. First he needed a source of income that would stretch his meager minister's salary and the miscellaneous landholdings that supported his growing family. A larger school would require extensive financial aid. This would involve creating a convincing rationale and a widespread promotion campaign. Like John Eliot, his illustrious predecessor, Wheelock never underestimated the need for political pressure to secure economic assistance. Wheelock's efforts in this direction earned him the sobriquet "religious politician."

The rationale for the "the great Design," Wheelock's grandiose title for his experiment in Indian education, possessed appeal. The minister-schoolmaster began by reminding New Englanders of their "great obligations" as "God's Covenant-People" and by chastising them for their "neglect of the precious Souls of our Fellow Creatures, who are perishing for lack of Vision." Further, he projected his plan as a practical remedy to appease the constant fear of frontier attack. The money spent on education, he argued, would serve New England as a better defense against Indian attack than expensive forts. He suggested, in a theme that would become familiar in the nineteenth century, that if the Indians were "brought up in a Christian manner . . . , instructed in Agriculture, and taught to get their Living by their Labour," they would no longer "make such Depradations on our Frontiers." He also recommended, in a modified echo of John Eliot and the Mayhew family, that Indians, rather than whites, be trained as preachers and teachers for "for carrying the Gospel into the wilds of America." Here he appealed to his supporters' pocketbook: "[a]n Indian may be supported with less than half the Expense that will be necessary to support an Englishman." Moreover, "the Influence of their own Sons among them will likely be much greater than of any *Englishman* whatever." There is little indication that Wheelock initially made the addition of girls to Moor's School a strong selling point, but when he did add them, he justified the action to his supporters with similar arguments.

With this rationale for "the great Design" in hand, Wheelock garnered his support. Although he had uneven success, he established an extensive network of contacts. Individuals and organizations in England and the colonies came to the aid of the growing number of male and female charity scholars. For Wheelock, however, it was an unending task. Even when the school became well established, financial pressure constantly drained his energies. In the two and a half decades that the minister-schoolmaster devoted to Indian education, from 1754 to his death in 1779, he constantly appealed for support. In addition, between 1763 and 1775, he published nine separate *Narratives*. These served as a continuing promotion effort for Moor's School and, eventually, Dartmouth College.

Once a measure of financial support appeared certain, Wheelock introduced one of the most interesting and least publicized aspects of his experiment: schooling for Indian girls. The notion of educating Indian girls formed a subject of some concern to New England missionaries during and after the Great Awakening. In the 1740s the Rev. John Sergeant, missionary for the Mohegan-Stockbridge Indians in western Massachusetts, and Rev. Dr. Benjamin Colman of Boston had stressed the role Indian women played in "the Care of the Souls of Children in Families . . . for the first 7 or 8 Years." Rev. John Brainerd, missionary to the Delaware in New Jersey, expressed similar concern about the need of education for the Delaware women in his community. These women, Brainerd believed, were "much better inclined in all respects than the men." Not only did they have better morals, they were more industrious. Since they were unable to support themselves, except by making baskets and brooms, Brainerd suggested to his Scottish financial supporters (the Society in Scotland for the Promotion of Christian Knowledge) that he establish a "female school" where the young women could be taught to spin and knit. This dream, like so many others held by Brainerd, never materialized.

Wheelock communicated with these men, but he also wrote to colonial schoolteachers scattered among the small Algonquian communities and to the more prestigious Sir William Johnson, ally of the Iroquois and superintendent of Indian affairs for the northern colonies. In the late 1750s, when Wheelock decided that Moor's School was financially able to include girls, he asked these men about potential students.

Between 1761 and 1769 Wheelock enrolled some 16 Indian girls at Moor's School. Their attendance provided perhaps a fourth of the total Indian enrollment. Some of these girls stayed only a few months; five, possibly seven, were there for at least two years; two of them remained for five years, and one for six years. They came from nearby groups, including the Narragansett, Mohegan, Niantic, and Pequot; from the Delaware; and from two Iroquois groups: Mohawk and Oneida.

Of these tribes, most of the Algonquian groups had been in contact with Europeans since the early 1600s. Of the Iroquois, the Mohawk, who were Sir William Johnson's neighbors, had been most exposed to European culture. Thus, Wheelock dealt with girls who knew about the rudiments of Christianity, who were accustomed to European trade goods, who spoke some English and may have had some schooling, who were almost all very poor, and whose material cultures had changed radically from pre-European days.

A practical schoolmaster, Wheelock based his plan for the education of these Indian girls on two considerations: the fact that they were female and his conviction that their education should not be a financial burden to the school. Wheelock believed that their schooling should be similar to that of young, white colonial women, whose intellectual skills were summarized in a gently ironic couplet borrowed from Abigail Adams:

> The little learning I have gained
> Is all from simple nature Drained.

New Englanders believed that women were fit for home and hearth. Hence, girls received the rudiments of a formal education—reading and writing—but most of their training was for the home. While parents often apprenticed colonial girls to another home for training in housekeeping, more often they learned these skills in their own family.

Herein lay a fundamental difference between colonial daughters and these Indian girls. Whereas the former were usually trained at home, Wheeler settled the latter in nearby community homes where families treated them as servants or possibly even as slaves. Wheelock argued that he did not have space to board the girls in his own home. For this reason he "Hired women in this neighborhood to instruct [them] in all the arts of good House wifery." Nonetheless, Wheelock did provide for their clothing, and he also assumed responsibility for their moral instruction and their basic educational skills.

For both Indian and white girls, instruction was limited to relatively few hours. Schooling for colonial girls often occurred only in the early morning or late afternoon, when boys were not using the schoolroom, but Indian girls received schooling for only one day a week. Wheelock did require homework, assigning his Indian wards to "write four lines on each Day they are Absent." He imposed this limitation on their formal schooling in order to minimize financial expense. Wheelock reasoned that he could afford to maintain the girls as pupils if they cost him only one day's schooling and dinner per week. On the one day the girls attended school they "were to be instructed in writing &c, till they should be fit for an Apprenticeship, to be taught Men's and Women's Apparel . . . . " Like their white counterparts, their education trained them to serve their husbands' needs. Woman's relation to man, wrote a New Englander in 1761, is to be "an Help to him." The education of these Indian girls, Wheelock explained in 1763, is "in order to accompany these [Indian] Boys, when they shall have Occasion for such Assistance in the Business of their Mission."

Unlike the girls, Wheelock kept the boys directly under his thumb, subjecting them to a rigorous, daily routine. Like all schoolmasters of the period, Wheelock adhered to the maxim: "Idleness in youth is scarcely healed without a scar in age." At Moor's School the day began before sunrise. Following early morning prayer and catechism the boys remained in the classroom until noon, where they received a classical training in Latin and Greek and sometimes even Hebrew. After a two-hour break they returned and worked until five p.m. Just before dark they attended evening prayers and public worship; then they studied until bedtime. This schedule alternated only on Sunday, when they spent the day in Sunday meetings and catechism classes.

Sometimes, however, this educational environment became more illusionary than real. Despite Wheelock's protests to the contrary, drunkenness, misbehavior, and running away composed a part of daily life. Striking a realistic note, Wheelock suggested that the girls be added "for the purpose that *these* Boy[s] may not be under absolute *necessity* to turn Savage in this manner of living for want of those who can do the female part for them when they shall be aboard [*sic*] on the business of their Missions and out of reach of the English." The inclusion of girls, however, may have merely increased Wheelock's chronic discipline problems at the school. A confession by Hannah Nonesuch, written on her first day in Lebanon, typified those pleas for forgiveness that Wheelock kept in his files.

> I Hannah Nonesuch do with shamefacedness acknowledge that on the evening of the 8th Inst I was . . . guilty of being at the tavern and tarrying there with a company of Indian boys & girls for . . . a frolick . . . I am heartily sorry, & desire to lie low in the dust & do now beg forgiveness of God, the Revd & worthy Doctor Wheelock, his family & school, and all whom I have hereby offended.
>
> March 1768

The story of three of Hannah's companions—Miriam Storrs (a Delaware, and a student from 1761–1767), Hannah Garrett (a Pequot, 1763–1768)—illustrate the problems that plagued Wheelock's "great Design."

Miriam Storr's was the second girl to enroll in Moor's School. She grew up in the small Delaware community served by John Brainerd, who remained with this remnant group of some forty Delaware families over a period of thirty years. Miriam came from one of the more religious families in this community. Her mother belonged to Brainerd's church, and Miriam had been baptized as an infant. She was the only girl among the six young Delaware whom Brainerd sent to Moor's school. She started on the trip to New London, Connecticut, with Elizabeth Quela, but Elizabeth's recurring illness forced her to turn back before the ship left. As the two girls were departing, Brainerd informed Wheelock:

> I feel tenderly concerned for these little girls, & as it is a very considerable thing for them to go so far away from their parents, I hope they will meet with the kindest & best treatment . . . .

On Miriam's arrival in Lebanon, Wheelock described her as "an amiable little black savage Christian." During the next six years she changed from an eleven-year-old girl to a young woman.

Wheelock provided for Miriam's physical needs: He purchased material for her clothing and found her a place to live. Shortly after she arrived, he hired a "proper Gentlewoman" to train her and her companions in "all parts of good Housewifery. Tending a Dary, Spining, the use of their needle." A few years later, as more girls arrived, he sought to hire a tailoress to equip them with more advanced skills. Wheelock's "Masters" taught Miriam the minimum reading and writing skills when she came to his home once a week for her lessons, while Wheelock himself assumed responsibility for the condition of her Soul.

Miriam's housekeeping duties probably prevented her from participating in daily worship at the school, but she and the other pupils attended church on Sunday, where she sat at the rear, on the side reserved for the women of the community. She probably attended the catechism classes held between Sunday meetings and there received a solid grounding in Calvinist religion. "Every *Grace* enters into the Soul through the *Understanding*," Cotton Mather had written in 1704, and understanding could come about only through a knowledge of the Scriptures and intense introspection.

The religious state of his pupils greatly concerned Wheelock. Shortly after Miriam turned thirteen, he noted her progress: "[Miriam] has of late," he wrote, "had such discoveries of the Truth, Reality, and Greatness of things revealed, as were more than Nature could sustain; she fainted under them . . . . " Miriam's religious experiences were reminiscent of the spiritual enthusiasm Wheelock had elicited during the Great Awakening. Yet there was no minimizing the difficulty of the religious aspect of boarding school life for both Indian girls and boys. As one of Miriam's companions wrote: "I have no peace of conscience."

In late 1767 or early 1768, when Miriam was sixteen or seventeen years old, she left the school. Had she been raised in a traditional Delaware community, she would already have been married and raising a family. Had she achieved the goal established by Wheelock—housewife, schoolmistress, or tailoress—she might have been able to adjust but she had not reached that goal and she found herself ill prepared to cope with colonial society. When she left school, she headed south through Connecticut to New York City. There, after several jobs, she wrote a letter of bitter disappointment to her former mentor. Composing the message required effort. The grammar was poor and the script almost illegible, but the meaning was clear: "Sir I have heard but one prayer since I went from Norwich," she lamented. "Since I went from thy house instead of prayers [I hear] filthy talk . . . . I have been under many trials . . . which caused me soo to weep nights." Nevertheless, she retained her faith: "I found no rest until I put my whole trust in God." Miriam soon tired of New York. Within a year she returned to her Delaware community. "Her poor old parents were overjoyed to see her," Brainerd wrote, and "I wish she might be a blessing to them." This proved a groundless hope, for Miriam did not progress as Brainerd and Wheelock had expected. Brainerd tried to apprentice her to a tailor so as to "perfect her trade" as a seamstress, but he reported no success. The only occupation she could pursue was the basic skill she had learned in Lebanon—housework. In the ensuing years Brainerd reported on her occasionally, each time an edge of despair in his words. "Miriam Store is not the thing I want her to be, by any means," he wrote in June 1769. "There is too much truth in that common saying: 'Indians will be Indians.' " Three and a half years later, at the age of twenty-three, Miriam was suffering from severe rheumatism and had "but poor use of her hands." There is no further mention of her name.

By the standards of Brainerd and Wheelock, Miriam's contemporary, Hannah Garrett, achieved more success. Hannah was descended from the Pequot, a tribe almost decimated in the Pequot War of 1636. When the remaining Pequot warriors were divided among the Mohegan, Narragansett, and Niantic tribes, Hannah's ancestors were among those sent to Narragansett territory in Rhode Island. Missionaries visited this area, but by the 1750s, when Hannah was growing up, the Narragansett had established their own Protestant church under the guidance of a well-known Indian preacher. The elementary school in Charlestown, which Hannah may have attended, was the first school for several of Wheelock's Narragansett pupils. In 1764 four girls attended Moor's School: Miriam, Hannah, Amy Johnson, and Mary Secutor. Within a year of her arrival Hannah was being courted by Joseph Woolley, an eighteen- or nineteen-year old Delaware who had studied with Wheelock for seven years. The courtship had just commenced when Wheelock sent Woolley to Onohoquawge to serve as a schoolmaster to the Mohawk children. En route, Woolley wrote to Wheelock asking him to advise Hannah's father of the marriage proposal. Hannah, a dutiful daughter, refused to take any further steps without her father's permission. Woolley feared a possible change of heart by Hannah: "I can't take it well f[r]om her, if Just at the End, she should turn the Contrary." But he and Hannah never saw each other again, for consumption soon cut his life short.

Another scholar began to court Hannah. David Fowler, a Montauk, and the younger brother of Mary Fowler Occom, Samson Occom's wife, began his studies with Wheelock when he was twenty-four, and by the time the fourteen- or fifteen-year-old Hannah arrived in Lebanon, he was already twenty-eight. During Hannah's third year in Lebanon Wheelock sent David Fowler to Canajoharie to teach the Oneida children. David had no illusions about living in the wilderness without a wife. On the eve of his departure he planned to marry Amy Johnson, a former pupil at Wheelock's school. This relationship soon cooled, however, and by the following spring David had determined to marry Hannah Poquiantup, a Niantic. "I find it very hard to live here without the other Rib," he wrote to Wheelock from Canajoharie. Fearing that Hannah Poquiantup might break the bargain they had made, he wrote again to Wheelock, "If she won't let her bones be joined with mine, I shall pick out my Rib from your House." David's fears of Hannah Poquiantup's refusal were soon realized. He returned to Lebanon and went directly to Wheelock's school on his spouse hunt with a determination born from two failures and one lonely winter. Evidently it was not too difficult for this thirty-one-year-old frantic bachelor to convince the seventeen- or eighteen-year-old Hannah Garrett to marry him. Wheelock duly commented on the courtship in an exchange between the minister and Fowler: ". . . how yo[u] & Hannah ha' Spent y[ou]r prec.[ious] Hours yesterday & t'day I know not—Or how yo[u] will live or w[he]n you will serve tog[ethe]r I know not. . . . "

Wheelock had wearied of David Fowler's romances. Probably with some relief he sent Hannah and David back to the Iroquois country. He and David continued to correspond, but if Hannah learned how to write at school, no evidence of it has survived. By David's account, however, she proved to be the wife he had hoped for. "I find very great Profit by having the other Rib join'd to my Body for it hath taken away all my House work from me," he wrote to Wheelock during the first winter following the marriage. In June of the following year Hannah bore their first child, a boy whom they named David.

Shortly after the birth of their son, Hannah and David returned to Montauk, where David taught school. Following the Revolution they moved with their six children to Brothertown, an Algonquian settlement on Oneida land which had been established by David, his brother-in-law, Samson Occom, and several other Indian leaders. Here they settled among their own people for the remainder of their lives. Hannah outlived her husband by four years and died in 1811.

Of the sixteen girls who attended Moor's School, Hannah Garrett was the only one who achieved the goal of marriage established by Wheelock. There is no record of any courtship for Miriam Storrs, and the brief account of the third girl in this trilogy, Mary Secutor, is underlined by disappointment. Like Hannah Garrett, Mary Secutor had grown up on the Narragansett reservation. She, too, probably attended the school in Charlestown before going to study with Wheelock in December 1763. Following her arrival, at the age of perhaps thirteen or fourteen, she matured sufficiently during the next three or four years for Wheelock to describe her as "well accomplished and very likely." Up to this point Mary appears to have been a model student.

On Mary's arrival she met Hezekiah Calvin, a young Delaware. Mary and Hezekiah saw each other for a year and a half before Wheelock sent seventeen-year-old Hezekiah off to keep school for Mohawk children. During the next two winters, Hezekiah taught school near Fort Hunter, but his mind was not on his teaching. The Narragansett girl back at Moor's School preoccupied his thoughts. "[N]othing was in my thoughts but being married," he later confessed to Wheelock. When he returned to Lebanon after the second winter among the Iroquois, he wrote to Mary's father, asking him for permission to marry her. "It may be no small thing I have to acquaint you with," he began, "the design that lay between your daughter Moley and me, Pardon me if I blush to Name it, that is *Matrimony* but I shall not attempt it without y[ou]r Consent & approbation." John Secutor opposed the marriage, and with no explanation he wrote to Wheelock, urging him to use his "reasonable powers to Dissuade my Daughter from such design." There is no record of Mary's feelings at this time, but in later correspondence she stated: "I have had more regards for Calvin than ever I had for any Indian in my life." Without the approval of Mary's father, however, the two young people were in a quandary. A few months later both Mary and Hezekiah apologized in written confessions for "gross sins"; they had been involved in drinking and other "vile" behavior. In the spring they wrote second confessions; by the following summer they had left school.

Hezekiah and Mary returned to their own people, but the appropriate moment for their proposed marriage seems to have passed. Mary's father finally gave his permission, but she was now plagued with uncertainty. "I love him well enough," she wrote to Wheelock, "but what to do I know not. . . . I hope I shall be Derected to do what is rite."

From Wheelock's point of view, his eight-year experiment with women's education must have been keenly disappointing, further aggravating his bitter feelings of failure about the young Indian men he had trained to serve as schoolmasters among the Iroquois, no more than half of whom, he wrote in 1771, had "preserved their characters." Only six of the girls who enrolled at Moor's School stayed longer than two years, and they had come from the more assimilated Algonquian communities. Of those six, only Hannah Garrett lived an exemplary life. Miriam Storrs disappointed both Brainerd and Wheelock; Mary Secutor's last letter dwelt on her indecision in marriage; Amy Johnson was consumptive; Sarah Wyog stood out in memory only as the instigator of a "frolick"; and Sarah Simon's last letter, which was filled with Calvinist angst, recited a tale of woe.

Wheelock provided these girls with practical skill, minimum reading and writing ability, and a Calvinist view of life, but he failed to convince them that they should adopt the cultural traits of the colonists. Wheelock and his contemporaries needed certain values in order to achieve individual success in the fluid, expanding economy and society of eighteenth-century America. Few New Englanders would have disputed the maxims so well epitomized in the sayings of Poor Richard: "A penny saved is a penny earned"; "Early to bed, early to rise, makes a man healthy, wealthy and wise"; "Light purse, heavy heart"; "God helps them that help themselves." Benjamin Franklin popularized these phrases, but his New England neighbors lived the precepts. When John Adams wrote to his wife, Abigail, on their children's education, he summarized the prevailing attitude:

> The Education of our Children is never out of my Mind. Train them to Virtue, habituate them to industry, activity, and Spirit.

Industry, diligence, frugality, temperance—each of these values shaped Wheelock's character as well. An ample supply of piety completed his framework for success. Ironically, the cultural values that served Wheelock so well were the very qualities he was least able to transmit to his pupils. This may have been due to their retention of native values that ran counter to those of the contemporary New Englander.

Historians recognize that the material culture of these girls' tribes changed radically after the early 1600s. Less accepted, however, is the possibility that their cultural values may have persisted, perhaps to a far greater extent than Wheelock and his contemporaries cared to admit. Wheelock had theorized some years earlier that the boarding school would remove Indian children from "the pernicious influence of *Indian* examples," but for Miriam and her contemporaries, the learning acquired at Moor's School was merely superimposed on their earlier education. Despite a century and a half of contact, these Indian groups continued to live cooperatively with nature. The scarcity of game had made hunting increasingly difficult, but they still fished and cultivated their patches of corn and beans. They were a people who balanced *being* with *doing*, contrary to the colonists who were bound to the maxims of Poor Richard. They remained a people of seasonal or, if you will, natural time, unpunctuated by the colonial hourglass, calendar, or notion of "wasting time." Their group orientation persisted: The family and community were of greater importance than any single member, and without this support the individual felt unable to cope with the world.

Wheelock's schooling did not destroy the family and community orientation of these Indian girls; nor did it prepare them adequately for the heterogeneous morality of colonial society beyond the small New England community. Miriam Storrs experienced this cultural shock during her search for a place in the colonial world. Even had Wheelock's influence succeeded, one additional factor would have continued to dissuade these Indian girls from participating in colonial society: This was the strength of racial prejudice. Prejudice was a fact of life for the Indian in colonial America. These girls met it in the homes of Lebanon; they met it at church, where they were seated *behind* the women of the community; they met it at school, from a mentor who had described one of them as a "black savage Christian," and whom another pupil accused of treating the girls as "slaves." The girls also encountered racial hostility in the post-school society, where colonists commonly said that "ye Indians are dispized by ye English." For many colonists the Indians "were mere tools used by grasping and uneasy men to obtain their own selfish ends." Racial prejudice, for some, probably became the *coup de grâce* that sent them back to their own people. Hannah Garrett, the most successful of the girls, never confronted white colonial society. She and her husband chose to live among communities composed of Indian people who had rejected many of the colonists' values.

Rejection of colonial society did not necessarily mean that the girls could easily return to their people. One senses that they felt dissatisfied with their lives at this stage. Moor's School and their experiences in Lebanon had given them a taste of colonial living. They would no longer be totally content with the traditional values of their people; nor could they be comfortable in colonial society. Their frustrations bespoke the uncertainty of imbalance. An Indian woman with a veneer of colonial culture who faced prejudice in colonial society and uneasiness in her native society confronted an enduring dilemma.

Many young Indians would share in the same dilemma in succeeding generations. Throughout American history, Indian children subjected to missionary, federal, or public schooling faced the agonizing decision of choosing parts of two cultures. The choice was seldom clear-cut. Often it was complicated by the peculiar circumstances of the education encountered by the child, by the persistence of that child's own culture, and by the pressures of racial hostility. Whether Indian children received an education at Carlisle Indian School or in Gallup, New Mexico, they encountered the same cultural dilemma which Wheelock had imposed on his pupils.

Even when Wheelock admitted disillusion with the earlier phase of "the great Design" and moved his school to Dartmouth, he still failed to comprehend the dimensions of the choice he imposed on his students, female as well as male. "It grieves & breaks my heart," he wrote in 1768, "that while I am wearing my life out to do good to the poor Indians, they themselves have no more Desire to help forward the great Design of their Happiness . . . but [there] are so many of them . . . pulling the other way & as fast as they can undoing all I have done." Had he walked in their path, perhaps he would have understood, but cultural myopia dimmed Wheelock's comprehension. To his death he remained convinced of the righteousness of his cause.

8

THE REVOLUTIONARY WAR AND THE INDIANS OF THE UPPER SUSQUEHANNA VALLEY

PETER C. MANCALL

By the era of the American Revolution the tribes of the Northeast had long and bitter experience with the outcomes of the white man's wars in colonial North America. The tribal groups living in the upper Susquehanna Valley in Pennsylvania represented survivors of earlier Indian-white wars and competition over the land and its resources. During the 1750s composite groups of Delawares, Shawnees, Mahicans, Nanticokes, and Iroquois dwelt in the Valley. These refugees had moved away from earlier conflicts, subordinated their differences, formed new villages, and reconstituted their societies in an impressive show of cultural resilience. Although pressures from land speculators and pioneer squatters produced some tensions, the Indians of the region enjoyed relatively peaceable relations with the Pennsylvania authorities. Nevertheless, when the American Revolution began, the situation changed dramatically. Most tribal people in the region joined the British rather than the land-hungry Americans. Although rational, this choice brought disaster. American armies ravaged their lands, and by the end of the war the tribes of the Valley had suffered much violence and destruction. The military campaigns brought fundamental changes in Indian-white relations, and by the 1780s few pioneers wanted the Indians to remain in the region. This discussion relates the events and ideas that brought disaster to the Susquehanna Valley Indians and shows the part the tribes played in bringing about their own destruction.

Peter C. Mancall is an assistant professor of history at the University of Kansas.

The Revolutionary War and its aftermath brought ruin to the Indians of the upper Susquehanna Valley. The majority allied themselves with the British, infuriating

Source: Peter C. Mancall, "The Revolutionary War and the Indians of the Upper Susquehanna Valley," *American Indian Culture and Research Journal*, 12, no. 1 (December 1988), pp. 39–57. Reprinted with permission of the author.

local colonists who mostly sided with the Continental Army. General John Sullivan's campaign of 1779 devastated the Susquehanna Indians' towns, as well as the communities of Indians living farther north and west throughout Iroquoia. At the end of the war these Valley Indians were displaced, impoverished, and ignored; they lived at the edges of the new republic but could not enjoy the benefits of citizenship.

While recent studies of the Revolutionary period have described crucial decades in the nation's past, historians still have not examined the influence of the Anglo-American crisis on Indians in sufficient depth. Barbara Graymont's *The Iroquois in the American Revolution* traces the experiences of the Six Nations but treats primarily the political and military aspects of these Indians' lives. Anthony F.C. Wallace's *The Death and Rebirth of the Seneca*, while putting the Revolutionary period into a broader historical and cultural context, focuses almost exclusively on the Senecas. But this westernmost tribe in Iroquoia managed to retain at least a portion of its land in the post-Revolutionary period, thereby distinguishing the tribe's history from that of many Indians who were completely displaced from their territory. The Indians who inhabited the upper Susquehanna Valley, many of whom were not members of the Six Nations, have received insufficient attention from scholars. Even Barry Kent's recent analysis, *Susquehanna's Indians*, contains little on the Revolutionary period, primarily analyzing the earlier Indian occupation of the region.

Scholars have tended to study the histories of particular tribal groups. Such an approach makes sense for much of eastern North America, where tribes generally inhabited specific regions. But the upper Susquehanna Valley does not lend itself to such tribally specific analysis. When colonists expanded their settlements in Pennsylvania and Maryland, displaced Indians migrated to the region, creating a multitribal society along the river's banks. Most of these refugee Indians built towns with members of other tribes or lived adjacent to groups with different tribal affiliations. While the Indians may have maintained their tribal identity, they often acted together to protect their territory or enhance trade opportunities. Before the Revolution the Indians of the upper Susquehanna Valley were able to create stable communities in spite of the repeated social and demographic crises that already had reoriented their traditional ways of life.

While the Indians of the upper Susquehanna Valley were thus no strangers to conquest and hostile invaders, the Revolution altered their lives more profoundly than had earlier misfortunes. The war completely destroyed their economy; the tribally mixed settlements never recovered. The extent of the Indians' economic decline, and the resulting threat to their communities, emerges in richly descriptive documentary evidence. Because many of the Susquehanna Indians allied themselves with the British, the correspondence of Crown military officials precisely describes the changing fortunes of these Indians. These sources, especially the many volumes of correspondence in the Haldimand papers in the British Library, reveal the concern of the British for the Indians' well-being and the impact of the Indians' declining prospects on the Crown's efforts to prosecute the war. These letters, written in the field, behind the lines, and even, at times, across the Atlantic, describe how the Valley Indians' economy degenerated during the late 1770s. Used in conjunction with other existing documentary sources, the evidence in the Haldimand papers on social and economic change can move the analysis of the Indians' wartime experiences beyond the largely political and military narratives that currently dominate the field. Such analysis can broaden our understanding of the Revolution in general and the specific impact of the Anglo-American crisis on Indians.

These documents reveal that Valley Indians lost the Revolutionary War not only because they were allied with the British. Indeed, even some who sided with the Continental Army lost their lands in the upper Valley after the war. The war and a postwar wave of settlement on former Indian lands destabilized the Indians' communities and prevented them from enjoying the emerging economic opportunities available to others in the early republic. After the Revolution, and perhaps as early as the mid 1780s, few if any Indians inhabited the Susquehanna Valley. Their dislocation was complete.

Before the war a number of different Indian groups lived in the upper Valley, generally clustered along the banks of the Susquehanna or one of its major tributaries. Most of these refugee Indians had fled their homelands around Chesapeake Bay or in the Delaware Valley when colonists encroached on their territory in the late seventeenth and early eighteenth centuries. During the eighteenth century the upper Valley had become a home for displaced Indians from other areas. Delawares, Shawnees, Conoys, Nanticokes, Tutelos, and Mahicans, along with members of Six Nations' tribes, often lived together in small, primary agricultural communities. Shamokin had Delaware, Mahican, and Tutelo occupants; Delawares and Shawnees inhabited Great Island, along the west branch of the Susquehanna; Mahicans and Delawares lived at Wyoming, where a Nanticoke town was so close that a group of missionaries believed it part of the same settlement. From the late 1720s to the early 1770s Otsiningo, near the confluence of the Chenango and Susquehanna rivers, had occupants from many tribes; in the early 1750s two missionaries found Onondagas, Shawnees, Oneidas, Tuscaroras, and Nanticokes at the town.

Like other eastern Indians, those inhabiting the upper Susquehanna Valley reoriented their economies in response to demographic decline and new trade opportunities. Many hunted indigenous fur-bearing animals and transported the pelts to local trade centers. Throughout the region Indians incorporated trade goods, such as metal axes and pots, into both daily activities and ceremonial occasions. Perhaps most important, many Valley Indians developed a taste for alcohol which traders gladly indulged, regardless of the complaints of local Indian leaders about the destructive impact of drinking on their communities. Periodic encounters with traders and other traveling Indians also exposed Valley Indians to various diseases, especially smallpox, which devastated their communities.

The Indians' prewar economy, like that of many primarily agrarian peoples, had strict seasonal requirements. Crops needed to be planted at certain times, kept free of pests as much as possible, and harvested at the appropriate moment. Failure to follow the traditional calendar easily led to food shortages and, if food could not be found elsewhere, disease and death. Hunting followed a slightly different calendar. Valley Indians, like the Iroquois and other northeastern Indians, hunted in winter when it was easier to track game, especially deer. Food obtained from the hunt could not be preserved like corn and was consumed when fresh. While limited storage and the adoption of livestock by at least some Valley Indians allowed them to maintain some control over annual food supplies throughout the year, most Indian groups still relied on the hunt for food during parts of the year.

Even when the population of fur-bearing animals dwindled because of over-hunting, Valley Indians continued to bring pelts to trading centers, such as Fort Augusta at the confluence of the Susquehanna's two branches. In spite of the decline of beaver stocks in particular, threatening the fur trade in many places, the storekeeper at Fort Augusta received more beaver pelts in 1763 than any other furs. His inventory reflected the diversity of the mid-century peltry trade; he listed the hides of twelve other species he was shipping to market. Still, colonial observers noted that agriculture, particularly corn, legumes, and tubers, supplemented by fruit, fish, and some game birds, dominated the Valley Indians' economy.

While Valley Indians managed to live peaceably together for the most part, they had to accommodate themselves to the Iroquois, who claimed suzerainty over the Susquehanna Valley after the demise of the Susquehannocks in the seventeenth century. Hostilities with other Indians and continued demographic decline had taken a toll on the Confederacy's strength. But while the Iroquois of the eighteenth century did not have the authority the Six Nations enjoyed in the seventeenth century, the League still held the most power in the upper Susquehanna Valley. Perhaps more important, colonial officials, especially Sir William Johnson, the superintendent of Indian affairs in the northern colonies, accepted the Iroquois' claims to control over much of the northern backcountry. Thus, in spite of tensions between the Susquehanna Indians and the Indians in the Confederacy, British negotiators assumed Iroquois control over the upper Valley. In the treaty-defined political world of the hinterland, the refugee Indians found themselves politically, and at times economically, bound to decisions negotiated between representatives of the British and the Iroquois.

The Iroquois used their favored status to negotiate with colonial officials, often deciding matters for other Valley Indians. At a treaty at Lancaster in August 1762, for example, the Iroquois at the meeting prevented Pennsylvania provincial authorities from building a trading house on the west branch of the Susquenhanna, even though it would have lowered the cost of goods for the Delawares in the region. Similarly, Shickellamy, an Oneida sachem, negotiated trade terms at Shamokin, even though most of the residents of the town were not from tribes in the League. Tensions between the Iroquois and other Indians prompted some Shawnees and Delawares to migrate to the Ohio country in the 1740s.

Valley Indians also had to contend with colonists who defied colonial author-ities and tried to settle along the Susquehanna on lands still belonging to the Indians. The struggle for the Valley erupted into violence on occasion. In August 1762, for example, a group of ninety settlers from the Susquehannah Company tried to settle at Wyoming. The group, based in Connecticut, claimed that they had purchased the land from local Indians, but Valley Indians, as well as provincial authorities, declared the sale invalid. When the settlers arrived to stake their claim, they encountered over five hundred Iroquois, Delaware and other Indian warriors returning from a treaty at Lancaster. According to one colonial observer, the Indians "ordered the Connecticut people to go away, and quit the Land, and said if they had not done so forthwith, the Indians would have killed every Man of them before they could have got into the Inhabitants." The Company members, wisely sensing the danger, left the area. The following year another group from the Susquehannah Company again sought to settle at Wyoming. They were less fortunate than their predecessors. The Indians, in the words of a colonist who arrived after the Indians departed, had "most cruelly butchered" nine men and one woman, leaving their mutilated corpses behind.

While some Indians aggressively defended their territory, others found themselves the victims of colonial assaults. The so-called Paxton Boys, a group of backwoods vigilantes, massacred a group of peaceful Indians at Conestoga in 1763; later they offered their services to the Susquehannah Company in its continuing campaign to gain control of northern Pennsylvania. Colonial attackers were not always so boastful of their accomplishments. Teedyuscung, a Delaware sachem living at Wyoming, died when his house burned, possibly an act of arson and murder by members of the Susquehannah Company seeking control of the area.

But while hostilities flared up periodically, Valley Indians and their colonial neighbors were usually able to live in harmony. At repeated treaty meetings provincial authorities in New York and Pennsylvania negotiated with Valley Indians over matters important to everyone in the area: the return of captives, the price of trade goods, the location of trade centers, the building of forts. Pennsylvania officials built a town for Teedyuscung and his community at Wyoming, completing the project even after an unknown group of Indians murdered one of the workers. Provincial officials also promised to prosecute colonial trespassers on Indian lands. A 1768 Pennsylvania statute even authorized the death penalty without benefit of clergy for squatters refusing to leave Indian lands. The following year the provincial legislature modified the temporary 1768 bill; thereafter violaters would be fined £500 and be imprisoned for twelve months. In 1773, responding to violations of the law, particularly by the so-called Fair Play settlers along the west branch of the Susquehanna who claimed lands beyond the Fort Stanwix treaty boundary, Pennsylvania Governor John Penn issued a proclamation promising to prosecute offenders. He feared that "the making [of] such Settlements doth greatly tend to irritate the minds of the Indians, and may be productive of dangerous and Fatal Consequences to the Peace and Safety of His Majesty's good Subjects." His proclamation, which he ordered distributed "thro' the back Counties," commanded colonial officials to enforce the law vigorously. While Penn primarily hoped to dissuade potential trespassers from going beyond the boundary line, his proclamation was also no doubt intended to reassure Indians in the upper Valley and elsewhere who feared the further expansion of colonial settlements into their territory.

At treaty meetings Valley Indians from different tribes often worked together to address local political and economic issues. Sir William Johnson often met with such groups of Indians from the Valley, many of whom visited his estate at Johnson Hall to negotiate specific matters. For example, a group of Tuscaroras, Nanticokes, and Conoys living in or near Oquaga visited Johnson Hall in April 1757 to discuss French efforts to woo Iroquois tribes away from their alliance with the English.

Such an action would break the Covenant Chain which, according to Adam, the Oquaga Indians' spokesman at the meeting, "our Forefathers made with our Brethren the English" and which these Valley Indians wanted to maintain. Johnson shared their belief in the desirability of preserving the Covenant Chain and promised to do all in his power to counteract the French threat. The Oquaga Indians also had more-mundane concerns relating to their village. At the end of the three-day meeting they asked for twelve hatchets and twelve hoes, "as they were too poor to buy them & in great want of them to cultivate the Land they had newly come on." Johnson agreed to provide them with the tools; he also gave them provisions for their return trip and replaced a keg of rum and a blanket that colonial soldiers had stolen from them.

Thus, in spite of the inroads of alcohol and European diseases, and even despite growing pressure to sell their lands to colonists, refugee Indians continued to inhabit the upper Valley. Even when Indian and colonial negotiators divided the region at the Fort Stanwix treaty of 1768, the Indians already settled on the eastern side of the boundary line, including communities along the west branch of the Susquehanna and at Wyoming, retained title to their villages and surrounding fields. The Indians also kept the territory between Owego and Oswego, which, they believed, could not be relinquished; as one Indian negotiator noted at the treaty, it was too "full of our Towns & Villages."

After the Fort Stanwix treaty Valley Indians continued to live peaceably with colonists even while colonists spread into former Indian territory and at times trespassed on lands the Indians still possessed. One group of Indians at Oquaga provided food and canoe-making tools to a group of colonists in November 1774, saving their lives even though the colonists were trespassing on Indian lands and surveying the region for colonial land speculators. Local Indians along the north and west branches of the Susquehanna also continued to trade with the new settlers whenever they had the opportunity.

Even when the Indians believed that colonists were illegally seizing their lands, they sought a peaceful resolution to the situation. Thus in 1775 a group of Indians went to Johnson Hall to complain that they had been deceived at Fort Stanwix in 1768 and had inadvertently ceded more land than they expected. The error, provincial officials pointed out, was not an intentional deception; the problem stemmed instead from a poorly drawn map used at the treaty which did not depict the Susquehanna's course accurately. Provincial officials, in the tradition of the recently deceased Sir William Johnson and others who sought negotiated solutions instead of violence, promised to solve the problem, but the outbreak of the Revolution soon prevented any easy answer. Of greater importance was the Indians' response to this overture: They accepted the promise and did not try to force the settlers off the lands. But the resolution to this crisis was only temporary. Once the Revolution began, Valley Indians soon realized that they could not press their claims peaceably with any real hope of success.

The stability achieved by the Indians before the Revolution quickly disintegrated in the late 1770s. The war, from the beginning, undermined these Indians' economy and made their survival precarious. British officials who commented on these events in depth isolated two intimately related factors contributing to the

Indians' decline. First, they wrote, direct military assaults of the Continental Army devastated Indian communities. Indeed, one of the Continental Army's stated aims was to destroy the backcountry Indians' economy, and they ruthlessly applied themselves to this task. Second, according to Crown officials, the Indians' commitment to the British war effort prevented them from reestablishing their economy. In particular, the participation of Indians in military affairs deprived communities of necessary labor generally devoted to maintaining local economies. While using their time to fight the Crown's battles, Valley Indians found themselves increasingly dependent on King George's treasury for food and clothing.

During the early years of the Revolutionary War most Valley Indians allied themselves with the British. Both local circumstances and existing relations between the Iroquois and the British influenced their decision. Valley Indians presumably hoped to receive material assistance from the British, thereby allowing them to provide for their communities. But their decision to join the Crown's forces was largely based on political considerations, especially on maintaining an alliance with Crown officials and protecting the Indians' territory. The earlier efforts of provincial officials to support Valley Indians in their claims against trespassing colonists no doubt made Valley Indians favorably inclined toward the Crown's position. When many Valley colonists began to ally themselves with the rebels, evident as early as 1775, Valley Indians apparently found the Crown's cause the best defense for their communities. Most likely, the Indians, sharing the logic of several of the tribes in the Iroquois confederacy, believed that fighting for the British would help preserve their territory. Indeed, Indians in the Valley might have followed the lead of others in their tribe living farther north in Iroquoia. Still, what was logical politically had unforeseen economic consequences.

The outbreak of the war put an end to the Indians' agriculture and hunting. When the Continental Army invaded the Indians' territory in 1779, the soldiers deliberately destroyed all vestiges of the Indians' economy. At Chemung one troop destroyed approximately one thousand bushels of corn and presumably burned extensive local supplies of pumpkins, beans, squash, and potatoes as well. At Newtown, according to one soldier, another troop destroyed 150 acres of fresh produce as well as "great Quantities of Beans, Potatoes, Pumpkins, Cucumbers, Squashes & Watermellons." The company traveling with Henry Dearborn was representative of many involved in Sullivan's campaign. At Chemung they burned forty acres of corn; at Chugnut they destroyed "plenty of cucumbers squashes turnips &c." Several miles away, at an unidentified location, the party discovered a field of "70 or 80 acres of fine corn"; the following day it took them so long to destroy the crop that their march was delayed several hours.

Continental Army soldiers destroyed important villages throughout the Valley, including Chemung, Newtychanning, Wyalusing, Chugnut, Otsiningo, and Owego. Their descriptions of the events demonstrate the callous nature of their actions. "This evening," Dearborn wrote in his journal in August, "the town of Owagea [Owego] was made a bone fire of to grace our meeting."

The effect of the depredations of Continental Army soldiers on the Indians' economy was immediate and obvious, yet the Indians also suffered in other ways and for other reasons. Indeed, their decline began before Sullivan's 1779 raid and stemmed directly from the nature of their commitment to the English. After the decision to join the British war effort, many Indian groups, including virtually all of the Indians from the upper Susquehanna Valley, moved to the Crown's stronghold at Niagara, joining thousands of other Indians forced to abandon their territory and rely on the British for provisions. Most important to the British, the cost of maintaining the Indians at Niagara itself proved increasingly difficult. Fighting the Continental Army prevented Indian men from hunting; Indian women, previously responsible for their communities' crops, could not tend their fields. British officials soon came to realize that the Indians were in danger of economic collapse.

John Butler, commanding the British military campaign in the backcountry, recognized signs of trouble as early as September 1778, when he toured the Indian country. "As the Young Men were already either out at War, or ready to go with me, they had nothing to subsist upon but the remains of the last Years Corn which was near expended, their hunting being neglected," he wrote to General Frederick Haldimand, the Governor of Quebec and a commander of British troops in North America. "Most of them too, were very bare of Clothes, however upon my promising them Clothing this fall they were satisfied." Difficult times continued. "A Number of the Mohawks, Onandagoes and Ochquagoes are to remain here, having not Homes to go to," Butler wrote from Niagara in February 1779. "The Ochquago Village being burnt by the Rebels, and the villages of the Mohawks situated in them of the Enemy."

By July 1779, even before Sullivan's campaign, the Indians were using up food supplies without replenishing them. "Although there was last Fall a considerable Quantity of Cattle in the Indian Country these have been chiefly consumed by the Indians themselves," Butler wrote to Haldimand.

> It is well known that they never raise more Corn, Pulse and things of that Kind which compose the principal Part of their Food than will just suffice for their own Subsistence: but they were so employed in various Excursions the last Summer that they did not cultivate the usual Quantity, and great Part of what they did cultivate was destroyed by some means or other before it came to Perfection.

Butler added that a number of travelers in the region, presumably other Indians or perhaps loyalists or Rangers working for the British cause, further depleted their food supplies. At various towns, both within the upper Valley and beyond, Butler found that the local Indians

> have not had an Ear of Corn the whole Winter and were obliged to live such as had them upon Cattle, such as had no Cattle upon Roots. This by the Time we came into the Country made Beef exceeding scarce and dear: what there was we have made Use of, and so intirely has the Country been drained that at Shimong [Chemung] where Cattle were by far the most Plenty there is not a Creature to be got.

The situation was so bleak that the Rangers had been sent to the Genesee Falls, where they could find enough fish to meet their nutritional needs. There, Butler concluded, they would not "have as many Indians about them to eat up their Provision," a fortunate circumstance because it was "impossible to avoid giving it [to] them when they are with you." Haldimand too, realized the problems of providing for both the Indians and other Crown soldiers and believed the situation had devastating implications for the British war effort. "For, after the troops have been sent into the Country," he wrote to Butler in September 1779, "to have them stand or obliged to abandon the Purpose of their Enterprise for want of Provisions, would be followed by much more fatal Consequences than if they had never undertaken it."

Still, British officials struggled to supply the Indians with necessary goods. They realized, as Butler informed Lt. Col. Mason Bolton, commander of the Crown's forces at Niagara, that this was essential for the Indians' continued commitment to the British cause. "The Indians seem in better Spirits & more determined than I have seen them since they left Chuchnut [Chugnut]," Butler wrote, "and if they get any Succour from Niagara I am in hopes I shall be able to persuade them to attack the Rebels on their March, at any Rate I shall do my Endeavour to get them to make a Stand."

British military officials realized that cattle could solve their problems, but they found themselves unable to procure sufficient head for the Indians' needs. The price for cows soared during the war. Mason Bolton, writing to Haldimand from Niagara in September 1779, noted that the price had risen from around £8 per head to £20 at Carleton Island and that those with cattle sought to move their stocks there to receive the better price. Bolton, wanting to keep the cattle near Niagara, refused their request, but faced a dilemma. "The Indians have not brought in Cattle this year," he wrote, "all we have purchased was a few Cows from the distressed Families."

Cattle rustling became common during military forays. As early as January 1778 soldiers had orders to bring cattle back from their raids in the upper Susquehanna Valley, presumably to feed both soldiers and Indians. "I shall collect all the Cattle of every kind I can," John McDonnell wrote to Butler in July 1779 from the Valley, "as I am Sensible that Provision will be an Object of the Utmost Consequence when all the Indians are Imbodied." One group of Indians and Rangers at Wyalusing in September 1780 managed to take the cattle around the settlers' fort, but provisions remained scarce; there was little game to be hunted and the party needed more supplies. In addition, as Continental Army soldiers discovered and as the Indians no doubt already realized, herding cattle through the upper Valley proved time-consuming and frustrating; cattle moved slowly along the region's paths and even, at times, fell off precipices to their death.

The Indians' dependence on the British for food and other provisions threatened the Crown's efforts, mostly because of the great expense involved. None realized this more than Haldimand when he urged Butler to cut costs and to encourage the Indians to begin cultivating during the spring of 1779. Several months later he informed Butler that the costs of the Indian Department had actually exceeded those of every other department, including the army and navy. "I must therefore recommend to Your most Serious attention the Strictest economy wherever there is a possibility of observing it," he wrote in August, "the Credit of every Person at the head of Departments being concerned, and what is Still of greater Import, the Public Good." But Butler believed such requests could not be satisfied. The costs of providing the necessary supplies, such as cattle, could actually raise the expenses of the Indian Department. At the same time, the Indians would remain firmly in the British interest only if they were provided with what they needed, a sentiment that even Haldimand realized by August 1779. "We are Still Strong for the King of England," David, a Mohawk, informed Haldimand, "and we will lose our Lives chearfully for him if you will Shew us he is a man of his Word, & that he will not abandon his Brother the Six Nations who always Shed their Blood for him."

This tenuous arrangement held out until Sullivan's troops destroyed the Indians' towns along the Susquehanna and its tributaries, when the situation for the Indians and their British allies became worse. Then a far greater number of Indians were forced to live near Niagara, dependent on the British. According to Butler, they had been "driven from their Country & [had] every Thing destroyed." Still, the Indians remained firmly allied to the British. "Notwithstanding the Losses the Indians have suffered by the Destruction of their Corn & Villages," Butler wrote to Haldimand in September 1779, "I am happy to acquaint your Excellency that they seem still unshaken in their Attachment to his Majesty's Cause, and declare as soon as they have placed their Women & Children in Security they will go and take Revenge of the Enemy."

Nonetheless, the situation became more and more bleak, leading the British to reconsider their support of the Indians. Mason Bolton, in late September, summarized the problem concisely: "The Indians bear this misfortune with more patience than I could possibly expect, and seemed determined to take revenge when an opportunity offers," he wrote from Niagara, "but the loss of their Corn &c and the Scarcity of provisions here to supply the number I shall have at this Post, makes it impracticable at present." Fearful that the British would have to support almost 3,700 Indians at Niagara, he later wrote to Haldimand describing the situation. "I am convinced your Excellency will not be surprised if I am extremely alarmed, for to support such a Multitude I think will be absolutely impossible." He prevailed upon Butler to convince as many Indians as possible to spend the winter at Montreal and wanted him to "inform all the Rest who have not suffered by the Enemy, that they must return home, and take care of their corn &c."

But the efforts to encourage the Indians to become self-sufficient, or at least to supply their own food, did not succeed quickly. The British continued to provide corn and hoes to many Indians from the upper Susquehanna Valley and elsewhere until at least May 1781. Over 1,500 Indians received assistance because their corn had failed.

Other factors prevented the Indians from reestablishing a stable economy in the Susquehanna Valley after the war. The winter of 1779–1780 was unusually severe, with snow up to five feet deep across much of western New York. Animals died for lack of forage, diminishing even further the ability of Indian hunters to capture necessary meat and pelts. In addition, the end of the war brought a period of epidemics among the Indians of the region: dysentery, measles, and smallpox devastated refugee communities. The resulting demographic decline—which, including military casualties, has been estimated at approximately 50% for the Iroquois from the early 1760s to late 1790s—made economic recovery much more difficult.

Land-hungry settlers and speculators, rushing to the region after the war, further prevented the Indians' economic recovery in the upper Susquehanna Valley and elsewhere. Even many Oneidas and Tuscaroras who had fought for the rebels were unable to maintain their land in the Susquehanna Valley. In 1785 they sold an enormous tract, encompassing what is today Broome and Chenango counties. The Indians initially did not want to part with the territory circumscribed by the Unadilla, Chenango, and Susquehanna rivers. This region was, as Petrus, an Oneida chief, declared in June 1785, "our Deer-hunting Country, and the Northern our Beaver-hunting Country." But under pressure they eventually sold much of the land to state-appointed negotiators in New York, thereby preventing the Oneidas and Tuscaroras from reestablishing communities in the upper Valley.

After the war some Indians tried to move back to the upper Valley. Way-Way, a Nanticoke born at Chugnut, was among them. She was, she recalled later, "a little gal when the white man destroyed our crops and run us off in the war." Like other Indians she moved to Niagara and then to the Genesee. After the war she returned to the upper Valley, joining other Nanticokes and some Delawares trying to reestablish themselves in the region. But economic recovery proved elusive. They found settlers living on their former lands, and while they remained in the area for two years, the Indians apparently never prospered; one settler's family, Way-Way recalled, provided them with flour "& all kinds of provisions," evidence perhaps of the Indians' inability to grow sufficient food for their community. Soon Way-Way left the Valley, eventually living with other Nanticokes among the Iroquois settled at Grand River, Ontario. Other refugees from the upper Valley probably joined displaced communities living in far western New York or southern Canada or migrated, like many Delawares, even farther west. Perhaps many found themselves living in what Anthony Wallace has termed "slums in the wilderness." The upper Susquehanna Valley did not, however, remain depopulated. Under the direction of a group of wealthy landlord-speculators, thousands of people moved to the region. Few, if any, of these new settlers were Indians.

In spite of its place in a long history of European colonial aggression against Indians, the Revolutionary War was a stunning assault on interracial relations. While the expansion of a commercial market weakened Indian communities before the war and helped prepare the region for colonial settlement, colonists and Indians continued to work together peacefully to resolve their differences and maintain harmony in this borderland. This desire for peace in the Valley proved a great help to local Indians who periodically had to cope with epidemic diseases and colonial trespassers. Most Indians and colonists had demonstrated a willingness to live near each other. After the Revolution few postwar settlers in the Valley wanted Indian neighbors; they associated the Indians with the war and never trusted them again. The Indians, their economy in disarray, could not reestablish stable communities in the region.

While the Revolution did not create racism against the Indians, it poisoned the minds of the settlers in the upper Susquehanna Valley. And those settlers, not the Indians, took control over the region after the crisis ended. The Indians of the Valley, caught in the larger struggle for power and land in eastern North America, could no longer find sanctuary along the Susquehanna. During the period when many others declared their freedom, Valley Indians found themselves dispossessed.

The economic decline of the Indians during the Revolutionary years has a greater meaning. In the intellectual ferment of the 1780s, those involved in creating the Constitution needed more than history and ideology to establish their new system of government. What they needed, and received, was the support of the people who would live with the government created by the Constitution. But when various states held ratifying conventions, few in attendance voiced eloquent pleas on behalf of the Indians. Even Indians who had fought for the Continental Army were excluded, along with those who had been allied with the British. Even more than the loyalists who fled to England and Canada, the Indians of the upper Susquehanna Valley, like many Indians elsewhere, were the real losers of the Revolutionary War.

9

ECONOMIC DEVELOPMENT AND NATIVE AMERICAN WOMEN IN THE EARLY NINETEENTH CENTURY

MARY C. WRIGHT

Historical studies of Indian women now focus primarily on their roles within traditional societies and their influence on the changes that the tribes experienced as they dealt with Europeans and Americans. This article considers the actions of women in the Pacific Northwest during the early decades of the fur trade there. The author finds that women, particularly upper-class women in the stratified societies of the region, exercised considerable power within the local economy. She shows, for example, that although the coming of the fur trade weakened traditional tribal cultures, it strengthened the position of some women within the villages because the traders needed the cooperation of prominent people. The text discusses several traditional female activities within the village economy that lent themselves to a successful prosecution of the fur trade. Upper-class women served as intermediaries or mediators in their own society. When the traders arrived, the women continued this action by helping the whites penetrate the Indian economy and social structure. They did this through intermarriage, with their own exchange and sales network, and as consumers themselves. The reading examines a process that made the economic subsistence actions of Indian women become less important during the 1800–1830 era. While that took place, women's role in the growing cash economy failed to grow, so they found themselves pushed farther out of public life and importance in tribal affairs.

Mary C. Wright is a doctoral student in history at Rutgers University.

Economic development and participation in the Euro-American market economy define a common experience among women that transcends time, place, and culture.

Source: Mary C. Wright, "Economic Development and Native American Women in the Early Nineteenth Century," *American Quarterly*, Vol. 33 (Winter, 1981), No. 5. pp. 525–36. Copyright © 1981 by the American Studies Association. Reprinted with permission of the publisher and the author.

99

Feminists and scholars of the Third World have pointed to the degradation of women's traditional economic and social power that accompanies Western "modernization." American historians have similarly described the situation facing women in New England during the late eighteenth and early nineteenth centuries, as self-sufficiency gave way to agricultural production for sale, incipient industrialism, and a money economy. Native American women, as this ethnohistorical exploration attempts to show, suffered a comparable fate with the advent of the fur trade in the Pacific Northwest.

For many Native Americans, the fur trade constituted the first contact with the Euro-American economic system, providing a beachhead for the subsequent conquest of the continent. As Francis Jennings has shown for the seventeenth century, the trade progressively weakened Indian societies by supplanting inter-tribal trade and undermining local craft production. Yet, paradoxically, the very success of the fur traders depended on Indian cooperation. While every member of the Indian societies felt, on some level, the influence of the trade and contributed to its success, Native American women's involvement was pivotal. On the one hand and in the context of traditional practices, Indian women actively adapted to new opportunities offered by the traders. Through their participation, Euro-Americans gained access to local knowledge, skills, and resources. As liaisons between Indian and white culture, as intermediary traders, food gatherers, and crafts manufacturers, and as customers, employees, and service personnel, Native American women insured the success of the fur trade companies. On the other hand, the participation of Indian women contributed to the ultimate transformation of their societies' traditional subsistence economy—in which women played an important and often managerial role—into a dependent part of the Euro-American market economy.

Since Indian women's subsistence activities faded and those with a cash value did not correspondingly grow, they gradually became trapped—just as had Euro-American women earlier and as Third World women would become later—into a sphere labeled domestic, with limited access to public arenas. Such limitation was tragic, for Indian societies until then had accorded women an honored place because of their crucial political and economic roles. Yet, according to definitions of gender held by white traders, women's assistance to the fur trade was informal and domestic. Thus, Indian women received neither recognition nor positions of power in keeping with the scope of their contributions; they remained nearly invisible. It has taken historians more than a century to discover the role Indian women played in the fur trade, but historical anonymity was the least of the consequences suffered by these women as a result of that trade. Denied power within the fur trading system so dependent on them, Indian women were unable to protect their societies' integrity in the face of further white expansion and economic development.

The Pacific Northwest Seaboard regions were the focus of expanding fur-trading activities in the early nineteenth century. With economic success as their goal, the first traders built upon existing native practices and patterns of trade and did not attempt to alter Indian culture except where it seriously interfered with their objectives. As the traders' substantial records make clear, Indian women of the Oregon Seaboard and Coast Salish societies played an important role in their enterprises.

The Euro-American traders found that in that region's Indian cultures, women had high status and important roles. By lineage, wealth, and spiritual powers, a woman could lead her community politically, achieve prominence as a shaman, or be as active in trade as the men. "It is as common to see the wife . . . trading at the factory, as her husband," observed Alexander Ross, clerk of the North West Company. Women spoke in council, and their opinions were sought on all important matters, including trade bargains. Although the position of women was not uniformly high, for slavery existed, women had opportunities and respect equal to the men of their station in the Seaboard and Coast Salish Native American societies.

In large part, the native women's power emanated from their role in the family and the importance of the kinship system to public issues. Indian society was not separated into distinct spheres; rather, functions of family were enmeshed with politics and economics. Intermarriage facilitated this merging. Exogamy was the rule, and intermarriage occurred between families of high status in separate villages and language groups. Women maintained dual memberships, since descent was calculated on a bilateral basis. They thus remained fully recognized members of their own kin group, and although they often resided with their husbands' people, they traveled, traded, and mediated between the two groups.

Indian women extended their role as mediators to the white traders. At times they warned the fur traders of attack by groups to whom they owed no allegiance. When hostilities did erupt, their knowledge of diplomatic practices and their active intervention on the Euro-Americans' behalf often saved the companies. A representative incident, recorded by the North West Company, occurred in 1814 when the Wasco/Wishram peoples attacked a fur trade brigade and captured their trading goods and furs. The company's officers approached Lady Coalpo for assistance, daughter of the powerful Chinook Chief Concomly, sister-in-law to the important Kalapuya Chief Casino, and wife of the Oak Point Chief Coalpo. Drawing upon her kinship and tribal authority, she retrieved the company's goods and was amply rewarded. Impressed, Hudson's Bay Company leader George Simpson ranked her as the third most powerful Indian in the Columbia District.

Among the Native American elite, observed Simpson, marriages were basically alliances "formed solely on political considerations." Duncan McDougall, the first white trader to take an Indian wife in Oregon, apparently had the same end in mind when he espoused Illchee, Chinook Chief Concomly's daughter, in 1811. That the Indians continued to feel such unions advantageous was illustrated in 1833 by a Chehalis chief's offer to his kinswoman in marriage to trader William F. Tolmie. The traders followed Indian customs to the point of offering bridewealth to the women's families, receiving in return property of equal value. Goodwill, trading opportunities, and assistance with hostile tribes came to the Euro-Americans through marriage to Indian women.

Intermarriage defined yet another influential role for Native American women, again to the benefit of trade. Women functioned as intermediary traders as they visited relatives and friends scattered throughout the region. One kinship obligation was the exchange of surplus food and goods for other forms of wealth possessed by affinal kin. Furs, *hiagua* (a type of shell circulated as currency), specialty items such as baskets or canoes, and slaves, as well as goods obtained from the Euro-Americans, circulated through the native women's distribution efforts.

The significance of women as intermediary traders probably increased with the arrival of seagoing fur traders in the late eighteenth century. By the 1810s, when white land-based trading operations began, this role was firmly entrenched. Profits to the intermediary—male or female—could be as high as fifty percent of the posts' price per pelt, so it was in the interest of the native traders to keep the Euro-Americans isolated from far-flung tribes. The fur trade companies soon recognized the ploy and attempted to counter it by sending trading parties throughout the territory and setting up small posts. To no avail—Indians still used the traditional networks of exchange, and the strength of the native trade system continued, to the exasperation of the white traders. The Hudson's Bay Company admitted its "Great disadvantage" as Chinookan traders sought to monopolize contacts between Indians and whites into the 1820s. As late as the 1840s control of the trade had not been totally wrested from native hands because, as John McLoughlin complained, "in the lower parts of the Columbia, and along the Coast the Indians are so independent [and] the skins pass through so many hands." The mutual obligations of kinship and the role of women as mobile traders enabled the Indians to withstand the considerable pressure to conform to the best interests of the Euro-American fur companies.

Native American women along the Oregon Country's coast traditionally filled other economic functions beyond the exchange of goods. They gathered considerable quantities of food and produced many of the tools and utensils their people used. Modern scholars point to the centrality of such contributions to women's social status. Several contemporary Euro-Americans also felt this productive work accounted for the women's high position. Thus in Seaboard societies, observed Clerk Ross Cox, women "assume an air of liberty and independence." Throughout the Pacific Northwest, native women controlled the food they gathered and the meat or fish (brought in by the men), which they processed for long-term storage. Women's control over food was underscored by their exchange of surplus food products in the native trade system.

Initially, control of provisions gave Native American women a crucial bargaining power over white traders. Out of necessity, Euro-Americans depended on women for the foodstuffs needed to sustain their trading operations. Although supplies were sent from the East by ship and overland to these isolated posts, local produce supported the forts. The camas, wapato, and other roots, fresh vegetables, and dried and fresh fruits gathered by the women offset the traders' potential scurvy. Sturgeon, smelt, salmon, dried shellfish, and other meats processed by the women augmented company provisions. When out on expeditions, the Euro-American trappers repeatedly procured fresh provisions from women. Without this aid, the fur trade companies could not have expanded as they did in the Oregon Country.

Efforts by the traders to supplant Indian sources with homegrown provisions had the reverse effect of opening up other opportunities which the women quickly seized. Potato cultivation was one of the most important adaptations. Gardens were planted around the fur trade posts beginning in 1811 in an effort to supplement imported and purchased supplies. Among the vegetables, potatoes were very successful. No records exist indicating that the whites purposefully undertook to teach their agricultural techniques to the Seaboard or Coast Salish people. Yet by the 1840s potato cultivation had spread throughout the region.

Several factors, as ethnologist Wayne Suttles argues, were responsible for the quick integration of potatoes into the Indians' food supply. First, women already gathered roots similar to potatoes. They had the tools, harvesting techniques, and recipes applicable to this new food. Second, Indian women married to white fur traders had access to seed potatoes and were able to witness potato planting and harvesting about the forts. Third, as the women traveled throughout the territory, they brought the new food to their kin and friends. Fourth, the crop needed little more care than was already given to clam beds, fishing sites, or root prairies under the stewardship of kin groups or particular individuals. The only men involved in the cultivation of potatoes, apparently, were slaves who helped clear the natural prairies for planting. Otherwise, this whole new activity was a female endeavor.

The utensils produced by women also filled an important role within native culture and in trade with the Euro-Americans. Each village or geographic group specialized in goods using resources available in the local area. Talent and techniques passed through families also added to a variety of specializations. Clatsop women, for instance, were famous for conical hats which kept off the ever-present Northwest rain. Decorated with woven designs of deer, fish, or dogs, the hats were in demand in the native trade system. Finely woven cedar bark mats, serving a multitude of uses from bedding to table settings, were also sought after. Baskets—some woven tightly enough to hold water, others large and sturdy enough for stored fish or berries—came from various groups. Euro-American traders used this roster of goods on their routes to fill the demands of native customers and to bring in the Indians' beaver pelts. In the mid 1820s, according to George Simpson, a first quality hat, for instance, was worth four cured beaver pelts.

Although native handicrafts played a part in white-Indian exchange, the fur traders emphasized European goods. Metal, cloth, and some food items appeared superior to native crafts or were unknown to Indian culture. These imported goods, the traders hoped, would create "new wants and habitudes" among the Native Americans and thereby increase their trapping efforts. The women's acceptance and dissemination of these innovations contributed to the penetration of the Euro-American market economy into the region. They, more than men, were trusted on the early trading vessels that visited the coast. In return for their assistance in mediating between the traders and the on-shore Indians, women often received "regales" of bread, molasses, and, to a lesser degree, rum. Thus established as prestige items, such foodstuffs by the 1820s had become the "prizes" of those natives "shrewd in trade," and they remained in high demand for decades.

Gifts of clothing to high-ranking women, as well as men, likewise served the interests of the traders. The physical appearance of the native women repulsed the traders. Women's breasts were left bare by their costume, a petticoat of twisted cedar bark (resembling a grass skirt), to which was added a cape of furs in the winter months. The paint, tattoos, feathers, brass anklets and bracelets, earrings, nose rings or plugs, and fish oil further contrasted Native American women to

Euro-American fashion. The traders were only too happy to instigate new styles to replace these, for economic as well as moral reasons.

Displays of material wealth counted high in Seaboard and Coast Salish culture. When a member of these societies exhibited a rare object or gave it away as potlatch wealth, others also sought it. Elite women fitted out in the traders' gifts and those Indian women married to whites initiated new patterns of consumption and provided models of newly appropriate fashions.

New cloth was plentiful, reported Patrick Gass of the Lewis and Clark expedition, even before land-based fur trade operations began. In the 1810s "ready-made clothes [were] in great demand," observed seagoing trader Peter Corney. Only lack of the "means to buy the goods" kept the Indians from following Euro-American styles of dress, Clerk Gabriel Franchere claimed.

The thorough infiltration made by the whites' trade goods is indicated by the "capeau, vest, pantaloons, and shirts" decorating the grave of an elite Wasco woman in 1832 for her use in the afterlife. As the early ethnographer George Gibbs reported in the 1850s, "it is only in remote districts, or among old people too poor or too obstinately attached to the habits of their youth to change them, that one now sees . . . the petticoat" originally worn by all women of the Seaboard and Coast Salish regions. The nakedness so abhorred by the traders thus came to be covered and, more to the point, covered by goods obtainable only from Euro-American sources.

Native American women, however, demanded practical goods from the fur trade companies. Prestige items such as food and clothing, as well as the bells, beads, vermilion, and other goods used for decoration, of course had their place. But of greater importance were the various metal goods offered by the whites. So alluring were their tools that theft was a continual problem for the Euro-Americans. Women sought new hatchets and knives to use in food gathering; awls, needles, and scissors for basketry and leather work; and brass, copper, or tin pots for cooking. Each of these standard trade goods carried by the fur trade companies eased the work traditionally done by the women and replaced tools or utensils they made from local resources.

The disruption of native productive practices caused by such imported implements worked to the advantage of the Euro-American traders. "Homespun articles here, as elsewhere," observed Gibbs, "give place to 'store goods' with advancing civilization." Subsistence activities of women, as well as men, were gradually replaced by the products, and thus demands, of a market economy replicating the patterns of work and consumption already apparent in the Euro-American culture of the northeastern United States.

As traditional productive practices gave way to exchange with white traders, Seaboard and Coast Salish women grasped opportunities for wage work in order to purchase these new goods. Most of this work, however, consisted of temporary projects or piece work, such as producing moccasins or doing laundry at the forts. Work as servants and agricultural laborers at the posts usually devolved upon those Indian women married to the white indentured servants of the fur trade companies. Instead of wages, they received provisions from fort supplies. Women served as partners to their spouses on the trapping expeditions begun by the companies to harvest furs in the 1810s through the 1830s. Aside from the "gifts" they received directly, the pay for their furs went under their husbands' names. Women, while doing labor for the fur trade, tended, therefore, to be invisible employees.

Examination of Euro-American salmon fishing provides a further illustration of the loss in economic power experienced by women. Traditionally, fish caught during salmon runs were equally distributed to all community and kin members. Once the fish were up on the banks, the women cleaned and processed them for storage and thereafter controlled their allocation. But in the 1820s the Hudson's Bay Company began to cure salmon for its own use in the Pacific Northwest and to export small quantities to Britain. They employed Indian women to clean and pack the fish, and here the women worked for pay or gifts, losing control of the end product.

Although traditional female productive functions were displaced by the use of imported goods during the fur trade, few new positions of economic opportunity replaced them. Prostitution became one "occupation" readily available to women. The early seagoing traders apparently instigated the institution, for by 1804, when Lewis and Clark spent several months wintering in Seaboard territory, the practice seemed firmly established.

Several Indian customs of the Seaboard and Coast Salish people facilitated the emergence of prostitution, although it could not have developed without Euro-American customers. First, premarital sexual experimentation was permitted to adolescents, both male and female. Virginity at marriage apparently meant little, although fidelity to one's spouse was rigorously upheld. Girls in their experimental stage may have been open to sexual overtures from the whites. Second, women slaves were easily exploited as prostitutes by their owners. Since slaves were outside the kin group and could earn wealth to further the social standing of their owners, Seaboard elites soon organized their female slaves for "the trade."

When a ship entered the Columbia River or a party of travelers entered the territory, a canoe of slaves, often headed by a high-status woman, soon appeared to barter sexual service for Euro-American goods. Some elite women married to white traders provided prostitutes for the indentured servants at the forts, many of whom were not allowed to marry. When the Hudson's Bay Company forbade the practice in the mid 1820s, the women resolved, according to George Simpson, "they would not conform to this innovation as it deprived them of a very important source of Revenue." The women were able to resist the reforms or at least to maintain their business outside the forts, for as late as the 1840s canoes of prostitutes under the supervision of elite Seaboard women still traversed the area for "the trade."

The traders, in their written records, detested the sexual mores of the Seaboard women. They seemed "devoid of shame or decency"; their behavior "insupportably odious." While the elite women who organized prostitution perhaps saw it as another entrepreneurial undertaking consistent with their desire to increase their wealth and social standing, to the Euro-American traders it was depraved—despite their willingness to engage in it. Prostitution existed, of course, in white society, but usually involved only lower-class women. Middle- and upper-class women were expected to be innocent of such worldly goings-on. But in this Indian culture, one trader remarked with derision, "all classes from the highest to the lowest indulge in coarse sensuality and shameless profligacy." The Euro-Americans considered it demeaning for elite Seaboard women to be involved, even on a managerial level, with prostitution.

For slave women the trade in prostitution was not only demeaning, it was deadly. Venereal diseases—virtually incurable at this time (although some native herbal remedies alleviated its more obvious signs)—spread rapidly among their ranks. An epidemic of the diseases broke out among the white traders in 1814 and they sought to curtail contact with the prostitutes to bring it under control. While the Euro-American men received medical attention (such as it was) for the malady, venereal diseases resulting from prostitution brought death to many female slaves. Once illness rendered them useless, the slaves were often abandoned by their owners. In the case of death, they did not even merit burial.

In sum, the fur trade brought mixed, but mostly detrimental, results to the Pacific Northwest Indians. It served as a transitory institution, eclipsed by later, more direct and relentless contact with Euro-American culture. In 1830 a recurring malarial epidemic broke out that decimated the Seaboard population; an estimated ninety percent died. A smallpox epidemic in 1836 seriously affected the Coast Salish villages. Protestant and Catholic missionaries began compaigns in the mid to late 1830s to convert the Indians to the religion and ways of the whites. The incursion of farmers for the United States in the 1840s only sealed Euro-American dominance of the territory, begun in the economic realm by the fur trade.

Ironically, in light of the Native American cultural upheaval caused by Euro-American influences, Doctor John McLoughlin argued in 1843 that the fur trade fostered positive change in Seaboard and Coast Salish culture. Looking back over twenty years of Hudson's Bay Company control of the trade in the Pacific Northwest, he felt that the Company had "introduced order, and a respect for property, and moral obligation" among the Indians, had converted their hostility to respect, and "in short . . . reclaimed them from a state of barbarism to comparative civilization."

One need not accept McLoughlin's ethnocentric idea of "civilization" to recognize that the earliest contacts between Indians and whites in the Pacific Northwest had turned on the active adaptation of Native Americans to the material goods and opportunities introduced by the traders. Native women, in particular, adapted their traditional economic and diplomatic roles to the new exigencies involved in exchange with the first white settlers. As mediators, customers, and support personnel, they insured the continued success of the trade. But in the long run, exchange with the whites proved a snare for Native Americans—both men and women. Penetration of the Euro-American market, the introduction of European goods, the decline of native handicrafts, prostitution, and the ensuing decimation by disease shifted the balance of power in the Pacific Northwest from the civilization known for centuries by the native inhabitants to a new "civilization," in which racial exclusion and subjugation would be paramount.

10

EARLY PAN-INDIANISM: TECUMSEH'S TOUR OF THE INDIAN COUNTRY, 1811–1812

JOHN SUGDEN

One often hears the question "Why were the Indians not able to unite, defend themselves, and drive the struggling Europeans back into the ocean?" For several decades scholars have examined what has become known as pan-Indianism to learn how and why existing divisions hurt the Native Americans in their competition with the invading whites. Those investigating these issues generally place Indian leaders into one of two categories: either political and military leaders or religious ones. This essay places the actions of the Shawnee diplomat and warrior Tecumseh into a context of the tribes having to fend off a flood of onrushing pioneers who wanted their traditional lands and the growing tensions that led to the War of 1812. By 1806 or 1807 the Shawnee's half-brother, the prophet Tenskwatawa, had become a powerful religious rallying point for the disaffected tribes of the Ohio Valley and lower Great Lakes region. Within three or four years, however, the more politically skillful Tecumseh eclipsed the prophet. This reading chronicles Tecumseh's efforts to persuade the major Southern tribes to join a defensive alliance against the United States. It provides some understanding of how Indian leaders strove to work together and of the obstacles they faced as they met overwhelming American pressures that eventually destroyed them.

John Sugden is Joint Director of Studies at Hereward College in Coventry, England.

Because the North American Indians were not literate peoples in the eighteenth and early nineteenth centuries, those facets of their history which did not directly involve the whites remain obscure. Intertribal diplomacy falls within this realm. Little was known about it, and much that was reported by Indian agents,

Source: John Sugden, "Early Pan-Indianism: Tecumseh's Tour of the Indian Country, 1811–1812," *American Indian Quarterly,* 10 (Fall 1986), pp. 273–304. Reprinted with permission of the publisher.

frontiersmen, and military officers came as inaccurate rumor. The material bearing upon the multitribal movement of Tecumseh and Tenskwatawa in the first years of the nineteenth century illustrates the problems in reconstructing the purely native dimension of Indian affairs. The American and British contemporaries of the Shawnee brothers were so vague about their activities that they credited extravagant fictions relating to the two leaders, and modern historians have often fared little better. In the case of Tecumseh's attempts to create an Indian confederacy, some have woven a mosaic of improbable legends about his journeys, while others have overreacted and implied that most of those travels never took place. Yet relatively little research has been conducted into them. Even the most famous of Tecumseh's journeys in the cause of Indian unity, that which embraced his canvass of the southern Indians in 1811, has been left relatively untroubled by serious investigation. Much the best account remains that by Robert S. Cotterill in *The Southern Indians*, published in 1954, but it was marred by the author's misconception of the nature of Tecumseh's mission, an erroneous belief which Cotterill shared with some of the Shawnee's white contemporaries that the chief intended no hostility to the United States and promulgated only peace.

Tecumseh's six-month tour of the Indian country between August 1811 and January 1812 was one of the most ardent efforts on behalf of eighteenth- and nineteenth-century pan-Indianism and was a significant prelude to Indian participation in the War of 1812. This reconstruction of the tour, inasmuch as that is possible, evaluates pertinent portions of the many reminiscent accounts of Tecumseh's journey and offers, for the first time, the contemporary reports of the chief's progress on the frontier. It establishes that Tecumseh was not on a singleminded mission to the Creeks, but intended a canvass of the remoter tribes of the frontier in both the North and the South; that he probably passed through the country of the Chickasaws, Choctaws, Creeks, Osages, the western Shawnees and Delawares, Iowas, Sacs, Foxes, Sioux, Kickapoos, and Potawatomis, and that he may have visited bands belonging to other tribes; that he was rather more successful in the North than the South; and that he owed much of his impact to the coincident series of earthquakes which centered upon New Madrid in Missouri Territory in 1811 and 1812.

The immediate context of Tecumseh's tour is too well known to bear detailed recapitulation. For some years the Shawnee brothers had been wrestling with the problems which the frontier had imposed upon the Indians: depopulation, debauchery, the disintegration of native values and culture, loss of land, the disruption of the Indian economies, and the exploitation of the natural environment among them. In response, Tenskwatawa acted the holy man, offering himself as the catalyst of moral and spiritual rejuvenation, while Tecumseh promoted a multitribal confederacy to resist Indian cessions of land to the United States and to forge a more nationalist Indian identity. The brothers attracted many adherents from the tribes of the Old Northwest and by the summer of 1810 were planning to extend their activities to two of the Southern tribes, the Creeks and the Choctaws. It was not until the July of the following year, however, that Tecumseh completed the first leg of the journey by leaving his village on the Tippecanoe in northern Indiana Territory and travelling to Vincennes, on the Wabash, to confer with William Henry Harrison, the Governor of the Territory and one of the pan-Indian movement's strongest opponents. At Vicennes Tecumseh was candid enough to inform Harrison that the chief intended uniting the Southern and Northern tribes in a peaceful alliance, and that "having visited the Creeks and Choctaws he is to visit the Osages and return by the Missouri."

It is worth attempting an assessment of Tecumseh's prospects among the Southern Indians, at that time principally Cherokees, Creeks, Seminoles, Choctaws, and Chickasaws. They were more populous peoples than many of the Northern tribes, although their numbers cannot be accurately ascertained. The Chickasaw tribe seems to have been relatively small, perhaps amounting to about 4,500 people; the Creeks, Choctaws, and Cherokees were larger, possibly numbering some 20,000 persons or more each, and able to field between them 15,000 or so fit warriors. The Cherokees occupied the mountainous regions of the southern Alleghenies and the Creeks the present states of Alabama and Georgia, the more numerous Upper Creeks on the Coosa and Tallapoosa rivers, and the Lower Creeks on the Flint and Chattahoochee. By the end of the eighteenth century a part of the Creek confederacy which occupied the swampy wilderness of Florida and which had been forged from various groups of Indians, most of them Creeks, were being designated Seminoles and assigned a separate identity. In the Tombigbee watershed of what is now northern Mississippi dwelt the Chickasaws, while to the south the Choctaws claimed territory as far as the coast of the Gulf of Mexico.

For more than a century these tribes had been affected by the imperialist ambitions of the great European nations, Britain, France, and Spain, and their history reflected the resulting tensions. The tribesmen had achieved greater material standards of living, but their livelihoods were no longer independent or indefinitely sustainable. Intertribal and civil warfare had been intensified by keener trade competition, the participation of the Indians in the rivalry of the great powers, and by the demands of white slavers. Their people had been debased by the traffic in liquor and their vitality sapped through the advent of new diseases against which they had little protection. Their culture, values, and beliefs were under siege. The Cherokees and Creeks had also been relinquishing territory to the British before the Revolution. Afterwards this pressure increased, although for a time the Creeks at least had been able to employ the resurgent Spanish colonies in the South to shore up their resistance to the United States.

From 1796 the Americans embarked upon a systematic program to "civilize" the Southern tribes, to encourage them to adopt white customs and religious beliefs, to replace their communal working of tribal lands with the farming of individually owned private plots, and to subsist upon agriculture, stock raising, cotton planting, and crafts rather than upon the traditional blend of farming and the chase. Through trading posts like Hiwassee in the Cherokee country, Fort Hawkins in the Creek Nation, Chickasaw Bluffs on the Mississippi, and the Choctaw post of St. Stephens, American agents gradually forged a new identity for their wards. The exercise was not wholly a cynical one, for philanthropy of a kind dictated much of the effort, but it reconciled itself to the arrogant destruction of Indian culture and ultimately to tribal dispossession and removal.

The process was accelerated by the development of mixed white and Indian bloodlines. Traders settling in the native villages had long been marrying Indian women and producing children and grandchildren who were to rise to prominence through their familiarity with a white rather than an Indian culture. Acquainted or raised with white men, they spearheaded the adoption of "civilized," or European, lifestyles by the Indians and eventually gained control of tribal affairs. By 1796 mixed bloods could be found in almost all of the Cherokee settlements, and men like John Ross, the famous Cherokee leader, however they might identify with Indian nationality and land tenure, had biologically and culturally more in common with American people than with the traditional Indian. The most prominent Creek of the period, Alexander McGillivray, was the son of a Scottish trader and a mixed-blood French woman; and when the Creeks were relocated in Oklahoma in the nineteenth century, it was said that considerably less than one percent of their population was full blood. By 1800 the mixed bloods had taken control of Chickasaw affairs, despite resistance from the full bloods. One of their principal chiefs, George Colbert, was a son of James Logan Colbert, another Scottish trader. Among the Choctaws the full bloods held out longer, and in Tecumseh's time the three district chiefs were such—Apukshunnubbee, Pushmataha, and Moshulatubbee. But their days were numbered too, and the future belonged to the descendants of white traders such as the Folsom brothers, Michael and Louis Le Flore, and John Pitchlynn. These leaders were hardly likely to be the most receptive listeners to Tecumseh's plans to revitalize traditional native culture.

The "civilization" process was most successful among the Cherokees, especially in the early nineteenth century when the agent Return Jonathan Meigs presided over a major transformation of the Cherokee way of life, a transformation epitomized by their adoption of a tribal constitution in 1808–1810. Benjamin Hawkins attempted a similar revolution among the Creeks. In addition to promoting a new economy, in part geared to producing for the market, he centralized power in the loose Creek confederacy by strengthening the authority of the tribal council and the town chiefs, thus exercising greater control. "Civilization" was simultaneously afoot in the Chickasaw and Choctaw country, although there it lacked proponents with the energy of Meigs and Hawkins and progress was not so marked.

From Tecumseh's point of view the Southern tribes did not offer the brightest of prospects. Under American guidance they were retreating rapidly from the traditional native culture that he espoused, and its appeal was largely alien to many of the increasingly influential mixed bloods. Tecumseh preached nativism, not "civilization." Moreover, the Shawnee perhaps knew that many, if not most, of the important leaders in the South would be against him. He could expect opposition not only from the American agents installed among the tribes—Meigs, Hawkins, James Neeley of the Chickasaws, and Silas Dinsmoor of the Choctaws—but also from those chiefs whose positions had been bolstered or indeed depended upon the backing of the United States. There were other difficulties too. Tecumseh's message of intertribal unity would not claim the full attention of tribes racked by traditional animosities, between Chickasaw and Choctaw, Choctaw and Creek, and Chickasaw and Creek, and his underlying current of hostility to the United States did not inspire confidence in an area which lacked the presence of a strong counter power. The tribes of the Old Northwest were being encouraged by the British, but in the South there was no comparable alternative to the United States as a source of arms, ammunition, powder, and provisions. Spain still held the Southern territory east of the Mississippi and south of the thirty-first parallel, except for New Orleans, but she manifestly lacked the ability to defend it.

However, Tecumseh was not without any advantage, and his cause had been signally advanced by renewed evidence of American land hunger. Every Southern tribe had been affected by what had always been part of the logic of the acculturation program, the view that once the Indians had been weaned from hunting they would require less land and be prepared to cede it, perhaps in payment of debts run up at the trading houses or through the bribery of leading chiefs. In 1802 and 1805 the Creeks had sold territory on the Altamaha and between the Oconee and the Ocmulgee, and they had seen the Americans blaze a horse path across their domain from the Ocmulgee to the Alabama. More recently, Hawkins had pressed the natives to grant the United States permission to cut another road to link the Alabama and the Tennessee, and he was anticipating overcoming the considerable Creek opposition to the scheme at the time Tecumseh arrived in the South.

Even more industrious, Meigs alienated Cherokee title to ten million acres of land in nine cessions between 1801 and 1823. The sales of 1804–1806 created dissension among the tribesmen and the assassination of one of the corrupted chiefs and subsequently contributed to the decision of a thousand Cherokees in 1809 to emigrate to lands west of the Mississippi, where they would be free from interference. The Chickasaws and the Choctaws, hitherto little molested on the land question, both ceded tracts to the United States during the decade before Tecumseh's visit, the former areas northeast of the Tennessee and the latter land about Mobile and between the Mississippi and Tombigbee rivers. Both tribes had also agreed to the Americans' constructing a road across their territory between Tennessee and Natchez on the Mississippi.

By 1811 the land cessions had fed a rising anti-Americanism which linked with conservative reactions against the "civilization" policies of the United States and their coadjutors. Tensions were brewing between those for and those hostile to land sales, between "progressive" Indians, many of them mixed bloods, and the predominantly full-blooded nativists, tensions between people not simply divided by attitudes and values but increasingly by wealth and power. On the Coosa and Tallapoosa rivers a conservative movement was underway among the Upper Creeks, while the Cherokees had even seen the flicker of a nativist revivalist cult not unlike Tenskwatawa's. In February 1811 three Cherokees claimed to have communicated with the envoys of the Great Spirit and to have learned from them his anger at the land cessions and the adoption of American customs and economic practices. The significance of the vision can be overstated, but it suggested the underlying unease that some Cherokees felt about the tribe's development. In May the Nation resolved to stand firm against the alienation of further title and to evict unauthorized white intruders from Cherokee territory.

In the exploitation of these tensions lay at once Tecumseh's best and worst prospects, for they foreshadowed not only Indian unity—between some of the Southern Indians and the Northern nativists—but also disunity; not merely hostility to the United States, but also conflict between and within the Southern tribes themselves.

It was natural that Tecumseh and Tenskwatawa should turn to the South, after working several years to harness the Northern tribesmen behind their inter-tribal nativist movement to resist land cessions and the debasing and disruptive influences of white culture. The large Northern Indian confederacies of the 1780s and 1790s had both attempted a canvass of the Southern Indians, casting the Shawnees, then living north of the Ohio, as a link. To the Shawnee tribe also belonged a rootless, roaming history that had broadened their experience with other Indians, and Tecumseh himself had not only spent part of his youth with the Cherokees but came from a Shawnee family that had once resided in the Creek Nation. The chief now stood ready to exploit his connection with the Creeks; it was said by some that his mother was a Creek and by others that he claimed to have been born at the Creek capital in Tuckabatchie on the Tallapoosa River. The evidence about the matter is both voluminous and confused, but it respectably establishes that Tecumseh enjoyed some blood relationship to the Creeks and expected it to enhance his credence in the South.

Harrison's letter of August 16, 1811, as well as Tecumseh's subsequent move-ments, indicates that the Shawnee pinned his hopes upon the Creeks and Choctaws but had no full-scale lobby of the Cherokees or the Chickasaws in view. If he was assuming that the Cherokees were too "civilized" to benefit from his counsel, he gravely miscalculated because the religious fanaticism which shortly appeared in the tribe suggests that the seeds Tecumseh might have sown would not have been completely fruitless. Most likely the Shawnee leader planned his itinerary after making preliminary overtures to various tribes, and that the responses from the Cherokees and Chickasaws had been discouraging. According to an American agent with the Chickasaws, James Robertson, about the beginning of July 1811 a group of Northern Indians called upon the Chickasaws and other Southern tribes to invite them to join a general confederacy. The ambassadors presented the Chick-asaws with tobacco and beads, expecting to receive gifts in return which they could carry home as a symbol of union, but they were disappointed and dismissed empty-handed. There are also late and unconfirmed traditions of communications between Tecumseh and the Creeks prior to the Shawnee's journey south.

Tecumseh's party left Vincennes on August 5, 1811, descending the Wabash toward the Ohio. It consisted of twenty persons, six Shawnees, six Kickapoos, six Indians form a Northwestern tribe—probably Winnebagoes—and two Creek guides. Apart from the Shawnee chief himself, the most important member of the group was the linguist—according to Hawkins, a Creek from Tuckabatchie who had been living with the Shawnees for twenty years. Several Creek and Choctaw traditions commemorate this figure. They name him as Seekaboo and assert that he was a mixed-blood Creek, related to Tecumseh and fluent in both Creek and Choctaw, and that he remained in the South to serve in the Creek war of 1813–1814 and the Seminole war of 1818. Whoever, his talents were indispensable to Tecum-seh's mission because of the multiplicity of tongues spoken by the Southern Indi-ans. There were even Creeks who spoke neither Creek nor Muscogee, but Hitchiti, Yuchi, or other languages. Although travelers might resort to signing or to intertribal trade jargons like Mobilian, an embassy like Tecumseh's demanded a skilled interpreter.

The absence of American eyewitness reports of the first stages of Tecumseh's tour suggests that the Northerners did not follow the Ohio to the Mississippi and descend that river past the trading post of Chickasaw Bluffs, but crossed the Ohio to travel overland through Kentucky and Tennessee. The envoys were soon in Chickasaw country, and late-nineteenth-century oral traditions have preserved several erroneous and at least one fantastic story about their activities there. From the two contemporary reports it can be learned that Tecumseh's party passed Levi Colbert's home in the Chickasaw Nation about August 27. The Northern Indians were secretive about their intentions, six of them refusing to disclose their tribal affiliation and none prepared to declare their business in the South. When the mixed-blood chief George Colbert, who acted at the time as the chief spokesman for the Chickasaws in their dealings with the Americans, visited Tecumseh and attempted to learn his purpose, he was told that the Northerners would make their mission known when they reached the Creeks. It seems that the Shawnee chief distrusted the Chickasaws, and not without reason, for the tribe soon filtered information about Tecumseh's appearance back to the American secretary of war. Nor was George Colbert himself a chief the Northerners were likely to respect, for he had already received his rewards from the United States for facilitating Indian land cessions and in not many more years would do so again.

Tecumseh moved south into what is now Mississippi. He had hopes of the Choctaws but apparently made little headway among them. Unfortunately no contemporary account of the visit has been found. It escaped Dinsmoor, the Choctaw agent, and it was not until the following year, when the significance of Tecumseh's activities was appreciated, that Governor William C. C. Claiborne of Louisiana Territory ordered one Simon Favre to investigate the degree of Choctaw hostility to the United States and to determine whether Tecumseh or Tenskwatawa had been tampering with them. In August 1812 Favre delivered the Governor's talk, defaming the Shawnees, to the tribe, but omitted to mention anything about Tecumseh's visit in his report of September 11.

In lieu, the traditional accounts gathered by Henry Sale Halbert and Horatio Bardwell Cushman in the late nineteenth century assume greater importance than they inherently deserve. Halbert worked as a teacher among the Choctaws between 1884 and 1899; and because his sources form the basis of any inferences that can now be made about Tecumseh's canvass of the tribe, they are worth describing. His first witness, George W. Campbell, had an account from a Creek-born Choctaw called Stonie-hadjo in 1833 or 1834, when Campbell was in his early twenties. About 1878 Halbert sent a narrative of Tecumseh among the Choctaws, based principally upon Campbell's information, to J. F. H. Claiborne, who embellished it for his *Mississippi* (1880). Fortunately the original statement furnished Claiborne survives, and several subsequent versions, by Campbell and Halbert, are also available.

In 1882 Halbert found a second informant in Charley Hoentubbee, the son of the Choctaw chief, Hoentubbee, who had extended hospitality to Tecumseh in 1811. Charley was believed to be sixty-two years old in 1822, and would have thus been about thirty-nine when his father died in 1859. He claimed to have often heard his father speak of Tecumseh, and provided a detailed narrative of the Shawnee's adventures. A third informant was J. M. Brooks, who was interviewed in 1883 and 1887. In the former year, Brooks was fifty-eight and consequently had only been about ten years of age in 1835, when a Choctaw called Red Pepper told him of Tecumseh's tour. Red Pepper used to visit Brook's father, who settled near Oktibbeha Creek in 1833. The last of Halbert's principal witnesses was a Choctaw called Himonubbee, who had been born about 1799 and was a boy in his father's house when Tecumseh passed through the Nation. His father, Hilamotubbee or Filamotubbee, attended the Shawnee's council at Hoentubbee's town, and much of his information correlates with the material from Charley Hoentubbee.

Although credit must be given Halbert for his diligence and sincerity, the flaws in his sources are obvious. Only one of the informants, Himonubbee, was himself an eyewitness, and he had been merely a boy in 1811. Nearly all of the material comes secondhand, and late. Stonie-hadjo, for example, had more than twenty years to confuse the events of Tecumseh's visit before he related them to Campbell, who then suffered another forty years to pass before offering Halbert the remnants. This type of information is always grossly unreliable. It is also possible that in his eagerness to compare and clarify his various accounts, Halbert—nothing if not an enthusiastic enquirer—fed witnesses with ideas during the interviews.

The details of Halbert's accounts and the extent to which they complement or contradict each other would require another paper to adequately discuss. In summary, they suggest that Tecumseh's party arrived in Choctaw territory on horseback at Oktibbeha Creek and were escorted to the village of Moshul-atubbee—at present, Mashulaville. From there they passed to Chief Hoentubbee's village, in the northwestern part of Kemper County, where they held a council in which they urged the Choctaws to join them in a war against the United States. The appeal was repeated at a number of Choctaw towns—Yazoo, Muckalusha, and Chunky Town—but with the same lack of success. At this point Halbert's informants disagreed as to whether Tecumseh immediately returned to Moshu-latubbee's village or first proceeded further south into present Jasper County to visit the Six Towns, Coosha, and Yahnubbee, settlements in the district of Chief Pushmataha. However, the Shawnee's principal council with the Choctaws was said to have been held on Moshulatubbee's ground, at a site near present Brooksville. To Tecumseh's clarion call for unity against the advancing American frontier, Pushmataha is represented to have replied, counseling his people to remain steadfast to the United States, and so they agreed to do. According to Charley Hoentubbee, his father, David Folsom, and other Choctaws finally escorted Tecumseh's party across the Tombigbee, where a flicker of cooperation marked their separation. A number of Choctaw horses were run off by Creek raiders, and Tecumseh assisted the Choctaws to defeat them in a succeeding skirmish.

It is instructive to contrast Halbert's reconstruction of Tecumseh's tour of the Choctaw country with an account given about the same time by Horatio Bardwell Cushman, who had spent most of his life with the Choctaw tribe. Cushman was no more successful than Halbert in finding eyewitnesses, and also founded his narrative upon secondhand sources, in this instance, evidently, missionaries who had been told of Tecumseh's visit by John Pitchlynn, the Choctaw interpreter for the United States who may have attended the Shawnee's most important council in the Choctaw Nation. In Cushman's version the Northerners arrived in Apukshunnubbee's district, not Moshulatubbee's, and convened a vast meeting of both Choctaws and Chickasaws on the Tombigbee River, the largest assembly of warriors that Pitchlynn had ever seen. The speeches made by Tecumseh and Pushmataha on the occasion are reproduced, a total of more than 2,500 words in which the Shawnee presents a lurid portrait of the ills bestowed by the white man upon the Indian and bemoans the fate of such remote tribes as the New England Pequots and Narragansetts! The argument is eventually resolved by reverence to an aged Choctaw seer, who declares against the "dark and evil designs" of the Northern ambassadors.

The account by Cushman has sometimes been quoted by historians, but it is manifestly preposterous. Eyewitnesses to councils such as those in which Tecumseh participated could not—even minutes after the event—have reproduced speeches in the manner provided by Cushman's oral traditions nearly ninety years afterwards. They might remember the gist of the argument and the occasional telling phrase, but little more. At best Cushman's story preserves a memory of the visit of Tecumseh; it is not a record of the visit itself, and it is riddled with traces of fabrication.

A much earlier tradition survives in a narrative of the Choctaws written in 1861 by Gideon Lincecum. Lincecum resided with the tribe in 1822 to 1825 and knew all three of the district chiefs of Tecumseh's time. His story is interesting because he has nothing to say about a visit by the Shawnee chief, but he does furnish particulars of a canvass of the Choctaws by one of Tecumseh's "prophets" in 1812. Inasmuch as the broader details of this tour are compatible with Halbert's interpretation of Tecumseh's own—the "prophet" on a lobby of the Southern tribes began his campaign among the Choctaws in the area presided over by Moshulatubbee and traveled as far as the Six Towns, where he was opposed by Pushmataha—it is conceivable that Lincecum's tradition confusedly commemorates Tecumseh's visit itself and not some subsequent appearance by one of his lieutenants.

Tecumseh must have left the Choctaws disappointed, but perhaps not surprised. The tribe was on poor terms with the Creeks, Cherokees, and Osages, with whom Tecumseh was implicitly suggesting they stand, and was firmly wedded to the Americans. They had not yet confronted the pressure for land to which the Creeks and Cherokees had been subjected. Two of their leading chiefs, Pushmataha and Apukshunnubbee, were pensioners of the United States as part of the spoils of a treaty ceding tribal land in 1805 and had been awarded lump sums on the same occasion for their cooperation. The third, Moshulatubbee, had inherited a similar pension from the previous chief of his district, a relation of the same name. He had greater sympathy for Tecumseh's cause, but evidently lacked the prestige, influence, and prudence of his older peers. In 1813 Pushmataha aptly summed up the great Shawnee's tour in his remark that Tecumseh "came through our nation, but did not turn our heads." However, most probably not all of Tecumseh's words fell infertile. During the Creek war of 1813 a small number of

Choctaws did join the hostiles, undoubtedly upon their entreaty, and some remained at large afterward. Twenty-five Choctaw warriors helped to defend a fort on the Apalachicola River against the Americans as late as 1816.

It has been widely claimed that Tecumseh's destination after leaving the Choctaws was Florida, where he won the support of the Seminoles. Such was not the case. Albert Pickett's *History of Alabama* (1851) popularized the idea, but its only foundation appears to be an account which Thomas L. McKenney obtained from Creeks at Tuckabatchie about November 1827. As published in *The Indian Tribes of North America* (1836–44) the tradition embodies superficially convincing detail, but reference to McKenney's subsequently published memoirs robs it of credibility. There some of the particulars of the Seminole visit are switched to Tecumseh's dealings with the Creeks at Tuckabatchie, and those details of it that remain—the Shawnee's promise that the Seminoles would be provisioned and armed by a British ship that would anchor off Florida— are clearly inapplicable to 1811, before the outbreak of the War of 1812. It was not until 1814 that a British man-of-war arrived at Apalachicola Bay to support the Southern Indians, and there can be no doubt that it was a memory of this event which had stolen into the traditions about Tecumseh.

Tecumseh's arrival at Tuckabatchie can be dated precisely, and precludes the possibility of the chief visiting Florida between leaving the Choctaws and haranguing the Creek council. The Seminoles were, however, then considered part of the Creek confederacy, and their representatives would certainly have heard Tecumseh at the crucial council at Tuckabatchie, to which delegates of most of the Southern tribes had been invited. Afterward, Tecumseh spent some time touring the Creek country, and it is then that he may have traveled to Florida, although there is no evidence other than McKenney's tradition that he did so.

Tecumseh's canvass of the Creek Nation is the most documented, the most legendary, and the most momentous of his visits to far-flung tribes, and yet it is repeatedly chronicled from unreliable traditional materials, of which the most quoted single account appears to be bogus. An analysis of the latter reminiscences yields instructive examples of the distortion, plagiarization, and invention which characterize material of that kind, but there is not space here to treat the subject adequately. Rather, the following account of Tecumseh's visit is furnished solely from contemporary or near contemporary sources, and the traditional stories are examined afterward for any additional pertinent observations they contain.

Tecumseh's advent upon the Creek scene coincided with the annual national council, attended by delegates from each of the Creek towns. In this instance it was to be an important one, since the main item for discussion was the American intention to build the new road through Creek territory. Hawkins had already made the proposal to the more amenable Lower Creeks, but feared that the Upper Creeks would resist it. The council was scheduled to meet on September 15 at Tuckabatchie, in what is now Alabama, and in August invitations were sent to the Cherokees, Choctaws, and Chickasaws, to consider a matter of concern more than to the Creeks alone. Hawkins did not intend that the feelings of the Indians would interfere with American interests. "I shall do whatever depends on me to obtain their assent to the just expectations of the government," he wrote, "and if they refuse their assent I shall let them know the determination of the Government that the thing must and will be done." It was, therefore, a moment ripe for Tecumseh. His message could be delivered simultaneously to members of all the Southern tribes and upon an occasion in which the United States was bullying them into more concessions on the land question.

Tecumseh's party arrived at Tuckabatchie the same day as did the nineteen-strong Choctaw delegation and forty-six Cherokees, September 19. The Cherokees told Hawkins that they did not oppose the road but hoped to discuss their land differences with the Chickasaws and the Creeks and problems of horse stealing with the latter. It was noticed that Tecumseh and his followers were armed with new British muskets; and as they kept their business to themselves, there was considerable speculation about their intentions. It was rumored that they wanted the Southern Indians to join them in a war upon the United States. One observer remarked that "A Cherokee chief observed to them [the Northerners] that if such was the object of their mission, they had better return without making it known, for his nation was well settled and intended to remain so."

Nevertheless, in the presence of Americans Tecumseh flatly denied hostility to the United States. And alluding to a war pipe almost certainly circulated by his own allies, he completely deluded Hawkins:

> There has been sent to this nation a war pipe from the Wappaumooke and Tooetooeh who are said to live high up on the west side of the Mississippi. The object of the war pipe is to unite all the red people in a war against the white people. It came through the Chickasaws. The chiefs here unanimously refused to smoke the pipe on its presentation and of course refused to join in the war. The Shawanese leader stated last evening that he had followed this pipe from the north and recommended its rejection to all the Indians he had seen and that the Indians should unite in peace and friendship among themselves and cultivate the same with their white neighbours . . .

It was not until the 20th that the council proper got underway, and the following day the subject of the road was raised. There followed three days of arguments. At the end of it, according to a white observer,

> the Indians still refused to give their consent. Col. Hawkins, at length, told them, he did not come there to ask their permission to open a road, but merely to inform them that it was now cutting. Colonel Hawkins did not apprehend any attempt would be made to stop the progress of the workmen employed on the road, as the best informed chiefs of the nations were in favor of it personally, but thought it impolite to give their public assent.

Hawkins himself maintained that by the time he closed the conference with the Creeks on the 28th he had "entered into a convention relative to the roads" and that the road "through the agency will be acquiesced in unanimously by the chiefs." Whether these reports are capable of reconciliation or not they indicate that Hawkins' dealings left a residual bitterness among the Creeks upon which Tecumseh could feed. The Shawnee bided his time, until Hawkins had concluded his business and left. A mixed-blood Creek later recalled, "I was there for the space of two or three days, but every day whilst I was there, Tecumseh refused to deliver his talk, and on being requested to give it, said that the sun had gone too far that day. The day after I came away, he delivered his talk."

That Hawkins left, leaving Tecumseh to do his worst is evidence that he considered the Shawnee harmless, an opinion reinforced by a letter from the office of the secretary of war which informed their agent that "This Dept. has been advised of the mission of the northern Indians, but it is believed that they were wholly unauthorized by their tribes." Hawkins appears to have made no attempt to learn what Tecumseh had said to the Creeks, but reported casually upon the subject in January, two months after Tecumseh's followers had done battle with the Americans at Tippecanoe:

> Tustunnuggee Hopoie of Tookaubatchee called to see me. He is a young man but of high rank and standing among and is one of the chiefs. . . . He told me the Shawano deputation spent a whole day in their square on the object of their mission. The speaker talked much of conversations with you on Indian affairs. After the day was spent he and some others attempted to discover the meaning of what they heard so as to detail it to me. But their opinion was the man was a mad man (Haujo Haugee) or a great liar in fact both, and that as they did not understand them, to take no notice of their foolish talks. He says the prophet and his brother are both men of Tookaubatchee, born there and who left there about 20 years past. There were three of them one is dead.

Judging from the support which Tecumseh was shortly enjoying from many of the Creeks, one suspects that this report was not as candid as Hawkins believed. Another contemporary statement of Tecumseh's speech has been found in a letter written by the Indian agent for the Cherokees, Return Jonathan Meigs. Gathering the Cherokees together on November 24 to distribute treaty annuities, Meigs spoke with those Indians who had been at Tuckabatchie and he took what he heard seriously enough to deride Tecumseh to the Cherokees. It was absurd for a member of a landless tribe to travel seven or eight hundred miles to lecture a people as advanced as the Cherokees. Meigs reported that Tecumseh's talk had been transmitted by order of the Creek tribal council:

> Brothers, The Spaniards, the French & the English had formerly been our fathers. The Americans are now our father. Brothers if any of these attempt to take away your lands, do not resent it. I think it probable that Guns will be fired in the northern Country, but I advise you to be still. If there should be any attempt to take away your lands it may be that some of these will help you. We advise you to live in peace and raise your Children.
>
> Brothers, there are two paths. One is light & clean, the other is covered with Clouds. If you take the light clean path you may be safe. If you take the dark path you may lose your lands. Perhaps the U. States may wish to exchange lands with you. We advise you to keep your lands. The lands we now have are not so good as we had formerly.
>
> Brothers, the Indians often suffer by taking bad talks; do not listen to bad talks.

The message seems confused in this summary, but Tecumseh appears to have warned the Indians about American land and removal policies. However, he was evidently careful enough not to have urged outright hostility to the United States. Indeed, as his own people were not yet at war, it would have been irresponsible of him to have done so. Probably the chief was seeking some commitment to his confederacy, to a united front against further land cessions, and only potentially to military action in defense of aboriginal territorial integrity.

Hawkins himself grew to acknowledge that he had misjudged Tecumseh, but only after part of the Creek confederacy had rebelled against the United States in 1813. Addressing the Big Warrior, speaker of the Nation, and other chiefs in 1814, the agent declared that Tecumseh had delivered the British talk in the square of Tuckabatchie. True, he had counseled the Indians to do neither the Americans nor their property harm, but his words had been double-sided. Tecumseh intended the Creeks to kill their old chiefs and the friends of peace; to slay the cattle, hogs, and fowls that symbolized assimilation into the white culture; to refuse to work in the American fashion and to destroy wheels, looms, and ploughs; to sing the song of the warriors of the northern lakes and perform their dance; to shake their bodies in the ritualistic manner of other supporters of the Shawnee Prophet; and to frighten the Americans with their warclubs and watch the Great Spirit enmesh their enemies in a swamp so that the Creeks could strike them the better. If they did all this, Tecumseh and his warriors would come to assist them, as soon as the British were ready for war.

Ultimately, Tecumseh's interference contributed to the Creek War, but his immediate impact is difficult to gauge. A contemporary credited him with enlisting as many as eighty-one Creek followers by December 1811, and some of them either joined his entourage or independently made their way north to visit members of the Shawnee's confederacy there. In March 1812 there was sufficient discontent in the Creek country to convince some settlers that an uprising was imminent and to bring the Big Warrior and other chiefs to the quarters of Governor David Mitchell of Georgia to affirm that they had no connection with Tecumseh and Tenskwatawa. Nevertheless, that Tecumseh had some claim upon members of the Upper Creeks appears from a conversation of the following summer in which he said that the Creeks stood pledged to join him in the war. It is fair to conclude, therefore, that Tecumseh was not unsuccessful among the Creeks, and in a year a fanatical movement had developed in Alabama which looked to the Shawnees for leadership. As a mixed-blood Natchez Indian recalled, "Tecumseh's new war songs and dances, was sung and danced in all the towns on the Tallapoosy."

The nineteenth century saw the appearance of several reminiscences of Tecumseh's visit to the Creeks, some of which became very influential. McKenney's account has already been mentioned. Between 1831 and 1845 a Natchez Indian, George Stiggins, brother-in-law to William Weatherford—in 1813 one of the hostile Creeks—produced a narrative of Creek affairs which included details of Tecumseh's tour. He obtained some of his information from Thomas S. Woodward, who knew the Creeks after the War of 1812 and who eventually left his own recollections, many of them demonstrably erroneous, in a series of letters written in 1858. More well known are the narratives of Pickett and Claiborne. For his *History of Alabama* Pickett employed Samuel Manac's deposition, cited above, Monetee, who suggested some of Pickett's wording, McKenney and Stiggins, but he did trace some witnesses of Tecumseh's tour and treated cautiously his account has value. The original material in it concerns the Shawnee visits to Creek towns other than Tuckabatchie, Tecumseh's preparation of Creek prophets to continue his work, and the appearance and reception of the Northerners at Tuckabatchie.

Claiborne's description of Tecumseh at Tuckabatchie in the alleged autobiography of the Frontiersman Samuel Dale, however, is fraudulent. The book was purportedly based upon what Dale had told Franklin Smith, Henry Garrett, and Claiborne at different periods and to be in many parts an almost verbatim transcript of his words. Although they adopt the style of the first person, as in conventional autobiography, the passages dealing with Tecumseh were largely based upon published sources, including McKenney, Pickett, and Drake's *Life of Tecumseh*. The story is cast in the exaggerated and sensational language of the dime novelist, with embellishments more likely supplied by Claiborne than Dale, and the speech put into Tecumseh's mouth is not only unhistorical (it has the British in Detroit!) but similar to ones the author concocted for other Indians in different circumstances. There are also small but significant discrepancies between the version of Tecumseh's speech given in *Sam Dale* and that Claiborne published twenty years later which illustrate the ways in which material was juggled. Samuel Dale may have been at Tuckabatchie—the point was disputed between Pickett and Woodward—but his supposed memoirs are unworthy of confidence.

The later reminiscent accounts have contributed two classic ingredients to the story of Tecumseh's canvass of the Southern Indians: the origin of the term *Red Stick* to denote a hostile Creek and the intervention of a comet and an earthquake. To take the red sticks first, it was in 1818 that a newspaper explained that the Red Stick Creeks took their name from a red wand which Tecumseh had carried on his tour and which he was alleged to have used for magical purposes. McKenney offered a different solution. The original red sticks were a primitive calendar. On his visits to the Southern tribes Tecumseh gave his followers bundles of red sticks and instructed them to discard a stick each day. When the bundle was exhausted, it was time to attack the white settlements. McKenney's editor, Frederick Hodge, was not impressed by the explanation and believed that the term originated in the red poles which were erected in the public squares of Creek "red," or war, towns upon the declaration of war. It seems, however, that McKenney may have been closer to the truth, because an eighteenth-century source refers to the Creek practice of using bundles of red sticks to coordinate the raising of war parties. Probably Tecumseh never employed them, but once the Creek War of 1813 was underway, the red sticks were circulated and gave the hostiles their name.

As for the earthquakes and comets, they have become standard fare in accounts of Tecumseh and the War of 1812. McKenney was the first to use the story. He reported that Tecumseh told the Big Warrior that he would prove he had been sent by the Great Spirit by giving the Creeks a sign. When he reached Detroit, he would stamp upon the ground, shake the earth, and bring down houses in Tuckabatchie. Shortly after Tecumseh had left the south, an earthquake occurred as he had prophesied, and the Creeks were so astonished that many now declared themselves to be supporters of the Shawnee chief. According to Stiggins, Tecumseh offered to prove his powers to the Creeks by ascending a high mountain and stamping the earth so that it would tremble. And so it proved:

> what heightened their [the Creeks'] astonishment into almost certainty, was a coincidence of Tecumseh's omenous remark in the public speech to the shock of the earth quake, and the appearance of the comet previous, on its forebodings of ill to their enemies he commented in an alarming manner, two such uncommon occurrences in succession aided with his comments occasioned the fabrication of the most dreadful tales.

Both McKenney and Stiggins attributed much of Tecumseh's success among the Creeks to his accurate prediction of an earthquake. Neither the earthquake nor the comet is difficult to document. The comet had been seen in France as early as March 1811 and was visible in the United States from the end of August, increasing in brightness throughout September and reaching its closest point to the earth in October, about the time Tecumseh was touring villages in the Creek territory. By December the comet was visible only faintly, and in early February of 1812 it disappeared from view. Stiggins's view that Tecumseh used the comet to his advantage is certainly plausible. He may have told the Creeks that it signaled his coming, since Tecumseh's name, in Shawnee, meant Shooting Star.

But the earthquake was even more important. Three series of shocks took place, the first beginning about two o'clock in the morning of December 16, 1811, apparently about sixty-five miles southwest of New Madrid in what is now northeastern Arkansas. In New Orleans the tremor was not felt, but steeple bells were rung in Charleston, buildings moved, furniture shifted, and clocks stopped. The village of Little Prairie, near the epicenter, was destroyed by floods. A second series of shocks began on January 23, 1812, and a third on February 7. Jared Brooks, a Louisville engineer and surveyor, counted 1,874 shocks in all between December 16 and March 15 and regarded fifty-three of them as of alarming proportions. At various times they were felt from New Orleans to Quebec Province in Canada, but they take their name today from the town of New Madrid, which was destroyed and evacuated in January and February of 1812.

The significance of these earthquakes, occurring just after Tecumseh had left the South and while he toured the West, cannot be overstated. The idea that Tecumseh foretold them, as McKenney and Stiggins said, need not be accepted, but he may have promised the Creeks that he would give them a sign of some kind and left them to fulfill his prophecy with the first unusual occurrence. The ensuing shocks greatly advanced the cause of Tecumseh among the Creeks and elsewhere, for the Indians interpreted them as evidence of divine disfavor and sought an explanation of the creator's wrath in the decline of the Indian territory and the gradual desertion of the traditional ways of life. Tecumseh's nativism and his condemnation of the land cessions seemed to be vindicated by the Great Spirit.

In the instance of the Cherokees the earthquakes revived a clamor for the restoration of old traditions and customs independent of Tecumseh's preaching. Affected by Christian beliefs, some Cherokees were convinced that the Day of Judgment had arrived and evaluated their conduct accordingly. On February 17, 1812, Chief Chulioah informed Moravian missionaries that "many Indians believe that the white people were responsible because they had already taken possession of so much of the Indian land and wanted still more. God was angry because of that and He wanted to put an end to it through the earthquakes." Rumor and fear ran rife throughout the Cherokee nation as earthquake followed earthquake. Early in March

> it has been revealed to one Indian by God that there would be an intense darkness and that it would last three days; during which all white people would be snatched away as well as all Indians who had any clothing or household articles of the white man's kind, together with all their cattle. Therefore, they should put aside everything that is similar to the white people and that which they had learned from them, so that in the darkness God might not mistake them and snatch them away with the former. He who does not believe this will die at once together with all his stock.

Preserved in missionary diaries, the Cherokee hysteria suggests the processes by which Tecumseh's followers among the Creeks turned Nature to account and forged a fanatical nativism which fed upon opposition to American land policies and dissatisfaction with Hawkins's "civilization" program. Moreover, it furnishes the context in which Tecumseh continued his tour. Amid such powerful portents as the earthquakes and the comet, the Shawnee chief could sharpen his appeal.

There is no reliable report of Tecumseh for the two months after the end of September 1811, but it is inconceivable that he lay idle, and he probably spent much of that time touring the Creek country. He could have visited some of the Cherokees, either in the mountainous area of North Carolina or in Tennessee. In the late nineteenth century there was a strong tradition among the Cherokees that Tecumseh had visited them, and it was said that one Anderson Springston had collected information about it but that his papers disappeared after his death in the Civil War. Stories were passed down of Tecumseh lodging at Talbot's Tavern in Nashville, of his being accompanied to the Cherokees by a Shawnee whose son, by a Cherokee wife, still lived among the nation, and of his visit to Chief Junaluska's Cherokees on Soco Creek in North Carolina. No convincing support for these traditions has been found, and much that was written about them was fictitious.

The records take up the Shawnee chief's trail late in November, as he passed through Chickasaw land again, on his way to the Mississippi. This time Tecumseh imparted his plans to Chinubbee (the Chickasaw "king"), but although the tribe was troubled with the incursions of white squatters and thieves, the Northerners could not elicit Chickasaw support:

> The Shawanoe Indians and some of the Kickapoos solicited the king of this nation for men to join the Prophet's party, but the old king told them that if they killed all his white Brothers that he would die too. I am told that there are some Creeks gone to join the Prophet's party, how many I have not heard—I do not think that any of this nation will join them unless some of them that are hunting over the Mississippi should meet with the party above named & might be persuaded to go with them, if they do it will be against the advice & without the knowledge of the headmen. The Choctaws I believe are engaged in a war with the Osages which keeps them employed, I do not presume that many of them will join the Prophet. I have been constantly advising this nation against & shewing them the consequences of joining the Prophet & of going to war against the Osages.

While the land was convulsed by earthquakes, Tecumseh traveled northwest, toward the epicenter of the shocks, west of the Mississippi. About his reported visit to the Osages, an embattled people who lived in what is now Missouri, Kansas, Arkansas, and Oklahoma, there has brewed much controversy because the only record of it is contained in John Dunn Hunter's *Memoirs*, published in 1823, a work which has not been without its detractors. By his own account Hunter was captured as a child by Indians and remained with them until he was about twenty years old. After the appearance of his book he became something of a celebrity, but he incurred the wrath of patriotic Americans, particularly when a British officer used the pages of the London *Quarterly Review* to link the *Memoirs* with an attack upon United States Indian policy. A storm of abuse was unleashed upon Hunter by Lewis Cass, Governor of Michigan Territory, who believed that his country's honor had been outraged.

Recently Drinnon has shown that the contentions of Cass and others to demonstrate that Hunter was an imposter with little knowledge of the Osages cannot be regarded as objective commentaries, but formed an orchestrated attempt to discredit Hunter. Cass's work displayed an animosity to both Hunter and Indians, and its allusions to the natives contained inaccuracies ill befitted a man affecting such pronounced expertise upon the subject. The attacks rallied supporters to Hunter, one of them the painter George Catlin, who asserted that he had met Indians who had known Hunter. An English defender declared that Hunter "bears the genuine mint-mark about him, and it is visible in everything he says, and everything he does." Research has not demolished that view, for on the one hand it has been unable to discover sources from which Hunter could have taken his material, and on the other it has vindicated much of what he said about the culture of the Osages.

Hunter's account of Tecumseh's visit to the Osages, therefore, demands more respect than it is generally accorded. The information adduced to contradict it is neither convincing nor accurate. The pioneer Pierre Menard, for example, gave his opinion that Tecumseh was not in Missouri in 1811 or 1812, but official records establish the opposite Menard's credibility falls to the ground, for he was either dishonest or ignorant. Nor does the statement of four Osage chiefs and a white man who knew them to the effect that Tecumseh never visited the tribe carry much weight. They had been assembled to provide evidence against Hunter, and possibly shaped their responses to please the questioners. That they wished to disassociate themselves from Tecumseh and his movement is indicated by their language ("We have heard of Tecumseh, as we have heard of the Devil.") Moreover, since the Osages were divided among several bands as far apart as Missouri and Oklahoma in 1811, it would have been quite possible for the Shawnee chief to have been in some villages and not others.

Far from being the improbable event portrayed by Cass and his coadjutors, a visit by Tecumseh to the Osages appears likely from the records of the United States War Department. As early as August 1811 Tecumseh actually informed Harrison that he intended returning from the South by Missouri and canvassing the Osages, and he was indeed in Missouri Territory the following December. Hunter's account of Tecumseh's appearance among the tribe at this time conforms so snugly with these records that it is probably authentic.

In 1811 the Osages were settled in three or four villages. The Great Osages, or White Hair's band, tenanted the head of the Osage River in what is now Missouri. Another part of this band had made its home at the mouth of the Verdigris River, a tributary of the Arkansas, in present Oklahoma, and were led by Chiefs Clermont and Cashesegra, while a smaller group, the Little Osages, under Nezumonee, lived in one or two villages on the Neosho, a branch of the Arkansas River. The Osages were constantly at war with other tribes, many of them allies of Tecumseh, but their relations with the United States were fluctuating. Their delegations had been received in Washington, and in 1809 an American trading house was established to serve them as part of a treaty signed by the Great and Little Osages at Fort Clark in November 1808. By this agreement the United States affirmed that it would maintain a garrison at Fort Clark for the protection of the tribes, provide $1,200 and annuities, supply a trading post, a mill, and a smith, and furnish the Indians agricultural implements. On their part the Osages agreed to a boundary running from Fort Clark on the Missouri, south to the Arkansas, and down the Mississippi, and they ceded all land east of that line, north of the southern bank of the Arkansas, and northward of the Missouri. The treaty was extended to the Arkansas Osages in August 1809.

It is difficult to gauge the mood of the Osages during the winter of 1811–12. There was dissatisfaction over the treaty, and in the autumn of 1811 an Osage delegation at St. Louis protested that the Indians had not understood that they had ceded so much land and claimed that the treaty was void because the United States had delayed ratification. Although the first annuities, covering both 1810 and 1811, were distributed in September, discontent continued. The Little Osages complained that the smith and mill provided under the treaty had been situated with the Great Osages. Agents of Tecumseh and Tenskwatawa had probably already reached the tribe, and they may have been encouraged by the intrigue rife within the Osage villages. According to Sibley, the Osages were "very much distracted by the jealousies and intrigues of the principal warriors, and for want of energy and decision in the chiefs." Such circumstances favored Tecumseh, for his appeal was strongest among the younger warriors eager to win reputations and weakest where older and more moderate men exercised firm control.

The earthquakes were perhaps the Shawnee chief's most cogent argument. Hunter remarked that

> the Indians were filled with great terror . . . the trees and wigwams shook exceedingly; the ice which skirted the margin of the Arkansas river was broken into pieces; and the most of the Indians thought that the Great Spirit, angry with the human race, was about to destroy the world.

Hunter's assertion that Tecumseh visited Chief Clermont's village on the Great Osage River is confused, for the band of that chief was in fact located on the Verdigris and it was the White Hair faction which occupied the Osage River. Both options are consequently preserved. Tecumseh could have crossed the Mississippi from Chickasaw land, struck the Arkansas, and journeyed upstream to the Osages of the Verdigris and the Neosho. By ascending the latter stream he might eventually have reached the headwaters of the Osage River. Alternatively he could have traveled directly to the Osage River by the Mississippi and Missouri. Hunter described how Tecumseh addressed the Osages in a strong speech, outlining the difficulties under which the Indians labored, and urging the Indians to join other tribes in resisting the Americans. He promised British support and referred to the earthquakes which troubled the Indians:

> Brothers, The Great Spirit is angry with our enemies; he speaks in thunder, and the earth swallows up villages, and drinks up the Mississippi. The great waters will cover their lowlands; their corn cannot grow; and the Great Spirit will sweep those who escape to the hills from the earth with his terrible breath.

In this account one of Tecumseh's companions was the Creek Francis, later the most important leader of the Red Sticks, but neither he nor the Shawnee himself could induce the Osages to join the confederacy.

If Tecumseh managed to lobby the Osages, it would have completed the itinerary the chief gave Harrison the previous summer. While in Missouri Territory Tecumseh certainly visited the Western Shawnees, and it is possible that he there learned for the first time of the destruction of his town on the Tippecanoe by Harrison's army in November. Perhaps it was in consequence that he did not turn immediately for home, but decided to extend the tour to the northwest to ascertain whether Tenskwatawa's defeat had damaged the confederacy's credibility in areas which had hitherto given it its staunchest support. William Clark, Indian agent at St. Louis, reported the chief's next moves:

> The Winnibago Bands, part of the Kickapoos, and some of the Pottowotomies are yet friendly to the prophet and may join him again in the spring. His brother Tecumsy returned from the Southern Tribes in Dec. last. He made great exertions to get the Showonees and Delaways of this Territory to join the prophets party, but without success. He proceeded to the Sacs and Sioux Country where his councils have been more attended to. I have had a watchful eye towards him and hope to counteract the effects of his plans in that quarter.

It was natural that Tecumseh should call upon his kinsmen. Shawnees had settled in Missouri Territory since revolutionary times, for the most part about Cape Girardeau on a Spanish land grant. In 1811 their main villages were on Apple Creek, south of present St. Genevieve, and on the Meramec River, where Chief Lewis Rogers lived. Migrant Delawares had also found homes in the region, on the Current River and at various sites in what is now southwestern Missouri. Tecumseh won little support from these peoples, and no details other than those furnished by Clark survive.

Traveling northward, the Shawnee chief passed across lands commanded by tribes more hostile to the United States, where the influence of both the Indian confederacy and the British had already been felt and where the atmosphere was highly charged by the battle of Tippecanoe. It was from these Indians, particularly the Sacs, Potawotamis, Kickapoos, and Winnebagoes, that Tecumseh and Tenskawatawa had drawn most of their adherents. As Tecumseh traced the Mississippi upriver, he would have encountered the Iowa Indians on the Des Moines. Between the mouths of the Des Moines and the Rock lived the populous Sacs, some of them grieving over land sales conducted by Harrison a few years before. Their close allies the Foxes, then rather more pacific, tenanted the region above the Rock and below Prairie du Chien, at the mouth of the Wisconsin. Proceeding further, above Prairie du Chien and to and along the Minnesota River, Tecumseh could have reached several villages of the Mdewakanton division of these Santee Dakota Sioux under chiefs like Tatankamani, Little Crow, and Wapasha. Eastward, in present Wisconsin, dwelt the Menominees and Winnebagoes. The Kickapoos occupied the Illinois River and the Potawatomis generally the area northeast of that—the head of Lake Michigan, and what is now southern Wisconsin, northern Illinois, Michigan, and northern Indiana.

These remoter tribes, close to the manipulations of the British, exhibited a greater propensity for hostility to the United States, and Governors Ninian Edwards of Illinois Territory and Benjamin Howard of Upper Louisiana were convinced they were facing an unfriendly combination of tribes poised to fall upon the frontiers. To standing difficulties the past year had been added further grievances. In the summer the Sacs and Foxes had been disturbed by the arrival at Prairie du Chien of an American agent, Nicholas Boilvin, with a party of whites claiming possession of the local lead mines that the Indians regarded as their own. Far more serious was the Battle of Tippecanoe, for Indian warriors had been killed by the American militia that day and according to native customs their blood demanded retribution. In the following few months a number of Americans were killed on the Mississippi, and it was rumored that as soon as the Winnebagoes could gather their warriors from the winter hunting they would fall upon the outlying forts and settlements en masse.

Agents of the United States insisted that the British were urging the tribes to war, at St. Joseph's and Fort Malden in Canada, on the Mississippi by means of traders like Robert Dickson, and through the circulation of wampum belts. The Americans were also aware of their impotence in regions where Britain offered the Indians greater access to the provisions and trade goods upon which they depended. The dry summer of 1811 had been followed by a sharp winter in which necessity alone drove many of the tribesmen towards the British. Although the King's servants did not primarily intend to provoke an Indian war, they foresaw the difficulties that lay ahead for Britain and the United States and were preparing the Indians to defend Canada. Inevitably they fueled tribal excitement.

Indian emissaries too, from Tecumseh and Tenskwatawa and the Potawatomi chief Main Poc, were striving for a united front against the Americans in the Northwest. In November, shortly before Tecumseh's reappearance, a Potawatomi called Latourt, or the White Pidgeon, left Indiana Territory and passed through the villages on the Illinois River to canvass the Sacs, Foxes, and Sioux with, it was said, a wampum from Tenskwatawa and an invitation from the British to visit them for arms and ammunition.

> Brothers, [the White Pidgeon was quoted] you promised me last year that you would be ready in the Spring; the Spring came, but no person was ready—the Fall is come, I look towards the setting sun, but do not discover you coming—You have not been true! yet I hope you will not fail to be ready early next Spring!

In such an atmosphere Tecumseh successfully toured the Northwest. On March 3, Edwards reported that

> Gov. Howard Genl. Clarke & myself unite in the opinion that we have good cause to apprehend a formidable combination of Indians and a bloody war. And if there is any confidence to be placed in the agents, sub agents and spies engaged in these territories in the Indian Department who have had an opportunity of forming an opinion no other event can be expected. The Prophet is regaining his influence. Tecumseh has visited the tribes on our North Western frontier with considerable success.

Tecumseh's activities among the Sacs and Sioux cannot be recovered. During winters the Sacs dispersed into hunting parties, but Captain Horatio Stark of Fort Madison, above the mouth of the Des Moines, recorded unusual behavior which may have reflected Tecumseh's movements. About January 8 the Sacs held "a very general Counsel" to determine whether the tribe should take the warpath. Stark was at first doubtful as to its issue, but he shortly accepted that a confederacy of Winnebagoes, Shawnees, Potawatomis, Kickapoos, and Sacs was planning to attack Fort Madison. At the same time, Howard was advised by one of his agents

> that the Sauk have sent a great quantity of wampum painted red to the Winnebagoes on Roc River, which, in the opinion of all the Indians, is war, and I presume that it is for an attack on Fort Madison, they being neighbours and having no communication with that garrison all summer.

The Americans exaggerated their danger, for the blow never fell, but they were not mistaken about the disposition of the natives. Nor was Tecumseh unwelcome among the Sioux, who already complained of the inadequate provisions to be had from the Americans and enjoyed a close relationship with the influential British trader, Robert Dickson. Ninian Edwards, for one, considered the Sioux part of the Indian alliance. "Strong circumstances are stated," he reported in March, "which seem to justify a belief that the Sioux have joined or are about joining the hostile confederacy, and if so it will be the most formidable one with which the western country has had to contend."

Tecumseh may have left the Sioux to call upon the Winnebagoes, the tribe which had probably supplied six of the warriors he had taken to the South, but there is no record of it. Turning home, no doubt reassured by the last leg of his canvass, the Shawnee chief would have crossed the headwaters of the Illinois and conferred with his Potawatomi and Kickapoo allies thereabouts. A British agent at Fort Malden, at Amherstburg, appears to have alluded to this on January 12, when he wrote that a Kickapoo had reported Tecumseh "to be on his return and has reached the farthest Kickapoo Town, and is there in Council with the different Nations."

Several bands of Potawatomis and Kickapoos were residing on the Illinois at the beginning of 1812 and estimates of their strengths were obtained by Edwards. Sixty Kickapoo, Potawatomi, Ottawa, and Ojibwa warriors under Sulky lived below Peoria. A little upstream, above Peoria, three more bands had their homes: 150 Potawatomi fighting men under Gomo, a similar number of Kickapoo warriors with Paonanatam, and Little Deer's Kickapoo village of 120 men. Another concentration of Indians was to be met near the mouth of or along the Kankakee River. There were two mixed bands of Potawatomis, Ojibwas, and Ottawas, one reputedly led by Wabeesause and the other by Pepper, and another fifty Potawatomi warriors on the Kankakee under the fierce Main Poc, a principal ally of Tecumseh. Then, to the northeast, not far from the American post of Fort Dearborn (Chicago), two bands of Potawatomis, Ojibwas, and Ottawas, one headed by Old Campignan and the other by Cowaabee, were believed to command 130 warriors. If the information gathered by Edwards is correct, Tecumseh passed through a territory able to field almost 900 warriors in all, and he apparently found them not unsympathetic to his cause. It was noted by the governor at the beginning of March that positive evidence had been received that the Potawatomis and Kickapoos had "lately held a council near Pioria in which it was determined to attack our frontiers."

The date that Tecumseh arrived home on the Tippecanoe has not been ascertained. It was possible to travel over the high, dry, and open country between the Mississippi and Tippecanoe rivers in about a week, but the Shawnee chief must have been delayed speaking to tribes along the way. The Miamis reported that Tecumseh reached the Tippecanoe with eight men in company during January, but a contradictory report suggested that he was still missing a month later. The Indian agent John Shaw gave out that a Miami Indian said that some Winnebagoes, Shawnees, and Kickapoos of Tenskwatawa's following remarked about February 25 that Tecumseh had not yet reached the Wabash, but that upon learning of the battle of Tippecanoe he had sent some men forward, two of them Creeks, to discover the news.

Taken as a whole, Tecumseh's tour of 1811–12 remains one of the most remarkable made in the interest of pan-Indianism. It endured for six months or more, over perhaps as many as three thousand miles, and into eight to twelve of the present American states. The Shawnee chief probably traveled the country of the Chickasaws, Choctaws, Creeks, Osages, the Western Shawnees and Delawares, Iowas, Sacs and Foxes, Sioux, Kickapoo, and Potawatomi. The success he enjoyed owed much to standing grievances of the Indians and to the disposition of the British, but it depended also upon timely occurrences, the New Madrid earthquakes and Harrison's imprudent engagement on the Tippecanoe, which inflamed rather than pacified the tribesmen.

The tour was a logical extension of Tecumseh's multitribal confederacy, an attempt to bring the Southern and Western tribes into an Indian union that would resist the advance of the American land frontier and discard many of the debasing influences of the whites. Legend has declared that Tecumseh went further and vehemently exhorted the tribes to war, but it is unlikely that such was the case. The chief expected conflict between Britain and the United States and knew the part he would urge the Indians to play, but a premature border war was not to his advantage, and he was probably primarily concerned with securing some commitment to his confederacy that could be called to account at the appropriate time.

In this respect the tour was an important prelude to the Indian War of 1812. It certainly planted the seeds of the Creek War, for the regular communication between the Creeks and Shawnees that stemmed from it foreshadowed the unprecedented native cooperation of 1813, when the American frontiers of both the North and the South were attacked by warriors espousing the creed of Tecumseh and his brother. But for the same reasons Tecumseh's tour cast not only a long but also a gloomy shadow, for it presaged the division, defeat, humiliation, and dispossession of the once great Creek nation.

11

BACKDROP FOR DISASTER: CAUSES OF THE ARIKARA WAR OF 1823

ROGER L. NICHOLS

Issues related to interracial trade and warfare continue to attract scholars' attention. The Arikara War of 1823 provides a good example of how intratribal as well as intertribal factors might combine to bring violence as often as Indian-white difficulties did. A culmination of many factors, the process leading to military confrontation proved more important than the eventual fighting. In this case the Missouri River fur trade had brought the tribe into close social and economic contact with the whites for some decades. Despite the disruption of village economic patterns, the introduction of epidemic disease, and considerable ecological devastation, these Indians remained at peace with the white traders. In fact, when war did occur in 1823, it came about at least as much because of factors within the tribe and disputes with other tribes as because of basic disputes with traders. Competition with the nearby Sioux and Mandan peoples, as well as misunderstandings of American diplomatic activities in the region, set the stage for trouble. When the fighting began, it caught both traders and government officials by surprise. Neither group understood the complexities of the situation nor had any idea of why the Arikara had attacked. As this narrative indicates, the Indians acted as they did because they understood their own economic decline as well as the personal motivations of village leaders as they competed with each other. The tribal people had understandable and rational reasons for their attack on the traders. Contemporary whites characterized the tribe as treacherous and undependable only because they failed to understand the local situation.

Roger L. Nichols is a professor of history at the University of Arizona and the editor of this book.

Source: Roger L. Nichols, "Backdrop for Disaster: Causes of the Arikara War of 1823," *South Dakota History*, 14 (Summer 1984), pp. 93-113. Reprinted by permission from *South Dakota History*. © 1984 by the South Dakota State Historical Society.

Rays from the setting sun illuminated the Saint Louis waterfront as the keelboats *Rocky Mountains* and *Yellowstone Packet* pulled away from shore and headed north into the Mississippi River current. With sails in place, flags flying, and hired musicians serenading spectators who lined the riverbank, William Ashley's party of seventy mountain men began its journey on 10 March 1823, heading north and west toward the Rocky Mountains. Weeks passed uneventfully as they toiled up the Missouri River. By late May they were traveling through present-day South Dakota, where events shattered their comfortable routine. Stopping briefly to trade for horses, the whites provoked a fight with the unpredictable Arikara Indians, who were then occupying two villages along the Missouri near the mouth of the Grand River. This incident, labeled "the worst disaster in western fur trade history," coupled with the retaliatory expedition against the villagers led by Col. Henry Leavenworth later that summer, came to be known as the Arikara War.

The conflict paralleled many early nineteenth century Indian wars in which, for what at the time seemed unclear reasons, Indian Americans attacked intruding white Americans. With surprise on their side, the Indians won the initial skirmish, driving the trappers from the scene. Once the frontiersmen recovered from their shock, however, an overwhelming force invaded the Indian country to punish the tribesmen. This counterattack succeeded. The Arikara fled, leaving the enraged whites to burn their abandoned villages.

Students of South Dakota history undoubtedly recall these events well. Nevertheless, a few details of the incident may clarify the situation and help to explain how and why this war occurred. Hurrying up the Missouri toward the Rockies, Ashley had not expected to visit the Arikara. In fact, reports of their hostility that spring convinced him that they should be avoided. Just south of the Indian towns, however, he learned that his partners in the mountains needed another forty or fifty horses for use that coming season. Thus, despite misgivings and with little advance thought, Ashley decided to halt. He hoped that the ninety-man party of trappers and boatman was large enough to persuade the Indians to trade rather than fight. After a short parley on 30 May the chiefs agreed to trade the next morning. On 31 May the trappers and Indians began their barter, but with limited success. Far from other sources of horses, the Arikara demanded top prices for their animals. Because Ashley had not anticipated this trading session, his stock of trade items may not have been adequate. When the trading ended that day, the whites had only nineteen horses and the Indians had balked at the amount and quality of the whites' trade goods.

Continuing signs of Indian discontent convinced Ashley that he should move quickly upriver with the few horses he had obtained. Unfortunately, bad weather made it impossible to travel the next morning. The whites were forced to remain, some guarding the animals on the beach while the rest huddled aboard the boats waiting for the storm to pass. At dawn the following day, 2 June, the Arikara warriors attacked. In a few minutes their musket balls and arrows destroyed the horses and killed or wounded most of the trappers on the beach. Caught by surprise and defeated soundly, Ashley's remaining men scrambled aboard the keelboats and fled downstream.

News of the Arikara attack reached Fort Atkinson, just north of present-day Omaha, Nebraska, and set into motion a combination rescue effort and retaliatory expedition. Col. Henry Leavenworth rushed six companies of United States infantrymen upriver, while Saint Louis trader Joshua Pilcher joined the troops with a force of nearly sixty trappers and fur company employees. Along the way, this so-called Missouri Legion recruited a force of nearly 750 Sioux allies. By early August 1823 the mixed group of soldiers, trappers, and Indians arrived at the Arikara villages, where the mounted Sioux auxiliaries swept ahead of the foot soldiers and launched a preliminary attack on their long-time foes. A stream of Arikara warriors poured out of the villages to meet them. After spirited fighting, the Arikara saw the regular troops moving up and fled back behind the village palisades.

The next morning, 10 August, Colonel Leavenworth ordered his artillery to shell the villages, but, through ineptitude or carelessness, the soldiers sent most of their shots whistling harmlessly overhead. Seeing this, the colonel ordered an infantry attack on the upper village. Although the soldiers fought bravely, the Indian defenders refused to budge. At that point, fearing both a possible heavy loss of his men and perhaps even the total destruction of the Indian towns, Leavenworth chose to negotiate an end to the fighting. Late that afternoon the whites persuaded several Arikara chiefs to join them for peace talks. Although divided and bickering acrimoniously among themselves, the invading forces concluded a treaty with the Indians the next day, but the wary Arikara abandoned their villages during the following night. On 15 August Leavenworth led his force back down the river to Fort Atkinson. No sooner had the soldiers left than several fur company employees burned the villages to the ground. As a result of this campaign, the Arikara scattered. Many of them moved away from their traditional home for more than a decade.

There is little dispute about these events. Yet both Indian and white motivations remain murky. To reach an understanding of the forces that led to the Arikara War, several factors have to be considered. The nature of Arikara village life and society provides one clue to the reasons behind the Arikaras' actions. The villagers' pattern of dealing with other American Indian groups in the Missouri Valley likewise offers some insights into their behavior toward all outsiders. Obviously these Indians had developed a bitter hostility toward the white traders, or they would not have risked an all-out war with them, and the growth of antiwhite attitudes needs to be examined. At the same time, white ideas about the Arikara and the traders' responses to the villagers provide the other necessary threads in the pattern. When taken together, the Indian and white motivations offer the basis for a clear perception of the conflict. Historical accounts of Indian wars often focus chiefly on white actions. In this circumstance, however, the Indian motivations, attitudes, and actions proved more important than those of the whites in shaping the course of events. The following discussion, therefore, focuses more attention on Arikara actions than on those of Ashley or the Leavenworth Expedition.

Among the developments that propelled the Arikara toward their 1823 encounter with Ashley's trappers were several long-term trends within the villagers' society that played increasingly important roles. A Caddoan people related to, or perhaps part of, the Skidi Pawnee, the Arikara lived in nearly permanent towns on the banks of the Missouri River throughout most of the eighteenth century. There, between the White and Cheyenne rivers in central South Dakota, they fished in the Missouri, farmed its banks and bottom lands, hunted on the nearby plains to the west, and participated in the existing Indian trade network. The most important long-term trends in their society resulted from their growing role as traders. In that capacity they increased their corn production and exchanged their surplus harvest with the nearby hunting peoples for meat, hides, and leather goods. This activity tied the villagers into trade patterns that connected aboriginal peoples from central Canada to the borders of Mexico, and from the Rocky Mountains to the Mississippi River and beyond.

In the mid-eighteenth century, or earlier, the Arikara traders added European goods to their traditional wares. People from the southern plains offered horses to the Missouri Valley dwellers, while manufactured goods and guns filtered south and west from Canada. Before long, European traders followed their goods into the Indians towns, forever altering aboriginal life. As the century drew to a close, the Arikara economy had undergone fundamental changes. Their earlier trade had been a matter of choice—an exchange of surplus goods with other tribal people. Now they shaped their economy to reflect their dependence on trading. True, they still hunted, but in most years their catch did not provide enough meat or hides to meet their needs. Nor did exchange of their surplus corn by itself supply these necessities any longer. Increasingly their aboriginal customers demanded guns, ammunition, and manufactured goods in addition to foodstuffs. By accident or design the villagers became ever more dependent on their white trading partners for survival.

Within most Indian communities "trade was embedded in a network of social relations" so that few individuals gained new status because of it. Direct trade with Europeans, however, brought opportunities for increased wealth within many tribes and bands. Before the fur-and-hide trade, clan chiefs and other village leaders maintained a superior status because of their social functions. Direct trading with whites meant that individual hunters might acquire more wealth than was possible under the aboriginal system. Chiefs might still take a share of this new wealth, but a growing individual participation in the trade with the whites produced new economic pressures within many Indian societies. There is little direct evidence that this pattern was of major importance in the Arikara villages, but the lack of evidence may reflect the inability of white traders, who provided the early accounts of the Arikara, to perceive their own impact on the villagers. This pattern seems to have occurred repeatedly among other aboriginal groups, and there is little reason to dismiss it as a factor among the Arikara.

While such changes reshaped the villagers' economic life, even more disruptive events rent the fabric of Arikara society. Soon after the first meetings between European traders and the Arikara, a series of major smallpox epidemics swept across the Missouri Valley and out onto the northern plains. Although the chronology and severity of these epidemics remain shrouded in antiquity, the combined results unquestionably proved disastrous. Modern scholars and eighteenth-century observers agree that the epidemics destroyed nearly three quarters of all the Indians in South Dakota. The disease struck the Arikara and other sedentary agricultural tribes a devastating blow, one from which they never fully recovered. As the pox swept through their villages, it killed or terrorized most of the inhabitants. Village, band, clan, and even family organization crumbled as aboriginal healers failed to halt the plagues. The result was catastrophic, and by 1795 most of the Indians had died. In that year a resident trader reported: "In ancient times the Ricara nation was very large; it counted thirty-two populous villages, now depopulated and almost entirely destroyed by the smallpox. . . . A few families only, from each of the villages, escaped; these united and formed the two villages now here." When Lewis and Clark visited the tribe in late 1804, they learned that the existing three villages, located near the mouth of the Grand River, included the survivors of some eighteen earlier towns along both sides of the Missouri.

While the smallpox epidemics killed most of the Indians and disrupted or destroyed their social cohesion, the consolidation of survivors in two or three villages also brought unforeseen and continuing problems. Individuals from at least ten distinct bands, each with different leaders and varying customs, as well as major linguistic differences, huddled together in their new settlements. A higher percentage of band leaders and chiefs survived than did the population as a whole. Pierre-Antoine Tabeau reported that there were more than forty-two chiefs living in the three villages in 1804. Each of the many chiefs, Tabeau noted, "wishes at least to have followers and tolerates no form of dependence" on others. This situation brought nearly incessant wrangling among contending leaders as their factions disrupted village life with "internal and destructive quarrels."

Not only did these pressures on the Arikara affect the nature and operation of their society, but they also had direct impact on their dealings with other Indians. In particular, their divided and quarreling leadership caused problems and made other situations worse than they needed to be, especially in relationships with the neighboring Mandan, Hidatsa, and Sioux. The Sioux, largest of these Indian groups, threatened all three agricultural village tribes. Although the Mandan, Hidatsa, and Arikara shared a similar function as middlemen in the area trade network and suffered alike at the hands of Sioux raiders, they quarreled and even fought with one another rather than presenting a united front in response to Sioux aggression. Not only did the Sioux "pursue a system of preventing trade to all [Indian] nations up the Upper Missouri," but they also raided the villagers' crops and horse herds repeatedly.

In the Arikara's case, the lack of clear leadership in their fractured society made it difficult for them to pursue any consistent policy toward their neighbors. In fact, it created an instability that caused other groups to see the tribe as dangerous and unpredictable. The Frenchman Tabeau complained that the splintered nature of Arikara village leadership led to endless conflicts as the chiefs and their followers robbed each other and threatened to fight others in their own communities. What was worse, in his opinion, was the Arikara's continuing inability to settle disputes with the Mandan and Hidatsa so the that the three agricultural tribes could unite to defend themselves against the Sioux. Tabeau felt certain that Arikara leaders realized that it was imperative to ally themselves with the Mandans; yet they could not do so. He noted that all their efforts to make peace with that tribe failed because of "individual jealousy" within the villages. Divided leadership or a lack of unity, then, destroyed "all the plans which tend to bring about peace" with their natural allies.

The situation also made their response to direct Sioux aggression ineffective much of the time. All the roots of the conflict between these two tribes are not clear, but certainly the Sioux looked down upon their sedentary neighbors, treating the Arikara as inferior beings who farmed and did other such women's chores for their benefit. Sioux arrogance grew steadily more intolerable, and by the early nineteenth century they acted as if they were the masters rather than the equals of their trading partners. When they came to trade, Sioux visitors did little bargaining over prices. Instead, they took what they wanted and gave the villagers whatever amount of skins and meat they deemed adequate. To amuse themselves and show disdain for the Arikara, they often pillaged and trampled gardens, beat and insulted Arikara women, and ran off the villagers' horses. Outnumbered, divided, and often leaderless, the Arikara seemed unable to respond effectively to Sioux assaults.

Customs related to wealth and status among the upper Missouri Valley tribes also kept their intertribal relationships in turmoil. For young men, status within the village resulted from acts of bravery. Usually such acts included either stealing horses or fighting men from the surrounding tribes. Once a raid took place, the victims often retaliated, and a cycle of violent competition and warfare continued for generations. The warriors had strong social and economic motivations for their actions, and with village controls weakened among the Arikara, there were few restraints to curb raids against erstwhile allies or friends. Not only did these attacks and counterattacks prevent any lasting peace, but practices related to success and failure on these expeditions also worsened the situation. If raiders returned home without success, the warriors would " 'cast their robes'...and vow to kill the first person they meet, provided he be not of their own nation." This custom explains many incidents that otherwise make little sense— particularly when the Indians visited their wrath on white traders passing through their country. Thus, the situation among the tribes of the upper Missouri region by 1800 was one of uneasy peace and bitter economic rivalry, punctuated by recurring raids and warfare.

As long as the Missouri Valley Indians dealt only with each other, matters remained relatively simple, but once white traders and trappers entered the scene, the situation became more complicated. Prior to the 1790s the Arikara had encountered few whites, but the next several decades brought increasing numbers of Euro-Americans into the region. The presence of white traders aggravated existing stresses and violence among the Indians by accident, and perhaps by design as well. For example, the incident in which Teton Sioux threatened Lewis and Clark during the summer of 1804 resulted directly from the efforts of those Indians to close the upper Missouri to white traders. The Sioux assumed that the explorers carried commercial goods and that the village people would get some of those trade items. In a series of stalling actions and near skirmishes they tried to prevent the whites from traveling further upstream. At the same time, the Arikara, Mandan, and Hidatsa lived in fear that their downriver rivals would restrict their sources of manufactured goods. Therefore, the village tribes did whatever they could to keep their trade channels open and reacted violently when they thought the whites had cooperated with their enemies or had pursued policies that might hurt them. These intertribal rivalries became so bitter that often the warriors' treatment of whites depended upon whether the traders had dealt with their Indian competitors.

Examples of this attitude abound. After Lewis and Clark ran the Sioux blockade of the Missouri in 1804, the Arikara welcomed them enthusiastically. The explorers spent five pleasant days among the villagers and reported that these people "were all friendly & Glad to See us." Nevertheless, the explorers' actions while they were with the Arikara triggered a major incident a few years later. Following their orders, Lewis and Clark persuaded Arikara leader Ankedoucharo to join a delegation of Missouri Valley chiefs going east to Washington, D.C. The Indians reached the capital in 1806, and while there, Ankedoucharo and several other chiefs died. It took until the spring of 1807 for the government to inform the uneasy villagers of their chief's death. The Indians had no way of knowing what had happened and suspected the whites of having killed their chief.

Angered by what they saw as American treachery, the villagers turned violently against the whites along the Missouri in 1807. Saint Louis trader Manuel Lisa encountered their hostility first in late summer, when several hundred armed warriors confronted his party near the villages. The Indians fired a few shots over the boats and ordered the whites ashore, but Lisa relieved the tension and escaped without a fight. At this point the United States government blundered onto the scene in its efforts to return the Mandan chief Shahaka to his North Dakota home. Shahaka had been among the group of Indian leaders taken east a year earlier, and in May 1807 Ensign Nathaniel Pryor started up the Missouri to escort him home. After an uneventful trip, the whites reached the Arikara towns in September, completely unaware of the Indians' anger or the earlier incident with Lisa's party. Pryor found the Arikara sullen and angry. At the upper village warriors attacked, and after a brief exchange of shots the unprepared whites retreated downstream. The government officials who dispatched the escort assumed that the Arikara had received news of their own chief's death peacefully, and they ignored or failed to realize that the Arikara and Mandan were at war with each other that summer.

It is not surprising that the Arikara met the whites with hostility. The government had only recently notified them of Ankedoucharo's death, and the Americans now arrived escorting an enemy chief past their towns. The Arikara's hostile response gave them an early reputation as a dangerous and unpredictable people. They were, after all, the only regional tribe to fight with United States troops up to that time. Their attack persuaded federal officials that they needed a strong force when they next tried to return the Mandan chief to his home village. Two years later an escort of militiamen under the command of Pierre Chouteau awed the Arikara enough that they apologized and promised to remain at peace.

Although no other major incidents occurred during the next few years, little happened to change American ideas about the Arikara either. Most traders treated them gingerly, remembering the attack on Pryor and his men. In 1811, however, the villagers appeared as protectors, not attackers, of two large expeditions of whites traveling through their country. That summer groups of traders led by Wilson P. Hunt and Manuel Lisa raced each other up the Missouri, both hoping to avoid the hostile Sioux. Neither succeeded, but both got past them without bloodshed. Less than a week later the traders met a combined Arikara, Mandan, and

Hidatsa war party of nearly three hundred men. At first the whites feared that the Indians would attack, but to their relief the warriors escorted them north toward their home villages.

Once again the bitter rivalries between the agricultural trading villagers and the Sioux hunters explain much of this apparent dramatic shift in behavior. For a change the Arikara and their northern neighbors had put aside their differences to form a defensive alliance against the Sioux. They welcomed the traders because the whites carried a crucial supply of manufactured trade items, especially weapons and ammunition. The Indians seemed apprehensive that without the safety their escort offered, the traders might be frightened enough to turn back downstream, as the Crooks and McClellan party had done just two years earlier after an encounter with the Sioux. Arikara actions in this incident reflected their determination to protect their economic status through continued trade with the whites. Their actions may also have indicated a growing Indian awareness of their dependence on the whites for the manufactured goods that had come to play such an important role in the upper Missouri trade patterns.

Bitter rivalries and divisions among the chiefs, however, continued to disrupt the Arikara towns and often kept visiting whites uncertain how to approach these people. In August 1812, for example, Manuel Lisa again had trouble with them. A few days before Lisa and his men reached the Arikara settlements, Le Gauche, "The Left-Handed," a hereditary chief, met them near the river. He visited for a short time—just long enough for Lisa to give him a few small gifts—before returning to the village. Lisa's presents to Le Gauche infuriated rival chiefs, and when the whites arrived at the village, they encountered silence and obvious anger. Lisa demanded to know what had happened. Once the disgruntled chiefs explained, he offered enough presents to soothe their hurt feelings. While this incident illustrated the continuing importance of internal village divisions in shaping Indian responses to outsiders, the Arikara's lack of violence in this case showed something else. By this time they seem to have realized that because they had few furs or hides to offer the whites, they had to remain on their best behavior in order to retain a local trading post. Without such a post, they had no reliable source of white goods.

During the war of 1812 and the confused years after that conflict, few Americans penetrated the upper Missouri region. In fact, before 1818 there seems to have been little regular commerce between the villagers and the Saint Louis merchants. From 1820 on, relations between Americans and the Arikara deteriorated steadily. Time and lack of documentation shroud many of the circumstances, and Indian motivations during that era must remain uncertain. Nevertheless, some patterns continued. By 1820 the Saint Louis traders had moved north to the Big Bend of the Missouri, where they had established a trading post among the Sioux, about 150 miles south of the Arikara towns. From that location the whites provided arms, munitions, and other trade items to the hunting bands of the region. The Arikara responded to the new trading activity with violence. In 1820 a large war party attacked and robbed two trading posts along the Missouri. Here one must assume that the villagers struck the whites out of frustration and jealousy. They had no dependable source of manufactured goods, while their Sioux enemies had several.

By the early 1820s even the most obtuse company trader should have been able to discern the relationships among the Arikara, their Indian competitors, and the white traders. The villagers' actions toward the Americans varied from vicious attacks, through strained relations, to enthusiastic friendship, depending on the internal social pressures on the tribe and the success or failure of their dealings with the Sioux. Instead of acknowledging these pressures, the traders seemed both uninformed and uncaring. Either attitude seems strange because their livelihood and their lives depended upon their ability to understand the situation clearly. Without any firm basis for their picture of the Arikara, most traders seem to have accepted the negative descriptions current about these Indians. Certainly, inter-mittent violence by the tribesmen colored the whites' perceptions of them, but it seems likely that the negative reports of their customs and appearance fed the traders' fear and loathing of these people. Revulsion at their practice of incest and high incidence of venereal disease, grumbling about the expense of having to maintain an unprofitable trading post in their vicinity, and the confusion and violence resulting from their shattered village society all helped to persuade the traders that the Arikara were indeed troublesome and dangerous. Before the 1823 incidents they had acquired a reputation as the most unpredictable and hostile tribe along the Missouri.

It is only with this understanding of the Indian situation and actions that the Arikara War of 1823 can be understood. The local, or short-range, causes of that conflict began in 1822, when William Ashley and Andrew Henry led a group of white trappers into the northern Rocky Mountains. There they went into direct competition with both Indian trappers and traders, a move guaranteed to disrupt earlier patterns of Indian trade. The logical result would be that white traders and trappers would supplant Indians in those activities. In the fall of 1822, however, that possibility remained in the future. Ashley's expedition stopped at the Arikara villages in early September to trade for horses. The chiefs welcomed the white men and probably made their usual request—that a trading post be established for them. Ashley, of course, had little interest in beginning an unprofitable trading post, for he planned to avoid stationary trading facilities and, by bringing his men directly to the mountains, to bypass Indian hunters altogether. Nevertheless, as part of his effort to tell the Missouri Valley tribes whatever he "thought most likely to secure and continue their friendship," he promised to supply the goods they wanted from Saint Louis the next spring. Ashley failed to recognize the significance of his promise to the village leaders and would pay dearly for breaking it. When no trader moved into their vicinity the next year, the Arikara must have realized that the whites had not meant what they said.

Had that been the only issue between the village chiefs and Ashley, the 1823 violence might have been avoided. Other problems existed, however. A major cause for Arikara hostility in the summer of 1823 grew out of an incident with some Missouri Fur Company employees. In March of that year a group of Arikara hunters had met some of these traders riding near Cedar Fort, a trading post established for the Sioux near the Big Bend of the Missouri. The traders were carrying hides to the nearby post, and the Arikara demanded that the whites surrender the goods to them, but the traders refused. Outraged, the Arikara robbed and beat them. Their anger grew out of seeing the traders helping the hated Sioux rather than from any general antiwhite feelings. The assault may also have resulted from Arikara frustration over their continuing inability to persuade the whites to keep a permanent trading post open near their villages, an ongoing source of friction between the Arikara and Saint Louis merchants.

Only a few days after the fight with the traders another and larger party of Arikara unsuccessfully attacked Cedar Fort, the Missouri Fur Company post. This time two of the Indians died and several others were wounded. One of those killed was the son of Grey Eyes, a prominent Arikara chief. Reports of the incident indicated that the Indians' failure to defeat the traders and plunder their goods had infuriated and humiliated the warriors and that they were not likely to be discriminating in their vengeance against whites. Unfortunately for Ashley's men, they ventured up the Missouri just in time to bear the brunt of this anger and frustration.

Ashley's actions toward the villagers almost certainly played some part in bringing about the Indian attack as well. As mentioned earlier, he had, in 1822, pledged to give the Arikara what they wanted most from the whites—undoubtedly a resident trader and thus a dependable supply of manufactured goods. Clearly he had little intention of keeping his promise. At the same time, he had tried to assure them that his own trappers posed no competitive threat to their efforts as Indian traders. The mountain men would gather and transport the furs themselves, but because the villagers usually traded buffalo hides rather than the pelts of smaller, fur-bearing animals, he hoped that no problems would result.

Before the ninety trappers and boatmen reached the Arikara towns in late May of 1823, Ashley had learned of the Indians' attack on Cedar Fort, and he reported taking "all the precaution in my power for some days before I reached their towns." Once there he anchored the keelboats in midstream and rowed ashore in a small skiff to meet Indian leaders and get their assurances of peaceful trade. Dissension between the two villages and among Arikara leaders was apparent as the village leaders came down to the shore, for they agreed to talk only "after a long consultation among themselves." The trader invited two chiefs, Little Soldier and Grey Eyes, aboard his skiff, and, to his surprise, the latter agreed. Grey Eyes was reputed to be the most antiwhite of the Arikara leaders and had also lost a son in the abortive raid at Cedar Fort that spring. His cooperation calmed Ashley's fears somewhat. The Indian leaders returned to their villages, and later that evening Grey Eyes reported that the Indians would be ready to open trade in the morning.

On 31 May the barter began, with the Indians bringing horses and buffalo robes to exchange for guns, ammunition, and other trade items. Business moved slowly, and when the whites had nineteen of the forty horses they needed, a dispute arose. Some Indians objected to the number and kinds of guns and the limited amount of powder the whites displayed. It is unclear whether they thought that Ashley's party offered too little for the horses or whether the Arikara merely wanted more guns and powder to use in their own trade with the plains tribes. In either case barter ceased for the day, and Ashley decided to take the animals they had already acquired and leave the next morning. Bad weather prevented this plan, and the mountain men had little choice but to remain. They could not move upstream against the strong wind and current, and to retreat downstream would only postpone the need to pass the villages. While they waited for the storm to pass, Chief Bear of the upper village invited Ashley to his lodge. The Indians assured the visitors of their friendship, and Little Soldier even warned of a possible attack by other elements in the tribe. His warning proved to be correct. At sunrise on 2 June a hail of arrows and musket balls drove the trappers back downstream.

Clearly, divided leadership and conflicting desires within the Indian towns contributed to the attack. By this time no formal Arikara tribe existed. The villages consisted of survivors of many earlier communities, and the Indians had never managed to restructure their society so that it functioned in an integrated manner. Ashley and his party noted confusion among the Indians over whether to trade or fight, but the traders seemed ignorant of how splintered Arikara society had become or how much danger this represented for them. The chiefs Grey Eyes, Little Soldier, and Bear all reacted differently to the whites' presence. The first was friendly and then became hostile. The second was aloof but later warned of danger, while the third remained friendly throughout the visit. The attitude of each town toward its guests was also different. The murder of one of Ashley's men took place in the lower village, and it was from there that Grey Eyes and his followers launched their dawn attack on the trappers. In the upper village, however, Bear and his followers vehemently denied responsibility for the fighting. Later that summer Colonel Leavenworth reported that "the people of the upper village would not give up their horses to pay for the mischief which the Chief Grey Eyes of the lower village had done."

The Leavenworth Expedition later in the summer failed to defeat the Arikara, but it ushered in a period of difficulty for the Indians. Once the invading white army left, the bands separated. Some fled north up the Missouri. A few people remained near the now burned villages and gradually resettled there. Others moved south and west into Nebraska to live with the Pawnee for a time. One band even traveled to eastern Wyoming. In 1837, after more than a decade, the bands reunited on the Missouri, just in time to be further decimated by the smallpox epidemic that swept up the valley that summer. Thus, these people, who had survived continuing warfare with Indian neighbors and sporadic fighting with the whites, succumbed instead to disease.

Many accounts of their role in the early history of South Dakota and the fur trade stress the Arikara's treacherous nature and the danger they posed to peacefully inclined traders. Certainly they killed and robbed enough white trappers and traders along the Missouri and on the nearby plains during the first third of the nineteenth century to deserve the negative reputation they acquired among whites. Yet, except for the two famous attacks—the first against Ensign Pryor in 1807 and the second against Ashley's men in 1823—their record appears to be little more violent or unpredictable than that of the Pawnee, Sioux, or Blackfeet during the same decades. In the Arikara's case, a bitter newspaper war of charges and countercharges between Henry Leavenworth and Joshua Pilcher, growing out of the 1823 campaign, helped spread the denunciations of the tribe. In the 1830s travelers, artists, and traders continued to add to the list of negative images fastened on the Arikara.

When all is said and done, however, the Arikara appear to have had some clear motivations for their actions. They remained friendly and at peace as long as the whites traded fairly and until they finally perceived the fur companies to be a major threat to their own economic well-being. They responded violently when whites aided their enemies, either their sometimes competitors the Mandans or their bitter foes the Sioux. The villagers assumed that it hurt them when the whites traded with their enemies. It is not surprising, then, that white traders were often in danger of retaliation. The Arikara strove repeatedly to keep a resident trader at or near their villages. When whites promised to locate a trader or post in their vicinity and then failed to do so, the Indians interpreted this failure as an unfriendly act and sometimes responded violently. It is also possible, of course, that certain Ariakara chiefs used the divisions and confusions within their society for selfish purposes, or even that evil men fomented trouble for narrow local reasons. Whether this happened or not, the Arikara War of 1823 was not unique. It resembled other Indian wars and incidents in many ways. It was unplanned, unnecessary, and a disaster for the tribal people. There were no heroes, stirring slogans, or major accomplishments. Instead, the survivors of a once powerful tribe struck out at their perceived enemies and suffered adverse consequences. Their actions, whether we of the modern world believe them to be rational or not, made at least some sense to them at the time. In the long run, the white man's diseases, not his guns, resolved the issue. The survivors of the smallpox epidemic of 1837 eventually settled among the Mandan and Hidatsa in North Dakota, where most of their descendants remain today.

12

NATIVE AMERICANS IN THE FUR TRADE AND WILDLIFE DEPLETION

JEANNE KAY

Increasingly students of Native American history have become interested in the relationships between tribal people and the physical environment. Popular thought depicts the Indians as the first environmentalists, and considerable evidence exists that shows how much care the tribes exercised when they used the riches of their physical surroundings. Nevertheless, Native American hunting and agriculture certainly had a direct and often major impact on the environment. Scholars now consider many aboriginal practices as examples of good resource management. The fur trade and its obvious destruction of wildlife stands as an obvious exception. Ethnologists, historians, and geographers have all shown how Indian hunting and trapping brought great destruction to many kinds of animals in North America. The obvious question that needs to be asked is: "Why were the tribal people so careless about wildlife while they seemed to use their other natural resources with such care?" In this discussion the author deals with that issue by examining the Menominee and Winnebago hunting and fur-gathering activities in central Wisconsin in the years 1620–1836. During that time the two tribes ranged over much of the area virtually uncontested, and a clear record of their annual movements and harvests of furs is available. The author's discussion shows that during those two centuries the fur trade caused less depletion of wildlife than has been assumed. It also explains how and why the hunters took pelts for the fur trade despite their reverence for nature and the power of the animal spirits.

Jeanne Kay is a professor of geography at the University of Nebraska.

Native Americans are generally acknowledged as the New World's first and foremost environmentalists. Native American religions stress that people are coequal

Source: Jeanne Kay, "Native Americans in the Fur Trade and Wildlife Depletion," *Environmental Review*, 9 (Summer 1985). Reprinted with permission from *Environmental Review* 9:2: 118-130, (Summer 1985). © Copyright 1985, The American Society for Environmental History.

with nature, descendants of "Grandmother Earth." How then, could some of them have depleted wildlife for the fur trade, as occurred in the eastern United States and Canada by the mid 19th century? The most comprehensive discussion of that question published to date is Calvin Martin's *Keepers of the Game*. Martin proposed that Indians believed their catastrophic post contact epidemics were caused by wildlife diseases, which together with a Europeanization of their values, shattered their protohistoric deferential relationships with wildlife spirits. However, various authors subsequently have criticized Martin's interpretations as unsubstantiated and have advanced their own solutions to the question, focusing primarily on the political and economic advantages of the fur trade to Native Americans.

This paper examines Native Americans (predominantly Menominee and Winnebago) involved in the fur trade of Green Bay, Wisconsin before European-American settlement (ca. 1620–1836,) when Indians were almost the sole hunters and trappers in the region. By investigating fur trade ecology, economics, and ideology, the paper attempts to explain why they depleted wildlife populations.

Ecological analysis suggests that the whole notion of fur trade-related wildlife depletion itself is only partly accurate. Several intensively trapped species were not endangered by the time that white settlers and Indian removals ended the old fur trade era. Nor were all areas heavily trapped. Lower inherent wildlife productivity, remoteness, or intertribal conflicts made extensive areas unattractive hunting destinations.

The economic explanation focuses on exchange rates between furs and trade goods. European trade goods eventually replaced a variety of Native products in the Indians' material culture. Yet the trade goods were expensive, and cost many more furs as trading units than would have been required to make comparable Native items.

Beliefs also played a part. Concomitant with Indian reverence for wildlife spirits were attitudes, prayers, and ceremonies which permitted taking wildlife pelts for the fur trade with no necessary change in ideology. These beliefs did not need to change dramatically with European intrusion. Rather they provided a latent cultural background within which wildlife depletion could occur.

Exchanges of furs for French goods probably took place in eastern Wisconsin between Ottawa middlemen and the indigenous Winnebago and Menominee by the 1620s. Beginning in 1640 the Iroquois Wars forced the Ottawa, Sauk, Fox (Mesquakie), Potawatomi, Miami, Kickapoo, Mascoutens, and several additional tribes from the eastern Great Lakes into Wisconsin. Control by Native middlemen over the fur trade declined after 1660 with the establishment of a French post at nearby Mackinac and the incursion of French traders into the region. The site of the modern city of Green Bay was an important trading location by 1670 because of its access to large Indian populations and to the interior via the Fox and Wisconsin river systems.

In 1717 the French built Fort La Baye at the mouth of the Fox River, where it served as a military and trading post until the British conquest in 1760. After that date several French families established La Baye as a permanent fur trade community. These families and several British traders who followed conducted the trade under a variety of flexible arrangements until 1815. The Green Bay trading area reached its maximum extent during this period of British rule, although its boundaries overlapped considerably with those of trading posts on Lake Superior and the upper Mississippi. Traders who resided in Green Bay traded and supplied Indians as far east as western Michigan and as far west as the Missouri.

American control over the region following the War of 1812 brought the Green Bay trading families into conflict with Astor's American Fur Company. For the supposed mutual benefit of Astor and the leading Green Bay traders, Astor's Mackinac agent organized them under a series of subsidiary partnerships as the Green Bay Company, or Green Bay Outfit, beginning in 1821. Discriminatory management by the American Fur Company plus increasing competition from independent American traders financially debilitated the resident French and British trading families, although they remained in the fur trade past the establishment of Wisconsin Territory in 1836.

During the fur trade period, the Menominee and Winnebago remained in eastern and central Wisconsin and thus became the principal trappers for the Green Bay trade. Of the immigrant tribes, the Sauk and Fox made a series of moves south and west, remaining within the Green Bay sphere until the early 19th century. The other tribes moved east of Lake Michigan in the 18th century. However, Chippewa (Ojibwa) from the Upper Peninsula migrated into the northern and eastern fringes of the area, usually sharing Menominee lands.

Lands west of Lake Michigan were divided between dense mixed coniferous and hardwood forests to the north and east and prairie and savannalike "oak openings" to the south and west. Bison from the prairies and oak openings and beaver from the numerous lakes and streams supported the Green Bay trade in the 17th century. As these wildlife populations declined, the fur trade diversified in the 18th century, taking increasing numbers of bear, elk, deer, raccoon, and fine furbearers. By the 1820s muskrat, deer, and marten were the mainstays of the Green Bay trade. Throughout its history the Green Bay trade was a productive one, although much of its success before American Fur Company control lay in its ability to exploit the rich Mississippi Valley, rather than the forests near Green Bay.

A paper which proposes to explain why Indian hunters and trappers depleted their resource might begin by questioning its initial premise. Did fur trade–related wildlife reductions in fact occur in the study area? Results of this inquiry suggest that the issue of declining wildlife numbers has been exaggerated. There seems little question that some species did drastically decline in number during the fur trade period. There is no way to determine actual wildlife populations before 1836, but tracing wildlife descriptions and fur traders' business records over time permits some general conclusions about population trends. Schorger and Kay determined that bison were probably extinct in eastern Wisconsin by 1700 and throughout the state by 1832. Elk probably disappeared from the Fox River Valley by the early 18th century and from southern Wisconsin by the late 18th century. They continued to be abundant in the Chippewa Valley, a tributary of the Mississippi, through 1836. Beaver were overharvested in eastern Wisconsin by 1740 and throughout the state by 1790. They were extinct in southern Wisconsin by 1825. However, moderate numbers of beaver continued to be trapped in northern Wisconsin and Michigan's Upper Peninsula in the 1820s and '30s. Evidence for white-tailed deer, black bear, and otter is problematic, but these species possibly declined in numbers by 1820.

However, other wildlife species important for the fur trade, particularly marten and muskrat, remained abundant in the Green Bay region. By twentieth-century standards, they were probably lightly exploited. Lists of fur returns in the resident French and British Green Bay traders' account books were examined. They include comprehensive records beginning in 1803 through the end of the study period in 1836. They show no declines in numbers of pelts for marten and muskrat, two economically important species. Other species recorded in the account books, harvested in low numbers without evidence of decline, are fisher, mink, lynx, bobcat, red fox, and wolf. Raccoon numbers varied widely over the 34-year record, probably reflecting the normally erratic fluctuations in the species' population. Low numbers of the other species could reflect depletion, but given their lack of negative trends, they probably indicate only their typically low populations in nature (fisher, lynx) or low economic value (mink, wolf).

Wildlife population trends inferred from the Green Bay traders' accounts must be further interpreted in view of influences other than overharvesting. One of the most significant of these was the increasing constriction of the Green Bay trading area over time, particularly after 1815. An American Fur Company order in 1824 cost the Green Bay Company partners much of the territory they had exploited before they joined the American Fur Company, including the productive wildlife habitat of the upper Mississippi Valley.

Other records suggest that Native Americans simply devoted less effort to hunting and trapping for the fur trade after 1820. Those with villages near the Great Lakes apparently fished for winter subsistence. Traders on the upper Fox River seldom mentioned wildlife depletion as the cause of their poor returns. Instead, they continually complained about competition from new traders and the Indians' diminished hunting activity. The resident traders noted good marten and muskrat seasons when the Indians fasted in their encampments or departed for other areas. Government annuity payments provided an alternative to fur trade income for 19th-century bands who ceded their lands, and the timing of payments often precluded the fall hunts. Therefore, an apparent decline in returns of pelts during the years of record (1803-37) could reflect factors other than wildlife depletion, while the stable or even increasing numbers for some species as depicted in the fur returns cast further doubt on supposed downward trends.

Some biological facts may help distinguish between those species which declined and those which did not. Bison, elk, deer, and bear are large, highly desirable meat sources, providing Indians with the greatest yield for their hunting effort. These species' ability to withstand hunting pressure was diminished by their comparatively low reproductive potential. In contrast, marten and muskrat are small animals capable of producing multiple offspring each year and were not favored food sources. Beaver was both a valuable furbearer and a food source; its visible dams and lodges made it an easy mark. Otter, too, had a costly and therefore desirable pelt.

Wildlife depletion, moreover, was not a spatially homogenous phenomenon. Certain areas within the Green Bay region apparently were lightly exploited. The most prominent of these was the Sioux-Chippewa war zone, which extended from the lower Chippewa Valley in Wisconsin westward into Minnesota. This contained the best wildlife habitat in the region, and it sparked intense competition between the two tribes. Neither could intensively exploit the zone for fear of attack from the other. However, it was occasionally hunted by neutral tribes, especially the Menominee. In contrast, low wildlife productivity would seem to explain why a large tract within the dense mixed forest (centered in Wisconsin's Taylor, Rusk, and Price counties) was little exploited. Although sometimes hunted by Chippewa, it is void of specific historical records of hunting grounds, trading posts, or other economic activities, although there are many records of such features elsewhere in the Green Bay region. Most of the site-specific indications of general game scarcity come from places which originally were mediocre wildlife habitat or from along the well-traveled, long-exploited routes. Remote areas were probably less intensively exploited because the Indians confined their winter hunting grounds to sites within a reasonable distance of trading posts.

Clayton and Gilman, examining nearby regions of the Middle West, also concluded that the old fur trade did not decline because of wildlife depletion. Tracing fur returns over many years, they noted that numbers of pelts recorded actually increased after the demise of the traditional fur trade companies. They concluded that the thousands of part-time white trappers, such as farmers trapping for "egg money," occupied the land both more intensively and extensively than did the prereservation Native Americans. Not only were there less than 2,000 Indian hunters in the Green Bay trade by 1830, but they tended to concentrate within certain favored hunting grounds. Wisconsin pioneer memoirs of game abundance at other sites throughout the state support Clayton and Gilman's conclusions.

Schorger's tabulations of wildlife sightings from published accounts both during and after Wisconsin's fur trade era indicate that, in fact, most real wildlife extinctions in the state occurred long after the fur trade period. The evidence is convincing only for state wide extinction of bison and regional extinction of elk and beaver in Wisconsin before 1836. Most real extinctions occurred after 1870 through market hunting and habitat disruption. Extirpated species included timber wolf, marten, fisher, cougar, wolverine, elk, moose, and woodland caribou, while lynx and badger became extremely rare. Reintroductions of some of these species have since been attempted by the state Department of Natural Resources.

Native Americans in the Green Bay region, with the exception of the Sioux on the western perimeter, were apparently eager to adopt European goods. Their perception of the utility of metal utensils and woolen cloth was probably the principal motive, although trade goods were also important in traditional gift-giving.

Quimby's study in historical archaeology in the Great Lakes region showed that trade goods replaced Native manufactures in Wisconsin tribes' material culture by 1760. Most tribes eagerly sought trade goods before that date, and archaeological sites show accumulations of trade goods from the time of initial European contact. Following Quimby's assertion, the mathematics which explain overhunting and trapping are fairly simple. Many trade goods had Native counterparts which required few or no wildlife products for their manufacture. Hatchets, kettles, weapons, and ammunition are examples. Some Indian manufactures which trade goods replaced, such as blankets and clothing, were made largely or entirely of wildlife products. However, the number of animals required to make Native items were usually much less than the number of pelts needed as exchange units in order to purchase equivalent European substitutes. Few records of Green Bay traders' transactions with individual Indians have survived, but they illustrate the point. In 1806, for example, an Indian's jacket cost fifteen muskrats. In 1828 a French trader charged for a yard of trade cloth the equivalent of twenty-four muskrats or eight to ten shaved deer skins. The few extant accounts of traders' daily transactions with the Menominee and Winnebago show that the most frequent purchases were for ammunition, while blankets and kettles were the most expensive purchases.

Alcohol may have been a trade good which especially contributed to wildlife depletion. Indians like the Sioux, who were not much interested in the fur trade, could be induced to participate only by exchanges and gifts of alcohol. Also, a blanket or kettle could easily last all year, but a hunter who wanted alcohol had to trade a steady supply of furs to meet his demand. Tragically, alcohol contributed to the decline of the Green Bay trade by the 1820s, when it was used so excessively in the increasing competition between traders that serious declines in Indian health and economic independence resulted.

The preceding comparisons do not indicate whether the increased hunting pressure on wildlife needed to procure European goods was sufficient to cause wildlife depletion. They do indicate an economic framework within which over-harvesting could occur. Even given a Native American belief in taking from nature only enough game to supply basic needs, the "need" for game to supply basic clothing or household utensils was simply greater within the fur trade economy and material culture.

The comments of Thomas Forsyth, trader and Rock Island Indian Agent, followed by those of Lewis Cass, governor of Michigan Territory, illustrate these points:

> The Indians admire our manufactories but more particularly guns and gunpowder, but many old Indians say they were more happy before they knew the use of firearms, because, they then could kill as much game as they wanted, not being then compelled to destroy game to purchase our merchandise as they are now obliged to do.

> The rifle was found a more efficient instrument than the bow and arrow; blankets were more comfortable than buffalo robes; and cloth, than dressed skins. The exchange was altogether unfavorable to them. The goods they received were dear, and the peltry they furnished was cheap. A greater number of animals was necessary for the support of each family, and increased exertion was required to procure them. We need not pursue this subject further. It is easy to see the consequences both to the Indians and their game.

This economic entanglement should, however, be distinguished from mere technological change. Although Indian adoption of European hunting and trapping technology has sometimes been blamed for wildlife depletion, the elimination of beaver and bison in the area predated widespread adoption of steel traps and rifles.

The heart of the question about Native American overhunting for the fur trade lies in the influence of their environmental beliefs. Societies' environmental attitudes are widely used by historians to predict or explain the consequences of their environmental activities, and Native Americans are frequently cited for their profoundly religious attitudes toward nature. Elsewhere I have argued that the ecological and cultural issues are so complex and little integrated for most societies that environmental ideology as an explanation of environmental impact is best viewed as a testable hypothesis, rather than as an axiom. This section argues that no radical change of Indian environmental ethics within the Green Bay region need be postulated to explain wildlife depletion. The documents do not clearly demonstrate a major shift in environmental beliefs, as Martin postulated in *Keepers of the Game*, although the force of some older environmental beliefs and rituals probably dwindled by 1836. Furthermore, the tribes' environmental ethos operated within a context of a whole variety of Native American beliefs and attitudes, some of which permitted excessive hunting and trapping.

One Native American belief consistent with wildlife depletion is that people are entitled to take from nature what they need to survive, though only what they need. As demonstrated above, the "need" for furs and skins increased under the fur trade material culture, creating a condition in which game depletion could occur without a change in the basic belief.

Moreover, the proscription against wasting game apparently did not motivate all the region's Indians all of the time. Some killed large numbers of deer during winters when an icy crust formed on the snow and the deer floundered. A few records indicate the Indian practice of "driving away game" to deprive one's enemies. A trader who accompanied the eastern Sioux on a summer deer hunt in 1812 recounted: "The meat of the slaughtered deer was very little cared for; I do not believe that more than one in ten was taken from the spot where they were skinned." An expedition geologist blamed Indian reactions to white settlers' encroachment for Indian hunting beyond subsistence needs.

Indians of the Green Bay region revered wildlife spirits, particularly of the black bear. However, this spiritual relationship between Indian and wildlife did not function within current European-American concepts of game management. Indians believed sustained success in hunting, for example, depended upon dreaming of desired game, of thanking and avoiding offense to the spirits of animals taken. Accordingly, killing large numbers of bears was consistent with venerating the species, because celebration of a bear's death with prayers, offerings, and feasts propitiated its spirit. Less elaborate thanksgiving offered to appease other animal spirits permitted taking many animals without violating spiritual harmony with nature.

The most important ideological issue, however, may be how Native societies reacted to acknowledged resource deterioration. The "balanace of nature" is dynamic, and any society, no matter how reverent toward the environment, could overstep its ecological bounds under a new economic system. When Wisconsin Indians noted declining numbers of game, did professed beliefs facilitate reversals in their environmental impact or have sufficient flexibility to change? The answer to that question appears to be negative. Indian initiative in events like the Shawnee Prophet's following or the Black Hawk War notwithstanding, the predominant response of the Green Bay Native Americans to game reductions apparently was fatalism. The Great Spirit had given Indians wildlife for their use, and when it was used up, they were prepared to fast or to find other means of subsistence. Fur traders' correspondence after 1820 shows that increasing numbers of Native Americans did not complete their winter hunts but simply fasted in their winter encampments or remained along Lake Michigan to fish from the ice.

Few records survive of deliberate wildlife preservation techniques, in the current European-American sense, by the Green Bay area Indians. Native Americans certainly knew and practiced ancient methods of increasing their game supply, such as burning vegetation to provide better habitat for grazing and browsing animals. Baron Lahontan, "discoverer" of fictitious lands, claimed that the region's Indians always left a few beaver to reproduce, a statement corroborated by early French writers for other areas. Such strategies as they may have practiced were apparently not in force by the 1820s, when geologist Keating stated:

> They appear, since their intercourse with white men, to have lost the sagacious foresight which previously distinguished them. It was usual with them, formerly, to avoid killing the deer during the rutting season; the does that were with young were in like manner always spared, except in cases of urgency; and the young fawns were not wantonly destroyed: but at present, the Indian seems to consider himself as a stranger in the land which his fathers held as their own; he sees his property daily exposed to encroachments of white men, and therefore hunts down indiscriminately every animal that he meets with; being doubtful whether he will be permitted to reap, the ensuing year, the fruits of his foresight during the present...

Fur traders' account books from that time further show Indian hunting and trapping practices at variance with European-American wildlife management. Large numbers of does, and juveniles of most species, particularly of bears and muskrats, appear in lists of fur returns. With old conservation attitudes less frequently observed, tribes of the region did not indicate that game declines triggered new or extra conservation techniques. In that respect, the Indians resembled the white settlers who followed.

The Indian beliefs just described were not responsible for game population declines, but rather they provided an ideological context or framework within which the declines could occur. The fatalistic view toward game depletion further precluded changes in either beliefs or hunting and trapping practices necessary to reverse the resource deterioration. The Indians' beliefs in taking from nature only necessities, of propitiating wildlife spirits, and of facing adversity fatalistically are entirely consistent with Native American reverence toward nature and environmental religion.

Why did the Indians deplete their game? Unfortunately there are too many holes in the network of necessary data to answer definitively. However, this paper suggests that the case for wildlife population declines in the Green Bay trade has been overstated by historians who erroneously viewed financial losses or poor returns by traditional fur trade companies as the result of overhunting and trapping. Indians in the Green Bay fur trade were too few, and the areas and species they intensively exploited were too restricted, for their impact to have approximated that of subsequent white settlers. To the extent that game diminished before 1836, the mathematics of fur trade exchanges and the permissive operation of certain beliefs were the principal factors. While the question of depletion must be answered individually for many regions before a definitive answer emerges, the Green Bay study can serve as an interpretation to be tested in other areas.

This paper is not an attempt to discredit Native American environmental beliefs. Religions are important objects of study and observance in their own right. The argument that favorable environmental attitudes explain enivronmental protection, however, does appear to have limited utility in the case of Native Americans in the fur trade. Additional ecological, economic, and ideological factors also clearly influenced the outcome. Current interpretations of Indian environmental actions in the fur trade often rely less on historical facts than on scholars' attempts to realign Native American ecology to fit the paradigm of modern environmentalism. Native American beliefs about nature developed long ago within a mystical oral lore, without reference to modern wildlife management or the current environmental movement. Given the profoundly personal spiritual basis of Indian religions, they should not be expected to correspond to scientifically rooted European-American environmentalism in all particulars.

Some scholars have argued, in support of a simple causal relationship between environmental beliefs and impacts, that Indians participated in the fur trade only as unwilling victims of European-American economics. The thrust of the argument is that Native American environmentalism was tarnished by Europeanization. That rationale, however, further denies the efficacy of Native environmental beliefs in wildlife preservation. It essentially implies that Indian environmental beliefs, though beneficent, were not effective in the face of change, and that Indians were poorer judges than historians about the products best suited to their needs.

The conclusion that environmental religions are uncertain predictors of Native American societies, impacts on game cannot rob Native worldviews of their wisdom. It can suggest that the underlying relationships between societies' ecological beliefs and impacts are yet to be determined.

13

CHEROKEE WOMEN AND THE TRAIL OF TEARS

THEDA PERDUE

Power relationships within traditional tribal societies differed widely from those accepted by Anglo-Americans during the eighteenth and nineteenth centuries. This selection shows that Cherokee culture was both matrilineal and matrilocal—that is, property, inheritance, and place of homesite all depended on the female side of the family. Under those circumstances, Perdue claims Cherokee women enjoyed substantial personal freedom as well as exercising some economic and political power. She posits a sort of aboriginal golden age in which women had considerable power because they held the land, raised the crops, and controlled all or most of the family food supply. Although some feminist scholars disagree with the notion of gender equality in the dim past, this reading tends to support that view. Perdue sees the situation as changing because of increasing contacts with the English and Americans on the frontier. She traces a gradual shift in which tribal people came to accept or have forced upon them Anglo-American ideas about gender divisions of labor and power. She sees this as a gradual decline of the authority of Indian women, in particular by the early nineteenth century, and gives examples of how the process worked. In her view the government officials, teachers, and missionaries did the most to upset traditional Cherokee sex roles, and by the removal era of the 1830s tribal leaders had adopted nontribal ideas about the role of women in their society. The removal experience brought the process to a close because frustration and family violence ended any significant authority the women may have exercised previously.

Theda Perdue is a professor of history at the University of Kentucky.

The Treaty of New Echota by which the Cherokee Nation relinquished its territory in the Southeast was signed by men. Women were present at the rump council that negotiated the treaty, but they did not participate in the proceedings. They may

Source: Theda Perdue, "Cherokee Women and the Trail of Tears," *Journal of Women's History*, 1 (1989), pp. 14–30. Reprinted with permission from the *Journal of Women's History*.

have met in their own council—precedents for women's councils exist—but if they did, no record remains. Instead, they probably cooked meals and cared for children while their husbands discussed treaty terms with the United States commissioner. The failure of women to join in the negotiation and signing of the Treaty of New Echota does not necessarily mean that women were not interested in the disposition of tribal land, but it does indicate that the role of women had changed dramatically in the preceding century.

Traditionally women had a voice in Cherokee government. They spoke freely in council, and the War Woman (or Beloved Woman) decided the fate of captives. As late as 1787 a Cherokee woman wrote Benjamin Franklin that she had delivered an address to her people urging them to maintain peace with the new American nation. She had filled the peace pipe for the warriors, and she enclosed some of the same tobacco for the United States Congress in order to unite symbolically her people and his in peace. She continued:

> I am in hopes that if you Rightly consider that woman is the mother of All—and the Woman does not pull Children out of Trees or Stumps nor out of old Logs, but out of their Bodies, so that they ought to mind what a woman says.

The political influence of women, therefore, rested at least in part on their maternal biological role in procreation and their maternal role in Cherokee society, which assumed particular importance in the Cherokee's matrilineal kinship system. In this way of reckoning kin, children belonged to the clan of their mother and their only relatives were those who could be traced through her.

The Cherokees were not only matrilineal, they also were matrilocal. That is, a man lived with his wife in a house which belonged to her, or perhaps more accurately, to her family. According to the naturalist William Bartram, "Marriage gives no right to the husband over the property of his wife; and when they part she keeps the children and property belonging to them." The "property" that women kept included agricultural produce—corn, squash, beans, sunflowers, and pumpkins—stored in the household's crib. Produce belonged to women because they were the principal farmers. This economic role was ritualized at the Green Corn Ceremony every summer when an old woman presented the new corn crop. Furthermore, eighteenth-century travelers and traders normally purchased corn from women instead of men, and in the 1750s the garrison at Fort Loudoun, in present-day eastern Tennessee, actually employed a female purchasing agent to procure corn. Similarly, the fields belonged to the women who tended them, or rather to the women's lineages. Bartram observed that their fields are divided by proper marks and their harvest is gathered separately." While the Cherokees technically held land in common and anyone could use unoccupied land, improved fields belonged to specific matrilineal households.

Perhaps this explains why women signed early deeds conveying land titles to the Proprietors of Carolina. Agents who made these transactions offered little explanation for the signatures of women on these documents. By the early twentieth century a historian speculated that they represented a "renunciation of dower," but it may have been that the women were simply parting with what was recognized as theirs, or they may have been representing their lineages in the negotiations.

As late as 1785 women still played some role in the negotiation of land transactions. Nancy Ward, the Beloved Woman of Chota, spoke to the treaty conference held at Hopewell, South Carolina to clarify and extend land cessions stemming from Cherokee support of the British in the American Revolution. She addressed the assembly as the "mother of warriors" and promoted a peaceful resolution to land disputes between the Cherokees and the United States. Under the terms of the Treaty of Hopewell, the Cherokees ceded large tracts of land south of the Cumberland River in Tennessee and Kentucky and west of the Blue Ridge Mountains in North Carolina. Nancy Ward and the other Cherokee delegates to the conference agreed to the cession not because they believed it to be just but because the United States dictated the terms of the treaty.

The conference at Hopewell was the last treaty negotiation in which women played an official role, and Nancy Ward's participation in that conference was somewhat anachronistic. In the eighteenth century the English as well as other Europeans had dealt politically and commercially with men since men were the hunters and warriors in Cherokee society and Europeans were interested primarily in military alliances and deerskins. As relations with the English grew increasingly important to tribal welfare, women became less significant in the Cherokee economy and government. Conditions in the Cherokee Nation following the American Revolution accelerated the trend. In their defeat the Cherokees had to cope with the destruction of villages, fields, corncribs, and orchards which had occurred during the war and the cession of hunting grounds which accompanied the peace. In desperation they turned to the United States government, which proposed to convert the Cherokees into replicas of white pioneer farmers in the anticipation that they would then cede additional territory (presumably hunting grounds they no longer needed). While the government's so-called "civilization" program brought some economic relief, it also helped produce a transformation of gender roles and social organization. The society envisioned for the Cherokees, one which government agents and Protestant missionaries zealously tried to implement, was one in which a man farmed and headed a household composed only of his wife and children. The men who gained power in eighteenth-century Cherokee society— hunters, warriors, and descendants of traders—took immediate advantage of this program in order to maintain their status in the face of a declining deerskin trade and pacification and then diverted their energy, ambition, and aggression into economic channels. As agriculture became more commercially viable, these men began to farm or to acquire African slaves to cultivate their fields for them. They also began to dominate Cherokee society, and by example and legislation they altered fundamental relationships.

In 1808 a Council of headmen (there is no evidence of women participating) from Cherokee towns established a national police force to safeguard a person's holdings during life and "to give protection to children as heirs to their father's property, and to the widow's share," thereby changing inheritance patterns and officially recognizing the patriarchal family as the norm. Two years later a council representing all seven matrilineal clans, but once again apparently including no women, abolished the practice of blood vengeance. This action ended one of the major functions of clans and shifted the responsibility for punishing wrongdoers to the national police force and tribal courts. Matrilineal kinship clearly did not have a place in the new Cherokee order.

We have no record of women objecting to such legislation. In fact, we know very little about most Cherokee women because written documents reflect the attitudes and concerns of a male Indian elite or of government agents and missionaries. The only women about whom we know very much are those who conformed to expectations. Nancy Ward, the Beloved Woman who favored peace with the United States, appears in the historical records while other less cooperative Beloved Women are merely unnamed, shadowy figures. Women such as Catherine Brown, a model of Christian virtue, gained the admiration of missionaries, and we have a memoir of Brown's life; other women who removed their children from mission schools incurred the missionaries' wrath, and they merit only brief mention in mission diaries. The comments of government agents usually focused on those native women who demostrated considerable industry by raising cotton and producing cloth (in this case, Indian men suffered by comparison), not those who grew corn in the matrilineage's fields. In addition to being biased and reflecting only one segment of the female population, the information from these sources is second-hand; rarely did Indian women, particularly traditionalists, speak for themselves.

The one subject on which women did speak on two occasions was land. In 1817 the United States sought a large cession of Cherokee territory and removal of those who lived on the land in question. A group of Indian women met in their own council, and thirteen of them signed a message which was delivered to the National Council. They advised the Council:

> The Cherokee ladys now being present at the meeting of the Chiefs and warriors in council have thought it their duties as mothers to address their beloved Chiefs and warriors now assembled.

> Our beloved children and head men of the Cherokee nation we address you warriors in council [.W]e have raised all of you on the land which we now have, which God gave us to inhabit and raise provisions [.W]e know that our country has once been extensive but by repeated sales has become circumscribed to a small tract and never have thought it our duty to interfere in the disposition of it till now, if a father or mother was to sell all their lands which they had to depend on [,] which their children had to raise their living on [,] which would be bad indeed and to be removed to another country [.W]e do not wish to go to an unknown country which we have understood some of our children wish to go over the Mississippi but this act of our children would be like destroying your mothers. Your mother and sisters ask and beg of you not to part with any more of our lands.

The next year, the National Council met again to discuss the possibility of allotting Cherokee land to individuals, an action the United States government encouraged as a preliminary step to removal. Once again Cherokee women reacted:

> We have heard with painful feelings that the bounds of the land we now possess are to be drawn into very narrow limits. The land was given to us by the Great

Spirit above as our common right, to raise our children upon, & to make support for our rising generations. We therefore humbly petition our beloved children, the head men and warriors, to hold out to the last in support of our common rights, as the Cherokee nation has been the first settlers of this land; we therefore claim the right of the soil. . . . We therefore unanimously join in our meeting to hold our country in common as hitherto.

Common ownership of land meant in theory that the United States government had to obtain cessions from recognized, elected Cherokee officials who represented the wishes of the people. Many whites favored allotment because private citizens then could obtain individually owned tracts of land through purchase, fraud, or seizure. Most Cherokees recognized this danger and objected to allotment for that reason. The women, however, had an additional incentive for opposing allotment. Under the laws of the states in which the Cherokees lived and of which they would become citizens if land were allotted, married women had few property rights. A married woman's property, even property she held prior to her marriage, belonged legally to her husband. Cherokee women and martilineal households would have ceased to be property owners.

The implications for women became apparent in the 1830s, when Georgia claimed its law was in effect in the Cherokee country. Conflicts over property arose because of uncertainty over which legal system prevailed. For example, a white man, James Vaught, married the Cherokee Catherine Gunter. She inherited several slaves from her father, and Vaught sold two of them to General Isaac Wellborn. His wife had not consented to the sale and so she reclaimed her property and took them with her when the family moved west. General Wellborn tried to seize the slaves just as they were about to embark, but a soldier, apparently recognizing her claim under Cherokee law, prevented him from doing so. After removal the General appealed to Principal Chief John Ross for aid in recovering the slaves, but Ross refused. He informed Wellborn: "By the laws of the Cherokee Nation, the property of husband and wife remain separate and apart and neither of these can sell or dispose of the property of the other." Had the Cherokees accepted allotment and come under Georgia law, Wellborn would have won.

The effects of the women's protests in 1817 and 1818 are difficult to determine. In 1817 the Cherokees ceded tracts of land in Georgia, Alabama, and Tennessee, and in 1819 they made an even larger cession. Nevertheless, they rejected individual allotments and strengthened restrictions on alienation of improvements. Furthermore, the Cherokee Nation gave notice that they would negotiate no additional cessions—a resolution so strongly supported that the United States ultimately had to turn to a small unauthorized faction in order to obtain the minority treaty of 1835.

The political organization which existed in the Cherokee Nation in 1817–18 had made it possible for women to voice their opinion. Traditionally, Cherokee towns were politically independent of one another, and each town governed itself through a council in which all adults could speak. In the eighteenth century, however, the Cherokees began centralizing their government in order to restrain bellicose warriors whose raids jeopardized the entire nation and to negotiate as a single unit with whites. Nevertheless, town councils remained important, and representatives of traditional towns formed the early National Council. This National Council resembled the town councils in that anyone could address the body. Although legislation passed in 1817 created an Executive Committee, power still rested with the Council which reviewed all Committee acts.

The protests of the women to the National Council in 1817 and 1818 were, however, the last time women presented a collective position to the Cherokee governing body. Structural changes in Cherokee government more narrowly defined participation in the National Council. In 1820 the Council provided that representatives be chosen from eight districts rather than from traditional towns, and in 1823 the Committee acquired a right of review over acts of the Council. The more formalized political organization made it less likely that a group could make its views known to the national government.

As the Cherokee government became more centralized, political and economic power rested increasingly in the hands of a few elite men who adopted the planter lifestyle of the white antebellum South. A significant part of the ideological basis for this lifestyle was the cult of domesticity in which the ideal woman confined herself to home and hearth while men contended with the corrupt world of government and business. The elite adopted the tenets of the cult of domesticity, particularly after 1817, when the number of Protestant missionaries, major proponents of this feminine ideal, increased significantly and their influence on Cherokee society broadened.

The extent to which a man's wife and daughters conformed to the idea quickly came to be one measure of his status. In 1818 Charles Hicks, who later served as Principal Chief, described the most prominent men in the Nation as "those who have for the last 10 or 20 years been pursuing agriculture & kept their women & children at home & in comfortable circumstances." Eight years later John Ridge, one of the first generation of Cherokees to have been educated from childhood in mission schools, discussed a Cherokee law which protected the property rights of a married woman and observed that "in many respects she has exclusive & distinct control over her own, particularly among the less civilized." The more "civilized" presumably left such matters to men. Then Ridge described suitable activities for women: "They sew, they weave, they spin, they cook our meals and act well the duties assigned them by Nature as mothers." Proper women did not enter business or politics.

Despite the attitudes of men such as Hicks and Ridge, women did in fact continue as heads of households and as businesswomen. In 1828 the *Cherokee Phoenix* published the obituary of Oo-dah-less, who had accumulated a sizeable estate through agriculture and commerce. She was "the support of a large family," and she bequeathed her property "to an only daughter and three grandchildren." Oo-dah-less was not unique. At least one third of the heads of household listed on the removal roll of 1835 were women. Most of these were not as prosperous as Oo-dah-less, but some were even more successful economically. Nineteen owned slaves (190 men were slaveholders), and two held over twenty slaves and operated substantial farms.

Nevertheless, these women had ceased to have a direct voice in Cherokee government. In 1826 the Council called a constitutional convention to draw up a governing document for the Nation. According to legislation which provided for election of delegates to the convention, "No person but a free male citizen who is full grown shall be entitled to vote." The convention met and drafted a constitution patterned after that of the United States. Not surprisingly, the constitution which male Cherokees ratified in 1827 restricted the franchise to "free male citizens" and stipulated that "no person shall be eligible to a seat in the General Council, but a free Cherokee male, who shall have attained the age of twenty-five." Unlike the United States Constitution, the Cherokee document clearly excluded women, perhaps as a precaution against women who might assert their traditional right to participate in politics instead of remaining in the domestic sphere.

The exclusion of women from politics certainly did not produce the removal crisis, but it did mean that a group traditionally opposed to land cession could no longer be heard on the issue. How women would have voted is also unclear. Certainly by 1835 many Cherokee women, particularly those educated in mission schools, believed that men were better suited to deal with political issues than women, and a number of women voluntarily enrolled their households to go west before the forcible removal of 1838–39. Even if women had united in active opposition to removal, it is unlikely that the United States and aggressive state governments would have paid any more attention to them than they did to the elected officials of the nation who opposed removal or the 15,000 Cherokees, including women (and perhaps children), who petitioned the United States Senate to reject the Treaty of New Echota. While Cherokee legislation may have made women powerless, federal authority rendered the whole Nation impotent.

In 1828 Georgia had extended state law over the Cherokee Nation and white intruders who invaded its territory, Georgia law prohibited Indians, both men and women, from testifying in court against white assailants, and so they simply had to endure attacks on person and property. Delegates from the Nation complained to Secretary of War John H. Eaton about the lawless behavior of white intruders:

> Too many there are who think it an act of trifling consequence to oust an Indian family from the quiet enjoyment of all the comforts of their own firesides, and to drive off before their faces the stock that gave nourishment to the children and support to the aged, and appropriate it to the satisfaction to avarice.

Elias Boudinot, editor of the bilingual *Cherokee Phoenix*, even accused the government of encouraging the intruders in order to force the Indians off their lands, and he published the following account:

> A few days since two of these white men came to a Cherokee house, for the purpose, they pretended, of buying provisions. There was no person about the house but one old woman of whom they inquired for some corn, beans &c. The woman told them she had nothing to sell. They then went off in the direction of the field belonging to this Cherokee family. They had not gone but a few minutes when the woman of the house saw a heavy smoke rising from that direction. She immediately hastened to the field and found the villains had set the woods on fire but a few rods from the fences, which she found already in a full blaze. There being a very heavy wind that day, the fire spread so fast, that her efforts to extinguish it proved utterly useless. The entire fence was therefore consumed in a

short time. It is said that during her efforts to save the fence the men who had done the mischief were within sight, and were laughing heartily at her!

The Georgia Guard, established by the state to enforce its law in the Cherokee country, offered no protection and, in fact, contributed to the lawlessness. The *Phoenix* printed the following notice under the title "Cherokee Women, Beware":

> It is said that the Georgia Guard have received orders, from the Governor we suppose, to inflict corporeal punishment on such females as shall hereafter be guilty of insulting them. We presume they are to be the judges of what constitutes *insult*.

Despite harassment from intruders and the Guard, most Cherokees had no intention of going west, and in the spring of 1838 they began to plant their crops as usual. Then United States soldiers arrived, began to round up the Cherokees, and imprisoned them in stockades in preparation for deportation. In 1932 Rebecca Neugin, who was nearly one hundred years old, shared her childhood memory and family tradition about removal with historian Grant Foreman:

> When the soldier came to our house my father wanted to fight, but my mother told him that the soldiers would kill him if he did and we surrendered without a fight. They drove us out of our house to join other prisoners in a stockade. After they took us away, my mother begged them to let her go back and get some bedding. So they let her go back and she brought what bedding and a few cooking utensils she could carry and had to leave behind all of our other household possessions.

Rebecca Neugin's family was relatively fortunate. In the process of capture, families were sometimes separated and sufficient food and clothing were often left behind. Over fifty years after removal, John G. Burnett, a soldier who served as an interpreter, reminisced:

> Men working in the fields were arrested and driven to stockades. Women were dragged from their homes by soldiers whose language they could not understand. Children were often separated from their parents and driven into the stockades with the sky for a blanket and the earth for a pillow.

Burnett recalled how one family was forced to leave the body of a child who had just died and how a distraught mother collapsed of heart failure as soldiers evicted her and her three children from their homes. After their capture, many Cherokees had to march miles over rugged mountain terrain to the stockades. Captain L. B. Webster wrote his wife about moving eight hundred Cherokees from North Carolina to the central depot in Tennessee: "We were eight days in making the journey (80 miles), and it was pitiful to behold the women & children, who suffered exceedingly—as they were all obliged to walk, with the exception of the sick."

Originally the government planned to deport all the Cherokees in the summer of 1838, but the mortality rate of the three parties that departed that summer led the commanding officer, General Winfield Scott, to agree to delay the major removal until fall. In the interval, the Cherokees remained in the stockades, where conditions were abysmal. Women in particular often became individual victims of their captors. The missionary Daniel Butrick recorded the following episode in his journal:

> The poor Cherokees are not only exposed to temporal evils, but also to every species of moral desolation. The other day a gentleman informed me that he saw six soldiers about two Cherokee women. The women stood by a tree, and the soldiers with a bottle of liquor were endeavoring to entice them to drink, though the women, as yet were resisting them. He made this known to the commanding officer but we presume no notice was taken of it, as it was reported that those soldiers had those women with them the whole night afterwards. A young married woman, a member of the Methodist society, was at the camp with her friends, though her husband was not there at the time. The soldiers, it is said, caught her, dragged her about, and at length, either through fear, or otherwise, induced her to drink; and then seduced her away, so that she is now an outcast even among her own relatives. How many of the poor captive women are thus debauched, through terror and seduction, that eye which never sleeps, alone can determine.

When removal finally got underway in October, the Cherokees were in a debilitated and demoralized state. A white minister who saw them as they prepared to embark noted: "The women did not appear to as good advantage as did the men. All, young and old, wore blankets which almost hid them from view." The Cherokees had received permission to manage their own removal, and they divided the people into thirteen detachments of approximately one thousand each. While some had wagons, most walked. Neugin rode in a wagon with other children and some elderly women, but her older brother, mother, and father "walked all the way." One observer reported that "even aged females, apparently nearly ready to drop in the grave, were traveling with heavy burdens attached to the back." Proper conveyance did not spare well-to-do Cherokees the agony of removal, the same observer noted:

> One lady passed on in her hack in company with her husband, apparently with as much refinement and equipage as any of the mothers of New England; and she was a mother too and her youngest child, about three years old, was sick in her arms, and all she could do was to make it comfortable as circumstances would permit. . . . She could only carry her dying child in her arms a few miles farther, and then she must stop in a stranger-land and consign her much loved babe to the cold ground, and that without pomp and ceremony, and pass on with the multitude.

This woman was not alone. Journals of the removal are largely a litany of the burial of children, some born "untimely."

Many women gave birth alongside the trail; at least sixty-nine newborns arrived in the West. The Cherokees' military escort was often less than sympathetic. Daniel Butrick wrote in his journal that troops frequently forced women in labor to continue until they collapsed and delivered "in the midst of the company of soldiers." One man even stabbed an expectant mother with a bayonet. Obviously, many pregnant women did not survive such treatment. The oral tradition of a family from southern Illinois, through which the Cherokees passed, for example, includes an account of an adopted Cherokee infant whose mother died in childbirth near the family's pioneer cabin. Although this story may be apocryphal, the circumstances of Cherokee removal make such traditions believable.

The stress and tension produced by the removal crisis probably accounts for a postremoval increase in domestic violence, of which women usually were the victims. Missionaries reported that men, helpless to prevent seizure of their property and assults on themselves and their families, vented their frustrations by beating wives and children. Some women were treated so badly by their husbands that they left them, and this dislocation contributed to the chaos in the Cherokee Nation in the late 1830s.

Removal divided the Cherokee Nation in a fundamental way, and the Civil War magnified that division. Because most signers of the removal treaty were highly acculturated, many traditionalists resisted more strongly the white man's way of life and distrusted more openly those Cherokees who imitated whites. This split between "conservatives," those who souught to preserve the old ways, and "progressives," those committed to change, extended to women. We know far more, of course, about "progressive" Cherokee women who left letters and diaries which in some ways are quite similar to those of upper-class women in the antebellum South. In letters, they recounted local news such as "they had Elick Cockrel up for steeling horses" and "they have Charles Reese in chains about burning Harnages house" and discussed economic concerns: "I find I cannot get any corn in this neighborhood, so of course I shall be greatly pressed in providing provision for my family." Nevertheless, family life was the focus of most letters: "Major is well and tryes hard to stand alone he will walk soon. I would write more but the baby is crying."

Occasionally we even catch a glimpse of conservative women who seem to have retained at least some of their original authority over domestic matters. Red Bird Smith, who led a revitalization movement at the end of the nineteenth century, had considerable difficulty with his first mother-in-law. She "influenced" her adopted daughter to marry Smith through witchcraft and, as head of the household, meddled rather seriously in the couple's lives. Interestingly, however, the Kee-Too-Wah society which Red Bird Smith headed had little room for women. Although the society had political objectives, women enjoyed no greater participation in this "conservative" organization than they did in the "progressive" republican government of the Cherokee Nation.

Following removal, the emphasis of legislation involving women was on protection rather than participation. In some ways this legislation did offer women greater opportunities than the law codes of the states. In 1845 the editor of the *Cherokee Advocate* expressed pride that "in this respect the Cherokees have been considerably in advance of many of their white brethren, the rights of their women having been amply secured almost ever since they had written laws." The Nation also established the Cherokee Female Seminary to provide higher education for women, but like the education women received before removal, students studied only those subjects considered to be appropriate for their sex.

Removal, therefore, changed little in terms of the status of Cherokee women. They had lost political power before the crisis of the 1830s, and events which followed relocation merely confirmed new roles and divisions. Cherokee women originally had been subsistence-level farmers and mothers, and the importance of these roles in traditional society had made it possible for them to exercise political power. Women, however, lacked the economic resources and military might on which political power in the Anglo-American system rested. When the Cherokees adopted the Anglo-American concept of power in the eighteenth and nineteenth centuries, men became dominant. But in the 1830s the chickens came home to roost. Men, who had welcomed the Anglo-American basis for power, now found themselves without power. Nevertheless, they did not question the changes they had fostered. Therefore, the tragedy of the trail of tears lies not only in the suffering and death which the Cherokees experienced but also in the failure of many Cherokees to look critically at the political system which they had adopted—a political sytem dominated by wealthy, highly acculturated men and supported by an ideology that made women (as well as others defined as "weak" or "inferior") subordinate. In the removal crisis of the 1830s, men learned an important lesson about power; it was a lesson women had learned well before the "trail of tears."

14

INDIANS IN LOS ANGELES, 1781–1875: ECONOMIC INTEGRATION, SOCIAL DISINTEGRATION

GEORGE HARWOOD PHILLIPS

Usually Native Americans are studied within their social units: bands, villages, or tribes. Not only do most Americans think of Indians in generic terms, but when they think of California tribal people at all, they recall pastoral scenes of Spanish missions in some romantic past. Striving to overcome such ideas, this essay considers the impact that the Spanish, Mexican, and American invasions of California had on the native people there. The author traces Indian experiences with the intruders from aboriginal times through the post–gold rush era. He shows how each of the three imperial powers saw and dealt with the local tribes. The Spanish recruited Indians to labor at the coastal missions, expecting to convert their charges to Christianity while pacifying the region. By the time Mexico gained its independence, most tribal workers labored on farms or ranches or at the missions. In the mid 1830s the government secularized the missions, granting much of the land to ranchers and allowing the Native American workers to remain or leave. Some returned to their tribal homes, but many migrated to the coastal towns and worked as day laborers. Much of the article examines the kinds of jobs open to Native Americans and compares the means used to control their labor first by Mexican and later by American local officials. This discussion explores the impact of white intrusion upon the tribal peoples and explains the process by which some Indians made substantial contributions to the southern California economy.

George Harwood Phillips is an associate professor of history at the University of Colorado.

Source: George Harwood Phillips, "Indians in Los Angeles, 1781–1875: Economic Integration, Social Disintegration," *Pacific Historical Review*, 49 (August 1980), pp. 427–451. (c) 1980 by the Pacific Coast Branch, American Historical Association. Reprinted from the *Pacific Historical Review* by permission of the Branch.

As members of sociopolitical units not yet significantly damaged by white contact, Indians had their greatest impact on post-Columbian, North American history. Bands, lineages, villages, chiefdoms, and confederacies rendered decisions and implemented policies concerning the white intruders that sometimes were of crucial importance in shaping the histories of regions and localities. On occasion, however, Indians actively participated in the historical process as individuals whose traditional corporate existence had been disrupted by white contact. Indians in the Los Angeles region are a case in point.

Seeking work, individual Indians began drifting into the pueblo of Los Angeles almost from the day it was founded. Settlers and Indians thereby established an economic relationship that continued for nearly a century. Unfortunately, historians have overlooked this relationship and have concentrated instead on the social disintegration of the Indian residents. The Indians underwent social disintegration, however, because they became tightly integrated into the pueblo's economic structure. So interconnected were the processes of social disintegration and economic integration that no investigation of Indian urban life would be complete without each receiving equal consideration. This article analyzes the Indian in the history of Los Angeles as both social victim and economic contributor.

At the time of Spanish intrusion into Alta California in 1769 the Indian peoples occupying most of present-day Los Angeles County, half of Orange County, and the islands of Santa Catalina and San Clemente spoke Gabrielino, one of the Cupan languages in the Takic family which is part of the Uto-Aztecan language stock. On the islands and along the densely populated coastal region, the Gabrielino lived in permanent village communities based on kinship ties. For subsistence they relied primarily on hunting, fishing, and collecting wild plants, although they may have engaged in some protoagricultural activity.

In August 1769 Gabrielinos, perhaps from the village of Yangna, located near the Los Angeles River, established friendly contact with the first Spanish expedition passing through their territory. They presented the Spaniards with shell beads and baskets of seeds. The Spanish reciprocated with tobacco and glass beads. That these villagers resided in an incredibly fertile region was not lost on at least one member of the expedition. Fray Juan Crespí remarked: "after crossing the river we entered a large vineyard of wild grapes and an infinity of rosebushes in full bloom. All the soil is black and loamy, and is capable of producing every kind of grain and fruit which may be planted." After the Chumash, their Hokan-speaking neighbors to the north with whom they shared many cultural traits, the Gabrielino became the most intensively colonized people in southern California. Where greater Los Angeles stands today, Spaniards created a mission, pueblo, and three privately owned ranchos in just thirteen years.

In September 1771 Mission San Gabriel Arcángel was founded, the fourth Spanish mission to be established in Alta California. It was moved to its present location, near the Indian village of Sibangna, in 1774. By the end of the year 154 neophytes (the term used to designate the Indian converts) resided at the mission. Ten years later 739 neophytes were associated with the mission, although many lived on inland mission ranchos. Politically and culturally San Gabriel was much the same as the other missions, but economically it differed considerably. More than the others, it emphasized viticulture, and its large vineyard was recognized as the *viña madre* of Spanish California. Many of its neophytes acquired the skills of planting, tending, and harvesting grapes and manufacturing wine and distilled spirits. They also became masons, carpenters, plasterers, soapmakers, tanners, shoemakers, blacksmiths, millers, bakers, cooks, brickmakers, cartmakers, weavers, spinners, saddlers, shepherds, and vaqueros. In short, the neophytes of San Gabriel as well as those of the other southern missions—San Fernando, San Juan Capistrano, San Luis Rey, and San Diego—became *the* skilled labor force of southern California.

In September 1781, ten years to the month after the establishment of Mission San Gabriel, a party of forty-four men, women, and children founded the pueblo of Los Angeles near the village of Yangna and only three leagues from the mission. Racially and ethnically the colonists were heterogeneous; only two adults were true Spaniards, the others being of Indian, African, and mixed ancestry. But to distinguish themselves from the California Indian population, they adopted the label *gente de razón,* or people of reason. Included were a few farmers, a hoemaker, a cowherd, a mason, and a tailor. By 1790 the population of the pueblo totalled 141 persons.

Privately owned ranchos, the first to be established in Alta California, were also created in Gabrielino territory. In 1784 the governor of the province granted soldiers Juan José Domínquez, José María Verdugo, and Manuel Pérez Nieto permission to raise livestock on vast tracts of land, provided their claims did not encroach upon the holdings allotted to the pueblo and the mission. Each grantee was required to construct a stone house, stock his rancho with two thousand head of cattle, and employ as many vaqueros as needed to manage the animals.

Based on crop growing and stock raising, the mission, pueblo, and ranchos were designed to be economically self-sufficient. The mission relied mainly on neophyte labor, but initially the pueblo and the ranchos recruited most of their workers from the gentiles (a term applied by the gente de razón to the unconverted, politically independent Indians). The gentiles, however, consented to work only when it did not interfere with their traditional subsistence activities. In 1784 Lieutenant Francisco Ortega noted the dependence of the pueblo on Indian labor and the independence of the Indian laborers: "I feel that only with the aid of the gentiles have . . . [the settlers] been able to plant the . . . crops of wheat and corn but as . . . [the Indians] are at present harvesting their abundant wild seeds, they justly refuse with this good reason to lend a hand in digging and weeding."

Apparently concerned about the familiarity established between settlers and gentiles, the governor attempted to regulate Indian-white relations in the pueblo. In 1787 he issued instructions to the corporal of the guard which outlined how the Indians were to be treated. Never were they to be allowed inside the settlers' houses, certainly not to sleep or even to grind corn. Indians from distant villages were not to settle permanently in the pueblo, while those who came for only a few days' work were to reside near the guardhouse, where they could be easily observed. Large groups were not to be allowed in the town for their own amusement. Tact and diplomacy were to be used to encourage the Indians already residing near the pueblo to move from the immediate area. A settler seeking to recruit Indian workers from outside the pueblo had to obtain permission from the authorities, and a person who traveled alone to a village without authorization was liable to a week's punishment in the stocks. The directive forbade forced labor and false promises and demanded that Indian complaints be heard. An individual caught mistreating an Indian was to be punished in the presence of the victim. If Indians were apprehended in the act of stealing or stock killing, they were to be told the reason for the punishment and then lashed fifteen or twenty times in the presence of their leaders. Most likely these instructions were often ignored, but they do indicate that the pueblo, a tiny foreign enclave in a vast Indian territory, was both suspicious of and dependent upon its Indian neighbors.

By the beginning of the nineteenth century a sizable body of Indians, most of them from beyond the Los Angeles–San Gabriel region, had settled, at least temporarily, near the town. The corporal of the guard, Francisco Xavier Alvarado, reported in 1803 that 150 of the 200 gentiles were from outside the immediate area. Six years later he noted that the resident Indians spent much of their time gambling and drinking and a few had been put in the stocks as punishment. About this time some of the gentiles probably contracted the same venereal disease that had recently infected a large number of the neophytes at the nearby mission.

When the gentiles were not available or when skilled labor was demanded, the pueblo employed neophytes from the southern missions. In 1810, for example, a hundred Indians from San Juan Capistrano assisted the settlers in raising hemp and flax. And in 1819 neophytes from San Luis Rey constructed a church, receiving one *real* ($12\frac{1}{2}$¢) a day plus board and lodging for their efforts. But until the mid 1830s the pueblo and the ranchos depended mainly on gentile labor.

This dependency became a major concern of the Spanish missionaries, and from their accounts emerges a picture of Indian industriousness and settler indolence. The padres were convinced that the employment of gentiles sapped the initiative of the gente de razón and prolonged traditional Indian religious practices. In 1795 Father Vincente de Santa María wrote: "The whole of pagandom . . . is fond of the Pueblo of Los Angeles, of the rancho of Mariano Verdugo and the rancho of Reyes, and of the Zanja. Here we see nothing but pagans passing, clad in shoes, with sombreros and blankets, and serving as muleteers to the settlers and rancheros, so that if it were not for the gentiles there would be neither pueblo nor rancho. . . . Finally these pagan Indians care neither for the Mission nor for the missionaries." The following year Father José Señan expressed a similar view:

> The main fault . . . lies in the indifference of the colonists and their disinclination toward hard work; they prefer to hold in hand a deck of cards rather than a hoe or plow. What little progress is being made must be credited to the population of neighboring gentile rancherías and not to the settler. The Indians cultivate the fields, do the planting, and harvest the crops. . . . Still more painful is the effect of all this upon the natives who, being in contact with the colonists, or *gente de razón*, should have been the first to receive Holy Baptism. But because of the bad example set them, and perhaps for their own private reasons, these natives still abide in the shadows of paganism.

A report on the condition of the Indians at San Gabriel, issued in 1814 by the mission's padres, echoed the same concern:

In the town and on the ranchos of the people of the other classes both men and women who are pagans assist in the work of the fields. Also they are employed as cooks, water carriers and in other domestic occupations. This is one of the most potent causes why the people who are called *gente de razón* are given so much to idleness. Since the pagan Indians are paid for their labor by half or a third of the crops, they remain content in the service of their masters during the season of planting and harvesting. The latter, with few exceptions, never put their hands to the plow or sickle. As a result of this another drawback arises, namely the [Indian] adults delay having themselves baptised. In the service of their masters, they live according to their pagan notions and practices.

By the time of Mexico's independence in 1821 Los Angeles had become a thriving agricultural community, a development noted by foreign visitors. A. Duhaut-Cilly passed through in the late 1820s and "counted eighty-two houses comprising the pueblo, which I inferred it might have one thousand inhabitants, including in this number two-hundred Indians, servants or laborers. . . . The principal produce consists of maize and grapes. The vine succeeds very well." About the same time, Alfred Robinson arrived. "The population of this town," he wrote in *Life in California,* "is about fifteen hundred; and has an alcalde, two regidores, and a syndico who compose its 'Ayuntamiento' or Town Council. In the vicinity are many vineyards and cornfields, and some fine gardens, crossed by beautiful streams of water. The lands[,] being level and fertile, are capable of great agricultural improvement." To irrigate the vineyards, gardens, and orchards an efficient water system was developed. It consisted of a *zanja madre,* or main ditch, which channelled the water from the Los Angeles River to the town and several branch zanjas, eventually numbering eight, which carried the water to the growers' plots.

The pueblo's first vineyard was planted about 1803, probably with cuttings from Mission San Gabriel. The grape was of the "mission" variety, best suited for the table, but also made into a brandy called *aguardiente* and a wine of poor quality. Louis Vignes, originally from Bordeaux, is generally credited with establishing California's commercial wine industry. He settled in the pueblo in 1831, imported cuttings from France, and soon had a large vineyard under cultivation.

As the pueblo's grape and other agricultural industries expanded, the demand for cheap labor increased sharply. Indians supplied this need. The census of 1830 put the number of Indians in the pueblo at 198 as compared to 764 gente de razón. The census taker divided the Indians into two classes: Domesticated Indians (ex-neophytes who had once been attached to the missions) and Domesticated Heathens (gentiles who had never been converted or missionized). At this time the gentiles outnumbered the ex-neophytes 127 to 71 in the pueblo and 157 to 104 in the entire district. According to the census taker, amicable relations prevailed between the gentiles and the gente de razón. "The heathens of the neighborhood," he noted, "who come here and work with the whites, are treated well and live a civilized and quiet life."

Within a few years, however, Indian-white relations in the town changed significantly. In August 1833 the Mexican government enacted a law secularizing the missions of Alta and Baja California. Originally designed to convert the missions into Indian pueblos and distribute land to the neophytes, in effect the law opened up thousands of square leagues to private white ownership and thus established the rancho the dominant economic and social institution of Mexican California.

Even with the promise of land, most neophytes exhibited scant interest in remaining at or near the missions. They drifted into the interior, sought work on the ranchos, or wandered into the towns. Although most of the neophytes from San Gabriel fled to the north, those from the southern missions of San Diego, San Luis Rey, and San Juan Capistrano overran the Los Angeles area. The census of 1836 identified 533 Indians in the district as compared to 1,675 gente de razón. Residing in the town proper were 223 ex-neophytes and 32 gentiles. Eight years later another census recorded 650 Indians in the town, over 400 coming from the southern missions. Thus, in the decade after secularization began, ex-neophytes replaced the gentiles as the town's Indian majority and the total number of Indian residents tripled.

Because the town's economic structure could not absorb such a dramatic increase in the work force, a large number of Indians remained perpetually unemployed. The social and political ramifications of this economic situation were extensive. Incidents of Indian drunkenness increased and alarmed the Mexican authorities. The problem was linked to the development of a retail liquor business that by the mid 1830s had become an important part of the local economy. But rather than regulate the business in order to curtail Indian consumption, the ayuntamiento increased its authority over the Indian consumers. In January 1836 it authorized the *regidores* (councilmen) to arrest all drunken Indians and assign them to work on the zanja madre which needed improvement. Although hardly an act of great repression, the authorization initiated a system of labor recruitment that steadily integrated Indians by force into the pueblo's economic structure.

Over the years, Indians established several settlements in and adjacent to the pueblo. The smallest consisted of Pipimares, Gabrielino-speakers most likely from Santa Catalina Island. These survivors of a once thriving island population had been removed to the mainland sometime in the 1820s. Those who eventually settled in the pueblo clustered together in a few huts and tenaciously maintained their distinct identity. The majority of the Indians, however, resided on a tract of city property that the ayuntamiento granted them in 1836.

Three Indian *alcaldes* nominally governed the main settlement. While possessing limited influence with the white authorities, these officials sometimes pressed for Indian rights. On April 27, 1838, for instance, Alcaldes Gabriel, Juan José, and Gandiel petitioned the ayuntamiento to force a white neighbor, Juan Domingo, to vacate land that belonged to the Indians. The Mexican authorities ruled in favor of the Indians, fined Domingo $12, and ordered him off the property. The Indian residents, however, achieved few such legal victories, and it was not long before their rights were severely curtailed.

In January 1844 the ayuntamiento passed a resolution stating that all persons without occupation or some manner of making a living were liable to a fine or incarceration. Upon discharging servants or day laborers, employers were to issue each a document indicating the circumstances of their release and whether they were at liberty to work for someone else. No servant or worker could be hired without this document, and those seeking employment for the first time had to secure a certificate from the authorities. Persons failing to present their documents were to be arrested and tried immediately and, if found guilty, jailed as prisoners of the city.

The resolution emerged in response to a sharp rise in Indian crime and violence, although the hostilities were primarily intra-Indian and confined to the main Indian settlement. Most of those arrested were charged with being drunk and disorderly and usually received a sentence of fifteen days of hard labor on public works projects. On occasion, however, Indian prisoners worked out their sentences in the custody of private citizens who paid their fines and who were responsible for their whereabouts and behavior.

In May and June 1845 the Indian residents became so disorderly that two petitions presented to the ayuntamiento sought their removal from the town. The commission that was formed to study the problem recommended removal, and late in the year the Indians were forced to move across the river, where they constructed a new settlement called Pueblito. The following year two more petitions called for the removal of the Pipimares. The first was rejected on the grounds that these Indians had resided in the town for years and that no complaint had been issued against them. The second petition, however, led to the formation of a commission which reported that the few Pipimares who remained should be domiciled on the premises of their employers or relocated in the main Indian settlement. The commission's recommendations were approved and the Pipimares were dispersed.

The new settlement of Pueblito became as crime ridden as the old. In February 1846 twenty-six citizens petitioned directly to the Governor of California: "When the 'Indian Rancheria' was removed to the 'Pueblito' we thought that the isolation of these aborigines would prevent the committing of excess and thefts . . . but we are sorry to say it has proved to the contrary. Taking advantage of their isolation they steal all neighboring fences and on Saturdays celebrate and become intoxicated to an unbearable degree." The petitioners were also concerned about the spread of venereal disease among the Indians, blaming it on the "vice" of polygamy. They feared that the Indian population would soon disappear if corrective measures were not taken. The Indians, they recommended, should either be placed in an area where they could be strictly policed or provided with living quarters by their employers.

Late the following year Rafael Gallardo submitted a petition to the common council (the city government under American rule) that sought to remove the Indians from Pueblito. On November 8, 1847 the council passed an ordinance authorizing the destruction of the settlement. This required housing servants and workers on their employers' premises, relocating self-sufficient Indians outside the city limits in widely separated settlements and assigning vagrants of either sex to public works projects or confining them in jail. Twenty-four dollars were raised to assist the Indians in moving, and by the end of the month Pueblito had been razed.

American rule introduced new and serious problems to the resident Indians. As unruly Yankees, Californios, and immigrants from Mexico (especially Sonora) and

Europe drifted into the pueblo, Los Angeles became one of the most volatile and lawless towns in the Far West. "Gambling, drinking, and whoring are the only occupations," wrote an American military officer in 1849," and they seem to be followed with great industry, particularly the first and second. Monte banks, cock fights, and liquor shops are to be seen in all directions." In *Reminiscences of a Ranger,* Horace Bell recalled "that in the years of 1851, '52 and '53, there were more desperadoes in Los Angeles than in any place on the Pacific coast, San Francisco with its great population not excepted."

Given the general disorder that characterized Los Angeles in the early 1850s, it is hardly surprising that the semblance of social stability the Indians had maintained under Mexican domination quickly gave way to internal dissension and conflicts. The worst incident of intra-Indian violence occurred in 1851 during a traditional gambling game called *peon*. A fight erupted between local Indians and Cahuillas visiting from the interior. "We found thirteen dead in the vicinity of the fight," recalled Joseph Lancaster Brent. "These all had their heads mashed beyond recognition, which is the sign manual of Indian murder; but these Indians did not scalp. Dead and wounded Indians were discovered everywhere, and it was a moderate estimate that fifty lost their lives." In May 1851 the common council prohibited the playing of peon within the city limits. The games continued, however, often resulting in Indian casualties and arrests.

Throughout the 1850s seldom a week went by without the local newspapers reporting incidents of Indian violence and crime. Bodies of dead—usually murdered and mutilated—Indians were a common sight in the streets. Nearly all the homicides went unsolved, the coroner usually rendering a verdict of "death by violence from persons unknown." Arrested for theft, forgery, rape, assault, and sometimes murder, Indians were whipped, imprisoned, and executed for their misdeeds. Perhaps the most revealing statement on intra-Indian violence—indeed, on town violence in general—came from the *Los Angeles Star* on September 13, 1856. Mentioning no specific cases, it reported with icy indifference and caustic cynicism that "Indians continue to kill each other. One or two instances of stabbings have come under our notice this week. We cannot learn that any white person had developed his manhood within the last seven days."

By the mid 1850s the Indian residents were obviously undergoing social disintegration, a process that drew comments from travelers and local citizens. An American visitor remarked in 1852 that he "saw more Indians about this place than in any part of California I had yet visited. They were chiefly 'Mission Indians' . . . [and] are a miserable squalid-looking set, squatting or lying about the corners of the streets, without occupation. . . . No care seems to be taken of them by the Americans." In the same year, Benjamin Wilson reported on the condition of the Indians of southern California, stating that those in the pueblo had "become sadly deteriorated, within the last two years." In 1855 a local physician estimated that nine tenths of the town's Indians were infected with syphilis.

Despite the social disorder, Los Angeles continued to develop economically. "The pueblo of Los Angeles is extremely rich . . . ," reported Eugène Duflot de Mofras in 1842. "Vineyards yield 600 barrels of wine, and an equal amount of brandy. . . .

El pueblo has in addition sixty *huertas*, or gardens, planted out to vines that cover an area roughly estimated at 100 hectares." A few years later Edwin Bryant noted: "The yield of the vineyards is very abundant and a large quantity of wines of good quality and flavor, and *aguardiente*, are manufactured here. Some vineyards, I understand, contain as many as twenty-thousand vines."

In late 1852 the *Star* estimated that there were 400,000 vines within the city limits and that each vine would conservatively yield five pounds of grapes. On the vine, grapes brought between two to six cents per pound in the town and its environs but averaged twenty cents a pound in San Francisco. In 1859 approximately 300,000 pounds of grapes and 150,000 gallons of wine—valued at $36,641 and $113,180, respectively—were exported. Three years later 6,340 tons of grapes were harvested, resulting in 352,223 gallons of wine and 29,789 gallons of brandy. And by 1875 the production of wine had risen dramatically to 1,328,900 gallons.

Indian residents did not share in the agricultural wealth of Los Angeles County. The federal census of 1850 identified only 334 Indians as taxpayers, and only three in the county and none in the town had enough personal wealth to be listed in a column labeled "Value of Real Estate Owned." Those listed were Urbano Chari, a farmer worth $500; Roman, a farmer worth $1,000; and Samuel, a laborer worth $250. Yet according to the state census of 1852 the county's Indian population of 3,693 approximated that of the whites at 4,093.

At this time about four hundred Indians were employed in the pueblo, many as domestic servants. The Benjamin Wilson report of 1852 asserted that the Indians, "with all their faults, appear to be a necessary part of the domestic economy. They are almost the only house or farm servants we have. The San Luiseño is most sprightly, skillful, and handy; the Cahuilla plodding, but strong, and very useful with instruction and watching." The town servant earned a maximum of a dollar per day, but most received less. For attending to most of the household duties, an Indian and his wife received fifty cents a day from their Anglo-American employer. Domestics, moreover, could be discarded with blatant callousness. Upon discovering that his young servant was terminally ill, a Spanish-speaking citizen, apparently to avoid burial expenses, hauled her out of town to die beside the road. Competition was fierce among the Indians for the limited number of domestic jobs, so employers had no difficulty in finding replacements. In May 1860, for example, an Indian informed a Mr. Laventhal that his servant had been killed the previous night and that he had come to take his place.

Most of the labor performed by the Indians related to the town's most important industry. Indians maintained the vineyards and repaired the irrigation ditches throughout the year, but during the fall harvest their services were of special importance. Harvesting just one large vineyard called for a large body of organized workers. William Wolfskill, for example, employed about forty laborers, two thirds of whom picked the grapes and hauled them to a central location. Indians also provided valuable, if extremely tedious, labor in the processing of the grapes. "There were no wine presses," recalled an Anglo-American resident, "and the grapes were placed in huge shallow vats placed near the 'sanja' or water ditch. The Indians were made to bathe their feet in the sanja and then step into the vats where they tread rhythmically up and down on the grapes to press out the juice.

Quite a number of Indians were in the vats at one time." Harris Newmark wrote in *Sixty Years in Southern California* that the Indians, "Stripped to the skin, and wearing only loin-cloths, . . . tramped with ceaseless tread from morn till night, pressing from the luscious fruit of the vineyard the juice so soon to ferment into wine."

During the 1850s and 1860s the Indian residents increasingly were integrated by force into the pueblo's economic structure. The impetus behind this development came from both state and local legislation. At its first session in late 1849 and early 1850 the California legislature authorized the mayor or recorder of an incorporated town or city to arrest, on the complaint of any citizen, Indians caught begging, loitering, or "leading an immoral or profligate course of life." Those arrested could then be hired out to the highest bidder for a term not to exceed four months. Imitating the legislature, the Los Angeles common council issued the following ordinance in August 1850: "When the city has no work in which to employ the chain gang, the Recorder shall, by means of notices conspicuously posted, notify the public that such a number of prisoners will be auctioned off to the highest bidder for private service."

Nearly every Monday morning for some twenty years local ranchers and growers assembled at the mayor's office to bid on the Indian prisoners. That the practice became callously routine is demonstrated in a letter written in 1852. The administrator of Rancho los Alamitos called upon his employer to "deputize someone to attend the auction that usually takes place at the prison on Mondays, and buy me five or six Indians." In his characteristically flamboyant yet often poignant way, Horace Bell described the system in which the Indians were caught.

> The cultivators of the vineyards commenced paying the Indian peons with *aguardiente,* a veritable fire-water and no mistake. The consequence was that on being paid off on Saturday evening, they would meet in great gatherings called peons, and pass the night in gambling, drunkenness, and debauchery. On Sunday the streets would be crowded from morn till night with Indians, males and females of all ages, from the girl of ten or twelve, to the old man and woman of seventy or eighty. . . .

> About sundown the pompous marshal, with his Indian special deputies, who had been kept in jail all day to keep them sober, would drive and drag the herd to a big corral in the rear of Downey Block, where they would sleep away their intoxication, and in the morning they would be exposed for sale, as slaves for the week. Los Angeles had its slave mart, as well as New Orleans and Constantinople—only the slave at Los Angeles was sold fifty-two times a year as long as he lived, which did not generally exceed one, two, or three years, under the new dispensation. They would be sold for a week, and bought up by the vineyard men and others at prices ranging from one to three dollars, one-third of which was to be paid to the peon at the end of the week, which debt, due for well performed labor, would invariably be paid in *aguardiente,* and the Indian would be made happy until the following Monday morning, having passed through another Saturday night and Sunday's saturnalia of debauchery and bestiality. Those thousands of honest, useful people were absolutely destroyed in this way.

Many Indian prisoners, however, paid their fines and thus were spared the indignity of the auction. In fact, the town government met part of its operating expenses with the revenue collected from Indians. On October 2, 1850 the common council authorized the recorder to pay the Indian alcaldes one real ($12\frac{1}{2}$¢) out of every fine collected from an Indian they had brought to trial. Evidently they did their work well, for on November 27 of the same year the council appointed $15.75 for the alcaldes. At the rate of eight Indians to the dollar, it seems that these officials had rounded up well over 100 souls, of whom 126 had paid their fines. The alcaldes so abused their authority that in September 1852 the council encouraged the mayor to curtail their activity.

The practice of arresting and fining drunken Indians brought a strong condemnation from the *Los Angeles Star* on December 3, 1853.

> It has long been the practice with the Indians of this city, to get drunk on Saturday night. Their ambition seems to be to earn sufficient money, through the week, to treat themselves handsomely at the close of it. In this they only follow white examples, and like white men, they are often noisy about the streets.—It has also been the practice with the City Marshal, and his assistants, to spend the Sabbath in arresting and imprisoning Indians, supposed to be drunk, until Monday morning, when they are taken before the Mayor and discharged on paying a bill of two dollars and a half each, one dollar of which is the fee of the Marshal. Sometimes of a Monday morning we have seen the Marshal marching in a procession with twenty or twenty-five of these poor people, and truly, it is a brave sight.—Now, we have no heart to do the Marshal slightest prejudice, but this leading off Indians and locking them up over night, for the purpose of taking away one of their paltry dollars, seems to us a questionable act.

Apparently the criticism went unheeded, for seven years later the *Star* was still issuing sarcastic broadsides: "On last Sunday, our vigilant City Marshal and his assistants brought *forty one* Indians to the stationhouse, generally on charges of drunkenness. We do not know whether the officers are becoming more vigilant, or the aborigines more dissipated."

The Indians purchased aguardiente at the numerous local taverns. According to the Wilson report, "In some streets of this little city, almost every other house is a grog-shop for Indians." In mid May 1851 Mayor Benjamin Wilson called for a city ordinance that would prohibit the selling of liquor to Indians, and later in the month the common council amended the existing police ordinance to achieve this end. Those convicted were to be fined not less than $20 or imprisoned for five days or both. But the ordinance was blatantly ignored, and on November 16, 1854 the *Southern Californian* demanded that the council take the necessary action to correct the situation and identified several grog-shop owners—Alexander Delique, Pedro María, Ferrio Abilia, and J. B. Guernod—as the worst offenders. So profitable was this business, however, that the tavern owners could sustain the fines levied against them. In 1855 Vicente Guerrero paid a fine of $30 but kept his business active. A week later he paid another fine—this one for $200!

Although a few of the white citizens of Los Angeles expressed sincere concern about the social disintegration of the local Indians and sought to ameliorate what was considered to be the cause of their decline, no one urged elimination of the labor system. This point was made by California's Superintendent of Indian Affairs who visited the town in 1855. "If it were practicable or desirable in their demoralized condition, to remove them to the Reservation," he wrote to his superior in Washington, D.C., "it could not be accomplished, because it would be opposed by the citizens, for the reasons that in the vineyards, especially during the grape season, their labor is made useful and is obtained at a cheap rate."

Because the pueblo and its environs had a surplus of cheap Indian labor, white workers found the region closed to their services and skills. The Wilson report claimed that in 1852 no white man would work for the wages received by the Indians. In 1860, according to Harris Newmark, "Small as was the population of Los Angeles County about this time, there was nevertheless for a while an exodus to Texas, due chiefly to the difficulty experienced by white immigrants in competing with Indian ranch and vineyard labor." Less objectively, the *Semi-Weekly News* on February 11, 1869 asserted that the Indian, "being brought into competition with that class of labor that would be most beneficial to the country, checks immigration, and retards the prosperity of the country." Ignoring their contributions to the development of the pueblo, the editorial complained that the Indians "build no houses, own no lands, pay no taxes and encourage no branch of industry. . . . They have filled our jails, have contributed largely to the filling of our state prison, and are fast filling our graveyards, where they must either be buried at public expense or permitted to rot in the streets and highways."

Indeed, Indians were filling up the graveyards, for by this time the town's Indian population was in rapid decline. Between 1850 and 1860 the number of Indians recorded in Los Angeles County dropped from 3,693 to 2,014. By 1870 the figure had plummeted to 219. Some may have blended in with the Spanish-speaking population and thus were not counted as Indians in the census reports. Presumably others left the town for the ranchos or the interior. But intra-Indian violence and contagious diseases account for much of the population reduction.

Many perished during the smallpox epidemic of late 1862 and early 1863. The disease, of course, respected no race or class, but social and economic factors largely determined its demographic impact. An American resident concluded that the Indians "succumbed *en mass*" because their constitutions had been undermined by years of dissipation. According to Harris Newmark, "The dread disease worked its ravages especially among the Mexicans and Indians, as many as a dozen of them dying in a single day; and these sufferers and their associates being under no quarantine, and even bathing *ad libitum* in the *zanjas*, the pest spread alarmingly." The *Star* reported in late January 1863 that two hundred cases had been identified and that two hundred persons had already died. Accurate death statistics are lacking, but since immunization was not compulsory and was initially resisted by the Indians, their toll must have been devastatingly high.

Irrespective of their declining numbers, Indians continued to be jailed and auctioned off to private individuals throughout the 1860s. J. Ross Browne attested in 1864 that Indians were "paid in native brandy every Saturday night, put in jail the next morning for getting drunk, and bailed out on Monday to work out the fine imposed upon them by the local authorities. This system still prevails in Los Angeles, where I have often seen a dozen of these miserable wretches carried to jail roaring drunk of a Sunday morning." And in early 1869 the *Semi-Weekly News* reported that farmers continued to assemble at the mayor's office on Monday mornings to obtain the services of the Indian prisoners. By the mid 1870s, however, the town's Indian labor force had practically disappeared. A newspaper article dated November 3, 1875 stated that a band of Luiseños from San Diego County would soon arrive to participate in the grape harvest. Los Angeles, it seems, was now importing its Indian labor.

From 1781 to the 1870s the white residents of Los Angeles relied almost exclusively on Indian labor, domestic and agricultural. Initially, local Gabrielinos, the so-called gentiles, constituted the town's work force, and given their political independence, they were not without some economic leverage. They labored for the gente de razón only when it did not interfere with their traditional subsistence activities. So long as the gentiles provided most of the labor, Indian-white relations remained firmly based on a practical exchange of service for goods. But once the politically powerless ex-neophytes replaced the gentiles, relations between Indians and whites quickly deteriorated into economic exploitation. The quality of Indian-white relations, therefore, was determined as much by which Indian group (gentile or ex-neophyte) constituted the labor force at a given time as by which white group (Spanish, Mexican, or American) was in political control.

The shift from gentile to ex-neophyte labor came with the secularization of the missions. Ex-neophytes overran the Los Angeles area, providing the pueblo with many more workers than it could absorb. The domestic servants who found steady employment did not fare too badly, but the agricultural laborers, whose work was usually seasonal, often suffered unemployment for long periods of time. The social consequences of this economic situation were despondency, drunkenness, and violence. As disorderly Indians became a major concern of the Mexican and then the American city administrations, stringent laws were enacted to correct the problem.

Beginning in 1836, when the ayuntamiento authorized the regidor to arrest drunken Indians and assign them to public works projects, a labor recruitment system developed that increasingly integrated Indians by force into the town's economic structure. After 1850, when the common council authorized the recorder to auction off jailed Indians to private individuals, the system ensured that the demand for labor was always met with a plentiful supply.

Although it is impossible to discern the percentage of Indian workers recruited by force during the 1850s and 1860s, any rise in the Indian crime rate would have resulted in an increase in the number of Indians arrested and put up for auction. And a rise in the number of Indians recruited by force would have reduced the number of those freely employed. Furthermore, since forced labor was cheaper than free, it was in the best, albeit short-term, interests of the growers to see that there were always Indians available for auction. By paying their workers, at least in part, in aguardiente, they virtually ensured that some Indians would be arrested for drunkenness and immediately forced back on the job market. Serving the same end were the grog shop owners who persisted in illegally selling to the Indians the brandy they acquired from the growers.

This kind of economic system could not be maintained over the long run, however, because labor recruitment depended in large part on the perpetuation of Indian social instability. In effect, the system bred its own destruction, for the process of economic integration generated a process of social disintegration, which in turn led to drastic population reduction. The resident Indians, it seems, were caught not so much in a vicious circle as in a downward spiral from which few escaped or survived. But they were more than just social victims; they were economic contributors as well. In their descent to disappearance, they engaged in activity, both productive and destructive, that contributed significantly to the social and economic history of the pueblo's first century.

15

INDIAN LAND USE AND ENVIRONMENTAL CHANGE IN ISLAND COUNTY, WASHINGTON: A CASE STUDY

RICHARD WHITE

As noted earlier, scholars of the Native American experience now give increasing attention to environmental themes. Few ethnohistorians now accept the idea that Indians lived in harmony with their natural surroundings—that is, that they used what they found without making any changes in the natural habitat. At the same time, the author demonstrates clearly that tribal people in the Pacific Northwest knew what their home territory offered while they both used local resources and modified their environment through conscious actions. The pioneers who first encountered these Indians had no idea that they did anything more than gather plants growing wild, but White proves that this was not the case. In fact, he claims that local villagers knew their environment thoroughly and used at least fifty separate varieties of plants each year. His discussion focuses on the actions of four Salishian tribes on Whidby and Camano islands in Puget Sound. He shows that through the use of fire and a simple technology, the Indians encouraged the growth of useful plants as they sought to improve their subsistence economy and their food sources. The pioneer whites had no understanding of local Indian diet customs and failed to realize that the tribal people had brought long-term changes in the environments of the two islands. White shows that the pioneers objected to the Indian custom of burning the prairie each year as dangerous and destructive. The discussion points out the different awareness of nature by whites and Indians during the middle of the nineteenth century. It also makes clear the Indians' interactive relationship with the environment before Anglo-Americans entered the region.

Richard White is a professor of history at the University of Washington.

Source: Richard White, "Indian Land Use and Environmental Change: Island County, Washington A Case Study," *Arizona and the West,* 17 (Winter 1975), pp. 327–338. © *Arizona and the West* 17 (Winter 1975). Reprinted with permission of the publisher.

The first Americans to settle in Island County, Washington Territory, in the late 1850s regarded the region as a virgin wilderness. Heavy coniferous forests and small prairies covered the several islands in Puget Sound which composed the county. On these islands Salish tribes followed age-old practices of fishing, hunting, and gathering, and whites presumed that these people had adapted to the land, enjoying its abundance and suffering its scarcities. The prairies and forests seemed obviously the creation of unrestrained nature. Few observers were aware that the Indians inhabiting the area had actually played an active role in shaping their environment, not indirectly, as any population shapes the ecology of a region merely by occupying it, but consciously and purposefully to fit their own needs. Through the use of fire and a simple technology, the Indians over many generations had encouraged the growth of three dominant plants on the islands—bracken, camas, and nettles—to supplement their regular diet of fish and small game and also had created the conditions that fostered immense forests of Douglas fir. A study of the early Salish experience in Island County demonstrates salient features in the process by which hunting and gathering peoples profoundly altered their natural environment.

At the arrival of white settlers, the Indian population in Island County, an area of approximately 206 square miles, lived wholly on two large islands, Whidby and Camano. In size, Whidby ranks second only to Long Island in the continental United States; Camano is about one fifth the size of Whidby. Small fertile prairies, located largely on the northern part of Whidby Island, comprised about five percent of the county. The remaining terrain was hilly, forested, and infertile.

Four Salish tribes—the Skagit, Kikialos, Snohomish, and later the Clallam—had lived on parts of these islands since about 1000 A.D. Each tribe was a loose aggregation of villages united by language and blood, rather than by a centralized political system. Anthropologists have classified all these tribes as saltwater, or canoe, Indians, who, despite differences in language and kinship, shared basically similar culture traits.

The Salish viewed the land as not only being occupied by humans, plants, and animals, but also by a vast array of spirits associated with specific animals or natural phenomena. This added dimension gave nature an ambience and additional meaning. Plants and animals took on not only economic but also religious significance. Although the settlers dismissed these ideas as superstitions, the Salish possessed an acute knowledge of the natural world. Their understanding of plant life, for instance, was both thorough and refined. They named and classified plants, observing subtle differences in taxonomy and habitat. This knowledge was not solely utilitarian; the Indians observed and studied plants whether they were useful or not.

The Salish quest for salmon—the principal food staple for all Puget Sound Indians—largely determined the location of their villages on the islands. Salmon fishing oriented the tribes toward the rivers, and tribal boundaries in the county were the logical continuations of mainland river systems which lay opposite the islands. As a result, the people of the Snohomish River settled on southern parts of Whidby and Camano islands, while the tribes on the Skagit River built villages on North Whidby. The Kikialos were strictly an island tribe, living on North

Camano, but their territory faced the Stillaguamish River and they crossed to the mainland each fall to fish its banks.

At the peak of Salish population (about 1780), the Salish villages contained from 1,500 to 2,500 people, living in more than ninety-three places. Most of the sites were summer camping grounds inhabited seasonally for fishing, hunting, and berry or root gathering; but the Salish occupied at least fifteen permanent villages on the islands. Since the Indians bought safe and protected coves for canoe anchorages and a local supply of fish and shellfish, the selected village locations were principally on northeast Whidby and Camano. Three large Skagit villages on Penn's Cove, on North Whidby, formed the population center of the islands. The Snohomish had three villages on South Whidby, while the Kikialos occupied six permanent sites along the western and northern beaches of Camano. Most of the land on southern Whidby and southern Camano had no permanent population.

The large concentration of nonagricultural people on the islands called for a sensitive adjustment to the environment and a willingness to use every available source of food. This adjustment was reflected in the Salish food cycle of hunting, gathering, and fishing. Although the cycle varied from tribe to tribe, the Salish moved periodically through their territories in Puget Sound following the annual pattern of abundance. From May to October hundreds of mainland Indians joined permanent residents on the islands for root gathering and hunting. For all the Indians in the county, gathering vegetable products comprised a crucial element of their food cycle. At least fifty plants, exclusive of trees, were used by the Skagit alone.

The Salish search for food plants ended in September, when the first salmon of the great fall runs started up the rivers, and the Indians moved off the islands and gathered on the riverbanks to take them. For two months incredible numbers of fish crowded the streams. The large groups of Indians who fished and the immense quantities of fish caught led early settlers to regard salmon as their major food. Salmon were indeed of fundamental importance, but the Salish had other sources of food and were prepared to survive the occasional failure of the salmon to appear.

The Indian food cycle confused most early white observers. At times they saw the Indians as incurably nomadic, wandering across the land in search of food. But this was hard to reconcile with the strong Salish attachment to their permanent villages and their reverence for the graves of their ancestors. The tenacity of this devotion both impressed and bewildered the Americans when they sought to displace them. They found Salish devotion to their villages and lands as formidable as the huge cedar houses in which they lived. Actually the permanent villages and seasonal wandering in search of food formed the poles of the Salish's physical relation to the land. Both were basic.

Even modern anthropologists have tended to view the Salish as moving easily over the land, adapting to natural abundance and leaving no trace, with the settlers inheriting the land much as the first Indians had found it. They described the Indians as living off the "spontaneous product of nature" for generations until they were eventually displaced. Both the settlers and scholars have presumed that the components of the Salish food cycle were gifts of virgin nature. But in the plant communities that existed at the time of early settlement, there was evidence of substantial Salish influence on the environment. Three plants in particular—bracken, camas, and nettles—found in abundance by surveyors and settlers, were closely tied to Salish cultural practices.

Prolonged human occupation of a site usually led to a local enrichment of the soil. Succeeding generations of Indians living at the same village inevitably produced considerable amounts of waste. Shells and bones, plant refuse, ashes from fires, and excrement of humans and animals all gradually rotted and provided the soil

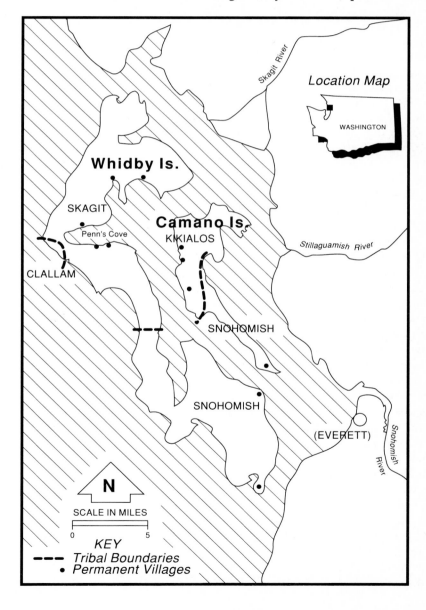

with significant amounts of potash, phosphorous, and nitrogen. These accumulations of waste also provided seedbeds for many of the ancestors of human food crops.

The nettle, for example, preferred rich soils and historically has been associated with human occupation. The nettle probably spread from the prairies, where it was a native plant, into the vicinity of the Salish villages. As with corn, constant proximity brought familiarity and eventually the discovery of uses for the plant. The Indians of Puget Sound made extensive use of the nettle. They extracted a medicine and a dye from it and peeled, dried, and rolled the bark into a two-ply string for fishing and duck nets. Moreover, as a wild nettle patch generally indicated rich ground, the Indians later used the plant as a guide in starting potato patches. According to their own testimony the Skagit Indians tended the nettles in a manner closely resembling cultivation. They kept the nettle patches free of weeds and burned the plant refuse in the fall after harvesting. The Salish clearly encouraged the nettle over other plant species of the prairies.

The Salish not only burned nettle patches but also regularly burned entire prairies in midsummer or early fall, when the rains had stopped and grass was tall and tinder dry. The first settlers on Whidby found these fires alarming, for they threatened their crops and houses. Because whites refused to tolerate the occasional destruction of their property, the beginning of American settlement saw the cessation of Indian burning on the prairies.

Few settlers gave much thought to the reasons behind these fires. One of the few who did was J. G. Cooper, a botanist with the railroad expedition that reached western Washington in 1854. Cooper recognized that the Salish had definite and sensible reasons for burning and concluded that if they ceased the practice the forest would soon encroach on the open lands. The Indians, he wrote, "burned to preserve their open grounds for game, and for the production of their important root, camas." The introduction of the horse, according to Cooper, had provided a further inducement for firing the grasslands. Fresh pastures sprang up in burned-over country. Cooper's comments on Indian land use were insightful but were largely ignored. Actually they fitted the inland Indians of southern Puget Sound better than they did the saltwater Salish of Whidby.

The Salish of Island County had no reason to burn to increase grazing areas, for they had no horses, nor were they dependent on large game animals for food. Even deer, a relatively minor source of food, were browsers that did not require extensive grasslands for feed. Undoubtedly, Indian burning encouraged game animals by enlarging their feeding areas, but this was not necessarily the rationale for burning. More likely the initial impetus for fires was to increase vegetable production.

The desire to encourage the growth of bracken, a fern which reached heights of seven feet on the prairies, and camas—which Cooper noticed dominating large expanses of open land—were the main reasons for setting fires. Both plants were staples of the Indian diet. The Salish ground dried bracken roots into flour, which they baked for bread. They boiled the fresh camas, eating them like potatoes, or dried and preserved the bulbs. The abundance of these plants on the prairies was not fortuitous. Rather than being major Indian food sources because they dominated the prairies, bracken and camas more likely dominated the prairies because they were major Indian food sources. According to Carl Sauer, the noted geographer, the very existence of people like the Salish depended on "acting intelligently within the range of their experience." Observing the changes that fire brought in its wake and using the altered landscape to their own advantage were "advantageous behavior" that enabled the Salish to survive.

In the Puget Sound region bracken was a pioneer invader of disturbed or burned-over lands. Burning facilitated the plant's spread over the prairies where the dense growth of native grasses often blocked its progress. Once established, the extensive root system of the fern, and the death of its topgrowth in the fall, protected it from fatal damage by fire and gave it an advantage over less resilient rivals. The encouragement of bracken would not have benefited a pastoral people seeking to enlarge their grazing lands. In fact, bracken was a poor feed after its first growth, and pastoral peoples lamented its increase. But the Salish were not herdsmen. They valued the fern as an important source of food and sought to promote its growth.

The camas plant benefited more indirectly from burning. Like bracken, its top growth died off in late summer and fall prairie fires did it little harm. Unlike bracken, however, the mere destruction of competing plants did not contribute to its spread. Direct human or animal intervention was necessary for the plant to widen its range. The Skagit moved camas bulbs into fresh areas, at first perhaps unwittingly, but later with zeal and care. Harvesting enabled the camas to increase, for dropped, split, and discarded bulbs spread the plant to new areas. Gathering the crop with a digging stick became a type of "unplanned tillage." According to Indian and white testimony, cultivation to ensure a better harvest eventually supplemented the digging and transplanting of mature bulbs. Such a technique approached true farming—as did other Salish practices. For example, they also worked in plant refuse around another food plant, the tiger lily. The Indians of the upper Skagit, and probably the Whidby Skagit, practiced a primitive cultivation of both the lily and the wild carrot. When the potato was introduced into Puget Sound, the Salish quickly became adept at the cultivation of that crop without any direct instruction by the settlers.

Indian modification of the vegetational community of the prairies was significant and purposeful. Salish practices involved a rational manipulation of the environment, and this manipulation had profound ecological effects. Burning destroyed conifer seedlings and shrubs that encroached on the prairies, while at the same time it encouraged bracken to become the dominant vegetation of the open lands. Other Salish practices helped spread camas and nettle plants. Unwanted trees or shrubs surviving the fires were pulled out by hand. When the whites arrived, they regarded the prairies as wild. They damned bracken for making plowing difficult, cursed the painful sting of the nettle, and praised camas as pig food. In fulfilling the biblical injunction of sinking plowshares into the earth, they imagined that they were putting the stamp of man upon the land. But the stamp of man was already firmly present.

Salish influence on the landscape extended beyond the limits of the prairies into the surrounding forests. Indians used wood extensively, especially cedar, but also fir, hemlock, and alder. Yet considering the abundance of the forests and the massive size of the towering trees, direct Salish use probably had little impact on forest ecology. The conifers of western Washington were so huge that it took the neighboring Makah Indians two weeks to fell a Sitka spruce by fire and axe. To cut the fir and cedar of Island County would have demanded similar labor. The occasional felling of one of these giants would have made only a minuscule difference in the forest as a whole.

For the Salish the forest yielded other products besides wood. They searched among the trees for berries, fireweed, and game, none of which favored deep forest, but thrived in the clearings and young successional forests that followed fires. The upper-river Indians, fearing the immediate destruction of existing game animals, were wary of fire, but the saltwater peoples of the lowlands apparently burned over berry fields without much hesitation. They particularly sought to promote the growth of fireweed and berries that formed part of the normal successional pattern on such lands. Berries were an important food, while fireweed, along with other materials, was used in the weaving of blankets. The very name *fireweed* given it by the settlers, showed the close connection between this plant and burning.

The first United States surveyors to examine Whidby and Camano islands in the late 1850s made significant comments on the condition of the forests at the time. There had not yet been a decade of settlement, and most of the islands were unoccupied and practically unexplored. The surveyors made two critical observations: (1) they noted that Douglas fir was the dominant forest species of the islands, closely followed by hemlock and Sitka spruce and cedar; and (2) they recorded that large areas in the forests had been burned.

In the hemlock-cedar climax forests in Island County, Douglas fir relied for propagation on the destruction not only of other trees but also of the mature fir itself. Fir not only thrived on catastrophe, it depended on it. Fir seedlings died in the dense shade of mature forests, while hemlock and cedar seedlings survived, spread, and eventually displaced the mature fir as they fell from age and disease. Without interference, the climax forest of the region would have been primarily cedar and hemlock. As Douglas fir of all ages and sizes abounded on the islands, mature forests obviously had been destroyed. This destruction clearly did not result from harvesting, nor was there evidence of extensive kills by disease or insects. The surveyors blamed the destruction on fire.

Normally the fires that had destroyed the virgin forests of Island County could have been ascribed to electrical storms. However, few thunderstorms occurred in western Washington. Thunderstorms swept the mountains on the mainland, but they would have had to be of staggering proportions to reach Puget Sound. Furthermore, such fires could never have reached Island County, simply because Whidby and Camano were islands. Yet fires were so extensive and common on the islands that, of the sixteen townships surveyed in the 1850s, six contained burned-over forests. In five of these the damage was substantial. This burning gave the Douglas fir its advantage and enabled the tree to dominate the forests of the islands.

Extensive forest burning in the county resulted either from prairie fires which accidently spread to the woods or from fires deliberately set to extend berry grounds. With the brisk winds that blew across the islands, a small fire could spread rapidly. As Indian fires were the main source of forest burning in Island County, and probably in the entire Puget Sound region, they played a critical role in determining the species composition of the forests. The result was a large stand of Douglas fir in the lowland forests of Puget Sound and a successional growth of groundsel, fireweed, berries, bracken, and fir, alder, and hemlock seedlings.

In the northern coniferous forests, burning had shaped woodland ecology for centuries. Fire formed a crucial part of the forest environment. It not only liberated mineral nutrients accumulated in the litter, humus, wood, and foliage of the old forest, but it simultaneously prepared seedbeds and triggered the release of some seed supplies. The periodic destruction of old forests kept a significant proportion of each region in young trees and thus reduced the susceptibility of the forest to insects and disease. In a sense, fires were so common and critical that the species composition that would have developed without fire would have been unnatural. The only unusual aspect of the situation on Puget Sound was that such a large percentage of fires were of human origin.

Fire shaped not only the forests but also the animal population that inhabited the woodlands. Both deer and elk were abundant in Island County when settlers first arrived, and according to Miron Heinselman, a forester who had studied forest fires, these animals were "best adapted to recent burns and early succession forests—not climax forests." Thus, by setting fires the Salish provided these animals with their habitat and increased their numbers—as well as the number of their predators, the wolves.

The Salish accomplishment in creating and maintaining their ecosystem was impressive. Because of this the Indian population of 1780 was larger than any human population on the islands before 1910. They populated their islands with spirits and powers, but they did not restrict their manipulation to magic. Their technology was limited, but they used it effectively. Unlike the Indians of the upper rivers, the Salish never suffered seasonal scarcities or periodic famines. Indeed, in terms of camas, berries, bracken, deer, and elk, the islands were a food-exporting region. This had been brought about by Indians learning, through observation and tradition, to alter natural communities to fit their needs, without destroying in the process the ability of these communities to sustain the cultures which had created them. Far from being creatures of their environment, the Indians had shaped their world and made it what it was when the whites arrived.

The stability of the environment the Salish had created in Island County depended on their continued burning, cultivation, and gathering. If they had ceased these activities, the ecology of the area would have been altered. With the coming of the settlers, however, the Salish not only curtailed these practices but began adapting new tools and techniques introduced by white farmers. As a result, the Salish environment changed at a staggering rate in the 1850s. Even as Indians lingered on the prairies and along the coves, pigs and cows destroyed the camas and farmers plowed up the nettles and bracken. The annual fires ceased, and the Indians found themselves powerless to sustain the world that they had created— and that, in turn, had sustained them.

16

THE NAVAJO AT THE BOSQUE REDONDO: COOPERATION, RESISTANCE, AND INITIATIVE, 1864–1868

KATHERINE MARIE BIRMINGHAM OSBURN

Throughout the nineteenth century American planners sought to move Indians into the majority culture and society. Usually such programs depended on experience and knowledge gained at school, in church, or on the farm. The officials delegated to help "civilize" tribal people assumed that the examples these institutions provided would help them achieve their goal of changing Indians quickly. Occasionally the elements combined successfully and a few Native Americans actually adopted much of the majority culture, but that proved uncertain and most Native Americans rejected the whites' overtures whenever they had a chance. This selection discusses the experiences of the Navajos after their 1863–64 defeat by federal troops in northern New Mexico. Having defeated the tribe, General James H. Carleton decided to force acculturation upon his captives. He moved the Indians into the southeastern corner of New Mexico, where the army herded them onto a forsaken area known as the Bosque Redondo. There the general ordered his subordinates to establish a reservation and to begin the process of forced acculturation. The author considers the variety of Native American responses and initiatives begun while having to farm in a sterile region, send their children to school, and see their culture gradually destroyed. Much of the article relates Indian efforts to avoid cooperating with the soldiers, to sabatoge its program, and to retain their tribal religion, economy, and identity. In 1868 the tribe signed a treaty with the United States that allowed the Indians to return to their traditional homeland, where they remain today.

Katherine Marie Birmingham Osburn is a doctoral student in history at the University of Denver.

Source: Katherine Marie Birmingham Osburn, "The Navajo at the Bosque Redondo: Cooperation, Resistance, and Initiative," *New Mexico Historical Review*, 60 (October 1985), pp. 399–413. Reprinted with permission of the editor.

Despite the traumatic experience of military defeat and incarceration in a strange and hostile environment, the Navajo at the Bosque Redondo, 1864–68, did not respond passively to the reservation experience. Rather, they devised active adaptive strategies using a pattern of cooperation, resistance, and initiative. While Navajo religion furnished the Indians with a means of devising their own responses to many problems they faced, it also acted as a basis for solidarity in an experience potentially devastating to the Navajo's cultural survival. Since Indian behavior worked against the military's purposes and functioning at the Bosque Redondo, Indians were a variable in the reservation's demise, actively participating in its failure—not merely observing its collapse. Thus, while administrative and military aspects of the Bosque are important, the Navajo's behavior warrants equal consideration.

As a result of the Kit Carson campaign of 1863–64, Brig. Gen. James H. Carleton, commander of the military department of New Mexico, moved the Navajo to a plot in southeastern New Mexico known as Bosque Redondo. There he had established a military post, Fort Sumner, and a reservation, where he planned to transform the Mescalero Apache and the Navajo into peaceful, Christian Americans. The Navajo who arrived at the Bosque Redondo were starving and impoverished, and over the next four years their miserable condition did not improve greatly. Shortages of food and fuel were continual, and the alkaline water caused dysentery. Other illnesses at the reservation included malaria, pneumonia, rheumatic fever, measles, and venereal disease. The Indians reported that sometimes military personnel beat them and that Navajo women were raped. Further, the Navajo were raided by other Indian tribes.

Despite this evidence, Carleton interpreted the Navajo's degraded condition as an indication that they were now passive and dependent. "It is a mockery," he wrote, "to hold councils with a people who . . . have only to await our decisions. [We should] care for them as children until they can care for themselves." In his view the Navajo were his to transform. The Indians initially proved cooperative. As a condition of their surrender the Indians agreed, as former Indian Superintendent James L. Collins noted in 1864, "to abandon their nomadic, marauding way of life, to settle on a reservation away from their cherished mountain homes, and to devote themselves to the pursuit of industry as their means of support."

Observers at the Bosque Redondo generally commented on how industriously the Indians worked. In 1865 the Indians testified before the Doolittle Commission, a Senate investigative committee, that they were more than willing to farm despite the problems involved. In addition, Michael Steck, superintendent of Indian Affairs in 1864, commented that "the tribe has for three centuries been engaged in planting and they are also far in advance of all other wild tribes in various fabricks such as blankets, baskets, ropes, saddles and bridle bits." Thus it appeared to individuals who visited the reservation in the early years that the experiment had tremendous potential and that the Indians were hard-working and cooperative.

Indian cooperation was, however, more complex than it first appeared. Although the Navajo recognized that farming was a necessity—because the rations provided by the United States government were inadequate—the Indians had more choice in this area than is initially apparent. In 1868, for instance, they staunchly refused to plant any crops, explaining, "We have done all that we could possibly do, but we found it to be labor in vain and have therefore quit it; for this reason we have not planted or tried to do anything this year." Thus cooperation, though mandated by hunger, was also a choice, for the Indians did refuse to farm. In this act they demonstrated their ability to decide for or against cooperation, regardless of the circumstances.

Similarly, the Navajo considered the benefits of the education programs at the Bosque and chose to accept training in carpentry, leatherworking, and blacksmithing. Delgadito, the Navajo headman, realized his people's need to repair their newly acquired farm implements and also concluded that they would now have to learn how to make a living. The Navajo also perceived that the trades provided them with such an opportunity. Accommodation in this realm, then, was a strategy born of immediate needs and of an understanding of the new economic realities facing the Indians.

While the Navajo appreciated instruction in the trades, they were much more reticent about the benefits of other types of education. For example, although General Carleton established a school at the Bosque Redondo in 1865, the Indians rarely utilized it. Apparently they were more interested in receiving the ration coupons that the school distributed than in procuring an education for their children. As post surgeon Dr. George Gwynther noted:

> I do not think that the juvenile savages shared either love of or aptitude for the alphabet, nor rightly appreciated the treasure to which it was the key; inasmuch as they often stipulated for additional bread rations as a condition of longer attendance at school.

The Navajo's resistance to the reservation school was a serious blow to Carleton's plans for acculturation. Yet the Indians claimed they were not opposed to education; they were simply more absorbed with the immediate concerns of daily survival and considered the benefits of education to be peripheral to more urgent matters, such as obtaining enough food to fend off starvation. Their attempt to procure money and extra ration coupons for sending their children to school demonstrates the Indians' shrewd survival strategy.

The Navajo gave top priority to procuring more food. They often tried pleading for larger rations. While officers struggled to find a solution, sometimes increasing the size of the ration, other times shifting its frequency, the Indians acted to meet their needs by their own methods. They stole any available food and also produced some three thousand extra ration coupons. By forging metal coupons, the Navajos were utilizing an old skill to meet a new need. In addition, since the number of forged tickets increased from January to May of 1865, the number of Indians who benefited from this practice probably increased. Apparently, however, this strategy profited some Indians at the expense of others.

Another method of obtaining extra food was prostitution, which was not a standard practice under less stressful conditions. Navajo women were generally considered to be modest and decent before and after the Bosque Redondo years. Indeed, the Navajo moral code discouraged promiscuity, and Navajo religion had a ritual designed for "the removal of prostitution or mania," called The Prostitution Way. While the Navajo recognized the degradation of prostitution at Fort Sumner, they also indicated that the women were compelled to set aside their moral prescriptions because of poverty and hunger.

Although some Navajo disregarded the moral injunctions of their culture against prostitution, the taboos governing residence were generally upheld. Carleton had originally planned to house the Navajo in neatly ordered barracks similar to the type of housing found in Pueblo villages. The Navajo, however, found this scheme unacceptable because their traditional housing was widely dispersed. Furthermore, they rejected the notion of permanent homes because of their beliefs about departed souls. "The custom of our tribe," the chiefs claimed, "is never to enter a house where a person has died, but abandon it." Consequently, they settled "in scattered and extended camps, unorganized by bands or otherwise."

The Navajo's refusal to adhere to Carleton's plans for their housing represents another assertion of their autonomy. Instead of conforming to the military's plans, the Navajo forced the military to restructure their administration procedures. As Nelson H. Davis complained, the dispersed Indians were difficult to control and his troops were severely taxed in their efforts to round up Indians for work. Thus the defiance of the Indians allowed them to continue their traditional settlement patterns in spite of their captivity and to exert some control over the decisions that affected their lives.

For similar reasons the Navajo refused medical treatment at the post hospital. The Indians explained that they shunned the hospital because "all that have reported there have died." Because of this belief, Dr. Gwynther insisted on removing from the hospital all patients who were near death. Thus the Indians' behavior helped to dictate hospital policy.

Resistance to the hospital can also be traced to the Navajo's preference for their native medicine men. Dr. Gwynther complained that "the relations of the sick person have [occasionally] carried the patient off clandestinely, to get such benefits as may accrue from the practice of their native medicine-men." The Indians admitted that the medicine men were often ineffectual in combatting diseases on the reservation, but explained that they lacked the plants necessary for native cures.

Army doctors viewed illness as a natural occurrence treatable with scientific methods, but the Navajo had a different interpretation. In the Navajo world view, illness is an example of disharmony in the cosmic order that the performance of a religious ceremony can correct. During the ceremony, the Navajo invoke their Holy People to rectify the disturbance of order. If the ritual is correctly carried out, the deities are obligated to grant the mortal's requests, for a principle of reciprocity governs the exchange. In this regard, Navajo oral tradition emphasizes the importance of healing ritual at the Bosque. Charlie Mitchell, a Navajo who had been a child at the reservation, explained that ceremonies were performed to prevent the Navajo from dying in captivity.

In seeking solutions to disease, the Navajo rejected Anglo cures but embraced some from other Indians. They borrowed, for instance, the Chiricahua Windway from the Apache at the fort. This ritual cures a variety of sicknesses: those caused by the winds—being knocked over by wind, cooking with a tree felled by wind, or sleeping in a place hollowed out by winds; those caused by snakes—eating food touched by a snake, injury to a snake, or snake bites; those from a cactus—because of cooking with tree cactus; or those by flooding. Another Navajo explanation for sickness at the Bosque Redondo was witchcraft. To help combat illness resulting from witchcraft, the Navajo also adopted the Apache's Suckingway ritual technique for curing a witchcraft victim: sucking out the witch's darts.

To bring about other cures, the Navajo also performed many of their own ceremonies. For instance, the Squaw Dance, a ritual of the Navajo Evilway, which purifies an individual from disease-inducing contacts with foreigners, was used at the Bosque. According to this ceremony some sicknesses are the result of the ghosts of aliens, either those whom a Navajo warrior has killed or those who died from other causes and with whom the Navajo may have had contact, sexual or otherwise. Touching the corpse or stepping on the grave of an "outsider" may also cause alien ghosts to torment a Navajo with sickness. Because the Navajo were in close contact with Apache and Anglos who died, they no doubt felt that at least some of their sicknesses necessitated the performance of the Squaw Dance.

Other reasons for enacting the Squaw Dance were probably connected with Navajo raids from the Bosque reservation. Since Navajo warriors were killing enemies during this time, they required a Squaw Dance to prevent or cure a retaliating illness. In March of 1866, as an example, seven Navajo went on a foray against the Utes who had killed one of their children. The Navajo pursued their enemies for approximately twelve days and then attacked them, killing five and capturing a ten-year-old Ute boy, twenty-four horses, and saddles and guns. Another account of a Navajo campaign from Fort Sumner does not end so happily. While on a raid in the Comanche country, the Navajo lost four of their war party. The raid had been doomed, the raiders concluded, when a coyote appeared one night in the warriors' camp. In October 1867 a contingent of Navajo retaliated against the Comanches for a raid on 9 September. The Navajo had pursued their attackers and killed twelve.

In addition to retaliatory raids, the Indians also committed offensive raids aimed at obtaining more stock. In this regard, settlers in eastern New Mexico claimed that Navajo from Fort Sumner attacked their homes and stole their livestock. Yet while some Navajo did engage in such activities, it is important to note that a large number of the complaints were probably exaggerated and that the Navajo were often blamed for depredations that other Indians committed. Regardless of blame, warfare conducted at the Bosque Redondo required ceremony to counteract the disturbance it wrought in the natural order.

The Navajo also performed the Fire Dance, a ritual of the nine-night Mountainway or Nightway ceremonies that restore harmony. The Fire Dance combines in a single ceremony the abbreviated forms of many ceremonials. Dancers representing a variety of other Holyway ceremonies, such as Beautyway, Windway, or Waterway, perform a portion of their chant. The patient receives the specific benefits of each without undergoing the entire ceremony. Thus the Fire Dance saves time and expense and would serve the Navajos by adapting their more elaborate ceremonies to the limited resources of the reservation.

The Fire Dance was also possibly connected with the food problems at the Bosque. Certainly corn-growing rites and the ritualistic treatment of food employed in the dance were relevant to experiences of the Navajo on the reservation. According to their eschatology an individual who has eaten another person's food without ritualistic preparation may be in danger of being transformed into that person. Therefore the Navajo may have performed Fire Dances as protection from being "transformed" by the white person's food. The recitation of rituals concerned with agriculture suggests that although the Navajos utilized the American's technology, they were convinced that their success in farming was contingent upon their controlling the forces of nature that were responsible for the harvest.

While the Navajo employed a variety of responses in order to survive at the Bosque, their ultimate goal was to return to their homeland. From April to August 1865 approximately 1,300 Navajo left the reservation, hoping to return to their old country, where roughly 1,000 to 2,000 Navajo remained, having escaped the roundup. General Carleton dealt sternly with the runaway problem, telling his newly appointed post commander Maj. William McCleave that he would kill every Indian found off the reservation without a passport. Despite this threat Indians continued to leave the reservation over the next several years. In 1868, for example, 250 to 300 more Navajo escaped.

The majority of Navajo, however, remained at the Bosque Redondo and attempted to obtain their liberty through pleading and ceremony. As early as 1865 the Indians begged for their release, warning that if they were forced to remain upon the reservation they would "all die very soon." They explained that they had been instructed by their Holy People to remain within the boundaries of three rivers, the Rio Grande, the Rio San Juan, and the Rio Colorado, and that their violation of this restriction was responsible for their current suffering. They extolled the productivity of their old country, where they had enough food and firewood and were safe from their enemies.

According to Navajo oral tradition it was not pleading alone that secured the Navajo's release, but also the performance of the Coyote Way ritual. Although some informants claimed that the ritual was divinatory, indicating that the government was now ready to free the Navajo, other Navajo attributed their freedom to this ceremony. The years of pleading had been unsuccessful, they claimed, until the performance of the Coyote ritual, "during which our leader was blessed with Coyote power." Because of this ceremony, the next request to leave was approved.

Moreover, the Navajo called on their religious ritual to aid them in interaction with the reservation personnel. Recognizing that Anglos controlled the reservation, the Navajo attempted, at the same time, to circumvent government officials and to procure release by petitioning their Holy People. To this day some Navajo believe that, ultimately, their Holy People, not the United States government, returned them to their current reservation. Whatever the cause of release on 1 July 1868, the Navajo signed a treaty with the U. S. government allowing them to return to their traditional homeland.

An examination of the Navajo's behavior at the Bosque Redondo reveals that the Indians worked toward two primary goals, survival and release, by using a pattern of cooperation, resistance, and initiative. Cooperation meant farming and learning the trades, while resistance was manifested in refusing formal education, barracks housing, and Anglo medical treatment. In addition, prostitution, forgery, raiding, fleeing, and ceremony represented Indian initiative. These varied activities indicate that the Navajo had no single survival strategy. In fact, solutions that individuals employed sometimes clashed with the interests of the tribe as a whole. For example, when Navajo leaders promised to curtail raiding, while other Navajo raided, the Indians were factionalized, increasing the potential for cultural disintegration.

Navajo religion, however, was an important element in avoiding this fate. Oral histories recount how special the ceremonies were to the Indians during captivity and indicate their belief that their Holy People sustained the tribe at the Bosque. In addition to providing comfort, religion was also a source of social cohesion. Navajo ceremonies require large gatherings of people, some of whom are involved with the ceremony while others come to meet friends and family. The largest number of spectators gather during the final day and night of a sing, and the patient's kinsmen are expected to feed them. Consequently there is social pressure on all nearby relatives to contribute time and labor to help defray the costs of a ritual. Thus kinsmen and neighbors are bound together by reciprocal obligations governing the ceremony.

Ceremony also functions ideally as a means of reducing intergroup tensions by redistributing wealth. The singer is expected to give a large portion of his fee to friends and relatives. Navajos who stint on ceremonies risk accusations of witchcraft, and prosperous Navajos must sponsor elaborate ceremonies to avoid similar suspicions. In a situation such as that at the Bosque Redondo, where resources were limited and tensions great, ceremony would have provided a means of reducing the stress the uneven distribution of resources generated. Religion, then, was the key to the Navajo's survival as a cultural unit during their stay near Fort Sumner.

The Bosque Redondo experiment failed for a number of reasons, most of which historians have discussed. The reservation was not economically feasible because of environmental and administrative problems, yet the failure of the Bosque Redondo cannot be understood without discussing Navajo activities. Clearly their behavior taxed the labors of the military in administering them—because of their dispersed settlement pattern—and in containing them—because they left the post without the proper papers. Their refusal to accept the Bosque Redondo, seen in their nearly constant begging to go home, also contributed to the realization that Carleton's plan was not workable. The Navajo at the Bosque Redondo were not passive observers of the reservation's rise and fall, but were instead active participants in the successes and failures of the experiment.

17

CANADA'S SUBJUGATION OF THE PLAINS CREE, 1879–1885

JOHN L. TOBIAS

As pioneers swept west across the plains of North America they encountered a variety of tribal people on either side of the border of Canada and the United States. Nevertheless, the process of settlement and economic development of the natural resources followed similar paths in the two nations. Indians occupied areas that the whites passed through and lands that they coveted. Eventually this brought the tribes and the governments in North America into competition and conflict. While the pace of settlement and the frequency or severity of the quarrels that resulted varied widely in Canada and the United States, much of the process appears similar.

In this essay the author suggests that Canadians have fooled themselves about nineteenth-century relations between the races in their West. He describes what he calls a persistent myth that Canadian officials followed honest, just, and humane policies in their dealings with the tribal people of the plains region. According to this idea the paternalistic and farsighted whites adopted policies that eventually allowed the Indians to become acculturated and then assimilated into Canadian society. Tobias finds this view of the past both one-sided and inaccurate. Instead he suggests that the Cree people proved both energetic and adaptive in their dealings with the whites and with the obvious need to change their lifeways when the game that had supported their traditional culture disappeared. The Canadian government, on the other hand, focused chiefly on manipulating the situation to its own advantage. In his discussion of policy implementation and the actions bureaucrats took in their dealings with the Cree people, the author gives a picture that looks depressingly like what happened in the American West at the same time.

John L. Tobias is a professor of history at Red Deer College.

Source: John L. Tobias, "Canada's Subjugation of the Plains Cree, 1879-1885," *Canadian Historical Review,* 64, 4 (December 1983), pp. 519–548. Copyright © University of Toronto Press, 1983. All rights reserved. Reprinted by permission.

One of the most persistent myths that Canadian historians perpetuate is that of the honourable and just policy Canada followed in dealing with the Plains Indians. First enunciated in the Canadian expansionist literature of the 1870s as a means to emphasize the distinctive Canadian approach to and the unique character of the Canadian West, it has been given credence by G. F. G. Stanley in his classic *The Birth of Western Canada*, and by all those who use Stanley's work as the standard interpretation of Canada's relationship with the Plains Indians in the period 1870–85. Thus students are taught that the Canadian government was paternalistic and farsighted in offering the Indians a means to become civilized and assimilated into white society by the reserve system, and honest and fair-minded in honouring legal commitments made in the treaties. The Plains Indians, and particularly the Plains Cree, are said to be a primitive people adhering to an inflexible system of tradition and custom, seeking to protect themselves against the advance of civilization and taking up arms in rejection of the reserve system and an agricultural way of life. This traditional interpretation distorts the roles of both the Cree and the Canadian government, for the Cree were both flexible and active in promoting their own interests and willing to accommodate themselves to a new way of life, while the Canadian government was neither as farsighted nor as just as tradition maintains. Canada's principal concern in its relationship with the Plains Cree was to establish control over them, and Canadian authorities were willing to and did wage war upon the Cree in order to achieve this control.

Those who propagate the myth would have us believe that Canada began to negotiate treaties with the Indians of the West in 1871 as part of an overall plan to develop the agricultural potential of the West, open the land for railway construction, and bind the prairies to Canada in a network of commercial and economic ties. Although there is an element of truth to these statements, the fact remains that in 1871 Canada had no plan on how to deal with the Indians and the negotiation of treaties was not at the initiative of the Canadian government, but at the insistence of the Ojibwa Indians of the North-West Angle and the Saulteaux of the tiny province of Manitoba. What is ignored by the traditional interpretation is that the treaty process only started after Yellow Quill's band of Saulteaux turned back settlers who tried to go west of Portage la Prairie and after other Saulteaux leaders insisted upon enforcement of the Selkirk Treaty or, more often, insisted upon making a new treaty. Also ignored is the fact that the Ojibwa of the North-West Angle demanded rents and created the fear of violence against prospective settlers who crossed their land or made use of their territory, if Ojibwa rights to their lands were not recognized. This pressure and fear of resulting violence is what motivated the government to begin the treaty-making process.

Canada's initial offer to the Saulteaux and Ojibwa consisted only of reserves and a small cash annuity. This proposal was rejected by the Ojibwa in 1871 and again in 1872, while the Saulteaux demanded, much to Treaty Commissioner Wemyss Simpson's chagrin, farm animals, horses, wagons, and farm tools and equipment. Simpson did not include these demands in the written treaty, for he had no authority to do so, but he wrote them down in the form of a memorandum that he entitled "outside promises" and which he failed to send to Ottawa. Thus the original Treaties 1 and 2 did not include those items the Saulteaux said had to be part of a treaty before they would agree to surrender their lands. Only in 1874, after the Indian leaders of Manitoba became irate over nonreceipt of the goods that Simpson had promised them, was an inquiry launched, and Simpson's list of "outside promises" discovered and incorporated in renegotiated treaties in 1875. It was only in 1873, after the Ojibwa of the North-West Angle had twice refused treaties that only included reserves and annuities, that the govenment agreed to include the domestic animals, farm tools, and equipment that the Ojibwa demanded. After this experience Canada made such goods a standard part of later treaties.

Just as it was pressure from the Indians of Manitoba that forced the government of Canada to initiate the treaty process, it was pressure from the Plains Cree in the period 1872–75 that compelled the government of Canada to continue the process with the Indians of the Qu'Appelle and Saskatchewan districts. The Plains Cree had interfered with the geological survey and prevented the construction of telegraph lines through their territory to emphasize that Canada had to deal with the Cree for Cree lands. The Cree had learned in 1870 about Canada's claim to their lands, and not wanting to experience what had happened to the Indians in the United States when those people were faced with an expansionist govenment, the Cree made clear that they would not allow settlement or use of their lands until Cree rights had been clearly recognized. They also made clear that part of any arrangement for Cree lands had to involve assistance to the Cree in developing a new agricultural way of life.

In adopting this position, the Cree were simply demonstrating a skill that they had shown since their initial contact with Europeans in 1670. On numerous occasions during the fur trade era they had adapted to changed environmental and economic circumstances, beginning first as hunters, then as provisioners and middlemen in the Hudson's Bay Company trading system, and finally adapting from a woodland to parkland-prairie buffalo-hunting culture to retain their independence and their desired ties with the fur trade. Having accommodated themselves to the Plains Indian culture after 1800, they expanded into territory formerly controlled by the Atsina, and as the buffalo herds began to decline after 1850, the Cree expanded into Blackfoot territory. Expansion was one response to the threat posed by declining buffalo herds; another was that some Plains Cree bands began to turn to agriculture. Thus, when the Cree learned that Canada claimed their lands, part of the arrangement they were determined to make and succeeded in making was to receive assistance in adapting to an agricultural way of life. So successful were they in negotiating such assistance that when the Mackenzie government received a copy of Treaty 6 in 1876 it accepted the treaty only after expressing a protest concerning the too generous terms granted to the Cree.

While willing to explore the alternative of agriculture, three Cree leaders in the 1870s sought means to guarantee preservation of the buffalo-hunting culture as long as possible. Piapot (leader of the Cree-Assiniboine of the region south of the Qu'Appelle River), and Big Bear and Little Pine (leaders of two of the largest Cree bands from the Saskatchewan River district) led what has been called an armed migration of the Cree into the Cypress Hills in the latter 1860s. All three men were noted warriors, and Big Bear and Piapot were noted religious leaders, but their prowess was not enough to prevent a Cree defeat at the Battle of the Belly River in

1870, and as a result they explored the alternative of dealing with the government of Canada, but in a manner to extract guarantees for the preservation of Cree autonomy. They were determined to get the government to promise to limit the buffalo hunt to the Indians—a goal that Cree leaders had been advocating since the 1850s. When Big Bear met with Treaty Commissioner Alexander Morris at Fort Pitt in September 1876, he extracted a promise from Morris that non-Indian hunting of the buffalo would be regulated.

Big Bear refused to take treaty in 1876, despite receiving Morris's assurances about the regulation of the hunt. Little Pine and Piapot also did not take treaty when the treaty commissions first came to deal with the Cree. Oral tradition among the Cree maintains that all three leaders wished to see how faithful the government would be in honouring the treaties, but equally important for all three leaders was their belief that the treaties were inadequate and that revisions were necessary. Piapot thought Treaty 4 (the Qu'Appelle Treaty) needed to be expanded to include increased farm equipment and tools and to stipulate that the government had to provide mills, blacksmith and carpentry shops and tools, and instructors in farming and the trades. Only after receiving assurances that Ottawa would consider these requests did Piapot take treaty in 1875. Big Bear and Little Pine objected to Treaty 6 (Fort Pitt and Carlton) because Commissioner Morris had made clear that in taking treaty the Cree would be bound by Canadian law. To accept the treaties would mean being subject to an external authority of which the Crees had little knowledge and upon which they had little influence. Neither Big Bear nor Little Pine would countenance such a loss of autonomy.

Big Bear had raised the matter of Cree autonomy at Fort Pitt in 1876 when he met Commissioner Morris. At that time Big Bear said: "I will make a request that he [Morris] save me from what I most dread, that is the rope about my neck....It was not given to us to have the rope about our neck." Morris and most subsequent historians have interpreted Big Bear's statements to be a specific reference to hanging, but such an interpretation ignores the fact that Big Bear, like most Indian leaders, often used a metaphor to emphasize a point. In 1875 he had made the same point by using a different metaphor when he spoke to messengers informing him that a treaty commission was to meet with the Cree in 1876. At that time Big Bear said: "We want none of the Queen's presents: when we set a foxtrap we scatter pieces of meat all around, but when the fox gets into the trap we knock him on the head; we want no bait...." A more accurate interpretation of Big Bear's words to Morris in 1876 is that he feared being controlled or "enslaved" just as an animal is controlled when it has a rope around its neck. In 1877, when meeting with Lieutenant-Governor David Laird, Little Pine also stated that he would not take treaty because he saw the treaties as a means by which the government could "enslave" his people.

The importance of these three leaders cannot be underestimated, for they had with them in the Cypress Hills more than fifty percent of the total Indian population of the Treaty 4 and 6 areas. By concentrating in such numbers in the last buffalo ranges in Canadian territory, the Cree were free from all external interference, whether by other Indian nations or by the agents of the Canadian government: the North-West Mounted Police. Recognizing that these men were bargaining from a position of strength, Laird recommended in 1878 that the government act quickly to establish reserves and honour the treaties. He was aware that the Cypress Hills leaders had the support of many of the Cree in treaty and that many of the Cree leaders were complaining that the government was not providing the farming assistance promised. As the number of these complaints increased, so did Cree support for Big Bear and Little Pine.

The Cree were concerned not only about the lack of assistance to farm, but when Canadian officials were slow to take action to regulate the buffalo hunt, Big Bear, Piapot, and Little Pine met with Blackfoot leaders and with Sitting Bull of the Teton Sioux in an attempt to reach agreement among the Indian nations on the need to regulate buffalo hunting. These councils were also the forum where Indian leaders discussed the need to revise the treaties. On learning about the Indian council, the non-Indian populace of the West grew anxious, fearing establishment of an Indian confederacy which would wage war if Indian demands were rejected. However, an Indian confederacy did not result from these meetings, nor was agreement reached on how the buffalo were to be preserved, because the Cree, Sioux, and Blackfoot could not overcome their old animosities towards one another.

When in 1879 the buffalo disappeared from the Canadian prairies and Big Bear and Little Pine took their bands south to the buffalo ranges on the Milk and Missouri rivers, most of the other Cree and Assiniboine bands also went with them. The Cree who remained in Canada faced starvation while awaiting the survey of their reserves and the farming equipment that had been promised. Realizing that many of the Cree were dying, the government decided that those who had taken treaty should be given rations. As well, the government appointed Edgar Dewdney to the newly created position of Commissioner of Indian Affairs for the North-West Territory; a farming policy for the Western reserves was introduced; a survey of Cree reserves was begun; and twelve farming instructors were appointed to teach the Indians of the North-West.

The new Indian Commissioner quickly sought to use rations as a means of getting control over the Cree. In the fall of 1879 he announced that rations were to be provided only to Indians who had taken treaty. To get the Cree into treaty more easily and to reduce the influence of recalcitrant leaders, Dewdney announced that he would adopt an old Hudson's Bay Company practice of recognizing any adult male Cree as chief of a new band if he could induce 100 or more persons to recognize him as leader. He expected that the starving Cypress Hills Cree would desert their old leaders to get rations. As a means of demonstrating Canada's control over the Cree, Dewdney ordered that only the sick, aged, and orphans should receive rations without providing some service to one of the government agencies in the West.

Dewdney's policies seemed to work, for when the Cree and Assiniboine who had gone to hunt in Montana returned starving, their resolve weakened. Little Pine's people convinced their chief to take treaty in 1879, but when Big Bear refused to do the same, almost half of his following joined Lucky Man or Thunderchild to form new bands in order to receive rations.

Taking treaty to avoid starvation did not mean that the Cree had come to accept the treaties as written; rather they altered their tactics in seeking revisions. Believing that small reserves were more susceptible to the control of the Canadian government and its officials, Big Bear, Piapot, and Little Pine sought to effect a concentration of the Cree people in an Indian territory similar to the reservation system in the United States. In such a territory the Cree would be able to preserve their autonomy, or at least limit the ability of others to control them; they would be better able to take concerted action on matters of importance to them.

Soon after taking treaty Little Pine applied for a reserve in the Cypress Hills, twenty-seven miles northeast of the North-West Mounted Police post of Fort Walsh. Piapot requested a reserve next to Little Pine's, while ten other bands, including most of the Assiniboine nation, selected reserve sites contiguous to either Little Pine's or Piapot's and to one another. If all these reserve sites were granted and if Big Bear were to take treaty and settle in the Cypress Hills, the result would be concentration of much of the Cree nation and the creation of an Indian territory that would comprise most of what is now southwestern Saskatchewan.

Unaware of the intention of the Cree and Assiniboine leaders, Canadian officials in the spring of 1880 agreed to the establishment of a reserve for all the Canadian Assiniboine and reserves in the Cypress Hills for each of the Cree bands that wished them. In 1880 the Assiniboine reserve was surveyed, but the other Indian leaders were told that their reserves would not be surveyed until the following year. In the interim, most of the Cree went to the buffalo ranges in Montana.

The Cree effort to exploit the remaining American buffalo ranges caused them much trouble. The Crow, the Peigan, and other Indian nations with reservations in Montana were upset by competition for the scarce food resource, and these people threatened to break the treaties they had made with the American government and to wage war on the Cree if the American authorities did not protect the Indian hunting ranges. These threats were renewed when the Cree began to steal horses from the Crow and Peigan. To add to their difficulties, American ranchers accused the Cree of killing range cattle. American officials, not wishing trouble with their Indians and wishing to placate the ranchers, informed the Cree that they would have to return to Canada. Most Cree bands—aware that if they did not leave voluntarily, the American government would use troops to force them to move north—returned to the Cypress Hills.

They returned to find that Canadian officials were now aware of the dangers to their authority posed by a concentration of the Cree. A riot at Fort Walsh in 1880, which the police were powerless to prevent or control, assaults on farming instructors who refused to provide rations to starving Indians, and rumours that the Cree were planning a grand Indian council to discuss treaty revisions in 1881 all caused the Indian commissioner much concern. To avoid further difficulties over rations, in late 1880 Dewdney ordered that all Indians requesting rations be given them, regardless of whether the supplicant was in treaty. There was little that the government could do at this time about the proposed Indian council or the concentration of Cree in the Cypress Hills.

In the spring of 1881 Cree bands from all regions of the Canadian prairies left their reserves to go south to meet with Little Pine and Big Bear. Even the new bands Dewdney had created were going to the council in American territory. What was also disconcerting to Canadian officials were the reports that Big Bear and Little Pine, who had gone to Montana to prepare for the council, had reached an accommodation with the Blackfoot and had participated in a joint raid on the Crow. To all appearances the Blackfoot, the Indian confederacy the Canadian government most feared, would be part of the Indian council.

The Indian council was not held because the raid on the Crow led American officials to intervene militarily to force the Cree to return to Canada. With Montana stockmen acting as militia units, the American army prevented most Cree and Assiniboine bands from entering the United States. As well, the American forces seized horses, guns, and carts and escorted the Cree to Canada. The Cree-Blackfoot alliance did not materialize, for soon after the raid on the Crow, young Cree warriors stole horses from the Blackfoot and thereby destroyed the accord that Little Pine and Big Bear were attempting to create.

The actions of the American military in 1881 were extremely beneficial to Canada. Not only did the Americans prevent the holding of the Indian council, but by confiscating the guns and horses of the Cree, the Americans had dispossessed the Cree of the ability to resist whatever measures the Canadian authorities wished to take against them. The Canadian authorities also benefited from Governor-General Lorne's tour of the West in 1881, for many of the Cree bands that had gone to the Cypress Hills in the spring went north in late summer to meet Lorne to impress upon him the inadequacy of the treaties and the need to revise them. Thus Lorne's tour prevented the concentration of most of the Cree nation in the Cypress Hills.

The threat posed to Canadian authority in the North-West by concentration of the Cree was clearly recognized by Dewdney and other Canadian officials in late 1881. They saw how the Cree had forced officials to placate them and to ignore their orders in 1880 and 1881. This convinced both Dewdney and Ottawa that the Cree request for contiguous reserves in the Cypress Hills could not be granted. Dewdney recognized that to grant the Cree requests would be to create an Indian territory, for most of the Cree who had reserves further north would come to the Cypress Hills and request reserves contiguous to those of the Cypress Hills Cree. This would result in so large a concentration of Cree that the only way Canada could enforce its laws on them would be via a military campaign. To prevent this, Dewdney recommended a sizeable expansion of the Mounted Police force and the closure of Fort Walsh and all government facilities in the Cypress Hills. This action would remove all sources of sustenance from the Cree in the Cypress Hills. Dewdney hoped that starvation would drive them from the Fort Walsh area and thus end the concentration of their force.

Dewdney decided to take these steps, fully aware not only that what he was doing was a violation of the promises made to the Cypress Hills Indians in 1880 and 1881, but also that by refusing to grant reserves on the sites the Indians had selected, he was violating the promises made to the Cree by the Treaty Commissions in 1874 and 1876 and in the written treaties. Nevertheless, Dewdney believed that to accede to the Cree requests would be to grant the Cree de facto autonomy from Canadian control, which would result in the perpetuation and heightening of the 1880–82 crisis. Rather than see that situation continue, Dewdney wanted to exploit the opportunity presented to him by the hunger crisis and disarmament of the Cree to bring them under the government's control, even if it meant violating the treaties.

In the spring of 1882 the Cree and Assiniboine were told that no further rations would be issued to them while they remained in the Cypress Hills. Only if the Indians moved north to Qu'Appelle, Battleford, and Fort Pitt were they to be given assistance, and at those locations only treaty Indians were to be aided. The Mounted Police were ordered to stop issuing rations at Fort Walsh, and the Indian Department farm that had been located near Fort Walsh was closed. Faced with the prospect of starvation, without weapons or transport to get to the Montana buffalo ranges, and knowing that if they were to try to go south the Mounted Police would inform the American military authorities, many Cree and all the Assiniboine decided to go north. Even Big Bear discovered that his people wanted him to take treaty and move north. In 1882, after taking treaty, he, along with Piapot and Little Pine, promised to leave the Cypress Hills.

Only Piapot kept his promise, and even he did not remain long at Fort Qu'Appelle. By late summer of 1882 Piapot was back in the Cypress Hills complaining about how he had been mistreated at Qu'Appelle and making the Cree aware of how they could lose their autonomy if the government could deal with them as individual bands. On hearing this report, the other Cree leaders refused to leave the Fort Walsh region and insisted upon receiving the reserves promised them in 1880 and 1881. North-West Mounted Police Commissioner Irvine feared a repetition of the incidents of 1880 if he refused to feed the Cree and believed that the hungry Cree would harass the construction crews of the Canadian Pacific Railway for food, which would lead to a confrontation between whites and Indians that the police would be unable to handle and that in turn might lead to an Indian war. Therefore, Irvine decided to feed the Cree.

Dewdney and Ottawa were upset by Irvine's actions. Ottawa gave specific instructions to close Fort Walsh in the spring of 1883. When Irvine closed the fort, the Cree faced starvation. As it was quite evident that they could not go to the United States, and as they would not receive reserves in the Cypress Hills, the Cree moved north. Piapot moved to Indian Head and selected a reserve site next to the huge reserve set aside for the Assiniboine. Little Pine and Lucky Man moved to Battleford and selected reserve sites next to Poundmaker's reserve. Big Bear went to Fort Pitt.

The move to the north was not a sign of the Cree acceptance of the treaties as written, nor of their acceptance of the authority of the Canadian government. Big Bear, Little Pine, and Piapot were aware that the other Cree chiefs were dissatisfied with the treaties and that if they could effect concentration of the Cree in the north they would be able to preserve their autonomy, just as they had done in the Cypress Hills in the 1879–81 period. Therefore, the move to the north was simply a tactical move, for no sooner were these chiefs in the north than they once again sought to effect a concentration of their people.

By moving to Indian Head, Piapot had effected a concentration of more than two thousand Indians. This number threatened to grow larger if the council he planned to hold with all the Treaty 4 bands to discuss treaty revisions were successful. Commissioner Dewdney, fearing the results of such a meeting in 1883, was able to thwart Piapot by threatening to cut off rations to any Indians attending Piapot's council and by threatening to arrest Piapot and depose any chiefs who did meet with him. Although Dewdney, in 1883, prevented Piapot holding a large council by such actions, Piapot was able to get the Treaty 4 chiefs to agree to meet in the late spring of 1884 for a thirst dance and council on Pasquah's Reserve, near Fort Qu'Appelle.

While Piapot was organizing an Indian council in the Treaty 4 area, Big Bear and Little Pine were doing the same for the Treaty 6 region. Little Pine and Lucky Man attempted to effect a concentration of more than two thousand Cree on contiguous reserves in the Battleford district, by requesting reserves next to Poundmaker, whose reserve was next to three other Cree reserves, which in turn were only a short distance from three Assiniboine reserves. Another five hundred Cree would have been located in the Battleford area if Big Bear's request for a reserve next to Little Pine's site had been granted. Only with difficulty was Dewdney able to get Big Bear to move to Fort Pitt. However, he was unable to prevent Big Bear and Little Pine from sending messengers to the Cree leaders of the Edmonton, Carlton, and Duck Lake districts to enlist their support for the movement to concentrate the Cree.

Dewdney was convinced that the activities of Big Bear, Piapot, and Little Pine were a prelude to a major project the Cree planned for the following year, 1884. He was also aware that his ability to deal with the impending problem was severly limited by decisions taken in Ottawa. The Deputy Superintendent-General of Indian Affairs, Lawrence Vankoughnet, was concerned about the cost of administering Dewdney's policies, and he ordered reductions in the level of assistance provided to the Cree and in the number of employees working with the Cree. In making these decisions, Ottawa effectively deprived Dewdney of his major sources of intelligence about the Cree and their plans. It also deprived Dewdney of a major instrument in placating the Cree: the distribution of rations to those bands which cooperated.

Vankoughnet's economy measures led to further alienation of the Cree. In some areas, notably in the Fort Pitt, Edmonton, and Crooked Lakes regions, farming instructors were assulted and government storehouses broken into when Indians were denied rations. The incident on the Sakemay Reserve in the Crooked Lakes area was quite serious, for when the police were called upon to arrest those guilty of the assault, they were surrounded and threatened with death if they carried out their orders. Only after Assistant Indian Commissioner Hayter Reed had agreed to restore assistance to the Sakemay band to the 1883 level and had promised not to imprison the accused were the police allowed to leave with their prisoners.

The violence that followed the reductions in rations convinced Dewdney that starving the Cree into submission was not the means to control them. He wanted to use coercion, but this required an expansion of the number of police in the West. Therefore, he recommended that more men be recruited for the Mounted Police. In addition, Dewdney wanted to ensure that jail sentences were given to arrested Indians so that they would cause no further problems. Having seen the effects of incarceration on Indians, Dewdney was convinced that this was the means to bring the Cree leaders under control. However, what was needed in his opinion were trial judges who "understood" Indian nature at first hand and who would take effective action to keep the Indians under control. Therefore, Dewdney wanted all Indian Department officials in the West to be appointed stipendiary magistrates in order that all Indian troublemakers could be brought to "justice" quickly. As Dewdney stated in his letter to Prime Minister John A. Macdonald: "The only effective course with the great proportion [of Indian bands] to adopt is one of sheer compulsion . . ."

Dewdney used the policy of "sheer compulsion" for only a few months in 1884. He found that his efforts to use the Mounted Police to break up the Indian councils and to arrest Indian leaders only led to confrontations between the Cree and the police. In these confrontations the police were shown to be ineffectual because they were placed in situations in which, if the Cree had been desirous of initiating hostilities, large numbers of Mounted Police would have been massacred.

The first incident which called the policy of compulsion into question was the attempt to prevent Piapot from holding his thirst dance and council in May 1884. Assistant Commissioner Hayter Reed, fearing that the council would result in a concentration of all the Treaty 4 bands, ordered Police Commissioner Irvine to prevent Piapot from attending the council. Irvine was to arrest the chief at the first sign of any violation of even the most minor law. To be certain that Piapot broke a law, Reed promised to have an individual from Pasquah's reserve object to the council being held on that reserve in order that the accusation of trespass could be used to break up the meeting, which all the bands from Treaty 4 were attending.

With a force of fifty-six men and a seven-pound gun, Irvine caught up with Piapot shortly before the chief reached Pasquah's reserve. Irvine and the police entered the Indian camp at 2 A.M., hoping to arrest Piapot and remove him from the camp before his band was aware of what happened. However, when they entered the camp, the police found themselves surrounded by armed warriors. Realizing that any attempt to arrest the chief would result in a battle, Irvine decided to hold his own council with Piapot and Reed. This impromptu council agreed that Piapot should receive a new reserve next to Pasquah, in return for which Piapot would return to Indian Head temporarily.

The agreement reached between Piapot and Irvine and Reed was a victory for Piapot. By getting a reserve at Qu'Appelle again, Piapot had approximately two thousand Cree concentrated on the Qu'Appelle River, and he was able to hold his council and thirst dance, for after going to Indian Head, he immediately turned around and went to Pasquah's. Reed and Irvine were aware of Piapot's ruse but did nothing to prevent his holding the council, for they were aware that the Cree at Qu'Appelle were prepared to protect Piapot from what the Indians regarded as an attack on their leader. Realizing the effect that an Indian war would have on possible settlement and that the police were inadequate for such a clash, the Canadian officials wished to avoid giving cause for violent reaction by the Cree. Piapot acted as he did because he realized that if any blood were shed the Cree would experience a fate similar to that of the Nez Perces, Blackfoot, and Dakota Sioux in those peoples' conflicts with the United States.

Dewdney and the police were to have a similar experience when they attempted to prevent Big Bear from holding a thirst dance and council at Pound-maker's reserve in June 1884. Dewdney feared that Big Bear's council, to which the old chief had invited the Blackfoot and all the Indians from Treaty 6, would result in a larger concentration of Cree than Little Pine had already effected at Battleford. Dewdney also believed that he had to undo what Little Pine had accomplished and refused to grant Little Pine and Lucky Man the reserve sites they had requested next to Poundmaker. Big Bear was again told that he would not be granted a reserve in the Battleford district. Dewdney believed that the Cree chiefs would ignore his order to select reserve sites at some distance from Battleford and that this could be used as a reason for arresting them. To legitimize such actions on his part, Dewdney asked the government to pass an order-in-council to make it a criminal offence for a band to refuse to move to a reserve site the Commissioner had suggested. In order to avoid violence when he attempted to prevent Big Bear's council and ordered the arrests of Lucky Man and Little Pine, Dewdney instructed the Indian agents at Battleford and Fort Pitt to purchase all the horses, guns, and cartridges the Cree possessed. He increased the size of the police garrison at Battleford and ordered the police to prevent Big Bear from reaching Battleford.

All Dewdney's efforts had little effect, for Big Bear and his band eluded the police, reached Battleford, and held their thirst dance. The Cree refused to sell their arms, and even the effort to break up the gathering by refusing to provide rations had no result other than to provoke another assault on a farm instructor on 17 June 1884. When the police sought to arrest the farm instructor's assailant, they were intimidated into leaving without a prisoner. When a larger police detachment went to the reserve on 18 June, the police were still unable to make an arrest for fear of provoking armed hostilities. Only on 20 June, when the thirst dance had concluded, were the police able to arrest the accused, and only then by forcibly removing him from the Cree camp. This was done with the greatest difficulty, for the police were jostled and provoked in an effort to get them to fire on the Cree. That no violence occurred, Superintendent Crozier, in charge of the police detachment, attributed to the discipline of his men and to the actions of Little Pine and Big Bear, who did all that was humanly possible to discourage any attack on the police.

The events at Battleford frightened all parties involved in the confrontation. Big Bear was very much disturbed by them, for he did not want war, as he had made abundantly clear to Dewdney in March 1884 and again to the Indian agent at Battleford, J. A. Rae, in June. However, he did want the treaties revised and establishment of an Indian territory. Agent Rae was thoroughly frightened and wanted Dewdney and Ottawa to adopt a more coercive policy designed to subjugate the Cree. Superintendent Crozier argued for a less coercive policy, for unless some accommodation were reached with the Cree, Crozier believed, out of desperation they would resort to violence.

On hearing of the events of May and June 1884, Ottawa decided that Dewdney—who was now Lieutenant-Governor, in addition to being Indian Commissioner—was to have complete control over Indian affairs in the North-West Territories. As well, the Prime Minister informed Dewdney that more police were being recruited for duty in the West and that the Indian Act was being amended to permit Dewdney to arrest any Indian who was on another band's reserve without the permission of the local Indian Department official. Dewdney was thus being given the instruments to make his policy of complusion effective.

Dewdney did not, however, immediately make use of his new powers. He still intended to prevent concentration of the Cree and rejected the requests Big Bear, Poundmaker, Lucky Man, and others made for a reserve at Buffalo Lake and later rejected Big Bear's, Little Pine's, and Lucky Man's renewed requests for reserves next to Poundmaker's. However, rather than following a purely coercive policy, Dewdney adopted a policy of rewards and punishments. He provided more rations, farming equipment, oxen, ammunition, and twine, and arranged for selected Cree chiefs to visit Winnipeg and other large centres of Canadian settlement. If the Cree were not satisfied with his new approach, he would use force against them. To implement this new policy, Dewdney increased the number of Indian Department employees working on the Cree reserves, for he wanted to monitor closely the behaviour of the Indians and, if necessary, to arrest troublesome leaders.

While Dewdney was implementing his new policy, the Cree leaders continued their efforts to concentrate the Cree in an exclusively Indian territory. Little Pine went south to seek Blackfoot support for the movement. Big Bear, Lucky Man, and Poundmaker went to Duck Lake for a council with the Cree leaders of the Lower Saskatchewan district. The Duck Lake council, attended by twelve bands, was initiated by Beardy and the chiefs of the Carlton District. Beardy, who acted as spokesman for the Carlton chiefs, had been relatively inactive in the Cree movements in the 1881–83 period. He, however, had been the most vehement critic of the government's failure to deliver the farm materials promised by the treaty commissioners. In the 1877–81 period, Beardy was a man of little influence in the Carlton area, but when Mistawasis and Ahtahkakoop, the principal Cree chiefs of the Carlton District came to share his views, Beardy's standing among the Carlton Cree rose dramatically.

The Duck Lake Council, called by Cree leaders who Dewdney thought were loyal and docile and of which the Commissioner had no foreknowledge, was a cause of much concern. Especially vexing was the detailed list of violations of the treaty for which the Cree demanded redress from the government. The Cree charged that the treaty commissioners lied to them when they said that the Cree would be able to make a living from agriculture with the equipment provided for in the treaties. However, rather than provide all the farming goods, what the government did, according to the Cree, was to withhold many of the cattle and oxen; send inferior quality wagons, farm tools, and equipment; and provide insufficient rations and clothes and no medicine chest. The petition closed with the statement expressing the Cree sentiment that they had been deceived by "sweet promises" designed to cheat them of their heritage and that unless their grievances were remedied by the summer of 1885, they would take whatever measures necessary, short of war, to get redress.

Dewdney originally assumed, as did some newspapers across the West, that the Duck Lake Council was part of a plot by Louis Riel to foment an Indian and Metis rebellion. Dewdney's assumption was based on the fact that the Duck Lake Council was held a short time after Riel had returned to Canada. It was also known that Riel had attended it and that he had advocated such an alliance and a resort to violence when he had met with the Cree in Montana in 1880. Further investigation, however, made quite clear that Riel had little influence on the Cree. To allay the growing concern about the possibility of an Indian war, Dewdney had Hayter Reed issue a statement that nothing untoward was happening and that there was less danger of an Indian war in 1884 than there had been in 1881. Privately Dewdney admitted to Ottawa and his subordinates in the West that the situation was very serious. After both he and Dewdney had met with Cree leaders throughout the West and after carefully assessing the situation, Hayter Reed stated that the government had nothing to fear from the Cree until the summer of 1885. What Reed and Dewdney expected at that time was a united Cree demand to renegotiate treaties.

What Reed and Dewdney had learned on their tours of the Battleford, Edmonton, Carlton, and Qu'Appelle districts in the fall of 1884 was that Big Bear, Piapot, and Little Pine were on the verge of uniting the Cree to call for new treaties in which an Indian territory and greater autonomy for the Cree would be major provisions. In fact, throughout the summer and fall of 1884 Little Pine attempted, with limited success, to interest the leaders of the Blackfoot in joining the Cree movement for treaty revision. Little Pine had invited the Blackfoot to a joint council with the Cree leaders on Little Pine's reserve scheduled for the spring of 1885. If the Blackfoot joined the Cree, Ottawa's ability to govern the Indians and control the West would be seriously jeopardized.

At the moment that the Cree movement seemed on the verge of success, Big Bear was losing control of his band. As he told the assembled chiefs at Duck Lake in the summer of 1884, his young men were listening to the warrior chief, Little Poplar, who was advocating killing government officials and Indian agents as a means of restoring Cree independence. Big Bear feared that if Little Poplar's course of action were adopted the Cree would fight an Indian war that they were certain to lose.

Dewdney was aware of Little Poplar's growing influence on the young men of Big Bear's and the Battleford Assiniboine bands; however, he wished to wait until after January 1885 before taking any action, because after that date the new amendments to the Indian act would be in effect. These amendments could be used to arrest and imprison Little Pine, Little Poplar, Big Bear, and Piapot and thereby, Dewdney hoped, destroy the movements these chiefs led. In anticipation of confrontations in 1885, Dewdney ordered that the guns and ammunition normally allotted to the Cree so they could hunt for food be withheld. In addition, Indian councils were prohibited, including the one scheduled for Duck Lake in the summer of 1885, to which all the Cree in Treaty 6 had been invited. Arrangements were made to place the Mounted Police at Battleford under Dewdney's command, and serious consideration was given to placing an artillery unit there also.

To get improved intelligence, Dewdney hired more men to work as Indian agents with the Cree. These men were given broad discretionary powers and were to keep the commissioner informed on Cree activities. As well, English-speaking mixed-bloods, many of whom had worked for the Hudson's Bay Company and had the confidence of the Cree, were hired as farm instructors. There would now be a farm instructor on each Cree reserve, with explicit instructions to keep the Indian

Agent informed of what was happening on his reserve. Staff who had personality conflicts with any of the Cree leaders were either transferred or fired. Only Thomas Quinn, Indian Agent at Fort Pitt and his farming instructor, John Delaney, were not removed before March 1885, although both were slated for transfer.

Dewdney found that his most important staffing move was the employment of Peter Ballendine, a former Hudson's Bay Company trader much trusted by the principal Cree leaders. Ballendine's job was to ingratiate himself with Big Bear and report on that chief's comings and goings. Ballendine won the confidence of Big Bear and reported upon how wrong Dewdney's earlier efforts to break up Big Bear's band had been. Because so many of Big Bear's original followers joined either Lucky Man, Thunderchild, or Little Pine's bands, Big Bear by 1884 was left with only the most recalcitrant opponents of the treaty. These individuals were only lukewarm in support of their chief's nonviolent efforts to get the treaty revised. They favoured instead the course of action advocated by Little Poplar. Ballendine believed that the government could expect trouble from the Big Bear and Little Poplar bands. However, Ballendine emphasized that there was little danger of a Cree-Metis alliance, for the Cree were refusing to meet with the Metis and were rejecting all entreaties from the Metis suggesting the two should make common cause. Instead the Cree, under the leadership of Big Bear, Beardy, and Little Pine, were planning their own council for the summer of 1885.

Ballendine also developed a new source of information in Poundmaker, who was also acting as a police informer. It was from Poundmaker that Dewdney and the police learned that Little Pine was attempting to involve the Blackfoot in the summer of 1884 and wanted to do so in January 1885, but was prevented from doing so because of temporary blindness—a possible sign of malnutrition from the hunger that most Cree experienced in the extremely harsh winter of 1884–85. Little Pine had sought to get Poundmaker to encourage Crowfoot to join the Cree movement, but Poundmaker refused to aid Little Pine, and when Little Pine recovered from his blindness, he went south to meet with Crowfoot.

While Little Pine met with Crowfoot, Big Bear was being challenged for the leadership of his band by his son Imases, also called Curly, and by one of his headmen, Wandering Spirit. These two men were spokesmen for the younger men of Big Bear's Band and wanted to work with Little Poplar. In the winter of 1885 Little Poplar was journeying constantly between Pitt and Battleford, enlisting support for his plan of action. Although Ballendine could not get precise information on Little Poplar's plans, he did report that by March 1885 Big Bear had asserted himself and that the influence of Imases and Wandering Spirit had seemed to wane.

On the basis of these and similar reports, Dewdney and the police were convinced that, although a number of councils were expected in 1885, no violence was to be anticipated from the Cree. Nevertheless, Dewdney wished to prevent the Cree from holding their councils. His strategy was to make the Cree satisfied with the treaties. He therefore admitted in February 1885 that the government had violated the treaties and ordered delivery to the Cree of all goods the treaties had stipulated. In addition, he ordered a dramatic increase in their rations. If this failed to placate them, he planned to arrest their leaders, use the police to keep the Cree on their reserves, and depose any chief who attempted to attend an Indian council.

Dewdney had the full support of Ottawa for his policy of arresting Cree leaders. The only reservations the Prime Minister expressed were that Dewdney have sufficient forces to make the arrests and that he provide enough evidence to justify the charges of incitement to an insurrection. Macdonald also volunteered to communicate with the stipendiary magistrates to assure their cooperation in imposing long prison terms for any Cree leader convicted of incitement. Macdonald was willing to provide this assistance because Dewdney had earlier complained that he could not use preventive detention of Indian leaders because the magistrates "only look at the evidence and the crime committed when giving out sentences," rather than taking into consideration the nature of the man and the harm that he might do if he were released at an inopportune time. All these preparations were complete when word reached Dewdney of the Metis clash with the Mounted Police at Duck Lake in March 1885.

The Riel Rebellion of 1885 provided Dewdney with a new instrument to make his coercive policy effective. The troops sent into the North-West to suppress the Rebellion could be used to destroy the Cree movement for an Indian territory. The Cree themselves would provide the excuse Dewdney needed virtually to declare war on the bands and leaders who had led the Cree movement for treaty revision. During March 1885 the Cree did engage in some acts of violence that Dewdney chose to label acts of rebellion.

These acts were unrelated to the Cree movement for treaty revision. In fact, these acts that led to the subjugation of the Cree were committed by persons not involved with the Cree movement for autonomy. It is one of the ironic quirks of history that the leaders of the Cree movement had little or nothing to do with the events that would destroy that movement to which they had devoted ten years of their lives. Nevertheless, they would be held responsible for the actions of their desperate and hungry people. To heighten the irony, it was the Metis movement, from which the Cree had held aloof, which would give Dewdney the excuse to use military force to subjugate the Cree.

The Duck Lake clash coincided with a Cree Council on Sweetgrass Reserve. The council of the Battleford area Cree had been called to consider how it could press for increased rations. When word reached the Cree at Sweetgrass of the clash at Duck Lake, they felt that circumstances would make Indian Agent Rae willing to grant them more rations. Thus the Cree, taking their women and children with them to demonstrate their peaceful intent, set out for Battleford. Fear and panic prevailed at Battleford, for on learning of the Crees' approach, the town's citizens assumed that the Cree had thrown in their lot with the Metis. The town was evacuated; most townspeople took refuge in the Mounted Police post.

When the Cree arrived at Battleford, they found the town abandoned. They sent word to the police post that they wished to speak to the Indian Agent, who refused to leave the safety of the post. The Cree women, seeing the abandoned stores and houses filled with food, began to help themselves. Then, fearing arrest by the police, the Cree left town. On the way back to their reserves, as well as on their way to town, the Cree assisted a number of Indian Department employees and settlers to cross the Battle River to get to the police post, thus demonstrating the pacific nature of their intentions.

Rather than returning to their individual reserves, the Cree went to Pound-maker's, for as the leader in the Battleford district to whom the government had shown much favour in the past, Poundmaker was seen as the man best able to explain to the government what had happened at Battleford. A second significant reason was the deaths of two prominent Cree leaders: Red Pheasant, the night before the Cree left for Battleford, and Little Pine, the night they returned. As it was the practice of the Cree to leave the place where their leaders had expired, both bands left their reserves and went to Poundmaker's, who, given the fears the whites had concerning a Cree and Metis alliance, might possibly defuse any crisis. Thus, in March 1885, Poundmaker became the spokesman of the Battleford Cree.

No sooner were the Cree at Poundmaker's than they were joined by the local Assiniboine, who insisted that a soldier's (war) tent be erected, for events at the Assiniboine reserves convinced them that an attack on the Indian camp was imminent. The Assiniboine explained that when word had reached them of the Duck Lake fight, a few of their young men sought revenge on farming instructor James Payne, who was blamed for the death of a girl. The girl's male relatives killed Payne and murdered farmer Barney Tremont. The Assiniboine now assumed that the Canadian authorities would behave in a similar manner to the Americans and blame all Indians for the actions of a few individuals.

Erection of the soldier's tent meant that the warriors were in control of the camp and that Poundmaker and the civil authorities had to defer to them. It was at this time that the Metis appeal for aid was received. The Cree refused to assist the Metis, although they expected an attack on their camp. Watches were set on the roads and protection was offered to the Metis at Bresaylor, for the settlers there had earned the enmity of the Batoche Metis. As long as no military or police forces came toward the Cree camp, the Cree remained on their reserves and did not interfere with anyone going to or leaving Battleford. The Mounted Police detachment from Fort Pitt and Colonel Otter's military unit arrived in Battleford without encountering any Indians. Nevertheless, reports from the police and local officials maintained that the town was under siege.

While the Battleford Cree were preparing their defences, Big Bear's band was making trouble for itself. Big Bear was absent from his camp when the members of his band heard about the fight at Duck Lake. Wandering Spirit and Imases sought to use the opportunity presented by the Metis uprising to seek revenge for the insults and abuses perpetrated against the Cree by Indian Agent Thomas Quinn and Farming Instructor Delaney. Quinn had physically abused some of the Indian men, while Delaney had cuckolded others before he brought a white bride to Frog Lake in late 1884. Big Bear's headmen demanded that the two officials open the storehouse to the Cree, and when they refused to do so, they were murdered. This set off further acts of violence that resulted in the murder of all the white men in the camp save one.

On his return to camp Big Bear ended further acts of violence. Although unable to prevent a minor skirmish between his young men and a small police patrol, he convinced his warriors to allow the police detachment at Fort Pitt to withdraw from the post without being attacked and to guarantee safety to the civilian residents of the Frog Lake and Fort Pitt regions. Big Bear then led his people north, where he hoped they would be out of harm's way and not engage in further acts of violence.

Beardy also lost control of his band. He and the neighbouring One Arrow band had reserves next to Batoche. Before the clash with the police, the Metis had come to the One Arrow Reserve, captured Farming Instructor Peter Thompkins and threatened the Cree band with destruction unless the Cree aided the Metis. Some of the younger men of One Arrow's band agreed to do so. The Metis made the same threat against Beardy and his band, and although a few of his young men joined the Metis, Beardy and most of his people remained neutral. It is doubtful that the Cree would have aided the Metis without the threat of violence. Earlier, the Cree of the Duck Lake region had threatened hostilities against the Metis, for the Metis had settled on One Arrow's Reserve and demanded that the government turn over to them some of One Arrow's Reserve. Ottawa, fearing the Metis more than the Cree in 1880, acquiesced. Over the next four years one task of the local Indian Agent and the police was to reconcile the Cree with the Metis of the Batoche region.

The Cree acts of violence in March 1885 were the excuse Dewdney needed to justify the use of troops against them. He maintained that the Battleford, Fort Pitt, and Duck Lake Cree were part of the Riel Rebellion. Privately Dewdney reported to Ottawa that he saw the events at Battleford and Frog Lake as the acts of a desperate, starving people and unrelated to what the Metis were doing. In fact, Dewdney had sought in late March to open negotiations with the Battleford Cree, but Rae refused to meet the Cree leaders. Subsequent efforts to open negotiations ended in failure because there was no way to get a message to Poundmaker, and after Colonel Otter's attack on the Cree camp, any thought of negotiations was dropped.

Publicly Dewdney proclaimed that the Cree were part of the Metis uprising. He issued a proclamation that any Indian who left his reserve was to be regarded as a rebel. As well, to intimidate Piapot and the Treaty 4 Cree, Dewdney stationed troops on their reserves. To prevent an alliance of Blackfoot and Cree, Dewdney announced that he was stationing troops at Swift Current and Medicine Hat. Dewdney took these steps, as he confided to Macdonald, because he feared that the Cree might still attempt to take action on their own cause, and he was concerned because in the previous year the Cree had attempted to enlist the Blackfoot in the movement to revise the treaties.

The military commander in the North-West, General F. D. Middleton, was not as concerned about the problems with the Cree. He wanted to concentrate his attention on the Metis. Although he did send troops under Colonel William Otter to Swift Current, he refused to order them to Battleford to lift the alleged siege until he received word of the Frog Lake massacre. Otter was then ordered to lift the "siege" and protect Battleford from Indian attack, but he was not to take the offensive. At the same time, General Thomas Strange was ordered to bring Big Bear under control.

Otter reached Battleford without seeing an Indian. He was upset that he and his troops would not see action. He therefore proposed that he attack the Indian camp at Poundmaker's Reserve. Middleton vetoed the plan, but Dewdney welcomed it as a means to bring the Cree under government control. Taking the Lieutenant-Governor's approval to be paramount to Middleton's veto, Otter launched his attack. The engagement, known as the Battle of Cut Knife Hill, almost ended in total disaster for Otter's force. Only the Cree fear that they would suffer the same fate as Sitting Bull after the Battle of the Little Big Horn saved Otter's troops from total annihilation.

The tale of the subsequent military campaigns against the Cree by Strange and Middleton and the voluntary surrenders of Poundmaker and Big Bear is found in detail in Stanley's *Birth of Western Canada* and Desmond Morton's *The Last War Drum*. With Big Bear and Poundmaker in custody, Dewdney prepared to use the courts in the manner he had planned before the Riel Rebellion. Both Cree leaders were charged with treason-felony, despite Dewdney's knowledge that neither man had engaged in an act of rebellion. Eyewitnesses to the events at Fort Pitt, Frog Lake, and Battleford all made clear that neither chief was involved in the murders and looting that had occurred. In fact, many of these people served as defence witnesses. As Dewdney informed the Prime Minister, the diaries and letters of the murdered officials at Frog Lake showed that until the day of the "massacre" there was "no reason to believe that our Indians were even dissatisfied much less con-templated violence." Ballendine's reports indicated that there were no plans for violence, that the Cree were not involved with the Metis, and that they planned no rebellion. Dewdney believed that the Cree had not "even thought, intended or wished that the uprising would reach the proportion it has . . . . Things just got out of control." As Dewdney related to the Prime Minister, had the people living in the region not been new settlers from the East and had they not fled in panic, much of the "raiding" and looting would not have occurred. In regions where people had not abandoned their homes no raiding occurred. Therefore, the charges against Big Bear and Poundmaker were designed to remove the leadership of the Cree movement for revision of the treaties. They were charged to elicit prison sentences that would have the effect of coercing the Cree to accept government control. The trials were conducted to have the desired result, and both Big Bear and Poundmaker were convicted and sentenced to three years in Stoney Mountain Penitentiary. Neither man served his full term, and both died a short time after their release from prison.

By the end of 1885 Dewdney had succeeded in subjugating the Cree. Big Bear was in prison, Little Pine was dead, and Piapot was intimidated by having troops stationed on his reserve. Dewdney had deprived the Cree of their principal leaders and of their autonomy. He used the military to disarm and impoverish the Cree by confiscating their horses and carts; he increased the size of the Mounted Police force and used the police to arrest Cree leaders who protested against his policies; he broke up Cree Bands, deposed Cree leaders, and forbade any Indian to be off his reserve without permission from the Indian Agent. By 1890, through vigorous implementation of the Indian Act, Dewdney and his successor, Hayter Reed, had begun the process of making the Cree an administered people.

The record of the Canadian government in dealing with the Cree is thus not one of honourable fair-mindedness and justice as the traditional interpretation portrays. As Dewdney admitted in 1885, the treaties' promises and provisions were not being fulfilled, and Dewdney himself had taken steps to assure Canadian control over the Cree, which were themselves violations of the treaties. Thus, he had refused to grant the Cree the reserve sites they selected and he had refused to distribute the ammunition and twine the treaties required. His plans for dealing with the Cree leaders were based on a political use of the legal and judicial system, and ultimately he made use of the military, the police, and the courts in a political manner to achieve his goals of subjugating the Cree. Only by ignoring these facts can one continue to perpetuate the myth of Canada's just and honourable Indian policy from 1870 to 1885.

18

FROM PRISON TO HOMELAND: THE CHEYENNE RIVER INDIAN RESERVATION BEFORE WORLD WAR I

FREDERICK E. HOXIE

By the last third of the nineteenth century the Western Indians faced wrenching changes in their way of life as their customs fell under the hammer blows of the advancing Anglo-American society. Repeated clashes with soldiers pushed the tribes onto reservations, and for the Sioux large parts of South Dakota became their reservation home. Agents, missionaries, teachers, boarding schools, and army forts there all served notice that a new day had arrived. When federal officials created the new Indian homelands, they saw those areas as temporary way stations along the Native Americans' path to acculturation and assimilation into the majority society. To speed that process, in 1887 President Grover Cleveland signed the Dawes, or General Allotment, Act, designed to split the communal tribal holdings into individually owned farms. That would require each adult reservation dweller to become an independent operator, at least in economic terms. Because the Sioux lived in isolation and lacked adequate credit or training, only a few of them could compete successfully. In fact, most studies of individual tribes depict the years between 1880 and 1920 as the nadir of the Indian experience as populations declined and disease swept through the malnourished people. Nevertheless the Sioux survived. Few of them became fully acculturated; rather they sought ways to face their changed situation and to adapt their customs and ideas. This essay discusses that process as it occurred on the Cheyenne River Reservation and as it provided the basis for the adaptations that took place after World War I.

Frederick E. Hoxie is the Director of the D'Arcy McNickle Center at the Newberry Library in Chicago.

Source: Frederick E. Hoxie, "From Prison to Homeland: The Cheyenne River Indian Reservation Before World War I," *South Dakota History*, 10 (Winter 1979), pp. 1–24. Copyright © 1979 by the South Dakota State Historical Society. All Rights Reserved. Reprinted with Permission.

There should be no doubt that the Great Sioux Agreement of 1889 was designed to destroy what remained of the Teton bands' traditional way of life. The Eastern reformers who drew up the agreement and the politicians who approved it were committed to replacing the old ways with new ones. Hunting, living in bands, accepting the rule of elders, following the wisdom of religious leaders, and traveling in an annual cycle across a large territory—these were all targets of the new law. Senator Henry L. Dawes, the author of the 1887 general allotment act that bore his name and the principal architect of the 1889 agreement, believed there was no alternative. As he wrote, "We may cry out against the violation of treaties, denounce flagrant disregard of inalienable rights and the inhumanity of our treatment of the defenseless . . . but the fact remains. . . . Without doubt these Indians are to be somehow absorbed into and become a part of the 50,000,000 of our people. There does not seem to be any other way to deal with them." By 1889 Dawes was convinced of his own wisdom. South Dakota had become a state. New rail lines were snaking across the plains, and thousands of settlers—some of them freshly arrived from Europe—were traveling west to share in America's last great land boom.

Dawes promised that the new land would satisfy white land hunger while it started the Sioux on the road to total assimilation. The agreement provided that (1) the tribes would cede 11 million acres west of the Missouri River to the United States; (2) five reservations would be established on the remaining lands (Standing Rock, Cheyenne River, Lower Brule, Rosebud, and Pine Ridge); (3) the government would create a fund to provide individuals with farming equipment, supplies, and schools; and (4) each reservation eventually would be allotted among the people who lived there.

Secretary of the Interior John Noble welcomed these steps. He wrote that "the breaking up of this great nation of Indians into smaller parts and segregating . . . separate reservations for each of said parts marks a long step toward the disintegration of their tribal life and will help them forward to . . . civilized habits." Like Dawes, the secretary believed that the pace of white settlement in South Dakota made it possible for the Teton bands to maintain their old ways. The 1889 law would force the tribes into the modern world.

Not surprisingly, tribal leaders among the Sioux agreed with Senator Dawes and the secretary. Still angry over the theft of the Black Hills and the government's refusal to live up to the 1868 Fort Laramie Treaty, tribal headmen wanted no part of additional land cessions. To them it was obvious that further reductions in the size of their nation would mean the arrival of still more whites, along with increased pressure from missionaries and educators and more demands that they turn to farming.

The 1868 treaty had stipulated that three fourths of the adult male members of the tribes must approve all future land sales. Seven years and four different congressional delegations were required before the tribes approved this new agreement. While several leaders won significant concessions during these negotiations, the 1889 agreement was a major defeat for the tribes. Its ratification was met with anger and depression. It is probably no accident that the announcement of the 1889 agreement and the fighting at Wounded Knee occurred within a year of each other.

But the events of 1889 and 1890 did not mark the last days of the Sioux Nation. Surprisingly, Lakota culture survived the programs designed to kill it. The 1889 agreement failed to destroy all the old ways. It failed to turn red men into white men. It failed to achieve the complete "disintegration" of tribal life. And the supreme irony: The reservations forced on the tribes did not become vehicles for "civilizing" and assimilating them; instead they became cultural homelands, places where a native identity could be maintained and passed on to new generations. Rather than graveyards for culture, the reservations created in 1889 eventually became centers for awareness and even for hope. To describe this paradox is to beg the question—why? How did the prisons of the nineteenth century become the cultural homelands of the twentieth?

When Cheyenne River Indian Reservation was established in 1889, it contained four distinct Lakota bands whose ways of life had not changed fundamentally for generations. Prior to 1889 the native people living near the Cheyenne River had been confined to the area around old Fort Bennett and urged to farm and adopt Christianity. But despite these restrictions and demands, there was little direct pressure on the Indians to break up their camps and leave the protected river bottoms where they had made their winter homes.

The bands had little contact with one another. Minneconjous lived on Cherry Creek in what would become the western end of the reservation. Sans Arc communities could be found along the Moreau River at places such as White Horse and On the Trees, running near what would become the northern border of the preserve. The Blackfeet and Two Kettle bands hugged the Missouri, spreading out between Fort Bennett and the Moreau. Most of these camps had a headman and some sort of government day school that operated sporadically during the year. Of course allotment had not yet begun.

While game was growing scarce and the government's rations were not always reliable, farming and stock raising had not yet become essential to the people's livelihood. Five district farmers visited the various communities, but as the superintendent reported in 1890, "they usually [had] very little to show for their work." People at the Cheyenne River Agency survived on a combination of rations, money from odd maintenance and freighting jobs, and whatever they could hunt or gather on the prairie.

The 1889 agreement undermined this peaceful routine. The government stepped up its efforts at the agency and broadened the scope of its activities. As Senator Dawes had promised, the campaign to "absorb" the Sioux into American society began in earnest. First, the Cheyenne River Agency was moved from Fort Bennett—which lay outside the new reservation—to Charger's Camp on the Missouri River. While the Minneconjous living on Cheery Creek were farther than ever from the superintendent's office, the Blackfeet and Two Kettle bands on the Missouri and the Sans Arcs on the Moreau were now close at hand. Second, a large boarding school was built next to the new agency. By 1904 this school had space for 130 students. In addition, up to 200 children began to be sent to BIA schools in Pierre and Rapid City and to the mission school at Oahe. These institutions, coupled with the day schools at Cherry Creek, Thunder Butte, Green Grass, On the Trees, and White Horse, could accommodate all of the approximately 650 school-age children on the reservation. Consequently the agency could now step up its campaign to force all young people to attend school. By the early 1900s it was almost impossible for a family to avoid sending its children away for an education, the principal goal of which was to separate the children from their traditions and their past.

School attendance also increased in response to the expansion of the Indian police and the Courts of Indian Offenses. In 1890, when the reservation was being organized for the first time, the superintendent at Cheyenne River noted that "many of the best Indians will not serve" on the police force. Whether this was because of the low pay offered them (as the superintendent thought) or because of the controversy surrounding the arrest and killing of Sitting Bull at nearby Standing Rock is unclear. What is certain, however, is that within ten years the Indian police were active in every part of the reservation. In 1896 policemen began to be selected from the districts, and police stations were erected at Cherry Creek and White Horse. The tribal courts, with judges selected from the four bands, met regularly and passed judgments on all but the five major crimes.

A third feature of the government's activism on the new reservation was the practice of stationing farmers in each district. During the 1890s subagencies were constructed at Cherry Creek and White Horse. Thunder Butte was added in 1909. These installations were permanent homes for the farmers who supervised individual family gardens and monitored the cattlemen who leased tribal pastureland. Through the efforts of these men, the area being cultivated at Cheyenne River began to grow. In 1895 only seven hundred acres had been planted in crops. Two years later that figure had nearly doubled, and by 1907 the superintendent reported that "at no time has there been so much farming . . . at this reservation." The gains in stock raising were equally impressive. In 1890, 500,000 pounds of Indian cattle were sold to the agency for rations. In 1899 *that* figure had doubled.

The year 1900 marked the beginning of allotment at Cheyenne River. Crews of surveyors worked methodically across the entire preserve. By 1909 they had made more than 2,100 homestead assignments. This process not only pushed families out onto their own land but brought home to each member of the reservation the fact that a new era had begun and that the government was determined to change their old way of life. The new reservation environment demanded that the Indians respond or perish.

Changes in Indian ways of life were apparent almost from the beginning of the government's assimilation drive. One of the most obvious of these was the dispersal of the population across the reserve. Rather than camping in concentrated areas and keeping to the place where their band had originally settled, young people began moving out on their own. For example, a man born near Fort Bennett in 1885 remembers today that "they allotted land to us and wherever our land was, was our homestead." As a result, he moved to faraway Iron Lightning and began farming his allotment. Men like him thus opened up new areas of the reservation. In addition to Iron Lightning, Thunder Butte in the extreme northwest and Red Scaffold in the southwest were both settled during these years. People lived near their land and began to think of themselves as part of something new—the Cheyenne River Sioux Tribe. As the superintendent reported in 1897, "the Indians of this reservation, while composed of what were formerly known as the Blackfeet,

Sans Arc, Minneconjou and Two Kettle bands of Sioux, are now regarded as one people, without any distinction as to band." While the superintendent was over-stating things—band designations are important even today—his perception was accurate. People on the reservation were now being defined as a single tribe. It was logical that they would begin defining themselves in the same way.

The second area of change involved the organization of reservation life. The Indian police and courts functioned as a unified whole and helped foster the idea of a reservation unit. Whether they were admired or hated, the policemen affected everybody, and they made it clear that Cheyenne River was a single place.

Another feature of this new tendency to organize the four bands into a single structure was the creation in 1903 of a twelve-man tribal business council. Prior to 1903 two kinds of councils had operated. The first was a general council open to all adult males assigned to the agency. This was the group that had been assembled to approve the 1889 agreement. The second council was an executive body made up of principal headmen. The new business council changed the old pattern in significant ways. First, members of the business council were elected from different parts of the reservation. Four men were chosen from each of the districts: White Horse, Cherry Creek, and the Agency District (Thunder Butte was added in 1909). And second, each councilman was elected by a local council, meeting at the sub-agency. These district councils also had to ratify all decisions involving money or the leasing of tribal property. While elders and traditional band leaders could still be chosen, this new system allowed younger people to rise to positions of influence. Nineteen hundred and three marked an important step in the gradual shift of leadership away from band leaders and toward people chosen for their ability to represent their constituents in a unified tribal government.

As the reservation neared its twentieth anniversary, in 1908, the people of Cheyenne River were surviving in their new environment. They were farming and raising cattle, relying less and less on government rations. Their children were attending school. Many of them were living in new settlements, and all of them were gaining a fresh image of themselves. They were a part of the Cheyenne River Tribe. While the members of this new tribe were themselves responsible for the changes that were taking place, it was clear that the government's programs had started the process.

But did the presence of these new institutions and new ways of life signify rapid assimilation? Does the fact that the tribes' adaptation began with the creation of the reservation mean that the Cheyenne River people were straying from their traditions and giving in to the white man? How did they respond to the erection of schools, the spread of allotment, and the rising power of the tribal police? Were the councilmen, the farmers, and the policemen all people who had been absorbed into the modern world? The behavior of the tribe during the remainder of the period before World War I reveals that answers to these questions should not be taken for granted. While first accepting a number of changes in their tribal organization and way of life, the people of Cheyenne River soon demonstrated that there were limits to their flexibility. They intended to remain a tribal people.

For the non-Indians of South Dakota the twenty years following the passage of the Great Sioux Agreement brought unprecedented growth. White population in the state rose by over 60 percent. New branch lines linked small towns to major railroads, putting cattlemen and farmers within easy reach of Eastern markets. South Dakota's boosters imagined that soon the state would finally live up to its publicity. This feeling intensified as the region emerged from the depression of the 1890s and wheat and beef prices began to climb to new heights. After bottoming out at fifty cents in 1895, wheat rose to almost a dollar a bushel in 1908.

Good times and the prospect of future prosperity brought new demands that the Teton reservations be reduced in size. Rosebud was the first to feel this pressure. In 1901 the tribe agreed to sell a large portion of its reservation to the government. The territory was not opened immediately, however, because a dispute arose in Congress over whether the government should pay for it. Some legislators argued for ratification of the agreement (and payment of the amount promised), while others suggested that they simply seize what they needed for settlement. The two groups were deadlocked until 1903, when the Supreme Court decided *Lone Wolf* v. *Hitchcock* and specifically authorized the national legislature to exercise its "plenary authority" in the disposition of all Indian lands. There was now no legal reason for Congress to pay the Rosebud tribe the money it had been promised. Armed with this invitation, the advocates of seizure won out, and a large portion of the Rosebud preserve was soon open to white settlement.

With Rosebud behind them, it did not take long for South Dakota's merchants and farm speculators to turn their attention to Cheyenne River. Opening the reservation to settlement would—in the words of one Pierre newspaper—be "the impetus of the development of Central South Dakota." "It means," the editorial continued, "the building of a great city right at Pierre." On December 9, 1907 Senator Robert Gamble (whose South Dakota backers called him "the empire builder") introduced a bill to take a portion of the Cheyenne River reserve for homesteading. At the same time, Philo Hall, the state's lone congressman, introduced a second bill that proposed to open *all* of the reservation's unallotted land. Both bills were forwarded to the secretary of the interior for his comments. Within a few days the secretary had instructed James McLaughlin, a thirty-five-year veteran of the Indian Service, to go to South Dakota and convince the residents of Cheyenne River to approve the idea.

But people on the reservation did not wait for McLaughlin before they let their feelings be known. Less than a month after the two bills were introduced, the tribe's general council met and spoke out against them. The group also appealed to the Indian Rights Association (IRA) for help. Writing on behalf of the general council, James Crow Feather noted that "we . . . consider ourselves incapable of plunging into the whirl of citizenship." The business council sent a second letter to the IRA that listed four reasons for opposing Gamble's and Hall's bills:

1. Our consent was never asked.
2. In our reservation we think the lands are rich in mineral deposits. We want these lands to be examined before opening for settlement.
3. The bill is not satisfactory to us.
4. What former treaties promise is not fully carried into effect yet.

After approving the texts of these two letters, the tribe's leaders decided to choose one delegate from each district to visit Washington. They selected Allen Fielder (Agency District), Percy Phillips (White Horse), and Ed Swan (Cherry Creek).

While willing to accept the government's schools and farming campaigns, the council rejected further land cessions out of hand. When Inspector McLaughlin arrived at Cheyenne Agency on March 16, 1908, he found James Crow Feather, the chairman of the business council, there to meet him. Bad weather kept most people from attending the conference with McLaughlin, but the inspector (with his BIA orders in his pocket) presented his case anyway. Crow Feather, speaking for the council, responded sharply, "There are many more of us people than are here today, . . . and we have a way of doing business in matters of this kind. . . . It is our business council. . . . This matter is of interest to the whole tribe. I am chairman of the business council and we have rules regarding this matter, and I would like to carry them out. . . . I would like to have all the people together when we do business regarding land."

McLaughlin ignored Crow Feather. He told the group that "Congress has the right to open the Indian reservations by legislative enactment without obtaining the consent of the Indians" and that they would be better off if they agreed to the change. After two days of fruitless speechmaking, the inspector returned to Washington.

McLaughlin's prediction that Congress would act on its own quickly came true. Less than two weeks after he left South Dakota, the Senate Indian Affairs Committee endorsed a bill to open nearly half the reservation to white homesteaders. Again James Crow Feather protested. In a letter to the commissioner of Indian affairs, he minced no words: "I do not like this way of doing business, because it is not according to the rules of the Indian Office, both here and in Washington. Mr. McLaughlin made a story of my people that did not represent them correctly. . . . As the bill now is it [is] against our will. This is not honest."

The tribal business council immediately dispatched the delegation they had selected in January. These men argued their case at the Indian Office, offering to open a small portion of the reserve but demanding the retention of mineral rights on whatever lands were taken. Unfortunately their efforts were in vain. They arrived in Washington during the first week of April. On April 15 the homestead bill passed the full Senate; five days later it was approved by the House Indian Affairs Committee. At that point, its ultimate passage was a foregone conclusion. President Roosevelt signed the bill on May 29, 1908.

Despite their defeat the tribal leadership continued to protest the new law. At its next meeting the general council adopted a resolution declaring that "the members of this reservation have been treated unjustly in the opening of a portion of this reservation." A year later the superintendent reported that "the people of this reservation cannot become reconciled to the idea that they did not have a proper voice in the recent ceding of the lands of this reservation to the United States." The tribe had lost a battle, but it was gaining valuable experience in dealing with assaults on its territory. Tribal spokesmen had met the government's agents with effective arguments. Delegates representing the three districts on the reservation had presented their case in Washington. The business council had responded quickly to the crisis and presented a unified position to opponents. If the tribe had more time to organize when the next attempt was made to push a homestead bill through Congress, perhaps then their protests would be heard.

The people at Cheyenne River did not have long to wait for a new attack. In 1909, within a few months of the arrival of the first homesteaders on the freshly opened lands, South Dakota's merchants and politicians began lobbying to open still more territory to white settlement. This time they wanted all the remaining tribal lands. Their goal was nothing less than the "final absorption" that Senator Dawes had predicted. South Dakota's Senator Robert Gamble introduced his bill to authorize the sale of all unallotted land on the Cheyenne River Reservation in December. The politicians' argument was by now familiar: "It is a matter of the utmost importance to the development of the state." While no one in Washington immediately opposed the idea, it was soon apparent that the new bill would not be rushed through as quickly as the first one had been. Homesteads opened by the 1908 law were only beginning to be settled, and it was obvious that they would go slowly. By the end of 1911—two years after the first filing—only a quarter of the available land had been claimed. Neither Congress nor the Indian Office felt any overriding need to go along with Gamble and his backers.

This time the tribe would have more time. The general council began its resistance by passing a unanimous resolution opposing the measure and authorizing a delegation of eight to go to Washington. Before this group left, Inspector McLaughlin reappeared but got nowhere. Only thirty-six people showed up for the "council" he summoned. With Congress eager to adjourn for the 1910 elections and the tribe unified in its opposition, it seemed clear that the bill would not come up for a vote. Gamble decided to put off the battle until 1911.

When the legislators reassembled in the fall of 1911, the senator was ready with a new version of his bill. Once again resolutions were passed at Cheyenne River condemning the idea, and once again Major McLaughlin appeared to argue his case. But the tribe refused to continue this now familiar charade. Percy Phillips, who had represented the White Horse district in trips to Washington in 1908 and 1910, was the first to speak when the representative from Washington arrived. "A delegation went to Washington concerning the same bill a year ago last winter," he exclaimed. "We went down there and we . . . would not have anything to do with the bill." Why, he asked, should the tribe discuss it again? Others spoke up. Charles La Plant, who was aware that the meeting was being recorded, protested that from McLaughlin's speech someone reading the transcript might get the impression that an official council was taking place. He reminded the inspector that "this is not what we call a general council." John Last Man was the most eloquent. Turning to McLaughlin, he said, "This bill has been before Congress for the last four years and you come every time to present it to us. . . . It seems like this bill called for the rest of our reservation being sold and the money to be used for the benefit of the whites. . . . [With the bill] this reservation is opened up and gone and used to the benefit of the white men and for them until the Indians die of starvation."

Finally, after listening to the inspector's familiar arguments, Chairman James Crow Feather announced that the business council had decided that "a delegation should be sent to the Indian Office . . . to discuss this matter with them face to face. . . . We are all well acquainted with you," he told McLaughlin, "and . . . we have come to the conclusion of sending a delegation to the Indian Office and that is our answer to this bill." Immediately after Crow Feather spoke, the meeting was adjourned. The next day, November 23, 1911, McLaughlin left the reservation. Three weeks later a new delegation was appointed by the tribe's general council. It consisted of representatives from each of the reservation districts. What is more, the tribe enlisted the support of the Cheyenne River superintendent and the head of the local boarding school. Both men wrote to Washington opposing the new bill, the school principal arguing that its passage would "be disastrous to these Indians."

In early April the tribal delegation arrived at the Indian Office to make its case in person. It consisted of Ed Swan from Cherry Creek (who was making his third trip to the capital); Oliver Black Eagle from Thunder Butte; Bazille Claymore from the Agency District; Straight Head, probably from White Horse; and Charles Jewett. The group not only opposed Gamble's bill but also presented six counter-proposals to the commissioner. These ranged from a suggestion that he join them in fighting against further homesteading bills, through requests that full payment be made for lands already opened, to demands that the Indian Office improve health care, education, and administration on the reservation.

Whether they realized it or not, the delegation's elaborate statement succeeded in so confusing the situation that passage of Gamble's bill was now almost impossible. The BIA would have to study their counterproposals and review the current management of the reservation before the commissioner could recommend that Congress pass the measure. And with so little pressure from potential settlers, Congress would not pass the bill unless the BIA approved it. The slow pace of the BIA bureaucracy now became an asset to the tribe. By the time an opinion could be offered, Congress was eager to adjourn and the proposal was buried. In the years to come, more attempts would be made to pass this bill, and while a similar effort was successful at Standing Rock in 1913, it never succeeded at Cheyenne River.

There is no written record of the tribe's reaction to its victory over Senator Gamble and South Dakota's boosters. In fact, because the bill was simply delayed and not voted down, reservation leaders might not have realized that they had won. For many it must have taken a winter without a visit from Major McLaughlin to convince them of their success. Less obscure were the dramatic changes that had occurred during the last generation in the tribe's style and system of leadership. Leaders were now chosen by districts and picked—at least in part—for their ability to deal with the business and political details that confronted them. In this respect it is significant that the 1910 and 1912 delegations to Washington both included men like Ed Swan and Percy Phillips, who had been to the capital before. Experience and familiarity with "white ways" had become another qualification for leadership. The business council, with four representatives from each district, had become an effective and flexible body. It could respond quickly to crises and speak credibly for the entire tribe.

Few would claim that the 1908 law that opened nearly half the Cheyenne River Reservation to white settlement was a blessing to the tribe or that the struggle to retain their remaining unallotted lands was beneficial. But what should be recognized in these events is the way they sparked people on the reservation to organize themselves to respond. The conflict heightened their commitment to the reservation and forced them to produce effective leaders. Senator Gamble's campaign to abolish the Cheyenne River preserve had a unifying and strengthening impact on the people who lived there. Equally significant, resistance to the Gamble bills was led by the business council—an institution created by white men. The white men had created it, but the tribe was now operating it.

Disputes over homesteading were not the only source of conflict between the tribe and the outside world during this period just prior to World War I. Law and order, education, and agriculture were also areas in which the hostility of outsiders allowed (and sometimes forced) the people at Cheyenne River to develop and maintain their own way of life. The final disposition of these issues was also a measure of the tribe's adaptation to their reservation environment.

Prior to the arrival of white homesteaders, the Indian police and the tribal courts had exclusive responsibility for law and order on the reservation. Policemen patrolled the entire preserve, keeping intruders and unauthorized cattle out and enforcing the superintendent's orders in Indian communities. The court met monthly in each of the four districts and heard cases involving violations of regulations (drunkenness, adultery) and disputes between individuals (conflicting claims to property, settlement of estates, and so forth). Once the homesteaders began arriving in 1909 and 1910, many people believed that the tribe would come under the jurisdiction of the new counties that would be organized on the opened lands. Some even expected the reservation institutions to disappear. The *Pierre Daily Capital-Journal* promised that with the new law "another district is unfolding to civilization. . . . No doubt good towns will spring up in this valley which is not so famed, but much larger than the renowned valley of the Mohawk." These predictions proved incorrect. Drought and dust storms accompanied the homesteaders to their claims. Instead of prosperous new farms and bustling boom towns, the open lands produced stunted crops and shattered dreams. In the summer of 1913 Farming Superintendent Charles Davis reported that "the reservation is the worst burned I have about ever seen. . . . At present there is no market for agricultural lands."

Because of their many hardships the white settlers had no interest in policing Indian communities. As a result few reservation residents were prosecuted in the state courts. In addition the scattered non-Indian communities made law enforcement more difficult. As Superintendent King wrote in 1912, "the opening of the . . . reservation . . . created . . . a community without law . . . this was quickly taken advantage of by bootleggers, gamblers, horse thieves, cattle rustlers and soldiers of fortune generally." Because the state did not act in the face of this rising crime rate, the duties of the Indian police and the tribal courts did not disappear but became even more important. While obviously an arm of the superintendent and not always popular, the reservation's law enforcement officers were respected in the community. Elderly members of the Cheyenne River Tribe still recall the effectiveness of the Indian courts during these years. For example, a man from Cherry Creek remembers, "They had a tribal court (when I was young). . . . That judge he didn't go to school, he have no education, but just a little. . . . and they'll have a court there. And a real court too, them days. . . . and there's a policeman, didn't go to school, he stands there. . . . That's the kind of law and order we had, them days, they were pretty strict. . . . But that's a real court they have."

A similar point can be made about the government schools on the reservation. Many people felt that the new county governments would accept Indian children into their schools and, as a consequence, that the BIA schools would disappear. The agency superintendent reported in 1914, for example, that he expected three day schools to "likely be abandoned for the next year, and the public schools organized in their place." This idea was killed in 1915, when South Dakota repealed a law that had opened its schools to Indians. From that time forward, only children whose tuition was paid by the government would be allowed to attend local white schools. As a result, most Indian children continued to be educated together, either in their own communities or in boarding schools. As in the area of law enforcement, rejection by white society caused tribal members to maintain their ties with each other.

Finally, the presence of boss farmers in each of the four districts helped hold the communities together. The farmers lived at the subagencies and were primarily responsible for supervising individual farms and acting as ombudsmen for all BIA business. Boss farmers were involved in arranging leases, distributing rations, assisting the tribal courts, and hearing complaints. Once the white homesteaders arrived, a new duty was added to this list: keeping settlers off tribal land and away from Indian cattle. Disputes arose almost as soon as the reservation was opened. The boss farmer was in a unique position. He was a white man, but he was a *federal* official. He knew the Indians well and was responsible for their government issue property. Cheyenne River may have been unusual, but most of its farmers seem to have been honest and willing to challenge local whites if they felt there was a reason. They did this, for example, in 1915, when Dewey County tried to tax the assets of allottees and when the South Dakota herd law was being used to capture and steal Indian cattle.

Through all of their activities, the boss farmers were living reminders to the native people on the reservation that they were a distinct community that could expect certain kinds of help and protection. Some of the favor of the strict life that focused around a boss farmer is conveyed by an elderly resident who remembers Cherry Creek in the years before World War I: "Cherry Creek used to be something like a town. They had a restaurant, a warehouse, . . . and a police headquarters, court house, and doctor's office, and carpenter shop and blacksmith shop—[they had] everything." "Everything" was at the subagency. It was where people went for their ration and lease money; it was where court was held; it was a place for visiting and keeping in touch with each other.

These patterns, established in the years prior to World War I, persisted through the 1920s. The tribal council continued to block congressional attempts to open more land or reduce their power. The Indian police and the tribal courts both functioned despite the influx of white settlers. County and state officials still had little interest in extending their jurisdiction to tribal members, and the Cheyenne River courts continued to be respected (this situation was not affected by the 1924 citizenship act). Reservation day schools and the boss farmer system remained important measures of the tribe's separation from the state government. In all these areas it was clear that the new reservation culture that had emerged at Cheyenne River would continue into the future.

Why did the Great Sioux Agreement, designed to "absorb" the four Lakota bands at Cheyenne River, fail? Why did this reservation—which was supposed to be a focus of government efforts to assimilate native people—remain an Indian preserve? The preceding discussion of events of the early twentieth century on the reservation has suggested some answers. The reservation became the setting for a new kind of culture, one that adopted certain non-Indian institutions but which used these to defend traditional values and goals. The reservation was a new environment for the people of Cheyenne River. It placed new restrictions on their activities and made new demands on them, and pressure from the outside world forced them back on themselves. As a result, they used many of the new reservation institutions as vehicles for self-defense and cultural survival. The tribal council, which the government had thought would be useful only when there was property to be sold or leases to be signed, became an effective force in the struggle to hold on to unallotted tribal lands. The courts and police system emerged as the only protection available against lawless homesteaders or errant fellow tribesmen. The schools—while bleak and often cruel—gave native children an alternative once they had been rejected by the white community. And the boss farmers, with all of their duties, created a focus for life in each district and served as a reminder of the kind of protection federal power could provide. All of these institutions—even though they were inventions of the government—were used to serve the interests of tribal members.

It would be incorrect to interpret this narrative as a simple defense of the Indian police or the tribal council or the BIA schools, for it is important to remember that each of these institutions was forced on the tribe. What is more, they benefited the tribe only because the people at Cheyenne River had rich traditions and a continuing loyalty to their culture. Those feelings of identity and strength, which overrode the horrors of the past, shaped the activities of those who were drawn to the new reservation institutions. The council opposed land openings, the policemen chased off cattle rustlers, and the people gathered at the subagencies because they never stopped feeling that they belonged to a special group and that they had an obligation to each other that was greater than the sum total of outside pressure. Thinking back to these early years, one of the tribe's oldest members recently recalled, "In 1912 they had a fair in Dupree [a town on the opened portion of the reservation] and I remember one white man, Congressman Henry L. Gandy, he said forty years from now there won't be no Indians. . . . He come near make it. . . . But we Indians will be Indians all our lives, we never will be white men. We can talk and work and go to school like the white people but we're still Indians." Beginning with that feeling, many of the people who participated in government-sponsored institutions worked to make those institutions serve the interests of the group. Without a sense of identity within the tribe, these institutions might have served their original purpose. And the reverse is true: If the traditions had remained without the new institutions, they alone might not have succeeded in keeping the tribal culture alive. The Gamble bill would have passed, law and order would have vanished, and reservation life would have had no focus.

Every culture is constantly changing. Values and traditions may persist, but ways of life are never static. The creation of the Cheyenne River Reservation caused dramatic changes in the lives of the people who were forced to live there. But despite these upheavals, the culture of those people survived. Thus we should view the early twentieth century not as a period of assimilation but as a time of rapid cultural change. The councilmen, the tribal judges, the policemen, and the rest were caught up in this process. They faced great pressures, but all through the crisis they worked to maintain their culture rather than to surrender it. For this reason the early history of the Cheyenne River Reservation should be understood not as a time of defeat and hopelessness but as a crucial period of adaptation and survival. Forced into a strange new world, these people used the tools available to them to protect and preserve the place they now call their homeland.

19

URBAN INDIANS AND ETHNIC CHOICES: AMERICAN INDIAN ORGANIZATIONS IN MINNEAPOLIS, 1920–1950

NANCY SHOEMAKER

Few Americans realize the extent of Indian migration from the reservations to the cities during the twentieth century. According to the United States Census Bureau, by 1970 half of all Native Americans lived in the cities, and that number continues to grow. This reading discusses the pre-1950 organizational activities of Indian groups in Minneapolis–St. Paul. In doing so it focuses attention on a time that has come to be regarded as increasingly important for those trying to understand where Native Americans fit into the pattern of ethnic group strivings of the past several decades. The author places such post–World War II groups and movements as the American Indian Movement (AIM) and the demands for Red Power of the 1960s and 1970s into the context of Indian migration to the cities dating back at least into the 1920s. Her study examines fraternal, social, and political groups that laid the foundations for the post-1950s actions. Minneapolis attracted Native Americans from several reservations because of proximity and economic opportunity. Indians who lived there for more than a short time came to think of themselves as separate and distinct from those who remained on the reservations, and they worried about losing their ethnic identity and tribal rights. Having to deal with that and facing the usual urban pressures, Indians began to found groups for mutual support. Some developed with only members from a single reservation, while others included people from several tribes. This discussion shows how the groups established in the Twin Cities during the past several decades built on the experiences of the earlier groups.

Nancy Shoemaker is a doctoral student in history at the University of Minnesota.

When Dennis Banks, an initial founder of the American Indian Movement (AIM), said in a 1976 interview that "urbanization was part of the downfall, part of the destruction of the Indian community," he articulated one of the most commonly held assumptions about American Indians' experiences in cities. Banks's statement is ironic, since AIM and other Indian organizations of the 1960s and 1970s emerged from Indian communities that urbanization had helped create. AIM began one evening in 1968 when several Indians met to try to prevent what they saw as discriminatory arrests of Indians in their south Minneapolis neighborhood. By organizing Indians living in specific communities to help each other, AIM members were acknowledging that Indians in cities belonged to ethnic as well as geographic communities. AIM's first meeting, its further development of Minneapolis-area projects in education and housing, and its proliferation nationwide suggest that urbanization has helped to reinforce American Indian identity.

Scholars studying recent American Indian history have exhibited a similar kind of historical shortsightedness. They generally share in Dennis Banks's assessment of the city as damaging to Indian communities. Because the federal government sponsored an urban relocation program for Indians in the 1950s, Indian urbanization is often treated as a by-product of misguided government policies. And the Red Power movement of the 1960s and 1970s is treated as a phenomenon of Indian ghettos, a response to poverty, unemployment, and alcoholism.

The experience of urban Indians before 1950 provides the necessary context for understanding post-1950 developments such as relocation, the growth of Indian ghettos, and the political activism of the 1960s and 1970s. In particular, Indian urban history before 1950 can offer insights on the twentieth-century emergence of an Indian ethnic identity. Scholars such as anthropologist Robert K. Thomas and historian Hazel Hertzberg have suggested that cities helped foster the development of a pan-Indian identity. To cope with social problems and discrimination, people who identified with a particular tribe or band came to identify themselves as Indian.

One way to express ethnic identity is to join an organization. While Indians living on reservations formed social and political organizations among members of the same tribe or band, urban Indians had many choices in determining the boundaries of their ethnic community. The Twin Cities—located between small Dakota communities in southern Minnesota and several large Ojibway reservations in northern Minnesota—offered opportunities for the Ojibway and Dakota, who had been enemies in the nineteenth century, to become allies in the twentieth.

While Indian urbanization resembles that of other ethnic and racial groups, especially the urban migration of blacks, there are important differences. Both blacks and Indians experienced a massive shift from rural to urban residence in the twentieth century, and discrimination forced both groups into ghettos. Members of both groups founded societies, clubs, leagues, and associations, but organizations founded by Indians reflected a different dynamic. Recent literature on the urbanization of blacks points to social class as an emerging dynamic among blacks in cities. Class distinctions also existed among urban Indians but were confounded by urban Indians' ambiguous relationship to reservations. For Indians, length of residence in the city greatly influenced such indicators of social class as occupation, income, and home ownership. Longtime residents of the Twin Cities distinguished themselves from newly arrived reservation emigrants by referring to the other Indians as "reservation Indians." And yet Indians with closer ties to the reservation had something urban Indians did not. Urban Indians found that living away from reservations threatened their rights to tribal membership as well as their ethnic identity.

From 1920 to 1950 Minneapolis Indians formed two kinds of organizations: political organizations for strengthening their tenuous tribal ties and social organizations for building urban communities. Members of these organizations identified strongly as Americans in their use of patriotic rhetoric and in their pleas for equal rights for Indians as American citizens. But they were more flexible in their ethnic identifications. Whether they referred to themselves as Ojibway (Chippewa) or as Indian depended on the organization's purpose. Political organizations seeking to maintain rights for members of tribes naturally needed to organize among members of the same tribe. Organizations with social or cultural goals organized multitribally and thus were pan-Indian. Membership between organizations overlapped, confirming that an organization's goals—and not the individual member's cultural attachments—determined the ethnic position of each organization.

Minneapolis Indians' detachment from reservation communities made the city itself an important influence on the goals and membership of organizations. Most 1920–1950 organizations emerged from the south Minneapolis neighborhood where AIM would later organize its first efforts. But the neighborhood itself offered a radically different urban environment for the first Minneapolis Indians. Before World War II living conditions for Minnesota's urban Indian population surpassed conditions on the reservations. The majority of reservation residents survived on some mixture of unskilled, seasonal labor and erratic welfare assistance. The city provided more stable employment and a wider variety of occupations; urban Indians had jobs as skilled workers, professionals, white-collar workers, and small business operators. The 1928 Meriam Report, a nationwide survey of conditions among American Indians, found that longtime Indian residents of Minneapolis and St. Paul lived comfortably in middle-class homes:

> The range in standards of living follows economic rather than racial lines. Indians newly arrived are found in cheaply furnished rooming houses with rents comparatively high, or scattered through low-rent neighborhoods in cheap flats of one, two, or three rooms in buildings where conditions are somewhat below a reasonable standard of living. Numbers of other well-established wage earners are rather attractively housed in pleasant one- or two-family dwellings in better sections. Some of the more successful have attractive homes in the less expensive suburbs.

In 1947 a Minnesota social worker specializing in Indian welfare similarly observed that some Twin Cities Indians enjoyed the best living conditions among Minnesota Indians, but Indians new to the city lived in cramped, inadequate housing in the poorer sections of town.

During World War II new arrivals rapidly began to outnumber long-time Indian residents. In the 1920s the Indian population in the Twin Cities numbered less than 1,000. By the end of World War II 6,000 Indians resided there. Plentiful jobs and high-paying defense work attracted Indians to the Twin Cities and other urban areas, but wartime and postwar housing shortages, combined with discrimination, forced Indians into substandard housing in what was fast becoming a slum area. A 1947 Minneapolis housing study uncovered stories of Indian families crowded into condemned buildings and of an apartment building where more than sixty-five people shared two bathrooms. In her book *Night Flying Woman*, Ojibway author Ignatia Broker described how, when she moved to Minneapolis during the war, a landlord overcharged her for a room not legally listed with the War Price and Rationing Board. It was a dingy basement room without adequate washing or cooking facilities: "[H]e would have made the illegal offer only to an Indian because he knew of the desperate housing conditions we, the first Americans, faced."

The more than 4,000 Indians who moved to the Twin Cities during the war created new areas of concern for Minneapolis's public and private welfare agencies and for those Indians well settled in the cities. Juvenile delinquency, prostitution, and especially the crowded, unsanitary living conditions created serious social problems in the growing Indian neighborhoods. On the home front World War II had helped create the Twin Cities' first Indian ghettos.

Before the war, however, there were no special social problems plaguing Twin Cities Indians. Conditions were so good that local public officials expected that most of its urban Indian population was assimilating and becoming part of the mainstream. On the basis of hundreds of interviews, the Meriam Report observed that urban Indians had succeeded in "adjusting themselves to white civilization." They had homes, clothes, and forms of recreation that were no different from those of other people in their respective economic classes. In Minneapolis and St. Paul, in particular, there was a high rate of intermarriage (46 of the 120 Indians interviewed had married non-Indians), and "the majority of persons in these cities who claim to be Chippewas are persons whose Indian blood is so diluted that its presence would never be guessed from their personal appearance."

The report also noted that city Indians were resisting certain native traditions as befit workers competing in the industrial marketplace:

> In city life the "sponging" permitted by this traditional Indian hospitality in its most aggravated form is rapidly disappearing. An occasional relative or friend, however, still tries to secure a foothold during periods of voluntary idleness, but the steady working Indian who rents a home and tries to survive in the presence of white civilization is more and more resisting this pressure to furnish food and shelter to drones.

Although the Meriam Report advocated these changes and even advised that the government sponsor a small-scale urban relocation program, some of the report's other observations on urban Indians make clear that "adjustment to white civilization" is more complicated than linear models of assimilation would suggest. The report found, for instance, that "in a number of cases a claim of only one-sixteenth, one thirty-second, or one sixty-fourth Indian blood was made, yet great insistence was put upon the right to be designated 'Indian.'" It also found that urban Indians socialized mainly with other Indians. Even though Indians belonged to white clubs and churches or lived primarily in white neighborhoods, most of their friends remained Indian.

Members of Indian organizations in the 1920s reflected the ambivalence toward assimilation the Meriam Report captured. Many of them had inter-married with whites, had joined mainstream clubs and churches, and had become "steady working Indians." They advocated assimilation and were preoccupied with making Indians economically self-sufficient members of American society. But by organizing along ethnic lines, they inadvertently set up barriers to assimi-lation. As they strove to become more American, they still emphasized their ethnic differences.

The first Indian organization active in Minneapolis was apparently a local social club affiliated with the American Indian Association and Tepee Order, a national fraternal society. Two World War I veterans, George Peake, Ojibway, and Warren Cash, Dakota, organized the Minneapolis affiliate soon after the war. Along with sponsoring dances and other social functions for Twin Cities Indians, the Tepee Order Club established a fraternity house for Indian students attending Minneapolis schools. Club officers Cash and Peake also tried unsuccessfully to organize a national Indian veterans' association.

The American Indian Association and Tepee Order's national organization, which included Peake and Cash among its officers, directed its greatest effort toward achieving public recognition of the Indians' contributions to American life. Annually the organization distributed promotional letters to local government leaders, churches, schools, and other social fraternities, urging them to participate in American Indian Day. Initially conceived of by another national Indian organi-zation, the Society of American Indians, American Indian Day was an accumula-tion of events including Indian speakers, music, and educational activities put together by local clubs in cities like Minneapolis, Denver, and Chicago. In 1923, when the national organization had its headquarters in Minneapolis, promotional letters for American Indian Day expressed hopes that "the day is not far when all our Indians will do away with their old mode of life, and accept the modern civilization, and we all be as one true American citizens." Club members seemed to celebrate their Indian heritage while anticipating a melting-pot demise of Indian cultural distinctiveness.

Other Minneapolis Indian leaders of the 1920s believed that Indians should be integrated into the American melting pot. Members of the Twin Cities Chip-pewa Council, the Minnesota Wigwam Indian Welfare Society (a local affiliate of a national organization), and the Twin Cities Indian Republican Club advocated assimilation while maintaining their own native identity by joining these ethnically based organizations. In the 1920s all three organizations had offices in one place, the home of Frederick W. Peake in south Minneapolis.

A graduate of Carlisle Indian School and a lawyer from White Earth Reser-vation, Peake moved to Minneapolis in 1915 and lived there until his death in 1934. While in Minneapolis, Peake continued to practice law and dabbled in real estate investment. Although Peake's organizations included members from Fond du Lac and Grand Portage Reservations, White Earth emigrants clearly dominated the membership. Some organization participants had probably known Peake at White Earth. And some, like Archie Libby, an officer of the Twin Cities Chippewa Council, probably had been a friend of Peake's at Carlisle Indian School.

There are other possible explanations for why Minneapolis Indian organizations attracted so many White Earth emigrants. White Earth's bitter factional politics, heightened by notorious land allotment frauds, may have provided some residents with experience in political lobbying and interest group organizing. Also, many political leaders, including Archie Libby, left the reservation shortly after World War I when a local economic depression set in at White Earth. However, the main reason for high White Earth participation may simply be that there were more Indians living in the Twin Cities with ties to White Earth than to other reservations. Because the federal government had tried to consolidate all Minnesota Ojibways, except the Red Lake Band, at White Earth in the late nineteenth century, it was the largest Indian reservation in Minnesota. By 1900 White Earth had a diverse population of about 3,000 Ojibways. A large proportion of them had acculturated to Christianity, wage earning, and pro-assimilation ideology. White Earth people predominated in Minneapolis Indian organizations probably because they were more likely to be city residents.

The Twin Cities Chippewa Council, a lobbying organization for Ojibway men dislocated from the reservation, was the most active of Frederick Peake's organizations. The council formed in response to 1924 congressional consideration of an Indian competency bill that would declare all Minnesota Ojibways legally "competent." The Indian Competency Bill proposed to release the Ojibways from government supervision and divide the tribal funds into individual payments to enrolled members of the tribe. Writing in support of the bill, Peake, acting as vice president of the Twin Cities Chippewa Council, suggested that government paternalism prevented Indian assimilation:

> [S]uch progressive measures as this [passing the competency bill] will be the means of getting the Indians to become a part of the melting pot, the same as other nations have been received by this Government and have become a part of it when they complied with the law provided for an emigrant to become a citizen.

The Indian Competency Bill never passed Congress, but the Council continued to lobby for per capita distribution of tribal funds as a solution to Indian dependency.

William Madison, another member of the Twin Cities Chippewa Council, would make similar pleas for "progressive" reforms ten years later to protest the Indian Reorganization Act. Like Peake, Madison had sold his White Earth land allotment shortly before World War I, moved to the city, and started a business. Before moving to Minneapolis, Madison lived in Missouri for about fifteen years. While there, he tried a variety of occupations, from working as a carpenter to owning his own cleaning and tailoring business. He may have moved away from White Earth for economic reasons, or he may have felt frustrated by a series of political disappointments at White Earth, where he tried several times to represent the tribe in its dealings with the federal government. Although Madison's grandfather was *me-zhuc-e-ge-shig*, a respected hereditary chief of the Mississippi Band of White Earth Ojibway, Madison's own efforts to influence political decisions at White Earth rarely succeeded. His political inclinations eventually met more success off the reservation, where he was a ubiquitous presence in local and national Indian organizations. Madison was one of the few Indians to participate in both the

Tepee Order and the Society of American Indians. In the early 1920s he edited the Tepee Order's magazine and in 1923 served as an officer of the Society of American Indians.

In keeping with the progressive ideals of the Society of American Indians, Madison believed strongly in the ability of Indians to better themselves. Along with participating in national Indian organizations, he started a local, pan-Indian social club, The Indians of Greater Kansas City, which urged other Indians to follow its members' example and move to cities. Like Indian reformer Carlos Montezuma, whom he particularly admired, Madison viewed the Bureau of Indian Affairs as an insidious institution, intent on maintaining Indians as dependents of the federal government.

When Madison moved to Minneapolis in the late 1920s, he naturally joined his friends at the Twin Cities Chippewa Council as an advocate of progressive reform for Indians, in particular for the Minnesota Ojibways. In 1934 the Council sent Madison to Washington to defeat what they saw as regressive legislation: the Indian Reorganization Act (IRA) and other Indian New Deal policies being formulated within Commissioner John Collier's administration.

Collier planned to reverse United States Indian policy's emphasis on the individual. By building up reservation land bases and economies and by emphasizing self-determination in reservation politics, Collier hoped Indians would achieve self-sufficiency as communities, not as individuals. The Twin Cities Chippewa Council attacked the proposed changes in tribal structure as just another attempt to deprive Indians of vital land and resources and predicted that the new policy would "reduce them to the old tribes and further prey upon them."

Collier's intentions to revitalize tribal authority on reservations also threatened the council's own ability to influence tribal affairs. As enrolled members of tribes, urban Indians had a personal stake in events and decisions occurring on their reservations, but their prime means of influencing tribal affairs was through the federal government since they could not participate first-hand in tribal politics. The council's vehement lobbying against the IRA resulted from an odd mix of progressive ideology, self-interest, and sincere concerns for reservation Indians. Progressive ideology helped shape their beliefs in individual success and influenced their rhetoric of assimilation, but self-interest dictated many of their actions.

The council's persistent attempts to influence both tribal enrollment guidelines and the distribution of tribal funds reflect its emphasis on pursuing the interests of nonreservation Ojibways. Tribal enrollment was an issue because urban Indians risked being removed from the tribal rolls. Before Collier's appointment as commissioner of Indian affairs, the Office of Indian Affairs had been trying to tidy up tribal rolls using reservation residence as one of the criteria for tribal membership. A series of court cases, culminating in the Patterson opinion in 1932, denied tribal enrollment to children born to Indians residing off the reservation. Consequently, many Ojibways moved back to their reservations in the 1930s.

Ojibways who stayed in the city tried to change enrollment requirements, but enrollment was a divisive issue. Members of the Twin Cities Chippewa Council agreed that Collier's focus on the reservation would reinforce the importance of reservation residence and undermine their rights as members of the Minnesota

Chippewa Tribe. But they could not agree on how to change enrollment requirements. William Madison argued that the degree of Indian blood should be used as the primary standard. Such a decision would have benefitted him and his family. He was listed as a full-blood on most government documents, but his children, those born after he left White Earth, were denied enrollment in the tribe. His children were half Ojibway since Madison's wife was white, but half was more than many reservation residents could claim. Other Minneapolis Indians could neither accept Madison's suggestions nor derive better ones since all proposed changes would exclude some of them.

The council, however, easily agreed on what to do with the tribal funds held in trust by the federal government. Throughout the 1920s it supported legislation that would distribute per capita payments of tribal funds to competent Indians. All the council members were "competent," some having proven their economic self-sufficiency by selling their land allotments and becoming wage earners in the city. As enrolled members of a tribe, council members periodically received interest from tribal funds, but funds continually dwindled because the government used that money to support reservation programs and facilities. Collier's plans promised to be even more expensive.

The council opposed the IRA, however, not just because it would delay a final per capita distribution of tribal money, but also because they had spent most of their lives believing that Indians should abandon the old way of life, assimilate, and seek individual success. In presenting the council's objections toward the IRA to the House Subcommittee on Indian Affairs, Madison argued that it would only prolong the Bureau of Indian Affairs' administration of reservations and would consequently encourage the Indians' dependence on the federal government:

> So far as I am personally concerned, I can make a livelihood in competition with others. They [the Bureau of Indian Affairs] are keeping the Indian down and that is un-American. They should be free like any other men. They should exercise their rights of citizenship like anybody else.

Because Madison and his fellow council members had achieved some success as individuals—as house painters, barbers, bankers, and lawyers—they thought individual success could and should be achieved by other Indians.

The Twin Cities Chippewa Council had organized to serve the particular interests of a few dislocated Ojibways, but members devoted some effort to purely charitable causes. Both Peake and Madison lobbied for more welfare relief for reservation residents (so long as tribal funds were not used) and organized a benefit dance in 1932 to raise relief money. Also in 1932, they lobbied the state for an exchange of state-owned land and Ojibway lands to give Minnesota Ojibways access to more of the lakes where wild rice grew. Wild rice was an important source of food and income for several Ojibway reservations. However, since they considered their organization primarily a tribal council with a political agenda, council members pursued welfare issues only occasionally.

One Indian woman, Amabel Bulin, initiated most of the Indian welfare programs that originated in Minneapolis before 1950. An enrolled Sioux and a graduate of the Bureau of Indian Affairs school at Tomah, Wisconsin, she later graduated from New York University, married a Scandinavian from Brooklyn, and settled into middle-class life in Minneapolis. In a 1954 newspaper interview Bulin described herself as a housewife, a member of women's clubs, and a faithful Catholic. She also bowled twice a week. She easily fit the Meriam Report's description of the assimilated Indians in Minneapolis who insisted on "the right to be designated 'Indian.'"

Beginning in the 1920s Bulin worked as a self-appointed, volunteer social worker. She located boarding homes for Indian children and temporary housing for reservation Indians taking advantage of the city's hospitals and schools. Young women from Minnesota, North and South Dakota, Wisconsin, and even Montana reservations used her as a connection for finding homes and jobs in the Twin Cities. During World War II she unsuccessfully tried to establish a boarding home for Indian women defense workers.

Amabel Bulin undertook some of these services at the request of several Indian Affairs agents in the upper Midwest, but her concern for young Indian women developed from her involvement in the General Federation of Women's Clubs. First, as a member of the Pathfinder Club, she helped provide educational scholarships to young women. In the late 1930s she formed her own affiliate to the General Federation of Women's Clubs, *Sah-Kah-Tay* (*Sunshine* in Ojibway). *Sah-Kah-Tay* was an all-Indian women's club that sponsored young Indian women who wanted to go to school or work in the city. Bulin later became the director of Minnesota's General Federation of Women's Clubs, Indian Division, where she carried out the division's usual programs of collecting clothing and food for distribution on Minnesota's Indian reservations.

Before World War II Amabel Bulin's social-welfare programs, like Madison's and Peake's occasional welfare activities, aimed to help reservation Indians. During the war she helped Indian women move from reservations to Minneapolis to take up defense work, but gradually she directed her efforts at meeting the needs of the Indians already living in the city. Before the war she served as a link between the reservation and the city; after the war she became a link between urban Indians and public institutions: courts, welfare offices, employers, and the Fair Employment Practices Commission.

Speaking in 1944 before the House Committee Investigating Indian Affairs, Amabel Bulin pointed to an alarming rate of juvenile arrests among Indians. She told stories of juvenile drinking and prostitution, which were increasing in the Indian neighborhoods of both St. Paul and Minneapolis. Although concerned that Indians were "forced to live in unwholesome surroundings or in a dirty, filthy city," the committee would ultimately propose abandoning Collier's policies in favor of reservation termination and urban relocation.

Public and private welfare organizations in the Twin Cities, similarly ignoring the growth of an Indian ghetto, also established urban relocation programs for Indians after the war. Hitler's anti-Semitism had created a heightened sensitivity about racism at home, and state and local governments sponsored labor and housing studies, educational brochures, and lecture tours about Minnesota's black, Hispanic, Asian, and Indian residents. Members of the newly formed Minnesota Interracial Commission perceived urban relocation to be the solution to the state's so-called Indian problem. In 1950 the commission also sponsored an Indian social club, American Indians, Inc., and recruited several Minneapolis Indians to help new arrivals from reservations find homes and jobs in the city.

At the same time, private charities like the St. Paul Resettlement Committee, which formed in 1943 to help resettle Japanese-Americans interned during the war, decided to fund the Twin Cities relocation of Turtle Mountain Ojibways from North Dakota. Public and private administrators of welfare programs believed that Indians were ready to move to the cities. Many Indians had already left their reservations to participate in the war effort as part of the military and as workers in defense plants. But administrators did not ask whether cities were ready for Indians. They showed remarkably bad timing in promoting urban relocation to cities already crowded by wartime migrations.

The changing city provided opportunities as well as hardships, however. Social organizations emerged from Indian neighborhoods. Before World War II Minneapolis organizations with pan-Indian membership developed out of other networks: Warren Cash and George Peake were World War I veterans, and Amabel Bulin maintained numerous contacts with Indian Affairs agents and women's clubs. It was not until World War II that pan-Indian groups coalesced in urban neighborhoods.

The Ojibway-Dakota Research Society was one such pan-Indian group. It grew out of an urban neighborhood where Indians from different tribes and reservations came to know each other. William Madison founded the Ojibway Research Society in 1942 with White Earth friends who were also members of the Twin Cities Chippewa Council. They wanted to preserve the Ojibway language and gain some public recognition of Minnesota's Indian heritage. The society met periodically to prepare brief papers on the Ojibway origins of Minnesota place-names. The society soon expanded to allow Ojibway women, and in 1944, members from other Indian tribes. Although they renamed the organization the Ojibway-Dakota Research Society, membership included some Crees and Iroquois. Meeting attendance averaged fewer than twenty participants, but membership lists show that more people were involved than could regularly attend.

The research society's changing composition during World War II shows how the urban environment was beginning to contribute to pan-Indian organizing. Early membership lists show a majority of people with White Earth backgrounds and even some people who still lived at White Earth, but almost half of the 1945 members were not Ojibway. Most members lived in the same south Minneapolis neighborhood. Madison, Peake, and other Ojibway organizers had lived in this particular south Minneapolis neighborhood since the 1920s. They originally located in this area, and wartime migrations concentrated more Indians there.

The development of pan-Indian organizations in the Twin Cities did not replace tribal organizations. As in the 1920s, pan-Indian organizations existed simultaneously with tribal organizations, and despite their different ethnic label, both types of organizations attracted some of the same people.

In the late 1940s Madison and some of the Ojibway members of the Ojibway-Dakota Research Society formed another organization, the Ojibway Tomahawk Band. This organization's principal activity seems to have been the publication of a monthly, sometimes bimonthly, newsletter, *The New Tomahawk*. Madison named the newsletter after *The Tomahawk*, the White Earth newspaper published forty years earlier by a friend of his, Gus Beaulieu, a proassimilation political leader at White Earth. The newsletter published information and opinion on current Indian-related legislation and pushed for rights guaranteed Indians as American citizens and rights guaranteed Indians by treaties. Minnesota Ojibways as far away as Washington and California received the newsletter, as did several of the Ojibway Tomahawk Band's friends and relatives still living on the Ojibway reservations in northern Minnesota.

The Ojibway Tomahawk Band pursued some familiar political goals but abandoned other issues. The old issue of tribal funds was no longer pertinent. By 1943 the fund contained only $32,424. Although Collier intended tribal funds for capital improvements, most of the Minnesota Chippewa Tribe's funds went toward daily expenses, education, and relief. Passage of the Indian Claims Act in 1946 made tribal enrollment requirements still an important issue for urban Indians, however. The Indian Claims Act declared that the federal government would settle all Indian claims once and for all. The Ojibway Tomahawk Band may have formed to take advantage of this federal initiative. If the government was planning to resolve all claims, the urban Ojibways wanted to ensure that their interests as members of the tribe would be considered. The Ojibway Tomahawk Band's newsletter persistently argued that urban Indians, although living off the reservation, still had "rights to tribal representation at least until the final settlement."

The possibility of a final solution to the tribal-federal relationship encouraged urban Indians to maintain their tribal identities. Of the Minneapolis Indian organizations that formed before 1950, the Twin Cities Chippewa Council and the Ojibway Tomahawk Band organized among Ojibways because they wanted to pursue issues relevant to Minnesota Ojibways. Consistently, the politically active urban Indians tried to secure what they considered to be their share of federal obligations to Indians. Because most federal obligations were based on earlier treaties and agreements with tribes or bands, urban Indians' unresolved relationship to the federal government gave tribal ethnicity a legal and political imperative.

Minneapolis Indians organizing for cultural or social purposes seem to have readily identified with other Indians from very different cultural and social backgrounds. Although their previous experiences were different, their experiences in the city were similar: they shared the same needs and the same grievances about their relationship to the larger society. Thus Minneapolis organizations without political goals tended to be pan-Indian. The local Tepee Order affiliate, *Sah-Kay-Tay* and Amabel Bulin's other welfare activities, and the Ojibway-Dakota Research Society all had Ojibway, Dakota, and other tribal groups represented among their members.

The effects of pan-Indianism on tribal identity were ambiguous. Because members of pan-Indian organizations had different cultural backgrounds, those organizations seeking to make the American public more appreciative of Indian contributions encountered problems. The American Indian Association and Tepee Order relied on romanticized Indian stereotypes. The Tepee Order used a pseudo-Indian dating system on correspondence, consisting of suns and moons, and gave officers titles such as "Junior Guide of the Forest" and "Great Sentinel." The

Ojibway-Dakota Research Society aimed at historical accuracy, but William Madison ventured into such schemes as selling "Madison's Indian Medicine" and publishing an Indian wild rice cookbook with native recipes, including "Spanish *Mah-no-min*" (rice in Ojibway). Tribal heritages had to find some common ground if Indian organizers were to promote the impact of Indian cultures on American life. That common ground often consisted of popularized images of Indian cultures.

Although symbols used by pan-Indian organizers had this synthetic quality, overall pan-Indian organizing probably reinforced tribal ethnic identities. Members of pan-Indian organizations always identified individual members by tribe, even though the organization labeled itself as Indian. One could not be Indian without belonging to a tribe or tribes.

Urban life presented a new environment, with new problems but also new solutions. As Indians residing away from reservations, urban Indians risked losing their ethnic identity. Legally, they risked being removed from tribal rolls, and emotionally, they risked losing the security and fellowship of their communities. Establishing Indian organizations in the city helped reservation emigrants maintain their tribal identities while expanding their ethnic identity to include a larger circle of people. Ignatia Broker described the positive side of urbanization when she eloquently observed that:

> [M]aybe it was a good thing, the migration of our people to the urban areas during the war years, because there, amongst the millions of people, we were brought to a brotherhood. We Indian people who worked in the war plants started a social group not only for the Ojibway but for the Dakota, the Arikara, the Menominee, the Gros Ventres, the Cree, the Oneida, and all those from other tribes and other states who had made the trek to something new. And because we, all, were isolated in this dominant society, we became an island from which a revival of spirit began.

The experience of Minneapolis Indians challenges most historical accounts of Indian urbanization. First, prerelocation urban Indian migration is important for explaining later migrations. As historian Kenneth Philp has argued, the federal government initiated its urban relocation program in part because many Indians on their own initiative had successfully settled in cities. Second, the activities and goals of these early organizations show that AIM and other Red Power movements were part of a continuous process. The first generation of Minneapolis Indian reformers—Frederick Peake, William Madison, and Amabel Bulin—had a progressive faith in legislative reform's potential to ameliorate the social and political situation of American Indians. Another generation of reformers would emerge in the 1950s and 1960s: social workers and other college graduates. This younger generation formed professional alliances with private and public institutions such as settlement houses, state and city social-welfare agencies, and church groups. Then, in 1967, a third generation of urban Indians founded AIM and rapidly began to utilize the radical reform methods that the civil rights movement had helped shape. Although the reform methods varied, urban Indian organizations have persistently addressed issues of education and welfare, treaty rights and federal Indian obligations, and what it means to be Indian.

20

INCONSTANT ADVOCACY: THE EROSION OF INDIAN FISHING RIGHTS IN THE PACIFIC NORTHWEST, 1933–1956

DONALD L. PARMAN

Native American people living in the coastal regions of the Pacific Northwest appear to differ widely from popular notions of what Indians are like. Instead of tepees, earth lodges, or hogans, they erected large plank houses, put to sea in immense canoes, and erected totem poles near their villages. They depended heavily on the sea and coastal rivers for their subsistence. Yet upon close examination it is clear that they faced the same issues as other tribes when facing the Europeans in North America. Disease swept through their ranks, invading whites took choice village and fishing sites, and gradually the Indians fell under the control of the United States. During the period of treaty negotiations and the establishment of reservations in the region, many tribes retained at least some of their fishing rights. Once the salmon-canning industry became well established in Washington and Oregon, however, both those states began a pattern of discriminatory legislation aimed at forcing the Indians out of the fishing business. This essay traces the emergence of that pattern and notes that not until objections were raised to the blatantly anti-Indian Initiative 77 passed in 1935 by the Washington legislature did BIA officials bestir themselves on behalf of the tribes. The narrative traces the halting steps that federal officials took during the next thirty years to protect or regain Indian fishing rights. It shows that greed and economic discrimination marched alongside the continuing efforts to destroy the tribal cultures through much of American history.

Mr. Parman is a member of the history department at Purdue University.

Source: Donald L. Parman, "Inconstant Advocacy: The Erosion of Indian Fishing Rights in the Pacific Northwest, 1933–1956," *Pacific Historical Review*, 53 (May 1984), pp. 163–189. © 1984 by the Pacific Coast Branch, American Historical Association. Reprinted by permission of the Branch.

The issue of Indian fishing rights in the Pacific Northwest has aroused national attention since the "fish-ins" of the 1960s and Judge George Boldt's controversial decision in *United States* v. *Washington* in 1974. Though that decision was favorable to the Indians, it represented only one development in a conflict that has ranged from the territorial period of Oregon and Washington to the present. The more recent controversies have been essentially a fight over remnants since Indians lost many of the most valuable fisheries in previous decades. Although Indian fishing rights have exerted an important influence on the development of the Pacific Northwest and have been (and are) a significant determinant in race relations, the topic has received little attention from historians. The present study will focus primarily on the New Deal and immediate postwar eras when changes in the Bureau of Indian Affairs, state-federal relations, and the national economy modified but did not appreciably alter the erosion of Indian fishing rights, an erosion that had been going on for decades and which wreaked havoc on traditional Indian lifestyles and violated the spirit and often the letter of earlier treaties.

Coastal Indians prior to white settlement had since time immemorial fished for both anadromous (fish which ascend rivers from the sea to spawn) and nonanadromous species, collected various types of shellfish, and hunted seals and whales. Groups living inland mainly caught anadromous fish. By the twentieth century, Indian fishing was largely restricted to migrating salmon and steelhead in three principal fisheries. The first of these encompassed the streams which entered Puget Sound, the second included those rivers which flowed directly into the Pacific Ocean, and the third and largest involved the Columbia River and its many tributaries. The latter can be considered as a separate category because the Columbia and its tributaries, most notably the Snake River, permitted salmon and steelhead to reach spawning grounds hundreds of miles in the interior. The Cascade Mountains, which traverse Washington and Oregon north and south, have also significantly affected Indian fishing. This range divides the Pacific Northwest into two climatic zones. The area to the west of the mountains has heavy rainfall, lush forests, and high humidity. The opposite conditions prevail to the east because the Cascades prevent moisture from reaching the interior. Precontact Indians west of the mountains were called "fisheaters" because the thick forests prevented them from doing much hunting and forced them to depend almost solely on the rich fisheries in the streams, Puget Sound, and the Pacific. Salmon caught west of the Cascades were difficult to cure because of their high oil content and the damp climate, and they could only be preserved by smoking. The much drier climate in the eastern interior created a more open country, which permitted precontact groups to achieve a balance among hunting, gathering, and catching salmon migrating upstream on the Columbia and its tributaries. The same aridity led the interior tribes to filet and dry their fish on racks without smoking.

It would be difficult to overemphasize the dependence of the coastal Indians on fishing and the taking of whales and seals both before and after white settlement. Bureau of Indian Affairs (BIA) field workers in the region during the late nineteenth century attempted to force the "fish-eaters" to become farmers and frequently complained about their charges' unwillingness to abandon aquatic subsistence for agriculture. Indeed, the agents' reports bear a striking resemblance to those emanating from the Great Plains reservations in the same period. While the agents in the Plains states condemned the Indians for an unwillingness to abandon hunting, those in the Northwest criticized their groups for refusing to give up fishing and hunting seals and whales.

The Cascades continued to influence Indian fishing practices in the present century. Salmon caught on the Columbia east of the mountains were considered inferior in taste and sold for a lower commercial price than those taken downstream or at sea. Indians who lived west of the mountains in the 1930s used very little of their catch for subsistence and sold nearly all of their fish on the commercial market. Indians east of the Cascades, however, continued to use a sizable portion of their catch for subsistence because of the ease of curing.

The special fishing rights of Indians in Oregon and Washington derive from a series of treaties negotiated in 1854–55 mainly by Isaac I. Stevens, governor of the newly formed territory of Washington. The treaties reflected the prevailing philosophy at the beginning of the reservation era by requiring the Indian groups to cede their large holdings to the government and to relocate on smaller reservations. Stevens pushed the negotiations with unusual speed because of the burgeoning white settlement in Washington Territory and, more importantly, because he hoped that Congress would authorize a transcontinental railroad terminating at Puget Sound. His desire for haste and his awareness of the Indians' attitudes about the importance of fishing and hunting, prompted him to include provisions in the treaties similar to the following:

> The right of taking fish, at all usual and accustomed grounds and stations, is further secured to said Indians in common with all citizens of the Territory, and of erecting temporary houses for the purpose of curing, together with privilege of hunting, gathering roots and berries, and pasturing their horses on open and unclaimed lands.

The rapid white settlement in the Pacific Northwest after the treaties increasingly interfered with Indian attempts to fish at off-reservation sites. Because salmon and steelhead runs took place in every stream in the region, Indians no doubt originally fished at hundreds of sites of varying importance. Many of these were lost when white farmers and ranchers occupied lands along streams and denied access to Indians trying to reach traditional fishing grounds. Lumbering had somewhat the same effect, as that industry grew rapidly to meet both local needs and those of California settlements. The practice of floating logs down streams sometimes created jams which blocked fish from reaching their spawning areas. White settlement seems to have forced the Indians to give up their less important fishing places and to concentrate at the more productive points.

The advent of commercial salmon canning in the Pacific Northwest threatened even the best Indian fisheries. The first cannery on the Columbia opened in 1866, and that river soon became the largest source of canned salmon in the world. Annual catches rose dramatically, reaching a peak of 40,000,000 pounds in 1883–84. Only Chinook, the largest and best flavored of the five salmon species, was processed up to that time. Even though other species were taken afterward, the catch on the Columbia gradually declined from the early twentieth century until 1937, when it seemed to stabilize at approximately half of the catch of the mid 1880s. The developments on the Columbia were not unique. Numerous canneries followed a similar pattern in the rich fishing areas of Puget Sound and on many of the smaller streams which flowed directly into the Pacific.

Canneries brought some economic advantages to Indian fishermen, but their long-range effect was negative. Since Indians had always engaged in the barter of fish, they readily caught salmon for sale to the canneries, some even using their traditional equipment at first instead of adopting the fishing gear of whites. Other Indians found employment in the canneries. The superior capital, large-scale methods, and aggressiveness of whites, however, quickly led to their domination of the prime fisheries of the region. The Yakima agent, for example, reported in 1894 that "the disputed fishery rights of the Indians along the Columbia has given me a vast amount of trouble." He went on to describe how canneries located at the prime fisheries had "inch by inch" forced the Yakimas from their best sites. The scene was repeated elsewhere. The Tulalip agent complained in 1897 that large firms had appropriated nearly all the best fishing areas at Point Roberts and Village Point on Puget Sound, where the Lummi Indians traditionally fished. By 1905 conditions had worsened. "The tremendous development of fisheries by traps and by trust methods of consolidation, concentration, and large local development," reported the Tulalip agent, "are seriously depleting the natural larders of our Indians and cutting down on their main reliance for support and subsistence. Living for them is becoming more precarious year by year."

As public fears arose about the decline of salmon and steelhead runs, Washington and Oregon reacted by passing laws to regulate the length of fishing seasons, size of catches, and types of equipment. The Washington territorial legislature in 1871 banned nets or traps which entirely blocked rivers so some of the fish could escape upstream. The same measure demanded that all dams must provide a passage for fish. Six years later the legislature began fixing seasons and established a fish commissioner to enforce the law. Oregon followed a similar pattern in 1877 by banning fishing during part of the season and creating a three-man regulatory board in 1887. Until well into the twentieth century state legislation lacked any scientific rationale but, according to a careful study, was based on an "intuitive feeling" that the fish runs were declining and certain types of equipment were responsible.

State regulation of Indian fishing and hunting started in a lenient manner but increasingly discriminated against Indian rights. The legislature of Washington in 1891 acknowledged the proviso in the Stevens treaties by exempting Indians from a new fishing law, and early game wardens in the Puget Sound area overlooked violations of state laws if Indians fished or hunted for subsistence. By the second decade of the twentieth century the attitude toward Indians had toughened. In 1915 Charles M. Buchanan, the Tulalip agent, appeared before the Washington legislature and detailed the Indians' recent legal problems. The state insisted that the Indians buy licenses to hunt or fish off their reservations, but officials refused to sell the necessary permits on the grounds that the Indians were not citizens of the state. At the same time, whites, claiming state authority because they possessed licenses, seized control of ancient Indian fishing sites on the shores of reservations.

Indians, Buchanan complained, were arrested not only when they left reservations to hunt, but also often while securing game within their own reservations. Although state courts released those arrested, the Indians had still faced humiliation, time in jail, and legal expenses.

The operation of state fishing laws and enforcement policies reflected the struggles of various interest groups (sportsmen, net fishermen, trap operators, canneries) to gain an advantage over each other. Unfortunately the competition often adversely affected Indian fishing as well. A notable example involved Washington state's practice of licensing fish wheels at prime spots for favored large canneries and simultaneously excluding Indians from traditional fishing grounds. Because of their small population, lack of political influence, and the hostility of whites, the Indians clearly did not figure in the design of state laws or their enforcement by officials.

Although the effects of state regulation must have been traumatic for Indians who were almost solely dependent on fishing, only glimpses of their reactions appear in agency reports. When the Washington legislature in 1897 imposed a tax on all nets used in state waters and banned such gear from within 240 feet of any fish trap, the Lummi complained bitterly that the measure and recent court decisions were aimed specifically at them. Their agent confessed that "no amount of explanation on my part" would change the Indians' opinion.

While it is clear from agents' reports and court cases at the turn of the century that Indians were encountering numerous and severe difficulties in having their fishing rights accepted by state officials and by private citizens, their problems did not cause BIA officials at Washington to take any major protective action. The first indication in central office correspondence of a response to Indian complaints was in 1914 when Samuel Eliot, a member of the Board of Indian Commissioners visiting the Northwest, reported that Indian fishing rights on the Quinault River and Quinault Lake needed protection. State regulations on commercial fishing should apply to citizen Indians, he stated, but not to the Quilleute who were still noncitizens. Except for the normal practice of referring Eliot's letter to the local superintendent, nothing evidently was done to meet his concerns. Nine years later the Quinault Indians complained that a weir installed by the Bureau of Fisheries to count fish had disrupted the fish run, and the BIA intervened to close the obstacle.

The event which brought Indian fishing rights into sharp focus was the implementation of Initiative 77 in Washington in 1935. This measure banned all fixed gear such as fish wheels, traps, and set nets from the entire state; established a line inside Puget Sound which severely limited commercial fishing in the southern portion of that body of water; and redefined legal fishing gear and closed areas for fishing. Initiative 77 was the handiwork of numerous sports groups, and perhaps small commercial fishing firms owned or associated with canneries. The effects of the new law were significant both immediately and in the long run as large-scale operators concentrated more on trolling and purse seining outside the restricted area, leaving the waters inside the line and the rivers to small commercial fishing interests and white sportsmen. The new regulations caused a sharp rise in the expenses of commercial fishermen, who could no longer use fixed gear in rivers, and they negated potentially simple and effective conservation practices that could

have been used to preserve the runs. More importantly, the new legislation hand-
icapped Indian commercial fishermen who lacked the capital necessary to buy the
larger boats and equipment required for trolling and purse seining outside the
restricted zone.

The Indians' attempts to adjust to the new situation caused the first serious
conflict between Northwestern fishing interests and the BIA during the New Deal.
At the start of the 1935 season Ken McLeod, secretary of the Salmon Conservation
League, wrote the Indian Office complaining strongly that the Swinomish of Puget
Sound had established two fish traps on their reservation for commercial purposes.
State officials then arrested three Swinomish on the grounds that the traps were
located off-reservation. Both a lower court and the Washington state supreme court
denied that the traps were outside reservation boundaries and ordered the Indians
released. Although the Swinomish emerged victorious, the arrests and suits created
considerable public controversy. The local superintendent complained that sportsmen's groups had agitated so much about Indians' preferential fishing rights during
the period that state officials had persecuted the Indians and threatened "their only
means of independent subsistence."

The attitudes of state officials of Washington and Oregon about Indian fishing
in the 1930s contrasted. Washington made few concessions for off-reservation
fishing at the "usual and accustomed places." The Washington attorney general in
1937 speciously argued that the Indian Citizenship Act of 1924 had abrogated any
special rights Indians had enjoyed earlier. Oregon, by contrast, did not demand full
compliance with its regulations and permitted some out-of-season fishing if the
Indians used the catch for subsistence. These differences apparently reflected the
existence in Washington of a major fishing industry, and close cooperation between
sportsmen's groups and state fish and game officials against a relatively large number of Indian fishermen. The population of Indians in Oregon was much smaller,
and their fishing was mainly confined to the Columbia River.

When Commissioner of Indian Affairs John Collier took office in 1933, he
vowed to defend Indian rights, but his reactions and those of his staff toward Washington state's attempts to regulate Indian fishing were surprisingly moderate. To
McLeod's complaints about the Swinomish fish traps, Collier stated that they were
located on reservation land and the superintendent would see that no violations of
state laws took place off the reservation. Assistant Commissioner William Zim-
merman, Jr., was even more candid about his position: "the state can make such
laws and rulings it desires governing fishing within its borders" so long as such
regulations applied equally to both races and were not enforced inside reservations.

The conciliatory attitudes of the Indian Office conformed with legal precedents established by state and federal courts. The U.S. Supreme Court, in *Ward* v.
Race Horse (1896) and *Kennedy* v. *Becker* (1916), had dealt with Indians arrested
while attempting to exercise treaty rights to hunt or fish on ceded land in violation
of state laws. The Ward case involved a Bannock arrested in Wyoming for killing
elk away from the Fort Hall Reservation. Although the Bannock treaty of 1869
guaranteed the tribe the right to hunt on "unoccupied lands" off the reservation,
the court ruled that the 1895 federal act which admitted Wyoming as a state had
failed to reserve any special hunting rights to the Bannocks. The Kennedy decision

dealt with Seneca Indians arrested on ceded land while fishing in violation of New York laws. Since New York was one of the original states, the decision could not turn on admission legislation. Nevertheless, the court held that the Senecas' treaty rights to hunt and fish on ceded lands were not exclusive but included the individual to whom the land was ceded, subsequent grantees, and all others entitled to hunt and fish. More importantly, all such rights were subject to state authority.

In rulings on attempts of whites to exclude the Northwest Indians from fishing at the "usual and accustomed places," the court adopted a more favorable attitude toward the Indians. This was in keeping with past federal court decisions which had held that Indian treaties which dealt with fishing or hunting must be interpreted as the Indians understood the provisions at the time of their negotiations. The most important ruling for the Northwest tribes was *United States* v. *Winans* in 1905. The case grew out of the Yakimas' long-standing problem of being excluded from fishing sites on the Columbia River. Winans Brothers, a cannery, had purchased land along the stream at a fishing site, obtained state licenses to operate fish wheels, and built a fence to keep the Indians from the area. The firm's attorney argued that his client's ownership of the land and the licenses gave it the right to exclude the Yakimas because the latter possessed no greater rights than a white person. The U.S. Supreme Court disagreed, endorsing strongly the Indians' right of access to the fishing site. Ingress to fishing areas, observed the court, "was a part of the larger rights possessed by Indians" at the time of the treaty negotiations. Thus the federal government had not given them a right of access to fishing sites, because they already possessed that right. The court noted, however, that Indian ingress was not exclusive because the treaty permitted whites to fish in common with the Indians. Since the latter had never abandoned their right of access, the federal government must protect their entry, a responsibility not altered by the admission of Washington as a state. In 1919 the U.S. Supreme Court affirmed and broadened the Winans decision when it ruled in *Seufert Brothers* v. *United States*. This time the plaintiff was an Oregon cannery which argued that the Yakima treaty extended only to the Washington side of the Columbia, and therefore the Seufert Brothers' attempts to close a Yakima's fish wheel on the Oregon side were legal. The court sustained a lower court's ruling in favor of the Indians on the grounds that before and after signing treaties the Yakimas freely crossed from one bank of the Columbia to the other to fish and had associated and intermarried with Oregon tribes along the river.

Although the case law of Indian fishing was often contradictory, certain general principles were accepted by the 1930s. Past decisions had affirmed the sole jurisdiction of the federal government over all reservation fishing on trust lands. The tribes had an unqualified right of ingress and egress across private lands to reach traditional fishing sites, as well as the right to camp and build temporary drying sheds at such locations. Their fishing activities at off-reservation sites, however, came under state authority. The states could not prevent Indians from fishing on an equal basis with whites.

From the perspective of the Indians, state regulation anywhere was unacceptable. The Indians also challenged statements in the Stevens treaties indicating that access to the "usual and accustomed places" off the reservations was guaranteed to whites as well as to Indians. As one observer noted in 1941, "the Indians have always contended that when fishing at the usual and accustomed grounds they are (a) free from state regulation and (b) entitled to the exclusive use of such places."

Although the BIA under Collier denied the Indians exclusive use of off-reservation sites, it did uphold their freedom from state regulation on the reservations. This position received sharp criticism from state officials and sportsmen's groups which accused the Indians of fishing for commercial purposes rather than for subsistence. Particularly outspoken was Ken McLeod, secretary-treasurer of the powerful Washington State Sportsmen's Council. In 1939 he complained to Interior Secretary Harold Ickes that the amount of fish sold commercially in Washington by Indians from 1935 through 1938 totaled over 17 million pounds with a value of $1,127,015. Moreover, he noted, the Indians had fished out of season and then shipped their catch to out-of-state buyers. Also disturbing were the Nisqually, Swinomish, and Quilleute, who had recently gotten temporary court injunctions permitting them to fish off-reservation without state regulation.

While McLeod's statistics may have been exaggerated, the influence of his and other sportsmen's groups helped force the Indian Office into action. Pressures also came from the Bureau of Fisheries, recently transferred from Commerce to Interior, which supported Washington sports groups and urged Ickes to acknowledge the problems created by Indian fishing practices in the Northwest. At first Collier found himself stymied by lack of statutory authority to regulate hunting and fishing on reservations. He feared that sportsmen's groups might pressure Congress into filling this legal vacuum by enacting a stringent conservation law for all Indians which would be badly suited for an individual tribe's needs. Although Congress never approved such a measure, Collier nevertheless asked superintendents to report on what tribal councils had done in recent years to regulate hunting and fishing. With few exceptions the responses indicated that conservation regulations were woefully inadequate.

Collier's approach to the problem was to embark on a policy of education and to encourage tribes to establish their own codes. Always short on technical personnel, he enlisted the cooperation of the Bureau of Fisheries and the Biological Survey to study wildlife conditions on reservations and to assist in drafting the local game codes. He also instructed superintendents in Oregon and Washington to make accurate tallies of fish catches because of the large disparities between their past estimates and those of the state officials.

Collier, in addition, sampled field workers' views on the appropriateness of Indian fishing rights. In 1940 he dispatched his assistant, John Herrick, to preside over a regional conference of Northwest superintendents as well as officials from the Indian Service and several other federal agencies. The central question, observed Herrick at the inaugural session, was whether the Indian Service should maintain Indian treaty rights or modify "some of those rights where they do not accord with conservation practices." Those in attendance expressed a greater willingness to accept a fish and game law imposed on the Indians by Congress. They also indicated concern about the Indians' subsistence needs and the effects of industrial pollution on fishing. Collier responded by ordering a major study of Indian fishing rights in the Pacific Northwest. In March 1941 he dispatched Edward

G. Swindell, Jr., an Indian Service attorney in Los Angeles, to Oregon and Washington, instructing him to identify the "usual and accustomed places" through interviews and to review pertinent treaties, statutes, and judicial decisions.

Swindell completed his voluminous report (483 pages) in 1942. He organized the material into three sections, with the first being a careful historical and legal survey of Indian treaty rights. Part two contained copies of the many affidavits he had collected in interviews, and the final section presented the minutes of Stevens's treaty negotiations and a digest of the treaties.

Swindell's findings were quite balanced. His legal analysis confirmed the prevailing view that Indians had no special rights on ancient fishing sites except for ingress and egress and freedom from paying state fees. On the other hand, his investigation of Indian fishing practices disputed the claims of sportsmen's groups and state officials. Indian commercial fishing, he stated, centered in three areas: Puget Sound, Gray's Harbor, and the mid-Columbia. Using an analysis by the Fish and Wildlife Service of fishing statistics supplied by Washington and Oregon, Swindell maintained that Indian commercial fishermen in Puget Sound had taken only 2.4 percent of the total catch in 1938, 2.8 percent in 1939, and 6.7 percent in 1940. The percentages were much higher in the Gray's Harbor area, where Indian commercial operators caught 49.4 percent of the fish in 1938, 26 percent in 1939, and 54.8 percent in 1940. The percentages were higher there because the Quinault and Queets rivers flowed through the Quinault Reservation, where the Indians caught and sold sockeye salmon free of state controls. Outside the reservation, state regulations prohibited the possession and sale of this species. Swindell estimated that Indian commercial fishing on the Columbia ranged from 8.6 percent in 1938–39 to 7.6 percent in 1939–40. Indian fishing, he concluded, was an important means of livelihood for many tribesmen, but it made up a very small proportion of the total catch in the Pacific Northwest.

Swindell admitted that unregulated Indian commercial and subsistence fishing had contributed to the reduced fish population, but he believed that other causes were far more important. Especially significant were numerous violations of state regulations by whites, the destruction of spawning grounds by erosion and flooding, the obstructions of runs in upper streams by irrigation dams, and young salmon swimming into unscreened irrigation canals. To Swindell the recent public furor over the Indians' damage to fishing was unwarranted and whites had made them scapegoats.

Despite the thoroughness of Swindell's report, it had no impact on the administration of Indian affairs. Evidently preoccupied with the war and resulting dislocations in his office, Collier thanked Swindell for his "careful research" and "painstaking work" but did little more than note that the "report will be filed for future reference purposes." It remained undistributed until a decade later.

Shortly before Swindell filed his report, the U.S. Supreme Court ruled in early 1942 on *Tulee* v. *Washington*, an important test of the Indians' treaty rights to fish in their "usual and accustomed places" without state regulation. The Tulee case grew out of a comprehensive new law passed in 1937 by the Washington legislature to control licensing of commercial fishermen. Included in the act was a license fee of five dollars for operating a dip bag net, the most common fishing apparatus used by Indians along the Columbia. State officials insisted that the new measure applied to Indians fishing at their traditional sites and, despite considerable resistance, forced them to secure licenses for the 1937 season. Sampson Tulee was arrested on May 6, 1939, for taking and selling fish without a license at Spearfish, Washington, and placed in the Klickitat County jail. As a member of the Yakima tribe, Tulee held treaty rights to fish where he was arrested, and federal attorneys quickly entered the case on his behalf. They first petitioned for a writ of *habeas corpus* before the U.S. District Court in Yakima on the grounds that the state could not force Indians to purchase licenses. Judge J. Stanley Webster denied their petition on the grounds that requiring a license did not violate the Yakimas' treaty rights. Tulee's attorneys then appealed to the U.S. Circuit Court of Appeals in San Francisco. That court ruled on April 3, 1940, that it would not act on the *habeas corpus* petition until the state courts had judged the case and Tulee had exhausted possible remedies at that level. The following month Tulee was tried before a jury in the Klickitat Superior Court, found guilty, and given a minor fine. The Washington Supreme Court heard the case in January 1941 and by a vote of five to three upheld the lower court's opinion.

The correspondence between the federal attorneys and the Washington attorney general's office indicates that both sides hoped that a judgment on the Tulee case by the U.S. Supreme Court would not only determine the legality of the Indians' payment of fees but define state authority at off-reservation locations. The ruling was not a total victory for either side. The high court noted that the "treaty takes precedence over state law and state conservation laws are void and ineffective insofar as their application would infringe on rights secured by treaty." The court limited itself only to the question of whether Tulee had to pay state fees. The remainder of the opinion was dicta, or nonbinding. The court noted that the state fees were both revenue producing and regulatory, but the latter function could be achieved by other means. Imposing fees on Tulee was deemed illegal because the state was charging him for exercising a right his ancestors had reserved. The practical effect of the ruling was that a state could not charge fees to Indians fishing on traditional sites, but the states could still regulate by such means as limiting seasons, prescribing types of fishing equipment, and imposing catch limits.

In addition to Collier's policies and the Tulee decision, another important development of the period that affected Indian fishing rights was the construction of large dams on the Columbia River that destroyed some of the best "usual and accustomed places." Unlike the numerous small dams built before 1930 on the upper tributaries and mainly used for irrigation, the Rock Island, Grand Coulee, and Bonneville projects spanned the Columbia itself and were aimed primarily at harnessing the enormous hydroelectric potential of the river. Cheap electricity was widely proclaimed as the key to the economic development of the Pacific Northwest, especially for future growth in such areas as metal refining, chemicals, and synthetic fabrics.

Interest in the huge new dams on the Columbia predated the New Deal by several decades. Numerous studies of individual dam sites had been made by federal agencies in the past, but the Rivers and Harbors Act of 1925 authorized surveys of all navigable rivers of the United States, except the Colorado, to determine the potential for hydroelectricity, navigation, flood control, and irrigation. The following year the estimates were presented in House Document 308, and the surveys of the Columbia River and its tributaries were published in 1933. The so-called 308 Reports laid the foundation for the vast construction program of dams in the Pacific Northwest during the New Deal and postwar eras. The Calvin Coolidge and Herbert Hoover administrations had initiated the surveys, but Franklin D. Roosevelt immediately sensed their political importance and used a promise to start construction to good advantage in his 1932 presidential campaign.

Of the three major dams built on the Columbia before World War II, only the Rock Island was privately constructed. Located in central Washington, a few miles below Wenatchee, the site was purchased in early 1929 by the Puget Sound Light and Power Company, which by the end of 1931 had completed the $28 million project. Fish ladders installed at both ends of the dam permitted salmon and steelhead to pass over the fairly low obstacle.

Unlike the Rock Island, which was built solely for power generation, the two government dams started in 1933 were multipurpose in nature. Grand Coulee Dam, built in northeastern Washington as a PWA project under the Bureau of Reclamation, began to produce electricity in 1942 and after the mid 1950s supplied water for vast reclamation projects in the state. Bonneville Dam, near Vancouver, Washington, was a PWA project under the Corps of Engineers and completed in 1938. In addition to power generators, Bonneville included a set of locks that permitted large vessels to go upstream as far as The Dalles.

Although the issue of "fish vs. power" became especially keen in the postwar period, the construction of Grand Coulee and Bonneville dams gave an unsettling preview of future threats to the Indian fisheries on the Columbia. The damages of Grand Coulee to the Colville and Spokane Indians were twofold: First, the dam was so high that fish ladders could not be employed to permit fish to surmount the obstacle and reach the extensive spawning areas upstream; and second, the huge Franklin D. Roosevelt Lake created by Grand Coulee flooded Kettle Falls, one of the largest and most productive Indian fishing areas on the Columbia. The impact of Bonneville was less serious. Although the Bonneville reservoir flooded Cascade Falls, another major Indian fishing site, ladders at the dam permitted passage of salmon and steelhead upstream. The largest and most important Indian fishing area at Celilo Falls remained available for the Yakima, Warm Springs, Umatilla, and other groups.

The Indian Office initially did not protest the loss of Indian fishing sites on the Columbia. Collier apparently did not consider compensation for the Indians until the Solicitor's Office notified him in 1936 that the Indians might be entitled to damages caused by Bonneville Dam. There is no evidence that the commissioner sought monetary rewards or took any special interest in the Indians' plight. In 1939 the Corps of Engineers reached agreement with the Yakima, Warm Springs, and Umatilla tribes on six substitute fishing sites on the Bonneville reservoir. The Corps included $50,000 in its 1941 appropriation bill to acquire the sites and build such facilities as drying sheds, toilets, and access roads, but the money was lost when President Roosevelt vetoed all new construction because of national defense needs. Funds for the "in-lieu sites" finally won approval in 1945, but hampered by other duties and difficulties in finding suitable locations, the Corps five years later had only purchased one site. The delays embittered the Indians, whose disappointment continued even when sites were allegedly completed. Access remained difficult and facilities inadequate. In one case a fishing site was on a cliff above the shoreline. The record of the Bureau of Reclamation at Grand Coulee was similar. That agency delayed compensation for flooding Kettle Springs until after World War II, when the Colville and Spokane Indians received "paramount use" of a fourth of the area of Franklin D. Roosevelt Lake for hunting, fishing, and boating.

With the close of World War II the drive to complete the system of dams on the main stem of the Columbia and on the lower Snake threatened Indian fishing rights anew. The postwar plans envisioned eight new dams on the Columbia and four to six on the lower Snake to meet the Pacific Northwest's burgeoning demand for hydroelectric power. The need for electricity in 1947 was twenty-five percent greater than during the peak wartime years, while population in Washington and Oregon had grown forty percent between 1940 and 1947, compared to a national average of only eleven percent. Pressure for the dams also came from advocates of improved navigation. The four new dams projected above Bonneville and those planned for the lower Snake would permit barge traffic from The Dalles to Lewiston, Idaho. The prospect of a cheap transportation link between Lewiston and the Pacific Ocean provide highly attractive to agricultural and industrial interests of eastern Washington and western Idaho.

The major impact of postwar construction on Indian fishing rights would be the dam at The Dalles, which would flood Celilo Falls, the only remaining Indian fishing site of importance on the Columbia. The estimated annual commercial catch by Indians at Celilo from 1936 to 1943 was valued at $250,000, while the annual value of subsistence fishing during the same period was $134,000.

Changed leadership of Indian affairs in the postwar years produced considerable concern about Indian fishing rights. Collier had been replaced by William Brophy, who was preoccupied with decentralizing Indian administration and frequently absent from office because of illness. Moreover, mounting congressional hostility toward the BIA signaled the beginning of the termination policy and greater indifference for Indian welfare. Still, the record of the BIA in protecting Indian interests during the "fish vs. power" conflict reflected improvement over that of Collier's administration in the 1930s.

The BIA found new allies in its efforts to preserve Celilo Falls by forestalling construction of new dams. Some of the private interest groups which had been most inimical to Indian fishing rights in the 1930s now joined with the BIA because the new dams threatened to eradicate salmon on the Columbia. The private groups included the Columbia Basin Fisheries Development Association, the Oregon Wildlife Federation, the Columbia River Fishermen's Protective Union, and the Izaak Walton League. Within the Interior Department, similar realignments occurred. The Indian Office joined forces with the Fish and Wildlife Service, successor to the Bureau of Fisheries. Both agencies contended that the proposed fish ladders, turbines, and spillways associated with the new dams might destroy the Columbia fisheries. The agencies also enlisted the support of the National Park Service, which was concerned about damage to public recreation if sport fishing was harmed.

In opposition to the BIA and its allies were the Bureau of Reclamation and the Corps of Engineers. The Reclamation Bureau, then in the midst of completing the vast irrigation works made possible by Grand Coulee, endorsed the new dams for their electrical output but saw no pressing need for additional irrigated land during the next ten to fifteen years. The Corps of Engineers wanted the navigation link from The Dalles to Lewiston completed as rapidly as possible. The resulting interagency battle reached a decisive stage in early 1947, when both the Fish and Wildlife Service and the BIA recognized the futility of defeating the comprehensive plan and sought instead to reschedule the construction of the proposed dams. They asked that the McNary and The Dalles dams and those on the lower Snake River be delayed for at least ten years. Regional power needs, they argued, could be met by increasing the generating capacity at existing dams and by building new dams on the headwaters rather than on the lower Columbia and Snake. The rescheduling would permit the Fish and Wildlife Service to work out a possible solution for preserving a portion of the fish run above Bonneville and to revive or reestablish runs on the tributaries below that point.

The policy statement issued in March 1947 by Assistant Secretary of Interior Warner W. Gardner accepted most of the proposals of the Fish and Wildlife Service and the BIA. He rejected attempts to stop construction of McNary Dam, since Congress had authorized the project and appropriated some construction funds, but he endorsed rescheduling the other projects. Gardner's later statements indicated that he was unwilling to establish a moratorium of any fixed time. Gardner also recommended compensating the Indians for the eventual loss of Celilo Falls. Monetary payments would never be entirely satisfactory to the tribes affected, he acknowledged, but he proposed that the Indians be given exclusive fishing rights at sites on the lower Columbia and use of fish carcasses at hatcheries. Gardner also urged the tribes to develop alternative economic programs for members displaced from fishing. The federal government, he insisted, must pay a just amount for the loss of Celilo Falls with that amount determined either by negotiation with the Indians or by court decision. The expense of the settlement should be charged to construction costs and not to a special appropriation. "There is no difference in principle," he stressed, "between flooding out a white man's factory and an Indian's fishery."

The outcome of the fish vs. power struggle in succeeding years did not fulfill all of Gardner's expectations or entirely satisfy the Indians, but it followed the principle of just compensation. Hopes of a moratorium were lost when Congress authorized The Dalles Dam in 1950 and made the first appropriation for construction the following year. A four-year study of the Indian catch at Celilo Falls by the Oregon Fish Commission, the Washington Department of Fisheries, and the Fish and Wildlife Service led the Corps of Engineers in 1951 to calculate the value of Indian fishing rights at $23 million. In 1953 the Corps negotiated settlements awarding the Warm Springs and Umatilla tribes over $4 million each. The Yakimas rejected the offer made to them and attempted unsuccessfully to block construction of the dam. They accepted a settlement of $15 million in 1954. All three tribes were represented by their own attorneys and aided by BIA officials during the negotiations. The receipt of the money was made contingent on the tribes devising economic programs to offset the loss of fishing revenues due to flooding of Celilo Falls. Later the Corps also negotiated a settlement with the Nez Perces, who belatedly claimed treaty rights, and paid the relocation costs of some Indians living at Celilo Falls. Unlike the endless delays and confusion of earlier settlements, the government acted promptly and offered reasonable compensation. The total award amounted to slightly under $27 million.

Typical of most claims settlements, the awards themselves created new difficulties. Some Indians later maintained that they had been promised in-lieu fishing sites on the lower Columbia, but the Corps of Engineers denied that such promises had been made or could have been made since it was impossible to secure new fishing areas downstream. Tribesmen who had moved to urban areas thought that using the settlement money to create economic programs on the reservations was unfair, and they demanded a per capita payment. The Indians who had actually fished at Celilo Falls complained that their settlements did not adequately compensate them for the loss of the fishing rights. Almost instinctively they sensed that the money would eventually be gone, although the fishing could have continued forever.

What sort of conclusions can be reached about Indian fishing rights in the New Deal and postwar period? Clearly Collier's record was lackadaisical. In contrast to his autobiographical accounts and the initial assessments by historians who depicted him as an aggressive defender of Indian rights and a reformer of major dimensions, more recent studies indicate that some New Deal Indian policies offered improvements but others were arbitrary and badly flawed. This view seems applicable to Collier's handling of Indian fishing rights. Despite the potential for improving the Indians' situation, Collier did not aggressively pursue a protective role but seemed content to respond in piecemeal fashion to problems.

Explaining these inadequacies presents difficulties because the records do not reveal a clear picture of Collier or his administration's motives. A partial explanation for Collier's weak role was his lack of familiarity with the complexities of Indian fishing rights. He apparently had never dealt with the problem extensively in the years before he became commissioner in 1933. An examination of his regular weekly (and later biweekly) reports to Interior Secretary Harold Ickes from 1934 to 1939 shows that Collier visited the Pacific Northwest only twice during the five years. Neither visit prompted him to comment on Indian fishing rights in subsequent reports. Collier did not broach the subject until July 1936, when the Solicitor's Office advised him that the Indians might be entitled to compensation because of flooding of fishing sites by Bonneville Dam. In sharp contrast, Collier's reports contain detailed information on the programs involving the Navajos and Pueblos. There may be more than passing validity to observations that Collier's inordinate interest in Southwestern Indians caused him to neglect Native Americans elsewhere.

On the other hand, Collier may have viewed the Indians of the Pacific Northwest as a kind of "cultural lost cause." In comparison to the Navajos, Pueblos, and other groups who had retained much of their cultural heritage, most Indians of Washington and Oregon had assimilated in dress, language, religion, economics, and psychology. While Collier expressed sympathy with Indians who caught and cured fish for subsistence, he seemed less interested in those who fished for commercial reasons. Moreover, given his strong interest in conservation, he may also have viewed state regulation of Indian commercial fishing as appropriate.

In Collier's defense, it must be noted that he lacked vital information needed to understand the situation in the Northwest. Reliable scientific data on salmon and steelhead runs did not exist until the late 1930s and the 1940s. Hatchery management was still quite crude, particularly in nutrition and disease control, while artificial propagation was widely regarded as a cure-all for decreased runs. Collier was unaware of recent technical findings, and until Swindell's study he lacked even general information on the destruction of spawning grounds by irrigation projects, the severe problems of stream pollution, the minor role of Indians in fish depletion, and the tendency of whites to blame all problems on Indians. Moreover, even Swindell was not fully cognizant of the severity of ecological disturbances caused by industrial pollution and the release by cities of raw sewage into rivers.

Collier became concerned about fishing rights only after 1939, when Congress threatened to impose stringent fish and game regulations on all reservations. Such restrictions violated his belief in Indian self-government and might have worked a serious hardship on Indians. To thwart the congressional threat, he encouraged tribal councils to regulate the taking of fish and game, supported the Tulee test case, and ordered Swindell's study. With the exception of the Tulee case, the dislocations of World War II halted even these modest efforts.

Different reasons explain Collier's failure to react to the threats to Indian fishing rights posed by Grand Coulee and Bonneville dams. The overwhelming importance of hydroelectric power to the Pacific Northwest during the 1920s and 1930s evidently convinced him that construction of the dams and destruction of Indian fishing sites were inevitable. The demand for electricity transcended partisan politics, and any attempt by Collier to block construction on behalf of preserving the Indian fishing sites would have been futile. Several legal peculiarities additionally hampered a defense of Indian fishing rights. The Indians did not hold title to the "usual and accustomed places" but rather enjoyed treaty rights to gain access to those "places" and to take fish. Thus this was not a situation where reservation lands were threatened by confiscation. Moreover, Indian tribes prior to passage of the Indian Claims Commission Act of 1946 could not file claims for damages against the federal government without special legislation, and Congress rarely gave such authorizations. Both these circumstances may help explain Collier's failure to seek damages for the loss of prime fishing sites on the Columbia. Certainly the war paralyzed efforts by the BIA to gain compensation, just as it stymied efforts to gain additional protection of Indian fishing rights against state regulation.

In the postwar drive to build dams, the situation changed rather dramatically. The creation of the Indian Claims Commission in 1946 doubtlessly made the BIA and other agencies aware that failure to indemnify the Indians for the loss of Celilo Falls would result in later claims cases. Moveover, the size of the $27 million settlement demonstrated that the BIA was fairly effective in meeting its trust responsibilities when the stakes were high, but less diligent and capable when handling the more mundane and day-to-day duties. In other words, the BIA previously had not always defended Indian fishermen from unfair treatment by state officials and private individuals because such episodes were commonplace and did not arouse wide public attention, but the postwar negotiations over the loss of Celilo Falls were reported widely in the national press and aired in congressional hearings. Such publicity and the importance of the issue motivated the BIA and the Corps of Engineers to act fairly and promptly in negotiating the rewards. Thus the Indian Office's traditional lack of strong constituency and a major voice in government was temporarily offset after 1945. The money awarded for the flooding of the last major Indian fishery on the Columbia may not have satisfied many tribesmen whose way of life centered around fishing, but the government rarely had met its responsibility as well.

21

BUILDING TOWARD SELF-DETERMINATION: PLAINS AND SOUTHWESTERN INDIANS IN THE 1940s and 1950s

PETER IVERSON

During the 1980s students of Native American history began to pay serious attention to the Indian experiences of the twentieth century. Such trends as population growth, urban migration, the development of pan-Indian groups and thought, and increasing success in dealing with the federal and state governments now receive careful attention. As tribal leaders and multitribal organizations strive for more authority over programs and funds earmarked for use in Indian communities, they call increasingly for self-determination—that is, for the right to decide their future. This selection examines the decades during and after World War II, when actions taken laid the groundwork for the more recent demands of self-determination. The text demonstrates how the process of rapid change worked when groups such as the National Council of American Indians and the later National Indian Youth Council mobilized opinion and directed attention to issues. Native American spokesmen and organizations lost several major battles, including the crucial fight over termination. Nevertheless, the discussion traces the development of a growing Indian self-awareness as tribes succeeded in developing or expanding local economic and cultural activities. At the same time, the author shows how tribal and pan-Indian groups increased Indian influence over policy creation and implementation. The narrative ties the developments of the 1940–60 era clearly to events of more recent decades.

Peter Iverson is a professor of history at Arizona State University.

Source: Copyright by Western History Association. Reprinted by permission. The article first appeared as "Building Toward Self-Determination: Plains and Southwestern Indians in the 1940s and 1950s," *Western Historical Quarterly* 16 (April 1985): 161–73.

Within the past decade more students of Indian history have turned their attention to the twentieth century. Until very recently the topical focus of this work has been primarily in the area of federal Indian policy, and the chronological focus, for the most part, has been on the years before World War II. This article represents a change in both topic and time. It attempts to analyze the period from World War II until the beginning of the 1960s, with specific consideration given to Indians of the Plains and the Southwest.

This era is often referred to in the literature as the era of termination. During this time many members of Congress and the Truman and Eisenhower administrations made sporadic but persistent efforts to reduce or eliminate federal services and protection for American Indians. The public rhetoric spoke of liberating the Indians by reducing governmental interference. Termination sought to immerse Indians in the mainstreams of their counties and states. This crusade resulted in significant hardship for many Indians. Tribes such as Menominees in Wisconsin or the Klamaths in Oregon saw their reservation status ended. Indians who relocated to cities, with or without federal sponsorship, confronted many dilemmas. State and local agencies proved unwilling or unable to shoulder responsibilities previously bestowed upon the federal government. Economic development programs on reservations usually did not markedly improve unemployment, housing, and other critical problems.

Yet to label these years as the termination era and to emphasize so exclusively the negative aspects of this generation is to present an incomplete picture. We cannot ignore federal policy in our consideration of any period, for it always has an important effect. But the 1940s and 1950s are more than a time of troubles. Just as new research is starting to reveal the late nineteenth and early twentieth centuries as a time when Indians in many areas made important and necessary adjustments to continue their lives as Indians, so, too, a closer examination of this more recent era shows it to be a period in which tribalism and Indian nationalism were reinforced. Indeed, to a significant degree the threat and the enactment of terminationist policy often strengthened rather than weakened Indian institutions and associations. In addition, the attitudes of state and local officials, as well as the perspectives of urban residents, encouraged Indians throughout the nation to recognize increasingly their common bonds and needs.

During the 1940s and 1950s, then, Indians in growing numbers tried to identify and take advantage of their own economic resources and tried to affirm their identities as members of tribes and as Indians. They rejected the conventional wisdom that they would be "less Indian" if they gained more education, acquired new jobs, or moved to a new residence. Actually, greater contact with the larger American society promoted greater awareness that the English language, new technological skills, and other elements of the American culture could be used to promote a continuing, if changing, Indian America.

A review of Indian actions in two important regions—the Plains and the Southwest—reveals a vital maturation in Indian leadership and a reaffirmation of Indian identity in the 1940s and 1950s. Far from vanishing, Indians emerged from this generation more determined than ever to be recognized on their own terms.

The more publicized activism of the late 1960s and 1970s thus may trace its origins to these ostensibly more quiet years.

World War II marks a critical turning point in modern American Indian history. Indians took great pride in their involvement in the war effort. For example, Cecil Horse, a Kiowa, remembered his son John winning a bronze star and a purple heart and in turn receiving from his people a war bonnet and a giveaway ceremony in his honor. Navajos celebrated their Codetalkers' role in the Pacific. In a publication of November 1945 the Office of Indian Affairs recorded the military honors earned by Indians and the investment by Indians in more than $17 million of restricted funds in war bonds. It quoted the instructions of Private Clarence Spotted Wolf, a Gros Ventre killed on December 21, 1944, in Luxembourg:

> If I should be killed, I want you to bury me on one of the hills east of the place where my grandparents and brothers and sisters and other relatives are buried. If you have a memorial service, I want the soldiers to go ahead with the American flag. I want cowboys to follow, all on horseback. I want one of the cowboys to lead one of the wildest of the T over X horses with saddle and bridle on. I will be riding that horse.

The war generated more than memories and emotions. It meant that Indians had become more a part of the larger world in which they lived. As Ella Deloria, the Dakota linguist, wrote in 1944: "The war has indeed wrought an overnight change in the outlook, horizon, and even the habits of the Indian people—a change that might not have come for many years yet." Through the service, through off-reservation experiences, and through wage work, Indian perspectives and Indian economies began to change. Returning veterans and other participants in the war effort recognized the significance of better educational opportunities. Navajo Scott Preston put it simply: "We have to change and we have to be educated."

Change also demanded organization. Indian delegates from fifty tribes, hailing from twenty-seven states, met November 15–18, 1944, in Denver to organize the National Congress of American Indians (NCAI). In the words of one of the congress' first presidents, N. B. Johnson, the delegates set "an example for speed, diplomacy and harmony." Within four days they "adopted a constitution and formally launched the organization in an effort to bring all Indians together for the purpose of enlightening the public, preserving Indian cultural values, seeking an equitable adjustment of tribal affairs, securing and preserving their rights under treaties with the United States, and streamlining the administration of Indian affairs." In subsequent meetings in Browning, Montana, in 1945 and Oklahoma City in 1946, those in attendance proved to be, according to Johnson, "a cross-section of Indian population: old and young, full-bloods, mixed-bloods, educated and uneducated Indians from allotted areas and others from reservations," all of whom "were dissatisfied with many phases of the government's administration of Indian affairs." Improved health care and educational opportunities, protection of Indian land rights, and increased Indian veterans' benefits were advocated. The National Congress of American Indians urged the U.S. Congress and the current administration "not to enact legislation or promulgate rules and regulations thereunder affecting the Indians without first consulting the Tribes affected."

Such, of course, would not be the case. In both the Truman and Eisenhower administrations the federal government proceeded to pass legislation and carry out policies contrary to the will of the vast majority of American Indians. For many Americans the Indian war record had prompted concern that Indians be treated fairly. O. K. Armstrong's influential article in the August 1945 *Reader's Digest* urged America to "Set the American Indians Free!" House of Representatives Majority Leader John W. McCormack read Armstrong's piece advocating the removal of "restrictions" from Indians and wrote to his colleague W. G. Stigler that he was "interested in seeing justice done for all—and this applies with great force to our fine American Indians." Cherokee/Creek historian Tom Holm has properly summarized what happened: "In the end, fighting the White man's war gained sympathy for American Indians but it also fueled a fire that they did not want and eventually found difficult to extinguish."

While they were not without effective allies, Indians had to lead the fight against Public Law 280, House Concurrent Resolution 108, and other features of termination. Protests against such measures soon resounded throughout the West. Through a variety of means, Indians attempted to ward off the implementation of a policy they realized could bring them great harm. In the early years voices from tribal councils and business committees rang out against a specific action in a particular locale. For example, Richard Boynton, Sr., and George Levi of the Cheyenne-Arapaho business committee telegrammed Oklahoma congressman Toby Morris to protest against the impending closing of the Cheyenne-Arapaho school in El Reno. Kiowa leader Robert Goombi argued that abolishing the Concho Indian School would be counterproductive. Yet as the wider pattern of the era emerged, multitribal associations were strengthened as a more effective means of presenting a more powerful Indian voice.

The National Congress of American Indians therefore continued to expand in its influence in the years that followed its establishment in 1944. Plains and Southwestern Indian peoples remained active in the executive ranks of the organization throughout the 1940s and 1950s. In the mid 1950s over half the elected members of the executive council would come from regional tribes, including the Osages, Gros Ventres, Gila River Pimas, Taos Pueblos, Blackfeet, Oglala Sioux, and Cheyenne-Arapahoes. Colorado River tribes, Hualapais, Omahas, and the San Carlos Apaches appointed additional representatives. Oglala Sioux Helen Peterson served as executive director; Papago Thomas Segundo was regional representative.

The NCAI filled two critical functions. It helped Indians speak out against termination, but it also advocated programs that would contribute to Indian social, political, and economic revitalization. Through publicity releases from its Washington office, specially called tribal forums, and other means, the congress directly confronted the forces favoring termination. John Rainer from Taos Pueblo thus in 1950 attacked Commissioner of Indian Affairs Dillon Myer for imposing "drum head justice" upon Indians by denying tribes the power to choose their own attorneys.

The organization did more than criticize. It manifested a maturing capacity to articulate counterproposals when it offered suggestions to reduce Indian poverty, improvements for health care and educational facilities, and provisions to use reservation resources more effectively. A specific example—the Point Nine Program—was formulated and adopted by the congress in November 1954. It addressed critical questions relating to such matters as land and water resources, planning, credit, land purchase, and job training. Pointing to the assistance provided by the United States to underdeveloped countries around the world, Helen Peterson and other leaders demanded that this country apply the same principles within its borders.

Indians addressed the issues of the day through other forums as well. The Association on American Indian Affairs (AAIA), under the direction of Oliver La Farge, helped publicize both the dangers of federal policy and Indian moves to oppose it. Thus when the NCAI mobilized Indian representatives from twenty-one states and Alaska to come to Washington, D.C., on February 25–28, 1954, to protest impending legislation, *Indian Affairs,* the newsletter of AAIA, not only gave extensive coverage but also proper credit to NCAI for its actions. Other institutions and organizations put together symposia for the examination of contemporary Indian well-being. Tribal spokesmen from the Plains and the Southwest participated vigorously in such gatherings, be it the annual meeting of the American Anthropological Association in Tucson in 1954 or the annual conference on Indian affairs at the University of South Dakota's Institute of Indian Studies.

By the end of the era new forums had been sought for the expression of Indian views. In 1961 representatives from sixty-four tribes, totaling approximately seven hundred delegates, met in Chicago to create the Declaration of Indian Purpose. They did not all agree with one another, but the so-called Chicago Conference was an important landmark in modern Indian affairs because of its size and its impact upon many of the participants.

Another example is the National Indian Youth Council (NIYC), which came into being soon thereafter. The NIYC had its roots in the annual conferences of the Southwest Association on Indian Affairs, beginning in 1956. This one-day session at the St. Francis Auditorium in Santa Fe brought Indian community people together with high school and college students, with the latter speaking to the former about their studies and the applicability of these studies to the communities. From this local beginning, the conference became regional in its focus in 1957 and was called the Southwest Regional Indian Youth Council. The council held annual conferences in the spring until April 1961, when the last meeting was held in Norman, Oklahoma. According to the Tewa anthropologist Alfonso Ortiz, "It was a core group from these youth councils, augmented later by alumni of D'Arcy McNickle's Indian Leadership Training Programs, who founded the NIYC in Gallup after the American Indian Chicago Conference was held in June."

Other experiences and associations prompted heightened pan-Indian feelings. Relocation programs to American cities brought Indians into contact with non-Indians indifferent to tribal distinctions. Prejudice sometimes spurred pan-Indian identification. The formation of Indian communities and intertribal marriages in the cities also could foster such sentiments.

The Cherokee anthropologist Robert K. Thomas and other observers have noted that this movement frequently had a pan-Plains quality to it. Thomas also suggested that within the Southwest something of a pan-Puebloism could be perceived Pan-Indianism, as it continued to evolve during this time, could be "very productive, as nationalist movements often are, in literature and the arts," but it also developed institutions dealing with non-Indians. One such development was the growth of powwows—a source of pleasure and pride for participants and enjoyment and education for spectators.

A final example of the pan-Indian movement in the 1940s and 1950s that should be cited is the Native American Church. It found significant support within the Plains and the Southwest, and leaders for the organization frequently hailed from these regions. At the tribal level, the Native American Church increased its membership during this period. Many Indians looked to participation within the peyote religion as a way of accommodating the various demands of modern life and reaffirming their identities as Indians. In Montana perhaps half the Crows and many Cheyennes embraced the church. Adherents included prominent tribal leaders such as Robert Yellowtail, Crow, and Johnnie Woodenlegs, Northern Cheyenne. Frank Takes Gun also emerged as an important, if controversial, church leader.

Attitudes toward the practice of the faith varied considerably, to be sure, from one Indian community to another and within communities. In the Navajo nation the peyote religion grew considerably in its membership during the 1950s, despite an antagonistic stance taken against it by the tribal chairman, Paul Jones. Raymond Nakai gained the chairmanship in 1963 in part because he pledged to stop harassing the Native American Church. On the Wind River reservation in Wyoming, Northern Arapaho political and traditional leaders became more conciliatory toward the well-established practice. As was true in many tribes, the Arapahoes often added the Native American Church to prior participation in other religious ceremonies, be they Christian or traditional.

The reservation continued in the 1940s and 1950s as a centrally important place for religious observances, but for other reasons as well. The guiding philosophy of federal policy dictated that reservations were economic dead ends. After all, people were supposed to relocate because there were not enough jobs being generated at home. Since the land, families, familiarity, and, indeed, everything that went into the definition of home continued to be valued so deeply, Indian communities within the Plains and the Southwest endeavored to keep more of their citizens at home. While organizations such as the NCAI could advocate local development of resources, such development had to be prompted and managed.

Navajo economic and political development has been described elsewhere in some detail. In the face of termination Navajos who distrusted state governments and desired to maintain a working ethnic boundary between themselves and whites had little choice during the era but to pursue a more nationalistic approach. With large sums newly available to the tribal treasury from mineral revenues, the Navajo tribal government became far more ambitious. Federal assistance through the long-range rehabilitation program also assisted internal Navajo development. While the 1960s and 1970s would bring more fully to fruition some of these plans and programs, the 1940s and 1950s were crucial in the reinforcement of a working tribal identity and a commitment to a revitalized tribal economy.

Arts and crafts came to command a more important place in many tribal economies in the Southwest. For the Navajos, silversmithing and weaving continued to be vital sources of income. Pottery also gained widening acclaim, particularly at San Ildefonso, but also in other Pueblo communities along the Rio Grande and at some of the Hopi villages. Silverwork at the Hopi and Zuni pueblos, basket weaving especially among the Papagos and Walapais, the paintings of such artists as Fred Kabotie, Hopi, and Harrison Begay, Navajo, and the sculpture of Alan Hauser, Apache, also found appreciative audiences. Though the boom in Indian art had yet to arrive, a foundation had been established.

Cattle ranching represented another important element in economic development. On the San Carlos Apache reservation the cattle industry underwent significant alteration. The tribal council in October 1956 approved Ordinance 5–56 to reorganize and consolidate existing associations and implement various reforms in grazing regulations and practices. Improved range management could be combined with maintenance of cooperative efforts among the people of San Carlos. Cattle sales created some income for most families in the tribe. The quality of the Apaches' Herefords consistently attracted cattle buyers from throughout the West and generated a positive image of the Apaches to the non-Indian residents of Arizona.

Similarly, the Northern Arapahos grained greater control over their tribal ranch established during the Indian New Deal. With the assistance of an attorney, the tribe eventually was able to hire a ranch manager and to have the ranch's trustees be Arapahos appointed by the Arapaho business council. This sizeable operation returned a consistent profit to each Arapaho. As with the San Carlos Apaches, the ranching enterprise contributed to tribal self-esteem, the status of the tribal government, and an enhanced view of the Arapahos among outsiders, including the Shoshones who shared the Wind River reservation.

In 1950 the tribal council of the Pine Ridge reservation in South Dakota passed a tax of three cents per acre for grazing privileges on tribal lands. The tax met with strenuous objections by white cattle ranchers. In the face of such opposition the Department of the Interior quickly assigned responsibility of collecting the tax to the Sioux. By 1956 white ranchers had challenged the tax in court, but in the following year the U.S. District Court judge ruled against them, contending that Indian tribes were "sovereign powers and as sovereign powers can levy taxes."

Greater assertion of Sioux power was not limited to Pine Ridge. Under the leadership of Chairman Frank Ducheneaux, the Cheyenne River tribal council approved a firm resolution against Public Law 280. Both on Rosebud and on Pine Ridge, tribal voters in 1957 overwhelmingly defeated the assumption of state jurisdiction in South Dakota on Indian reservations. Opposition to repeated efforts to institute state jurisdiction led in 1963 to the formal organization of the United Sioux Tribes.

By 1959 the Rosebud Sioux tribal chairman, Robert Burnette, had filed complaints of discrimination under the Civil Rights Act of 1957 before the Civil Rights Commission. Burnette contended that Indians in South Dakota had been excluded from juries, had been beaten and chained in prisons, and generally had been greeted as people without equal rights in the state. While the commission was not very responsive to Burnette's allegations, the very act of publicly challenging local conditions indicated that a more activist stance would be assumed in the 1960s.

In the Dakotas, Wyoming, Arizona, and elsewhere, then, the growing importance of attorneys could be observed. For many tribes the establishment of the Indian Claims Commission in 1945 had prompted their first acquisition of some form of legal counsel. While the Bureau of Indian Affairs in the 1950s had often discouraged tribal use of attorneys or tried to dictate the choice of a specific firm, by decade's end it was clear that legal assistance would play a vital role in many realms of tribal life.

Williams v. *Lee* is a useful example of this evolution. Called by Chemehuevi attorney Fred Ragsdale "the first modern Indian law case," *Williams* v. *Lee* involved a non-Indian trader on the Navajo reservation who sued a Navajo in the state court to collect for goods sold on credit. While the Arizona Supreme Court ruled in favor of the trader, the U.S. Supreme Court reversed this decision. Justice Hugo Black, on behalf of the Court, stated: "There can be no doubt that to allow the exercise of state jurisdiction here would undermine the authority of the tribal courts over Reservation affairs and hence would infringe on the right of the Indians to govern themselves." This landmark decision served as a crucial statement in support of tribal sovereignty, presaging additional legal battles to be waged in the years to come.

In any reappraisal of the 1940s and 1950s, it is important to not overstate the case. The negative aspects of the period remain, even with the vital developments outlined above. And in a treatment of this length, some events of magnitude must be slighted. For example, the damming of the Missouri River created great hardship for the Indian peoples of that area. Scholars have correctly underlined the problems that seemed to exist everywhere, from the most isolated reservations to the largest city.

Nonetheless, a more careful examination yields a more balanced picture. In overdramatizing the difficulties of the time, we may not give sufficient credit to the enduring nature of Indians in this country. By the end of the 1950s tribal resources were more studied and better understood; tribal council leadership was often more effective. The Salish scholar and writer D'Arcy McNickle appreciated the transition that had taken place. He spoke in 1960 of the growing Indian movement toward self-determination. Indians in the future, he suggested, would "probably use the white man's technical skills for Indian purposes." McNickle affirmed that "Indians are going to remain Indian . . . a way of looking at things and a way of acting which will be original, which will be a compound of these different influences."

The 1940s and 1950s not only witnessed a change in Indian policy and a resurgence of pressures to assimilate Indians into the larger society, but they also saw maturation and growth of Indian leadership at the local and national levels and efforts to develop tribal institutions, as well as a reaffirmation of identity and a willingness to adapt and change in the face of new conditions. In the immediate future seemingly new demands would resound for self-determination. Yet these demands were firmly based upon a foundation gradually constructed in the previous generation.

22

INDIANS AND IMMIGRANTS: A COMPARISON OF GROUPS NEW TO THE CITY

ARTHUR MARGON

As part of the effort to get the federal government out of the Indian business, in 1952 the Bureau of Indian Affairs established a relocation program. This offered some vocational training for persons leaving the reservations in the hope of finding employment in the cities. It also established offices in up to a dozen major urban centers all over the country that were to provide counseling and job placement services. Bureaucrats assumed that this would make the transition from reservation to big-city life reasonably smooth, but a high percentage of the relocatees quit their jobs and returned home. Many students of the urbanization process have concluded that elements in Indian tribal culture explain the difficulties Indians experienced in their adjustment to an urban environment. Margon rejects that view. He claims that a substantial minority of the Native Americans in cities did succeed in making the transition from their reservations and that urban Indians have demonstrated many responses to the city that were similar to those of other minorities. This 1977 essay considers the types of problems Indians encountered, compares and contrasts their experiences to those of other minorities in urban areas, and shows how and why Indians succeeded or failed in their adjustment to the cities.

The author is on the faculty of the New School of Liberal Arts, Brooklyn College, City University of New York.

Ten years ago popular impressions of Native Americans labeled them as members of an expiring race, wilting on their reservations and doomed to extinction as independent peoples. It was an image which— in the face of a high population growth rate and assertive Native Americans seeking to explore alternatives to assimilation

Source: Abridged from Arthur Margon, "Indians and Immigrants: A Comparison of Groups New to the City," The Journal of Ethnic Studies," Vol. IV, Winter 1977, pp. 17–28. Copyright © 1977 by *The Journal of Ethnic Studies*. Reprinted by permission of the publisher.

into the "mainstream" of American life—has passed from the scene. More recently, even the metaphor of a reservation-bound people is being undercut. According to the 1970 census, 45 percent of the Native Americans lived in urban places, and projections showed that by the early 1970s a majority of the group would be living in the towns. Urban life has become a central factor in contemporary Native American culture, one which may, in the long term, be as important to Indian culture as the nineteenth century's forced movement onto the reservations. Viewed in this light, our understanding of the Native Americans' city-ward migration, and of their adjustment to urban life, is crucial to any understanding of contemporary Indians.

Then-President Richard Nixon summed up the prevalent image of the urban Indian in his 1970 Message of the American Indian. He noted that "approximately three-fourths are living in poverty," and portrayed the group as "lost in the anonymity of the city . . . drifting from neighborhood to neighborhood; many shuttle back and forth between reservations and urban areas. Language and cultural differences compound these problems." Others noted that many Indians found it impossible to find stable jobs and became either vagrants or welfare cases. Indeed, the visible segment of the urban Indian population exhibits classical signs of social disorganization. Urban Native Americans appear on police blotters out of all proportion to their size as a population group. Their children drop out of school at alarmingly high rates. Alcoholism rates are high, and public drunkenness is a nagging problem. Job instability is high; the poverty is often extreme. Sex ratios and marriage rates are disturbingly out of line. On a personal level, stories circulate of women and children who never leave their tenement apartments, of demoralization and depression, of an inability to relate to the demands of the urban and bureaucratic environment. In short, studies of the urban Indian replace the stereotypes of the noble savage, the reservation Indian, and the relocatee finding a "happy hunting ground" in Minneapolis or Los Angeles with the image of a disorganized and desperate people unable to cope with the modern city. The common view holds that Native Americans are beset with special, nearly insurmountable difficulties because of the dissonance between their traditional cultures and the demands and patterns of modern urban living.

How accurate are these images? How difficult are Native Americans finding the transition to city life, and in what ways are they having problems? What is the relationship between their difficulties and their cultures? There have been many studies of Native American urban migration, most aiming at explaining the process or at formulating remedial policy recommendations. They form the basis for reevaluating both these images of Indians moving to the city and our picture of how the culture-contact process is operating. It is also possible to compare the Native American experience with city life with how other groups adapted upon coming to the city so as to better comprehend the Native American experience. What follows is an attempt to compare Native American experience with that of other immigrant groups newly arrived in the city, focusing primarily on one area of concern: How much of group experience is the special provenance of the group, and how much an aspect of the process of moving to and coping with an alien, urban environment? Put another way, to what extent is the Native American experience unique, and in what ways is that singularity a reflection of the cultural background of Native American peoples?

While Native Americans have lived in cities and towns throughout American history, their urban residence first began to receive public notice in the early 1950s. However, we tend to forget the way in which these people moved to the cities. The migration of Native Americans has been consistently linked to the federal government's termination and relocation policies. Stemming from the Relocation Act of 1952, these programs sought to move Native Americans from the reservations to selected cities, where they would presumably find enlarged job opportunities. Simultaneously, the federal government launched a policy geared to ending the special relationship between the Indians and the United States government by turning the management of the reservations over to tribal councils or corporations and ownership of the reservation land either to the corporation or to individual tribesmen.

These policies have taken much of the blame for the difficulties Indians encounter in adjusting to urban life, yet it is important to note that Native Americans had been moving to the cities since the 1920s, with the single exception of the Depression decade. During much of that time (well before the inception of the relocation program) Indians were taking up urban residence faster than any other population subgroup, sometimes at a rate of four times that of the black population. In light of this it would be enlightening to know what percentage of the urban Native American population actually arrived in the city via federal relocation programs. Unfortunately such statistics do not exist. Virtually all of the available data concern BIA relocatees, and most studies of urban Indians—while noting that Indians often came to town on their own—are in reality studies of BIA relocation programs. However, if hard data on nonrelocation urbanites is lacking, it is possible to establish boundary figures for the impact of these programs on the Native American trek to the cities. According to the federal budget, just over 100,000 Native Americans were assisted by the BIA relocation programs between 1952 and 1970. According to the 1970 census, however, about three times that many Native Americans live in the cities. Thus, had all the federally assisted relocatees remained in town, the programs would account for less than one third of the urban Indians. Even with their children, "first and second generation" relocation Indians could account for only about one half of the total urban Indian population.

We know that all the relocatees did not stay in town. Again hard data are unavailable, but estimates vary between a 30 percent and a 70 percent rate of return to the reservation for relocatees. Whatever the precise statistics, it is apparent that relocation programs, while a visible component of Native American urbanization, do not form the framework for migration of most Indians into the cities. Most Native Americans living in urban surroundings, whether permanently, seasonally or transiently, are not there as a result of Bureau of Indian Affairs relocation programs.

Relocation has been important as an expression of the unique relationship between Native Americans and the United States government. It has often defined and modified the migration experience of individual Indians. However, the causes of Native American urbanization and the social difficulties involved in resettlement are not products of these policies but of deeper trends within American society and the contemporary world. Outside the United States, for example, Canadian natives have also been flocking to that nation's cities since the Depression, although neither the provincial nor the national government has advocated the kind of relocation schemes spawned in Washington, D.C.

Statistics aside, there is evidence that many Native Americans migrate to the city and adapt quite successfully to urban life. Investigators who work with client files in Indian centers and BIA offices form a picture of the Native American community which they often find unrepresentative of the kinds of experiences and individuals they encounter in field interviews in urban Indian "neighborhoods." This is not only the case in large metropolitan areas, but is present in smaller cities as well. Even in Rapid City, South Dakota, where the Native American settlement is a rundown shantytown at the city's edge, researchers were surprised at the difference between the grim statistics of maladaptation and the large number of Native Americans apparently capable of making it in their new surroundings. In a similar vein, a student of the Indians in Canadian cities uncovered through interviews a broad range of responses to urbanization and pointedly noted that the successful adaptors were a substantial minority of the subjects studied.

Explanations of these differences between successful and unsuccessful adaptations vary. The most systematic study of the urbanization process, as opposed to the experience of a group of Native Americans, begins with the assumption that the move from reservation to city "is a movement within a basically alien culture" and concludes that the Native American's culture will cause him "difficulties in both the cities and the reservations." Other researchers tie "success" in urbanization to previous education, marital stability, and sometimes even to good or bad fortune. Among some Western tribes from large reservations, especially the Navajo, observers find a correlation between location of reservation residence and urbanization experience: Those living in the most isolated, most traditional sections of the reservations have the greatest difficulties adjusting to the cities. Some writers stress the different traditions which Native Americans bring to the city. When the "Indians" of Chicago come from five or six dozen tribes, and the Los Angeles area hosts members of over 100 different tribes, urban adaptation, those researchers claim, becomes a series of unique adaptive situations. Whether studying social deviation, discussing styles of relating to the bureaucracy, or analyzing adaptation to general urban conditions—in short, whatever the relevant definition of "successful" urbanization—explanations of Native American experience and behavior are grounded in correlations with Native American culture traits. As one student of the problem sees it, "In many respects the urban Indian's problems are merely extensions of the problems he encountered on the reservations."

Students of urban Indians characteristically portray city-Indian problems as growing out of the Native Americans' "heritage or participation in small rural folk communities with a basis of aboriginal tradition" and emphasize the unique cultural bases of Native American adjustment problems. This orientation raises two obvious questions: are the observed behavior patterns specific to Native American migrants, and—unique or not—to what extent are they culturally defined and to what extent do they reflect the common experience of newcomers in the city? These cultural factors may explain the difficulties many Native Americans have in the city, but they can account for "successful" adaptation only by assuming that individuals who "make it" in town must give up their "Indianness." Students of urban Indians, however, find large numbers of successful and partially successful adaptations to city life. Often they explicitly note that the individual's traditional culture has not prevented acculturation to the city. Sometimes, paradoxically, the urban experience heightens the sense of Indianness. Many Indians still self-identify as reservation Indians after many years of living in the city. For these people "it is through urban life and its relative stresses that they come, perhaps for the first time, to identify themselves as Indians. Life in the city makes clear to them the differences between their life style and the world-views of the rest of American society." The differences, however, do not keep them from functioning successfully in town.

In fact there is a strong similarity between the behavior of Native American and other immigrants to the modern city because many of the traits which are seen as "Indian" can be found in many peoples of poor-rural and small-town origin. A comparison of the cultural values of Native Americans and rural Bohemian-Americans, for example, concludes that "the process of cultural change in Indian communities has significant elements in common with what takes place in immigrant-founded enclaves across the northern states," thus questioning the link between Native American behavior patterns and their unique culture even *before* urbanization beclouds the issue. Similarly, it appears that Navajos in Denver are "no more inflexible in adapting to the Western work ethic"—a major contention of observers who stress how the Indian's preindustrial cultures cause his difficulties in the city—"than any other migrant group . . . actually [both] educational background and their pre-migration wage-work experience revealed their potential for economic adjustment and eventual cultural assimilation."

None of this alleviates the real difficulties thousands of Native Americans have in adjusting to urban life, nor is it intended to minimize the differences in styles, expectations, and demands between reservation and city. The Mohawks' success relative to other tribal groups may, as one scholar has written, be fortuitous. In addition to their positive training, Navajo migrants bring notions and behavior patterns into town which inhibit a successful adjustment to city life. Since it operates so inconsistently, "culture" does not convincingly explain the Native Americans' difficulties with the city.

If Native American culture does not necessarily inhibit adaptation to urban life, just how does it affect the Indian attempting to cope with city life? Those who hold that Native American culture patterns are so different from the norms held by other urbanizing groups that Indians are faced with unique adjustment difficulties usually make three assertions: that urban Native Americans follow a special migration pattern (often with BIA assistance) from reservation to city; that Indians are exceptionally unstable urbanites, uniquely unable to remain in town and driven to return frequently to the reservation; and that the members of dozens of tribes face special problems in adjusting to the common identity, Indian, which they are often forced to adopt in the cities.

On first reading the literature of Native American urbanization, it appears that the group does indeed follow a peculiar pattern of migration from country to town. Perhaps because of the overemphasis on the BIA involvement in relocation, students of the migration have concentrated on large-city Native American residents and said little about how the people got to town. Interviews with relocatees leave the impression that Native Americans typically move from the reservation into a large city. However, in her study of the migration, Elaine Neils notes that Indians seem to be heading for both small towns and large cities. Although she is somewhat perplexed by this divided stream of migration, she speculates that traditionally Indians "have begun their urban experience in cities nearer home, and then moved further on," and that "individuals continue to follow this pattern. . . . " In addition, there is an urban dimension to reservation life, the administrative centers on the reservations where stable jobs and urban patterns exist within the context of reservation culture. In an administrative sense, these towns connect the reservations to the larger American society. But in a cultural sense, too, they occupy "a level of integration intermediate between the Indian and the nearest cities." They often form a first stop in the individual Indian's unassisted move into the city; second stops are often intermediate-sized cities. Chicago Indians, for example, often reported that they had "made repeated visits to the small towns and regional centers near the reservations."

Migration to the city is not typically a wrenching move directly from the depths of the reservation into the confusions of an urban slum environment. Whether viewed as a "series of steps" or an "extended sphere of movement," the pattern of Native Americans moving by stages into the metropolis is strikingly similar to that noted forty years ago by Arthur Schlesinger, Sr., who wrote how, in the 1880s, rural Americans "moved from the countryside to the nearest hamlet, from the hamlet to the town and from the town to the city." To the extent that BIA relocation programs disrupted this cycle by fostering direct migration to large cities, the Native American experience has indeed been unique. But in this instance the "special experience" is less a result of Indian than Anglo-imposed norms. Native Americans have not followed a special migration pattern from the country to the city.

The question of what paths Indians did take to the city is directly related to how long they remain and to how many of the migrants give up on urban life and return to the reservations. The most recent studies assert that "one of the most visible and noted characteristics of Indian living in cities has been their mobility, in a pattern of movement that seems to be peculiarly Indian." An example of this pattern is the Mohawk steelworker community, where men move around the continent while the women remain close to their extended families. However, the job-related mobility of the men is less important than their feeling that the city is not home, that retirement will be to the reservation in Quebec, that the children should be educated there, and that the group's urban base (Brooklyn, New York) is close enough to the reservation that families can visit frequently. In short, we have skilled, well-employed urban Indians still in close contact with the reservation, still migrating back frequently, surviving by integrating new lives into the old ways. Similar behavior has been observed by many urban Native Americans and among members of virtually all of the tribes.

What is the significance of this behavior? Does it demonstrate that the city is a uniquely "poor environment for a solitary tribal man"? or that centuries of non-Western, preindustrial norms—that is, Native American culture—make the Indian an especially difficult subject for urbanization? This is certainly the prevalent, romantic view, but much contrary evidence exists. In Los Angeles, Indians seem to come to town and react to the city in a "pattern of responses not significantly different from that [of] European-Americans who had migrated to a large city from a rural or small town background." These Indian migrants tend to make fewer reservation visits as the years go by, "while at the same time they increasingly tend to idealize the physical and cultural aspects of reservation life."

Such a description has obvious resonance with the experience of many Caucasian immigrants to American cities and is an important corrective to the tendency to overromanticize the cultural basis of the Native Americans' difficulties in the cities. Even in terms of migration behavior, or "persistence rates," the supposedly high Indian mobility looks more normal when compared to the experience of other population subgroups. As noted earlier, statistics are shaky, but it seems that about half of the Indians who come to live in the city actually return to live on the reservations. This estimate probably includes many, but not all, of the Native Americans who spend a part of the year in town and summers or other long periods at the reservation. In short, the statistics describe a group in which something more than one half of the first- and second-generation urbanites leave the cities, either permanently or seasonally, for a return to the "homeland."

This is not an especially high rate of out-migration. Only about one-half of the total population remained in Boston for as long as a decade throughout the nineteenth century, and urban historians have found similar low persistence rates in many cities throughout the nineteenth and early twentieth centuries. More recently, many black Americans (and many Southern whites, as well) have made semiannual trips southward an integral part of their urban lifestyles. These families, much as the Mohawk, do not have one address; they divide the year between a rural home and an urban one. In the nineteenth century, too, such patterns were common. Italian immigrants, for example, were notorious for their seasonal migratory patterns.

In fact, the assumption that stable urban residence is the norm against which urban Native Americans must be measured rests on a misreading of American immigration history. Most groups which have come to this country's cities, whether from abroad or from our own countryside, whether from Caucasian or other racial stock, whether from Western, non-Western, industrial or preindustrial cultures, have followed patterns of mobility similar to those characteristic of Native Americans. Indeed, the concept "immigrant" had no legal meaning prior to the 1920s, and the equation of immigration with permanent relocation is a relatively recent phenomenon. Many south Europeans said, upon arriving in the United States, that they intended to go home when they had accumulated some money. Their actions are more telling than their intentions, and Simon Kuznets calculates that between 1890 and 1910 forty percent of the "immigrants" to the United States returned to their homeland. His figure is an extrapolation; nevertheless, it seems clear that Native Americans return to the reservations at rates similar to those achieved by homeward migrants from earlier groups of more distant origin. The "wanderlust" so romantically associated with many Native Americans bears a striking resemblance to the experience of other economically disadvantaged groups during the early stages of urbanization. Native Americans are not exceptionally unstable immigrants whose inability to cope with urban life drives them, in disproportionate numbers, to return to the reservations.

If the Native American's culture fails to explain his difficulties in settling down in the city, it is no more successful in accounting for the tensions tribesmen undergo when, in an urban environment, they find themselves identified by Anglo society as Indians. The problem arises because the term *Indian* is so obviously an abstraction. Indeed, the term *urban Indian* reflects an even higher level of abstraction, since over 100 separate tribal traditions are represented, often within the same city. Undoubtedly, Anglo society's reduction of many peoples into a single category, urban Indian, heightens conflicts for individuals within the community as a whole.

In describing the urban Indian, students report that in both tribal and class terms the processes of group identification are creating an "Indian" in much the same way as they created an "Italian" or a "Jew." As Murray Wax has noted, the same forces operate on a class as well as a tribal basis among Native Americans, and many middle-class Indians avoid their Indian self-identity to avoid the "stigma" of a general Indian identification. However, even the most sensible of observers, comparing the immigrant middle class's tendencies to renounce their impoverished fellow ethnics with the middle-class Native Americans who "dissociate themselves from both the tribal Indian, whom they consider backward, and from the lower class Indian, whom they consider inferior," claims that the Native American case is unique. Indians and other immigrants are undergoing different experiences because "the German Jews [for example] could not evade being identified with and held responsible for their lower class co-religionists . . . " while "the tribal nature of Indian life, and the pattern of diffuse responsibility for the Indian condition" allow Indians to evade identification with poor or embarrassing tribesmen.

Obviously, Native American tribalism puts different pressures on an individual than do either Jewish traditions or those of other European ethnic groups. But the Native American who rejects his identity to avoid uncomfortable associations is following a path which was open to members of other ethnic groups, although closed to Afro-Americans. Differences in cultural background may alter the form of rejection, the rationalization of it, the presence or lack of guilt associated with cutting loose from the group. Individuals may retain an ethnic or racial self-identification and still function comfortably in the city. But neither Native American nor European ethnic can publicly retain his identity *and* avoid identification with his group, whether tribesman or coreligionists.

In short, even the complex tribal origins of Native Americans do not define a situation different in kind from that faced before World War II by the still unhomogenized members of European ethnic groups. Much of the Native American experience, viewed as a group phenomenon, is in fact very similar to the experiences of most other groups of new city residents in our nation's past. On a personal level, reports on social disintegration and deviance echo the reported behavior of other ethnic and racial groups first coming to the city. And even reports that the urban Native American ignores available government services because of "impatience with the slowness of the agencies, and ignorance of their existence" find their echo in, to cite a well-known example, the attitudes and behavior patterns of immigrants from southern Italy.

If carried to its logical conclusion, however, this view may become as misleading as the romanticized notion of the culturally based uniqueness of Native American experience in the city. The weakness of both views lies in their tendency to collapse two sets of variables, those relating to the immigration process and those relating to the content of personal experience. But given the "increasing phenomenon of the urban Indian who attempts, and often succeeds, in maintaining his identity in the city" it may be necessary to begin studying the ways in which Native American cultures help the migrant to withstand the shocks of urbanization and make an adjustment to urban *milieu*.

While most scholars would agree with Stuart Levine's plea to recognize the Native Americans' uniqueness, few have answered his call "to raid the issue of that uniqueness." Reassessments of the functions of traditional cultures in the urbanization process have been under way for other groups for some time and have elaborated the ways in which old-world or rural cultures often formed the framework for individual adjustment to the city. Perhaps it is *not* Native American cultural traits but "the lack of an enclave structure, of a surrogate social structure in the city" which casts the young, single, noncommitted Native American adrift and heightens his problems in the city. In other words, not the presence but the absence of a well-defined subworld in which traditional norms can mediate between him and the city may cause the Native American migrant's particular adjustment problems. And that enclave structure may itself fail to appear not because of any incompatibility between traditional tribal culture and the city, but instead because of the combined effects of low absolute numbers of Indian migrants and the multiplicity of tribal traditions within the small migrant group.

The myths and misunderstandings surrounding the migration from reservation to city arise in part from the use of culturally specific factors to explain phenomena which are not specific to the culture group under discussion. Migration pattern, mobility, tribalism vs. Pan Indianism, and various forms of social disorganization and deviance are best explained as facets of the process of urbanization, not as outcomes of a specific cultural tradition. If we can drop the assumption that traditional cultures can only function to hinder adaptation to a core culture and focus instead on the ways members of a minority group utilize traditional norms to assist their adjustment to new and potentially disruptive environments, the meaningful uniqueness of minority cultures will become clearer. No longer trapped by questions of "whether the urban Indian can obtain equality of opportunity and still resist the movement toward assimilation," we can begin to learn how a minority's culture supports its members in time of strain.

23

JIM CROW, INDIAN STYLE

ORLAN J. SVINGEN

Throughout most of American history, certainly before the 1930s, few Indians participated fully in national political life. Although the 1924 Indian Citizenship Act granted full political rights and citizenship to all Native Americans in the United States, in much of the West custom or law limited Indian voting. This was not particularly difficult because earlier federal actions made state discrimination seem easy and defensible. Perhaps of equal importance, during the nineteenth century most tribal people had sought to remain independent or at least separate from the rest of society. Clearly, few reservation dwellers wanted full participation in national politics or those of their home states. This essay traces the things that inhibited Indian voting and civil rights in Montana and other parts of the West. The author shows that as early as the Montana Enabling Act of 1889 state leaders had excluded tribal members from the voting rolls. That pattern continued as white politicians prevented reservation dwellers from voting. The tactics, similar to those used against the newly freed blacks in the South during the late nineteenth century and against Hispanic people in the Southwest more recently, effectively kept Native Americans from any meaningful role in state or local political activities. Although the favorable ruling in the 1986 Windy Boy v. Big Horn County *ended the most obvious tactics to dilute Indian political power, discrimination and controversy over voting rights continue to the present.*

Orlan Svingen is an assistant professor of history at Washington State University.

In June of 1986 Judge Edward Rafeedie ruled that "official acts of discrimination . . . have interfered with the rights of Indian citizens [of Big Horn County, Montana] to register and vote." Civil rights expert and ACLU attorney Laughlin McDonald later observed in the *San Francisco Examiner* that racism against Indian people in Montana was even worse than he had expected. "I thought I'd stepped

Source: Orlan Svingen, "Jim Crow, Indian Style," *American Indian Quarterly*, 11 (Fall 1987), pp. 275–286. Reprinted with permission of the publisher.

into the last century," McDonald explained. "Whites were doing to Indians what people in the South stopped doing to blacks twenty years ago." Big Horn County Commissioner and area rancher Ed Miller "longs for the good old days" when Indians remained on the reservation. Angered by Rafeedie's ruling, Miller threatened to appeal the decision to the Supreme Court. "The Voting Rights Act is a bad thing," Miller complained. "I don't see no comparison with Negroes in the South." Before Janine Windy Boy and other plaintiffs filed suit against Big Horn County, "things were fine around here," Miller lamented. "Now they [Indians] want to vote," he exclaimed. "What next?"

On June 13, 1986, United States District Judge Edward Rafeedie ordered that "at-large elections in Big Horn County violate Section 2 of the Voting Rights Act. . . . " and "that a new system of election must be adopted." Judge Rafeedie's decision culminated a three-year process begun in Big Horn County by Crow and Northern Cheyenne voters who refused any longer to accept second-class voting rights.

The case began its way into court in August of 1983, when Jeff Renz and Laughlin McDonald, ACLU attorneys for the plaintiffs, submitted a "Motion for Preliminary Injunction" preventing the defendant, Big Horn County, from holding a general election on November 6, 1983. The motion called for a hearing before Federal Judge James Battin in Billings, Montana. The motion and subsequent suit against Big Horn County charged that the at-large system in county commissioner and school board elections in Big Horn County diluted the Indian vote so as to disenfranchise American Indian voters.

The plaintiffs in *Windy Boy* v. *Big Horn County* argued that the at-large scheme denied the plaintiffs' rights to participate in elections and to elect representatives of their choice to county and school board offices. In Big Horn County, where non-Indians constitute fifty-two percent of the population and American Indians form forty-six percent, at-large elections violated the Fourteenth and Fifteenth Amendments and Section 2 of the 1965 Voting Rights Act. They asked the court to bar further at-large elections until new districts could be apportioned for the Board of Commissioners and School Districts 17H and 1.

The case turned on the 1982 amendment of Section 2 of the 1965 Voting Rights Act. Amended Section 2 declares unlawful any election procedure or voting law which "results" in discrimination because of race, color, or membership in a language minority. In an earlier decision, the Supreme Court had held that Section 2 violations required proof of purposeful discrimination. Recognizing that intentional discrimination is difficult to prove, Congress amended Section 2 stating that no voting procedure can be imposed by a "State or political subdivision in a manner which results in a denial or abridgement of the right of any citizen . . . to vote."

Centuries of conflict dominate Indian-white relations and created the setting wherein late-nineteenth- and twentieth-century civil rights violations began. By the time Congress passed the Indian Citizenship Act in 1924, a sophisticated structure of anti-Indian policies was clearly already in place. Just as passage of the Fifteenth Amendment precipitated countless barriers for the freedmen, the Indian Citizenship Act also failed to elevate American Indian civil rights on an equal footing with non-Indians.

Until 1924 the various states ignored Native Americans and passed numerous unchallenged laws eliminating Indian people from the political process. In 1924, however, non-Indians harboring anti-Indian attitudes now confronted Indian people armed with the protection of the Fourteenth and Fifteenth Amendments.

In addition to federal Indian policies of dispossession, wardship, and concentration, specific territorial and state laws affected Indian people. In 1871 Montana Territory denied voting rights to persons under "guardianship" and outlawed voting precincts at Indian agencies, trading posts in Indian Country, or "on any Indian reservation whatever." In 1884 *Elk* v. *Wilkins* held that Indians were not made citizens under the Fourteenth Amendment because they were not persons born subject to United States jurisdiction. As such, Montana was not obliged to allow Indians to register to vote in state and county elections. The Montana Enabling Act of 1889 opened voting rights to all male citizens without regard to race or color, with the exception of Indians not taxed. At the turn of the century two more Montana laws restricted voting rights to taxpayers only and to resident freeholders listed on city or county tax rolls. Although certain American Indians could become citizens under the Dawes and Burke Acts of 1887 and 1906, Montana systematically denied voting rights to Indian people. The state denied residency to Indian citizens living on reservations and excluded those from voting who maintained relations with a tribe. In 1911 the state legislative assembly declared that anyone living on an Indian or military reservation who had not previously acquired residency in a Montana county before moving to a reservation would not be regarded as a Montana resident.

By 1916 Robert Yellowtail, a leader in Crow politics, compared racism against American Indians with the policies used against black Americans. Singling out discriminatory practices in public accommodations and schools, Yellowtail charged that Hardin, Wyola, Lodge Grass, and Crow Agency had drafted their own "Jim Crow" laws in Montana. Just as emancipation and Reconstruction had failed to elevate freedmen into the mainstream of America, the Citizenship Act fell short of incorporating Indian people into the larger society. Instead, a pattern of separation emerged, widened by state laws diluting the effect of citizenship.

In 1924 Congress extended citizenship to all Indians born in the United States. Application of the Fourteenth Amendment meant, moreover, that they were citizens of the United States "and of the State wherein they resided." Having all the basic political hardware, congressmen could say, just as was said after Reconstruction, Indians have all the "tools" for political equality; now they are on their own. But historians recognize that black Americans did not achieve equality with Southern whites after Reconstruction. What followed emancipation and the Reconstruction amendments was the white response to the abolition of slavery—segregation. In addition to facing a closed society, black Americans confronted an alien electoral system. Many lacked an understanding of political issues. Large numbers were illiterate or semi-illiterate; and as Joel Williamson has explained, some even sought relief in withdrawal from associations with the white race.

Was the 1924 Indian Citizenship Act an Indian emancipation proclamation? After that legislation had formally ended the "wardship" status for Indian people, did non-Indians respond by creating a de facto form of segregation in its place? The reservation system certainly lent itself to separating Indian people from non-Indians. Instead of fearing the Africanization of Southern society, did Big Horn County and other Indian counties in the North fear an Indianization of the political process? Did non-Indians redefine their relationships with Indian people by creating an Indian version of the Black Code or Mississippi Plan? Were Indian voting rights afforded the same consideration as non-Indians? Did Indian children receive an educational experience on a par with non-Indian children? Were Indian people summoned for jury duty? And what accounts for signs appearing in Hardin businesses declaring "No Indians or dogs allowed," or public outhouses with "Whites" and "Indians" scrawled over the separate doors? Although Indian people had won legal and political rights, a pattern of separation had become firmly entrenched in the minds of non-Indians—a mind-set fostered by years of acceptance of the ideology of white racial superiority.

Shortly after the passage of the Citizenship Act, the *Hardin Tribune* focused on newly won Indian voting rights. News accounts and editorials drew front-page attention to Indian voting potential and pondered its impact on upcoming elections. Robert Yellowtail attracted a great deal of news coverage when he ran for state office in the fall of 1924. The *Tribune* estimated 5,000, then 9,000, Montana Indians would vote in the 1924 elections, and it closely monitored the number of Indian people who registered in Big Horn County. Clearly Big Horn County's non-Indian population dreaded the possibility of an Indian being voted into county or state office.

Three years later, state machinery hobbled Indian voting potential when the Montana legislative assembly passed a law in 1927 dividing Montana counties into three-commissioner districts. The law established at-large elections for county commissioners who were elected to six-year terms, on a two-year staggered basis. In order to be elected, each candidate had to win a countywide election. On the surface, and in counties with a homogeneous population, at-large elections appeared to make county-elected officials more responsive to the wider needs of a county. It can be argued, moreover, that at-large elections were progressive responses to the call for greater democracy in the United States. To ethnic minorities, however, Indian people included, at-large elections erased their chances for minority representation because it required a majority vote in a countywide election. As of October 1986 no American Indian had been elected to the Board of County Commissioners in Big Horn County.

Who is to say what the motives were for instituting the at-large election process? Did some support it to genuinely enhance the democratic process while others saw the plan as a subtle method for diluting the "political efficacy" of American Indians in counties with large Indian populations? Or was the at-large election scheme originally a racially neutral phenomenon which was subsequently corrupted for invidious purposes?

The legislative history of Senate Bill 17 establishing at-large elections reveals no overt anti-Indian bias, but its sponsorship by three senators, two of whom were from Indian counties, suggests more than coincidental ties. Senator Christian F. Gilboe from Valier, Montana, represented Pondera County, which included a portion of the Blackfeet Indian Reservation. Senator Seymour H. Porter, another sponsor to the bill, from Big Sandy, represented Choteau County, which embraced the Rocky Boy Indian Reservation. The motives behind Senate Bill 17 may remain debatable, but the results of the at-large election scheme promoted by Senators Gilboe and Porter are eminently clear to Indian people in Big Horn County.

Ten years later more state actions crippled Indian voting in Montana. In 1937 the state mandated that all deputy voter registrars must be qualified taxpaying residents of their respective precincts. Because American Indians were exempt from certain local taxes, the state's action excluded Indian people from serving as voter registrars, thereby undermining Indian voter registration on the reservation. In the same year, Montana canceled all voter registration and required the reregistration of all voters. Indian registration had risen steadily, but after the 1937 cancelation process, Indian voting numbers remained depressed, not returning to the pre-1937 levels until the 1980s.

The events of 1924 did not inaugurate an enlightened period of goodwill between Indian and non-Indian voters. Between 1924 and 1934 Indian candidates ran for state and county offices, but none won. The at-large election scheme and subsequent state actions had effectively disenfranchised American Indians in Big Horn County.

After 1937 it was clear that non-Indians had not welcomed Indian people into the political fold of state and county politics in Big Horn County. Despite the 1924 citizenship legislation, attitudes about Indians and about their political participation had changed very little. Comparing Indians elected to office before and after 1924, absolutely nothing had changed. Indian voters did not even enjoy the personal satisfaction of being sought out on a coalition basis by non-Indian candidates. Through racially polarized voting, Indian candidates were systematically defeated by non-Indian voters who elected non-Indian candidates. To Indian people in Big Horn County, voting rights conferred by citizenship were meaningless.

Comparing Indian voting rights problems with the black historical model offers dramatic parallels with Jim Crowism and segregation. Both groups confronted the separation of races and second-class treatment. The black experience is useful because it dramatizes the seriousness and the pervasiveness of Indian discrimination. Throughout Southern society black Americans had interacted with whites, but on rural reservations Indian people confronted fewer non-Indians. The relative isolation of the reservation and its inhabitants allowed racial tensions and discrimination to go unnoticed within American society.

The black experience also draws needed attention to Indian voting issues because it invites society to conclude that Indian people have suffered indignities no longer tolerated by the courts of black Americans. Nonetheless, the black model has a narrow application to the American Indian experience because blacks and American Indians represent different culture patterns. Many distinct factors affect Indian voting patterns in ways peculiar to Indian people. For example, illiteracy and semi-illiteracy rates among Indian people make it difficult to participate in elections based on the English language. Dale Old Horn, Department Head of Crow Studies at Little Big Horn College, explains that Crow is the primary language of his people. Political and social events at Crow, moreover, are conducted in Crow and English to guarantee the widest understanding. So when it comes to voting, rather than seek assistance from non-Indians in getting ballots interpreted, some Indian people simply avoid the polls.

Old Horn and Mark Small, a Northern Cheyenne rancher in Big Horn and Rosebud County, identified BIA paternalism as another peculiar Indian problem. State laws that all but denied the constitutionality of the 1924 Citizenship Act left Indian people traditionally dependent on the federal government and its agent, the BIA. The Bureau, Small noted, created a "false sense of security" among Indians and persuaded many to believe it would take care of their concerns. This action, in effect, promoted dependence, helplessness, and statewide voting inactivity among American Indians. By ignoring the questions of Indian civil rights, Old Horn and Small agreed that the Bureau had retarded the development of full citizenship for Indian people. The question needs to be asked: If the government is guilty of fostering federal paternalism among Indian tribes and thereby promoting state voting inactivity, is the federal government guilty of violating its trust responsibilities in the area of Indian civil rights?

Another cultural expression affecting the voting rights question is the matter of tribal sovereignty. Some Indian people avoid confronting state and county voting rights issues because involvement with the state might be seen as inviting state jurisdiction over tribal politics. Demanding equal rights in Montana county and state elections might touch off a new round of termination discussions. Non-Indians promote these fears, Small explained, by challenging Indian people with the question: "We don't vote in your tribal elections, so why are you trying to vote in ours?"

Another far-reaching issue involving voting rights is the avoidance of bigotry and racism. Janine Windy Boy, the lead plaintiff in the Big Horn County suit and President of Little Big Horn College in Crow Agency, explains that it is a foregone conclusion: "You just don't go where you aren't wanted." Being branded a "pagan, heathen, savage, or a blanket-assed Indian" is reason enough, Old Horn observed, for some Indian people to avoid the election process. Gail Small, an attorney in Lame Deer and an enrolled member of the Northern Cheyenne, explains that Indian people have been "put down" by non-Indians so frequently that some actually internalize the criticism. "After you are told you are incompetent long enough," Small said, "some [Indian people] start believing it." These attitudes, which have historically opposed Indian political participation, have created a deep sense of alienation among Indian people toward state government.

What, then, accounts for the political wasteland for Indian people in Big Horn County extending up to the 1980s? I have argued that the historic relationship between Indians and non-Indians in the pre- and post-1924 period created a setting which was hostile to Indian participation in federal, state, and county elections. The post-1924 years inherited the wardship concept and perpetuated a system, which, whether by design or not, excluded Indian people from participation. Despite being struck down by laws, the historic barriers and stereotypes against Indian voting rights among non-Indians promote the attitude that it is inappropriate for Indian people to vote in state and county elections.

Voting rights cases involving American Indians are not new. Ample case law beginning in the mid 1970s demonstrates that Indian people meeting age and residency requirements cannot be denied voting rights. Exemptions from certain taxes no longer limits their right to vote, and election districts must be apportioned under the "one person, one vote" principle. The 1975 amendment to the Voting Rights Act requires voter registration facilities in Indian communities, and it affords special language arrangements for language minorities. Fred Ragsdale, Jr., an Indian law specialist at the University of New Mexico Law School, explains that Indian voting rights are not matters of Indian law. Ample case law precedents make this a simple citizenship question under federal law. Referring to previous voting rights cases, Ragsdale believes that "the easy ones are over with," and henceforth decisions will turn on the quality of factual questions, proof, and statistics.

If case law supporting Indian voting rights is so clearly defined by the courts, what accounts for violations of the Voting Rights Act in Big Horn County? The clearest answer is the at-large election scheme, described by Jeff Renz, co-counsel for the plaintiffs, as a form of reverse-gerrymandering in Indian counties. One might expect that Indians, who comprise 46.2 percent of the Big Horn County population, would have elected at least one Indian to county or state office sometime in the past sixty-two years. In response to this disturbing statistic and to the case in general, the defendants who are non-Indian officials of Big Horn County offer curious responses: (1) past problems cannot be blamed on us today, (2) nothing in Big Horn County hinders Indian voting rights, and (3) no official discrimination against Indians exists in Big Horn County.

The cumulative impact of nineteenth- and twentieth-century federal Indian policies, state legislation, and racial tensions has created a cultural setting intolerant of American Indian voting rights. What else accounts for the defendant's responses to the plaintiff's charges? The skeptic, however, may argue away each separate example cited, dismissing them as the results of pre-1924 citizenship laws, pre-1965 voting procedures, or unenlightened racial attitudes. But when considered within a historic chronology—the way Indian people consider them—their impact is staggering.

Let us next turn to some of the current specific problems Crow and Northern Cheyenne people confront in Big Horn County. In terms of county employment, for example, out of 249 employees, the highest number of Indians employed by Big Horn County totaled six in 1985—or 2.4 percent of the county work force. Of the one hundred members on twenty county citizen boards, only two Indians have ever been appointed. Membership on these boards is significant because they promote programs and provide valuable experience and countywide name recognition for their members. Despite offers from tribal police to serve subpoenas against Indian jurors, only three Indians served on coroner's juries in Big Horn County between 1966 and 1983.

During the 1970s and 1980s Indian people in Big Horn County became more vote conscious, and a voter registration drive produced as many as two thousand Indian registrants. At first, county officials cooperated, but as the numbers grew officials began rejecting registration cards containing minor mistakes previously overlooked. This was followed by a refusal to provide Indian people with additional blank forms with the excuse that new ones were being printed—even though information on old and new forms was identical. Another excuse from the Clerk and Recorder's Office was that the Office had already given out large numbers of registration cards to Indians and that no more would be forthcoming until those already given out were returned.

Then in 1982 four Indian and pro-Indian candidates entered the Democratic primary election and defeated their non-Indian opponents. The outcome shocked non-Indians in Big Horn County and prompted immediate anti-Indian sentiment. Little League baseball teams from Crow Agency, for example, encountered racial hostility just after the election, and non-Indian Democrats charged the organizers of the voter registration drive with fraud and accused them of stealing the election. The chairman of the county Democratic party admitted that "we sort of got caught with our pants down." Disgruntled non-Indian Democrats left the party and formed the Bipartisan Campaign Committee (BCC), whose sole purpose was to challenge Indian candidates from outside the Democratic party. The BCC had no Indian membership, it supported no Indian or "pro-Indian" candidates, and opposed only Indian and "pro-Indian" candidates. Its campaign literature informed readers that the Democratic candidates elected in the 1982 primary were not "qualified" and that they did not "reflect the majority opinion of the voters in this County." The Democratic Indian and "pro-Indian" candidates won, but only after narrowly surviving a BCC write-in campaign.

In 1984 Gail Small, a Lame Deer attorney and a graduate of the University of Oregon Law School, ran for state representative in House District 100. Small later described her campaign as one characterized by race. For example, while campaigning east of Tongue River on Otter Creek, she knocked on the door of an area rancher and introduced herself as a candidate for state representative. She explained that she was particularly interested in natural resources and water issues—both vital to this coal-rich region. The rancher responded by pointing off in the distance, where the ruins lay of a blockhouse fortress used in the so-called Cheyenne Outbreak of 1897. "It was just yesterday that we were fighting you off," he replied to Small, "and now you want me to vote for you?" His response typified Small's reception by non-Indian voters and persuaded her to never again run for office.

In both 1982 and 1984 elections many Indian people who had registered to vote came to the polls only to learn that their names were not on the list of registered voters. Despite showing proof of registration, election judges refused to allow them to vote. Others who had voted in primary elections found their names removed from the general election registration list. Clo Small, a former precinct committee woman, explained that for years she and her husband, Mark Small, had voted in Busby, but for no apparent reason, in the 1982 school board election she was told that her voting precinct was in Kerby—approximately twenty miles south of Busby. Her husband's precinct remained Busby.

In a related incident, Mark and Clo Small drove from Busby to Hardin, Montana to obtain voter registration cards. Small hoped to obtain a large number so that he could help register Northern Cheyenne people living inside Big Horn County. Leaving his wife in the car outside the courthouse, Small went to the Clerk and Recorder's Office and requested voter registration cards. The clerk handed him eleven and instructed him to sign for the numbered cards. Small explained to the clerk that he had driven considerable distance and that eleven registration cards were hardly worth the trip. The clerk responded: "We are out of them." Angry and suspicious, Small returned to the car and explained to his wife what had happened. Clo Small, a non-Indian, decided to try her luck. When she walked into the Clerk and Recorder's Office moments later and asked for voter registration cards, the same clerk handed her a three-inch stack of cards.

Windy Boy v. *Big Horn County* offers historians a wide range of ponderables. Despite full citizenship and recent favorable decisions, Indian people still confront official discrimination against their most fundamental civil rights—social and cultural aspects aside. Clearly the attitudes of their non-Indian counterparts have not kept pace with gains Indian people have made in the courts in recent years. Non-Indians rely on pat responses such as "Indians should look to the federal government for help" or "Indians don't pay taxes, so why should they vote in white elections?" While these attitudes persist, counties with large Indian populations will continue to oppose, challenge, and hamstring the voting rights of Indian people.

By amending Section 2 of the Voting Rights Act to consider the "results" of voting procedures rather than requiring proof of intentional discrimination, Congress has said "Let's not quibble over how intentionally or unintentionally voting rights are being denied." If election practices "result" in discrimination, a violation of federal law has occurred. This sounds simple and straightforward, but it becomes complicated when applied to the reservation setting, when compared with historic Indian policies, and when considered within the context of Indian-white counties controlled by non-Indians.

It is time for historians to survey nineteenth- and twentieth-century American Indian issues with a broader perspective. Rather than applying a litmus test to isolated laws frozen in time and concluding that they were equally demanding to all citizens, let's ask ourselves what is the cumulative long-term impact of these policies and laws on a culturally distinct language minority.

In the aftermath of Judge Rafeedie's decision civil rights prospects for Crow and Northern Cheyenne people are, at best, mixed. On the positive side abandonment of at-large districting enabled Indian people of District 2 to elect John Doyle, Jr., as Big Horn County's first Indian county commissioner. Doyle's election reverses decades of discriminatory voting practices and illustrates the strength of Indian voting power freed from vote dilution.

On the negative side, however, anti-Indian sentiment seems as strong and defiant as ever. In the spirit of former County Commissioner Ed Miller, who complained that the Voting Rights Act was "a bad thing," the defendants filed a motion of appeal in August of 1986. Subsequent to that, the *Hardin Herald* reported that an anti-Indian jurisdiction group known as Montanans Opposed to Discrimination (MOD) had become interested in the case. Composed primarily of white ranchers, MOD backed a local Secret Concerned Citizens Committee (SCCC), whose objective was to seek the basis for criminal prosecution of two of the plaintiffs in *Windy Boy,* Janine Windy Boy and James Ruegamer, and also Clarence Belue, a former "pro-Indian" county attorney in Big Horn County. Using a $5,000 donation from MOD, SCCC sought to uncover evidence of wrongdoing for prosecuting all three. These actions, however, came to center on Windy Boy and Belue. Charges against Belue resulted in his review before the Montana State Bar Association.

Also in the wake of the decision and prior to the November 1986 election, Janine Windy Boy received a telephone call from an agent of the Federal Bureau of Investigation in Billings, Montana, asking to meet with her. The FBI explained it was investigating complaints lodged against her with the U.S. Attorney's Office. The complaint alleged that Windy Boy, President of Little Big Horn Community College at Crow Agency, had misused her office by allowing Democratic candidates and tribal officials to use community college facilities rent free. The FBI concluded its inquiry after Windy Boy met with agents in Billings and delivered documentation disproving the allegations.

Clearly a political setting in Big Horn County free of distrust, suspicion, and racism remains a long way off. Historic political inequality, oppression, and Indian hating requires more than one election to usher in a period of racial harmony. One court decision such as Windy Boy means nothing more than non-Indians in Big Horn County can no longer "officially" ignore the county's Indian population. Rafeedie's decision may weaken racist foundations in the county, but the old patterns of distrust, suspicion, and harassment will continue until Indian people are no longer viewed and treated as political refugees in a white man's world.

24

FULL BLOOD, MIXED BLOOD, GENERIC, AND ERSATZ: THE PROBLEM OF INDIAN IDENTITY

WILLIAM T. HAGAN

All of the contributors to this collection assume some definition of Indianness and the nature of tribal societies. Yet the issue of just who is an Indian, who decides that, and what criteria are used has remained unclear throughout American history. Do the Indians decide? What authority should the government have in this matter? Have federal laws, administrative actions, or court decisions laid down any clear guidelines on this issue? In this essay the author suggests that few answers to these questions are clear and accepted. In general, federal officials have insisted that for a person to be considered an Indian he or she needed to have some Indian blood and a formal connection with some recognized tribal group. Just what percentage of blood and what evidence is needed to establish that fact vary widely. In addition, proof of a person's tie to an organized tribe might differ as well. Formal status as a tribal member is important because of things as varied as voting rights in the corporate activities of Alaskan native people or membership in social and religious societies in parts of the West. The author claims that during most of American history the federal government dealt with the tribes without giving much careful thought to the nature of Indian status and tribal membership. Then he traces what guidelines have come into being and the impact they have had on Native American societies down to the present.

William T. Hagan is a professor of history at the University of Oklahoma.

One of the most perplexing problems confronting American Indians today is that of identity. Who is an American Indian? The question is raised in a bewildering variety of situations. Contingent on its resolution can be the recognition of a group

Source: William T. Hagan, "Full Blood, Mixed Blood, Generic, and Ersatz: The Problem of Indian Identity," *Arizona and the West*, 27 (Winter 1985), pp. 309–326. © *Arizona and the West* 17 (Winter 1975). Reprinted with permission of the publisher.

by the federal government, voting rights in a multimillion-dollar Alaskan corporation, or acceptance of an individual as a member of a pueblo's tightly knit society. Nor is this a question which has arisen only recently. It has been a problem for individuals, tribes, and government administrators since the birth of this nation.

Four centuries to the year after Christopher Columbus began the semantic confusion over how to label the original inhabitants of this hemisphere, Commissioner of Indian Affairs Thomas Jefferson Morgan spoke to a more important issue. He devoted six pages of his 1892 annual report to the question: What is an Indian? "One would have supposed," observed Morgan, "that this question would have been considered a hundred years ago and had been adjudicated long before this." "Singularly enough, however," he continued, "it has remained in abeyance, and the Government has gone on legislating and administering law without carefully discriminating as to those over whom it has a right to exercise such control."

Nearly a century after Commissioner Morgan expressed surprise at this state of affairs (1980), the Department of Education spent $90,000 to try to establish a useful definition of the term *Indian*. Another government agency, the Branch of Federal Acknowledgement, plans (1984) to spend millions to try to determine which of nearly a hundred tribes applying for federal recognition should merit it.

The founding fathers provided little guidance in the Constitution on matters relating to Indians. They included no legal definition of the term *Indian*, and in fact mentioned the word only twice. The federal agencies responsible for the conduct of Indian affairs, first the War Department and then the Interior Department, failed to fill the gap, and it was left to the courts to grapple with the problem of Indian identity.

In a series of cases in the nineteenth century the courts dealt with the issue but never formulated a simple definition to put the issue to rest. According to Felix Cohen, author of the monumental *Handbook of Federal Indian Law* (1971), the courts did find two considerations most significant in determining Indian identity and status. These considerations were enunciated in *United States* v. *Rogers* in 1846. First, the individual must have some Indian blood; and second, those Indians with whom he/she claimed affiliation must accept him/her as a fellow tribesman.

Cohen adds that ethnological evidence also has been used in determining full-blood status. A notorious example was in a series of cases involving the inhabitants of pueblos in New Mexico. In 1869 the supreme court of New Mexico Territory held that the residents of the pueblos were not Indians, in part because they were "a peaceable, industrious, intelligent, honest, and virtuous people." Presumably, if they had been militant, indolent, stupid, dishonest, and immoral, they would have qualified as Indians. In 1912 a United States circuit court employed similar reasoning. It ruled in the case of a family dropped from the Lower Brulé Sioux tribal rolls that their having one-eighth Indian blood was evidence of "sufficient Indian blood to substantially handicap them in the struggle of existence." Therefore, the court ruled, the members of the family should be considered to have full-blood status and be reenrolled with the Lower Brulé Sioux.

In the second half of the nineteenth century the relative affluence of some tribes attracted numerous enterprising non-Indians, and the question of Indian identity assumed new significance. The Five Civilized Tribes, for example, were inundated by outsiders, many of whom sought membership in those tribes. By 1890 non-Indians made up more than seventy percent of the population of Indian Territory, the home of the Cherokees, Choctaws, Chickasaws, Creeks, and Seminoles. Some of these non-Indians were blacks who before the Civil War had been slaves owned by the tribesmen. After the war, the United States had prevailed upon three of the tribes—the Cherokees, Creeks, and Seminoles—to grant full citizenship to their ex-slaves. By 1890 the Choctaws had granted some privileges to their freedmen, but the Chickasaws were still holding out.

White men, however, constituted the great bulk of non-Indians living among the Five Civilized Tribes in the post–Civil War era. Some of these whites married Indian women, fathered mixed-blood children, and applied for tribal membership. The Cherokees, Choctaws, and Chickasaws permitted this. Many other white men, without a shadow of a legal claim, attempted to secure a place on tribal rolls in order to enjoy the economic benefits—principally access to land—of being a member of one of the Five Civilized Tribes.

The situation was further complicated for the Cherokees by the requests of Eastern Cherokees, descendants of those who had not removed to Oklahoma, to be admitted to the rolls of the Cherokee Nation. This led to a lawsuit in which the Eastern Band sued the United States and the Cherokee Nation. The finding of the U.S. Supreme Court in 1885 was a signal victory for the right of the Cherokee Nation to determine its own criteria for citizenship, and the decision would be used as a precedent to ensure the same authority for other tribes.

Within a few months after the court ruled for the Cherokee Nation, the agent for those Indians was directed to cease issuing citizenship certificates and to publicize the fact that in the future this would be a matter to be adjudicated exclusively by the Cherokee Nation. Encouraged by this ruling, the Cherokees created a three-man commission to handle claims to Cherokee citizenship. The tribe also moved to expel individuals who had filed for citizenship prior to the time the matter was removed from the agent's hands. Some of those ousted protested to the federal government that they were being forced off land after having made substantial improvements in the way of fencing and buildings. The Indian Commissioner expressed considerable sympathy for those squatters who could show some evidence of Cherokee blood, and he refused to assist the Cherokee Nation in ridding itself of these intruders. They were usually American citizens, and the federal government clearly placed their interests above those of noncitizen Indians.

The Five Civilized Tribes were not alone in suffering from non-Indians who hoped to acquire tribal membership and access to tribal property. A well-publicized example was the claim of the Murphy family to membership in the Sac and Fox band holding a reservation in Kansas. Largely because of the Indian Rights Association, the well-known organization of friends of the Indian, the Murphy claim was finally defeated, although not before it had caused the band considerable aggravation and expense over a period of about ten years.

The Murphy claim had arisen through a mixed-blood tie. In the 1870s, as a matter of charity, the Sac and Fox had adopted an elderly and impoverished visitor, a Menominee woman. After the woman died, her daughter, who had married a white man named Murphy, applied for adoption. After refusing her petition more than once, the Sac and Fox Council finally adopted her, although it specifically excluded her several mixed-blood children. Nevertheless, in 1889 the Murphy woman's offspring applied for adoption by the Sac and Fox in order to get access to the reservation in Kansas. Their petition denied, the Murphys sought help from the Indian Bureau. At considerable expense the government conducted two investigations of the Murphy claims. Both upheld the refusal of the Sac and Fox, but the complainants were undaunted.

Aided by the senators from neighboring Nebraska, the Murphys obtained a favorable ruling from an Indian commissioner and took possession of land on the Sac and Fox reservation, including a house occupied by an Indian. The Indian Rights Association intervened at this point and was able to get the Murphys removed from the property. The Murphys then took the matter to court, where they lost. They even tried to obtain recognition as members of the Sac and Fox band through a special act of Congress, only to have the bill die in committee. The ten-year-long struggle cost the Sac and Fox an estimated $10,000 in legal fees.

The Murphy claim had originated with the mixed-blood children of a woman adopted by the Sac and Fox. A common problem for all tribes was the question of rights to be accorded white men who married Indian women and the offspring of such unions. In 1888 Senator Henry L. Dawes, who the previous year had authored the celebrated severalty act, sponsored another piece of legislation. This bill prohibited a white man married to an Indian from acquiring from his wife's tribe any land or special privileges as a result of that marriage. The law, however, did not speak directly to the status of the mixed-blood children who were the product of such marriages.

Prior to the passage of this 1888 law there had been a contradiction between common law and tribal practice. Common law held that descent is patrilineal, and therefore the children of an American citizen and an Indian woman were themselves American citizens. Among most Indian tribes, however, descent is matrilineal. In discussing the problem of Indian identity in his 1892 report, Indian Commissioner Morgan stated that in the past the government had accepted tribal definitions of membership. Tribes usually had accepted mixed-bloods into full membership if their mothers were tribal members, a situation which had implications for land titles for some settlers.

A common provision of treaties negotiated by the Peace Commission of 1867–68 was a requirement that any subsequent purchase of land from the tribe involved would not be valid unless approved by three fourths of the adult males of that tribe. To meet this requirement, the government had routinely sought the signatures of mixed-bloods to validate purchases of tribal land. Under the circumstances, Commissioner Morgan advised continuing to allow tribes to accept mixed-bloods into full membership. To hold that this group were not Indians "would unsettle and endanger the titles to much of the lands that have been relinquished by Indian tribes and patented to citizens of the United States." As always, ensuring settlers' land titles took precedence over concern about the shabby tactics required to get enough Indian signatures on a sale of tribal land.

By the end of the nineteenth century the principle had been established that— barring action by Congress—the tribes were the final authority in determining their membership, even if the Indian practice of tracing descent matrilineally ran counter to common law. This tribal right was reaffirmed in 1978 in a case involving Santa Clara Pueblo, which, incidentally, traces descent patrilineally. A woman who had married outside the pueblo sought to have overturned a pueblo ruling that children born of that marriage were not members of the tribe. The woman had sued on the grounds that the pueblo's action was a violation of the 1968 Indian Civil Rights Act. The Supreme Court refused to interfere with what it regarded as the pueblo's authority to regulate its own "internal and social relations."

After the flurry of activity generated by non-Indians trying to cash in on severalty program allotments had subsided, there was a period in the early 1900s during which Indian identity was broadly defined in a generic sense by some Indian spokesmen. These years saw the emergence of what Hazel Hertzberg has described as Reform Pan-Indianism. Hertzberg detailed the problems that "Red Progressives" had in determining who qualified for membership in the organization they launched in 1911, the Society of American Indians. The society provided for three categories of membership, with the first two limited to those of Indian blood. Only members of these two categories could hold office in the organization.

As expected from a group of middle-class Americans of varying degrees of Indian ancestry, the founders of the society did not confine membership to just those who held tribal memberships. For example, the self-styled Seneca Arthur Parker, a founding father of the organization, was three-quarters white. Of even more importance, his mother was not Seneca—which meant that within that matrilineal tribe he was not considered truly Seneca. The best he could claim was adoption by the tribe. Thus, to qualify for one of the two memberships reserved for Indians in the society, a person needed to be only one-sixteenth Indian, if not on a tribal roll. An even smaller blood quantum was required if the applicant was on a tribal roll.

During the 1920s new leadership in the society turned away from the pan-Indianism of the founders and began to emphasize tribal affiliation and tribal cultures. Factional struggles within the organization caused a shrinking membership and a diminution of its influences. By the end of the decade the best-known Indian to the general public was not a leader in the Society of American Indians, but Sylvester Long Lance, whose claim to be Indian was debatable.

Long Lance was the 1920s version of today's Jamake Highwater, the self-proclaimed Blackfoot who in recent years has parlayed his declarations of Indian heritage into publishing and television contracts. Both Sylvester Long Lance and Highwater had roots among the remnants of Southeastern tribes who lived a troubled existence sandwiched between the much larger white and black populations. Sylvester Long, as he was known as a child, had been born into a North Carolina family of mixed black-Indian ancestry, a family which white North Carolinians designated Negro. Long, however, was admitted to Carlisle Indian School as a Cherokee. After service in the Canadian Army during World War I he settled in western Canada, where he was known as Sylvester Long Lance. In 1922 he was adopted by the Blackfoot tribe and given the status of an honorary chief and a new name, Buffalo Child. By the late 1920s Long Lance had published his life story— considerably embellished—entitled *Autobiography of a Blackfoot Indian Chief*. Reprinted twice, the book, together with articles Long Lance wrote on Indian life for *Cosmopolitan, Good Housekeeping,* and other popular magazines of the day, made him a celebrity.

While Sylvester Long Lance capitalized on his Indian roots, however remote, Congress continued to wrestle with the proper definition of *Indian*. In 1931 it restricted membership in the Eastern Cherokee Band to those at least one-sixteenth Cherokee. Three years later the Wheeler-Howard Indian Reorganization Act, which inaugurated the Indian New Deal, defined three categories of people:

1. All persons of Indian descent who were members of a recognized tribe under federal jurisdiction.
2. All persons who were descendants of such members who on June 1, 1934, were residing within the present boundaries of an Indian reservation.
3. All other persons of one-half or more Indian blood.

Clearly membership in a federally recognized tribe was the easiest and only sure way to prove eligibility for government programs under the Wheeler-Howard Act.

Besides furnishing its own definition of Indian, the act also encouraged tribes to compile membership rolls and in the process define membership criteria. These have varied widely. A common criterion required one-quarter blood in a particular tribe, although one-half was sometimes demanded. No degree of blood of the tribe concerned was specified in a few cases. And it grew complicated in some instances. The Osages, for example, developed three categories of tribal membership. One qualified the individual, as the holder of a headright or a portion of a headright, to share in certain tribal income. Then there was the general membership roll, a place on which qualified the holder to vote in tribal elections. The third membership category related to officeholding and was restricted to those with at least one-quarter Indian blood, regardless of tribe, as long as the individual was on the Osage rolls.

By the late 1960s and early 1970s new forces again focused on the issue of Indian identity. One was the rising popularity of Indianness. The activism of Red Power militants had inspired new pride among Native Americans, while at the same time the Indian image profited from their portrayal in television commercials and popular writing as the first conservationists. The remarkable increase the 1980 census showed in the number of Americans who chose to identify themselves as Indians reflected this new perception of Indians by the public.

This led to the appearance of more ersatz Indians, as they were described in 1974 in a Philadelphia newspaper article reprinted in *Wassaja,* a publication of the Indian Historical Society. The individual who inspired this reporting was one Lightfoot Talking Eagle. Talking Eagle's claim to be a Susquehannock "sun priest" had been denounced by the American Indian Society of Pennsylvania. Nevertheless, Talking Eagle had appeared on television and had delivered public lectures in his role as a sun priest. The article in the Philadelphia paper went on to denounce others who fraudulently claimed Indian ancestry to qualify for student aid reserved for Indians, to help merchandise their handicrafts, or simply to satisfy their yearning for identification with a group enjoying, at least temporarily, considerable public acceptance.

The enterprising reporter who uncovered this story even contacted *Wassaja's* editor, Rupert Costo, for his comment on Talking Eagle. Costo, an enrolled Cahuilla, acknowledged the problem but neatly sidestepped offering a definition of *Indian*, maintaining that tribesmen were learning to cope with the problem and that in time it would be overcome. The president of the American Indian Society of Pennsylvania was less optimistic: "It is apparent the $2.00 head band and the Hong Kong medallion, with a self declaration, is going to be a method . . . by which the Indian population is going to boom."

And there were other incentives for discovering Indian ancestry. These included the well-publicized, multimillion-dollar judgments being awarded tribes in land claims cases. Every announcement of a large judgment seemed to trigger the memories of some Americans that their family trees included an Indian, usually a chief's daughter, a princess. Another incentive was the rapid increase in federal assistance programs available to Indians. This growth had its origin in President Lyndon Johnson's war on poverty, and the programs continued to proliferate under his successors. By 1980 there were over seventy programs, administered by many different government agencies, which could be tapped by Indians.

Eligibility for these federal programs, most of which were administered by offices other than the Bureau of Indian Affairs, varied from agency to agency. The Indian Health Service tended to be more flexible in its interpretation of eligibility, giving considerable latitude to the Indian communities to identify those meriting health services. In contrast, the Bureau of Indian Affairs reserved the exclusive right to determine who participated in the programs it administered. In Oklahoma, for example, in an effort to reduce the cost of the program, the bureau has an "informal agreement" with the state that the federal government will provide welfare payments only for those Cherokees with at least one-quarter Indian blood, with Oklahoma responsible for all others on the tribal roll.

Other agencies had their own definitions of *Indian*. School boards, anxious to collect subsidies from the federal government for educating Indian children, were first told by the Department of Health, Education, and Welfare that the child must be at least one-quarter Indian blood to merit assistance. That requirement was relaxed by the 1972 Education Act, which was passed at the full flood of the nation's concern for minorities and the disadvantaged. The new law more broadly defined Indian and provided for grants to local agencies for a wide range of projects to improve the educational opportunities of Native American children. The intent, as the report of the Senate committee handling the bill made clear, was to help remedy "the consequences of past Federal policies and programs." The policies and programs referred to were the termination and relocation efforts of the 1950s and 1960s, with their resultant "impoverishment and educational deprivation of many of the so-called non-federal Indians."

With so much government assistance and community status riding on being identified as Indian, and with tribal membership being the most frequently employed criterion, tribal affiliation assumed new significance. This was highlighted in two articles in the *American Indian Journal* in 1980. The first was by Jamake Highwater, who appeared on the membership rolls of no tribe, but maintained that both of his parents were mixed-bloods. He attacked the "exclusivity and cultural snobbery" of those tribal members who tended to look down upon individuals of Indian ancestry with no tribal status (the so-called generic Indians). According to Highwater, the "grand climax" of his "professional and personal life" came when he was adopted by Blackfeet in Canada, the same people who had extended honorary membership to Sylvester Long Lance a half-century earlier. Highwater used the term "professional and personal life" advisedly because he had used his Indian ancestry to advance himself professionally as an author and TV producer.

The companion article to Highwater's was designed to show another side of the issue. It was written by Ron Andrade, an official of the National Congress of American Indians. Andrade defended the conservatism of tribal enrollment practices. He identified the desire to share in supposed tribal wealth as the principal motivation of those seeking tribal membership and labeled them the "Indians of convenience." However, Andrade cited other possible motivations, such as living out childhood fantasies of Indian life and the desire to associate with a culture which might offer more stability than what characterized American society in the 1970s.

Andrade was concerned that, by relaxing their standards for membership, tribes would lose things more valuable than money. He feared that tribal cultures and traditions would be dangerously diluted by an influx of strangers who would "jeopardize the entire future of the tribe." Other Indians feared a more massive dilution from another quarter.

Just as there have been thousands of individuals in the last twenty-five years desiring admission to the rolls of federally recognized tribes, there were nearly a hundred groups seeking federal recognition as tribes. In the early 1960s these ranged from tribes recently terminated to groups that had preserved some kind of tribal identity but had never enjoyed federal recognition, with all the psychological and financial advantages that go with it.

Further variations in status were discernible on close examination. Some tribes had federal recognition but no access to federal assistance programs. Some were recognized by the states in which they lived but could participate in only selected federal programs. Other tribes were recognized by states but enjoyed no federal services. There were many tribes, particularly in the East, which were recognized by neither state nor federal government.

A refinement in the art of categorizing tribes was illustrated by the Coushatta case in Louisiana. The Coushattas have lived in the lower Mississippi Valley for hundreds of years. As late as the 1950s, before they fell victims to termination, the Coushattas had received limited education and health services from the federal government. In the Indian renaissance of the early 1970s the Coushattas began to agitate for state and federal recognition. First, Louisiana offered recognition, and then the federal government accepted them as eligible for the partial services available to the "landless tribes" category. To be qualified for the full range of federal programs, however, the Coushattas needed a land base. This technicality was taken care of with the assistance of the Association on American Indian Affairs, which purchased fifteen acres and deeded it to the Coushattas for a reservation. The Coushattas then turned over their newly acquired homeland to be held in trust, finally meeting all criteria for recognition as wards of the United States.

While the Coushattas were winning their battle, other tribes and bands that had been terminated in the 1950s and early 1960s were actively seeking restoration of recognition. As political entities they no longer enjoyed a special relationship with the federal government, although their individual members were still eligible for aid programs, particularly in the health and education fields.

The termination plan for the Utes of the Unitah and Ouray Reservation had been particularly unfortunate. It has created two classes, according to blood quantum. Those over one-half Ute were classified as full-bloods and remained wards of the federal government. Those one-half or less were classified as mixed-bloods, given a share of tribal assets proportional to their numbers, and terminated. The arrangements, however, did not take into consideration hunting and fishing rights on the million-acre Ute reservation. This arbitrary division of the Ute people has, in the thirty years it has been in force, produced real tension between the two groups and spawned lawsuits and near violence.

Restoring federal recognition to the Utes and Coushattas inspired little opposition, as contrasted to the resistance met by those groups seeking federal recognition for the first time. Nevertheless, beginning in 1956 with the Lumbees of North Carolina, a number of tribes, who never previously enjoyed it, have managed to secure the status of wards of the federal government. For the Lumbees the victory initially was tempered by the provision that their federal recognition carried with it no federal services.

In the 1960s the combination of greater pride in Indianness, the millions of dollars available in Indian programs, and the publicity accorded the land claims cases led to first a trickle and then a flood of applications for federal recognition. The American Indian Policy Review Commission, created by Congress in 1970, estimated in its 1977 report that more than a hundred tribes, comprising over 100,000 Indians, were being denied the "protection and privileges of the Federal-Indian relationship." By the end of 1983 nearly one hundred petitions for recognition had been received by the Bureau of Indian Affairs.

The report of the Policy Review Commission had concluded: "Every Indian tribal group which seeks recognition must be recognized; every determination that a group is not an Indian tribal group must be justified soundly on the failure of that group to meet any of the factors which would indicate Indian tribal existence." The commission also proposed that the government aid tribes financially in the expensive task of researching their history in order to meet government criteria.

Nevertheless, there were forces opposed to the federal government recognizing any more tribes. The Interior Department was not sure it even had the legal right to unilaterally grant recognition. As a result, the department was not prepared to push for recognition of particular tribes until Congress took action, either in individual cases, as it had done with the Lumbees, or by authorizing a formal recognition procedure for all applicants. Members of Congress, for their part, were not anxious to rush into a policy which could result in land being removed from local tax rolls and thousands being added to eligibility lists for federal aid programs.

Nor were the already recognized tribes eager to share the federal pie. In 1978 Veronica Murdock, then president of the National Congress of American Indians, appeared before the Senate Select Committee on Indian Affairs, which was considering guidelines for recognition. Murdock expressed concern that "indiscriminate recognition . . . could have adverse impact on all Indian tribes." It would, she argued, "diminish the significance of tribal claims to sovereign rights" and, unless appropriations increased proportionately, "mean slicing the 'Federal funding pie' too thin."

As early as 1969 a bill had been introduced into Congress to extend recognition to all organized tribes in the United States. However, not until 1977, when Congress was asked to restore some of the tribes terminated in the 1950s, did the need for recognition procedures attract much attention. By that time nearly twenty-five applicants were in line.

To meet the need, the Bureau of Indian Affairs prepared an addition to the Code of Federal Regulations. After the initial draft had been circulated and amended, in June of 1978 new procedures for recognition of Indian tribes were published in the *Federal Register*. In general, their objective was to acknowledge those groups which had "maintained their political, ethnic and cultural identity."

To implement the new procedures, a Branch of Federal Acknowledgment was created within the Bureau of Indian Affairs. But this was only one of three methods available to a tribe seeking federal recognition. Congressional action remained an option. Another possibility was to take the expensive and possibly protracted route through the federal courts. Between 1970 and 1983 eleven tribes won recognition through the administrative procedure, five were acknowledged by act of Congress, and three were beneficiaries of court action. In the same period three groups were denied recognition.

The Mashantucket Pequot was one of the tribes that achieved federal recognition by an act of Congress, and its experience offered hope to every small cluster of Native Americans with aspirations for federal status. In 1974 the Pequot tribe consisted of a paltry fifty-five members, whose only common possession was 212 acres of land in Connecticut. Under the leadership of a dynamic young chairman, the Pequots incorporated and began aggressively seeking support, first from Connecticut, and then the federal government. Winning state recognition facilitated the Pequot request for federal funds, even though they still lacked federal recognition. In what must be some sort of record for grantsmanship, the tiny Pequot tribe was able to secure HUD, CETA, and other funds, culminating in a grant of over $1 million for fifteen units of housing.

Meanwhile, with the aid of an anthropologist employed from a grant by the Indian Rights Association, the Pequots prepared a petition for federal recognition. They also publicized plans to sue local landowners for property the tribe had lost in the nineteenth century. In 1983 this case was resolved by an out-of-court settlement, endorsed by Congress, by which the federal government granted recognition to the Pequot tribe and provided $900,000 for the purchase of eight hundred acres to add to their reservation. For its part Connecticut turned over to the tribe twenty acres, including a cemetery containing the graves of Pequots, and spent $200,000 on reservation roads. The tribe has ambitious plans for more housing, a museum, and a gift shop. In these and other projects state and federal aid figured prominently. Most recently the Pequots have received one federal grant of $128,750 for the purchase of a pizza restaurant and $300,000 to help launch a bingo operation.

Given the cornucopia of grants and awards that had enriched the Pequots in ten years, it is not surprising that the tribe's population has risen six-fold, from the fifty-five of 1974 to more than 350. If history tells us anything, it is just a matter of time until this booming tribal population will be torn by dissension over just who is a Pequot and entitled to share in the bonanza.

Indian identity remains a serious question for several constituencies. From the standpoint of the acknowledged tribes, there hopefully will come a time when no new tribes will be recognized. Otherwise, assuming that the U.S. Treasury is not bottomless, the size of the slices of the federal pie must shrink as more share it. Many taxpayers also would subscribe to the view that the time must come when no more individuals or groups will be given federal recognition and access to the federal trough. Moreover, as Ron Andrade pointed out, tribal members have to be concerned that continuing to admit new members to tribes can result in dilution of the cultural heritage. But can we ignore the desires of the individuals and tribes seeking acknowledgment of their Indianness? At stake for these people is a recognition which is important to them for psychological as well as economic reasons. Clearly, Indian identity is a complex and persisting problem. It has been a serious issue for Indians and the federal government for over 150 years and shows every indication of being around for many more.

25

INDIANS IN THE
POST-TERMINATION ERA

ROGER L. NICHOLS

*In the happy glow of victory after World War II American officials began talking of
freeing the Indians as the United States armed forces had freed other peoples around
the world. For Native Americans this supposed freedom came in a package labeled*
termination *and consisted of an end to federal services and responsibilities to the
tribes unfortunate enough to be chosen to receive the new policy. By 1960 this effort
had failed, and the government turned its attention to other ways of dealing with
the tribes. During the 1970s and 1980s the Indian experience proved eventful,
exciting, fruitful, and frustrating all at the same time. New federal programs, court
decisions, and administrative actions have combined to improve the lives and status
of some Indians. Native American leaders and the officers of pan-Indian
organizations learned how to deal with the bureaucrats effectively and now often
garner millions of dollars in grants and programs. Yet those successes mask
continuing difficulties for Native Americans as individuals and groups within the
general society. As an ever decreasing number and percentage of Indians live on
reservations, the majority who have moved away continue to lose parts of their
cultural heritage. The Red Power movement and public demonstrations brought
tribal grievances to public attention, but neither Indian leaders nor the federal
government has implemented workable programs for the continuing difficulties.
This selection focuses on federal efforts to deal with Native Americans on such
issues as self-determination, educational reform, religious freedom, and the
acknowledgment of new tribal groups. It shows what actions have been taken and
the extent to which they have succeeded or failed.*

Roger L. Nichols is a professor of history at the University of Arizona.

During the past two decades the position and role of tribal people within the
United States has undergone major changes. Existing tribal governments exercise

Source: Roger L. Nichols, "Indians in the Post-Termination Era," *Storia Northamericana*, 5, no.1
(1988), pp. 71–87. Reprinted with permission of the publisher.

more direct and a wider variety of authority than at any other time in this century. Indian leaders and multitribal organizations know how to attract publicity and favorable media attention, as they so quickly demonstrated during President Ronald Reagan's June 1988 visit to the Soviet Union. In his press conference there the President said "maybe we made a mistake" by allowing the tribes to retain their cultures. "Maybe we should not have humored them in that, wanting to stay in that primitive lifestyle." His remarks brought immediate demands for public apologies and an embarrassed response from the administration. In addition to their increased skills at gaining publicity for their ideas, tribal leaders now direct or control some federally funded programs on the reservations, and Indians, in fact, largely staff the ever hated Bureau of Indian Affairs. A casual glance at the contemporary situation, then, might suggest that Indians now enjoy relative well-being within the political, economic, or social spheres of American life, but that is not yet the case.

Nevertheless, there have been significant changes and improvements in the status of Indians in American society. These resulted from many factors, some of which affected other minority groups as well. During the late 1960s and into the 1970s new federal laws, court decisions, and administrative policy changes within the government provided new or expanded opportunities for tribes and for individual Indians as well. The cumulative effect of the social reforms within American society regarding civil rights, equal treatment for all citizens, and a growing awareness that American society included a host of ethnic groups altered perceptions of Native Americans and allowed them opportunities not often available decades earlier. Tribal leaders gained increased experience at dealing with federal bureaucrats and sharpened their skills as administrators. All of these trends combined to help tribal people develop an increased awareness of their position within the general society, a stronger sense of cultural pride in Indianness, and, for some, heightened awareness of their local tribal cultural, linguistic, and religious identity.

Despite such achievements for both tribes and individuals, long-term difficulties and unresolved issues continue to plague the dealings of Indians with the rest of American society. These need to be seen in the context of some frequent and basic changes sweeping through Indian communities by the 1980s. For at least the past decade a majority of all Indian people lived off the reservations, many of them in the major urban centers of the country. As a result, regardless of how well a tribe does, it now increasingly speaks for an ever shrinking portion of the total Indian population, and because most government policies still focus on tribal units rather than on individuals, many of the new trends and programs virtually ignore the majority of Native Americans.

From the days of George Washington down to 1970, basic American policy was to destroy Indians as an identifiable ethnic and cultural group. Warfare, removal, reservations, education, and a host of other efforts combined to encourage tribal people to give up their communal, village and family-oriented culture and adopt the more individualistic approach of the majority within American society. True, during the 1930s John Collier's so-called Indian New Deal had made an effort to encourage tribal survival, but that program disappeared by the 1950s, when the hated termination policy held sway. That effort had as its goal to end any special link between the federal government and the particular tribes to be terminated. It brought immediate and continuing objections from many Indian groups, but nevertheless throughout the 1960s it continued in force. In 1970 President Richard M. Nixon sent a special message to Congress in which he denounced termination, called for Indian self-determination, and presented a list of enlightened proposals to Congress.

The new approach being called for by the President echoed earlier demands being made by tribal people themselves. Vine Deloria, Jr., for example, noted that "termination is used as a weapon against the Indian people in a modern war of conquest," and he demanded a new policy. Gradually Indians asked for more local tribal control over their lives and reservations than the government had allowed them to exercise in the past. Self-determination became a popular rallying cry, but it in turn soon gave way to demands for tribal sovereignty—for nearly complete freedom of action on the reservations. The present relationship between Native Americans and the rest of society resulted from the joining of such powerful streams as the move for self-determination and then tribal sovereignty on the Indian side and the veritable avalanche of legislation and favorable court decisions during the past two decades by the federal government. One other significant thread in this evolving pattern was a conscious effort by tribal chiefs and other Indian leaders to obtain rights lost or ignored throughout much of American history. This included an effort to strengthen tribal or general Indian cultural identity as well as actions leading to the reconstituting of tribes long thought to have been extinct or who had never received federal recognition in the first place. The contemporary situation, then, includes shifting federal actions that allow the tribes more responsibility for their own welfare, Indian efforts to expand their rights, their continuing fears that too much freedom for the tribes is little more than a disguised return to the discredited termination of the 1960s, and the long-term struggle to gain or regain federal recognition for groups that have been considered marginal in the general society.

Most scholars agree that by the early 1970s the cumulative impact of the civil rights movement of the preceding decade, the Black Power movement, and a rising consciousness among Indians led to the so-called Red Power activities that occurred during President Nixon's term in office. Books by the articulate and caustic Vine Deloria, Jr., expressed the pent-up frustrations of a new generation of educated Indians unhappy with the existing situation and seeking to strike out at the entire society to bring about basic changes in American life. What these writings did was to keep Indian-related issues in the public eye at a time when fundamental social changes occurred throughout American society. Such writings also helped explain the motivations of young Indians who sought to gain national attention with tactics that included the occupation of Alcatraz Island in the San Francisco Bay after the government closed its famed prison there and the brief takeover of the *Mayflower II* on the New England coast. These actions and others, such as the Trail of Broken Treaties and the occupation of the village of Wounded Knee, South Dakota, some months later, all demonstrated graphically Indian demands for changes in their relationship with the United States government.

Increasing public awareness and sensitivity to issues related to ethnic groups may be seen in the startling shift of the federal government in its dealings with tribal people. Only a few months after President Nixon announced the termination policy dead, his administration followed that declaration with specific and favorable actions toward Indians. In 1970 the administration agreed to return Blue Lake and the immediately surrounding lands to the people of Taos Pueblo in northern New Mexico. The dispute over the lake, which the Indians considered sacred, dated back to 1906, when the government had incorporated it in the Carson National Forest, and its return to the Indians seemed to mark a new sensitivity to tribal feelings.

The Alaska Native Claims Settlement of the next year, 1971, also illustrates the acceptance of rights held by Indians and other native people that went far beyond anything the government had considered prior to that time. The rush to exploit the rich natural resources of Alaska by the middle of the twentieth century, particularly once Alaska gained statehood in 1959, brought matters there to a head. By the late 1960s state officials, the major oil companies, and the federal government decided that the claims of Indians, Eskimos or Inuits, and Aleuts needed to be settled. As a result, after lengthy congressional hearings in 1971 the Alaska Natives Claims Settlement Act became law. More complex than most legislation affecting native people, this measure represented a clear victory for the tribes in their dealings with the government.

As the decade of the 1970s proceeded, the federal government continued to give Indians more control over their own lives. Those who wanted to get the government out of the business of administering expensive and apparently unending services to the tribes joined forces with others who thought that continuing governmental supervision could only result in a sort of smothering dependency among tribal peoples. This collaboration helped produce substantial legislation in such areas as education, housing, law enforcement, and even religious freedom. Certainly any effort to grant a larger degree of personal freedom to Indians stood in direct contrast to the regulations and actions taken by federal bureaucrats for an entire century as they strove to destroy tribal cultural ideas and practices.

For purposes of this discussion, federal actions aimed at increased tribal self-determination, educational reform, and religious freedom seem most significant. A scathing 1969 report on Indian education by the Senate Special Subcommittee on Indian Education started the changes. Evidence in the report suggested that in some ways few effective changes had occurred in Indian education since the famous but then forty-one-year-old *Meriam Report*. In the early 1970s Congress passed new legislation that called for the appointment of Indian people to serve on advisory boards for local schools. In addition, it provided for new special grants to improve Bureau of Indian Affairs schools as well as public schools serving large numbers of reservation children. A departure included establishing a National Advisory Council on Indian Education, consisting of Indians and Alaska Natives to be appointed by the President. Of more direct importance, however, was the creation of the Office of Indian Education within the Department of Health, Education, and Welfare (HEW). This meant that now two federal departments, HEW and the Interior Department, acting through the Bureau of Indian Affairs, played a role in restructuring the system of Indian education. The two federal departments turned their attention to different aspects of Indian education as the

Office of Education in HEW focused on off-reservation Indians and Alaska Natives, while the BIA continued its support of government boarding schools and reservation schools.

Indian demands that non-Indian teachers and other school employees respect tribal customs brought a new set of guidelines from the BIA. These called for the acceptance of certain native cultural expressions, such as allowing boys to wear their hair in long braids and permitting all students to wear Indian clothing as long as it did not "disrupt the educational process." The regulations also reminded school officials and employees to recognize their students' right to express their religious and cultural beliefs freely. Repeated complaints from Indian communities that neither the tribal governments nor the parents had much to say about what the schools taught the children bore fruit gradually. This may be seen in some of the provisions of the 1975 Indian Self-Determination and Educational Assistance Act. That legislation provided for advisory committees of Indian parents in communities where the local boards included a majority of non-Indians. Of more significance, in 1975 legislation allowed a tribal government to direct the complete operations of BIA schools on its particular reservation. This did not solve all of the problems of Indian education, but indicated the government's willingness to give tribal people more direct control of the educational process.

During the late 1970s Congress continued to make adjustments in federal educational plans and programs for the tribes. In fact, in the 1978 Education Amendments Act the lawmakers moved back in the direction of more federal control of education, particularly on the reservations. It reduced the tribes' powers to contract for educational services, placing the responsibility on the BIA Office of Indian Education Programs. While seeming to offer increased authority to the BIA, the new legislation also reaffirmed the authority of local Indian school boards over not just budgetary matters but both the operations and personnel at the schools. Indian higher education as it exists today resulted from federal encouragement and funding beginning in 1969. That year the Navajo Community College began its classes. Supported primarily with federal grants, the school received some $5.5 million for construction of its first buildings and its early operation cost. The Navajo college success persuaded Congress to help other tribes, and the 1978 Tribally Controlled Community College Act sought to encourage Indian higher education. As a result, for the first time a modest number of Indian adults of all ages had some opportunity to receive college or technical training on or near their reservation homes.

While Navajo Community College got off to a good start, it soon foundered because of quarrels between tribal officials and some of the non-Indian staff and faculty. After several years of controversy Dean Jackson, a respected Navajo educator, became president in 1981, and since then the college has experienced solid improvements. This particular school functioned much as most traditional residential colleges in the United States with a fixed campus and a few courses being offered in nearby communities. Because of the vast size of the Navajo Reservation and the broad dispersion of the people in 1973, tribal leaders added a branch of the school at Shiprock, New Mexico. The new center proved convenient for a large population in the northeastern corner of the reservation and so made higher education available to a larger potential number of the tribe than the single campus at Tsaile Lake, one of the more isolated parts of the reservation. By the 1980s the student body included only five percent non-Indians and only about ten percent Indians other than Navajos. Not only is this school the oldest of the Indian colleges, but it has been the most successful in terms of attracting students and offering a reasonably wide variety of courses.

Following the Navajo lead, other tribes took tentative steps to found colleges or to conclude cooperative agreements with existing colleges and universities in several Western states. During the 1970s eighteen more tribally controlled colleges came into being. Ranging from Michigan in the East to California in the West, and from Montana in the North to Arizona in the South, these schools began operations. Organized and supported by various groups of Sioux, Chippewa (Ojibwa), Mandan, Arikara, Hidatsa, Lummi, Omaha, Winnebago, Cheyenne, Blackfeet, Crow, Salish-Kootenai, Assiniboine, Hopi, Hoppa Valley, and Soboba, the new colleges served tribes with an aggregate population of nearly 220,000 people and by 1980 enrolled just under 5,000 students. Most of the schools had enrollments of under 250 students, and many of those attended only part-time. These institutions varied widely in the variety and level of courses they offered, with some being primarily vocational in nature, while others provided clearly academic classes. In either case the schools existed to meet the obvious educational needs of the reservation communities and pointed in the direction of continuing Indian movement toward the actual rather than potential self-determination.

With tribal communities moving along the road to more direct control over their educational institutions, reformers looked for other issues that might need attention. A century of close federal regulation of reservation affairs had left Indians with many curbs on their personal freedom. Religious persecution, a lack of civil rights, overt discrimination, and a sense of frustration and powerlessness had led to the 1960s Red Power movement. Responding to growing awareness of ethnic inequality, in 1968 Congress passed an Indian Bill of Rights and ten years later passed the American Indian Religious Freedom Act. Continuing persecution of Indians for religious and cultural actions remains a significant issue. Even within the community of tribes, differences appear. For example, during the late 1950s the Navajo Tribal Council decided to curtail peyote use on the reservation. After considerable discussion the tribal leaders banned the introduction, sale, use, or even possession of peyote in Navajo country. This brought the Tribal Council into open conflict with local affiliates of the Native American Church, who claimed that the tribal action violated their First Amendment right to freedom of religion. In this case the Indian peyote users faced their own tribal government in federal court, and to their dismay they lost. The court ruled that the United States Constitution does not apply to the Indian tribes because as "domestic dependent nations" they were considered as entities distinct from both federal and state governments. The decision indicated that the relief the peyote users sought could be obtained through congressional action, and this occurred with the passage of the 1968 Indian Civil Rights Act. That law was tied to the civil rights legislation of the late 1960s, and its goal was to protect individual Indians from misconduct by tribal or reservation officials. Usually, however, they were not the problem. Rather it was federal officials, particularly government employees, including those of the BIA, who most consistently discriminated against tribal people and undercut their basic rights. For example, federal fish and game officials rigorously enforced regulations against possessing the feathers of eagles and certain other protected species of birds. To the Indians, however, the feathers were central to their ceremonies and worship practices. When Native Americans crossed into and out of the United States traveling into Mexico or Canada, agents of the Border Patrol regularly demanded to inspect sacred medicine bundles carried or worn by Indian men.

In response to repeated complaints over such matters, Congress passed the 1978 American Indian Religious Freedom Act to prohibit such tampering with Native American religious practices, at least in theory. The legislation made little impact on this issue or on the negative practices for several reasons. One was that often the federal government itself proved to be the biggest violator, and federal officials did not cease their intrusive practices. Of more significance, however, was the fact that the law was little more than a pious statement. It provided no enforcement machinery. Instead it called on the President to direct federal agencies to examine their activities "to determine the appropriate changes necessary to protect and preserve Native American religious cultural rights and practices." Once each agency completed its survey, it was to report its findings and proposed suggestions for new congressional legislation. The following year (1979) the Department of the Interior issued the *American Indian Religious Freedom Act Report*. This document listed the areas of major dispute, involving such things as land and religious sites, cemeteries, sacred objects, museums, and religious ceremonies. In addition to this compilation the *Report* included pages of suggested legislative changes. Unfortunately, few federal officials or agencies paid much attention, so few changes occurred. In fact, when Indian spokesmen called for civil rights hearings in 1982, Congress failed to respond.

Nevertheless, the issue remains a major point of contention between tribal people and the federal and state governments to the present. For example, as recently as 1986 the United States Supreme Court ruled that despite the use of eagle feathers in certain Indian religious ceremonies, Native Americans' rights to obtain or possess such feathers did, in fact, fall under close federal regulation. The court ruled that congressional legislation protecting eagles demonstrated its desire to abrogate past treaty rights of some tribes to hunt the birds. This restriction of Indians' ability to get or possess eagle feathers strikes at the heart of several time-honored ceremonies of a number of tribes, so clearly earlier federal legislative actions have not resolved this issue to the satisfaction of the Indians.

The dispute over the use of hallucinogenic peyote fruit, or buttons, in the rituals of the Native American Church has stirred conflict throughout the twentieth century, and to date the use of this drug has not been fully accepted. Despite apparent legalization of peyote use resulting from the 1978 American Indian Religious Freedom Act, some users were still harassed under the 1965 Drug Control Act, which included peyote on its list of prohibited narcotic substances. Several state legislatures have moved against peyote users, chiefly because of the drug scare during the 1960s, and those efforts have had a long-lasting effect. In Texas, for example, legislation limits the possession of the drug to people of at least one-quarter Indian blood who can prove their active membership in the Native American Church. This law and recent moves by the Native American Church, North America to limit membership to Indians complicates the issue of peyote use. The most recent authoritative study of peyote religious practices suggests that most users are not formal members of the NAC of NA, and many accept into their ceremonies whites who accept the local teachings.

Another issue related to religious and cultural practices is the demand that Indian burial remains, whether skeletal or artifacts, must be returned to the tribes. These demands received widespread attention after 1978, when the Native American Rights Fund and the American Indian Law Center joined forces with the fifteen-member Native American Religious Advisory Board to gather data from traditional leaders among the tribes. They presented their findings to the President and Congress, but little specific action resulted. Nevertheless, the data gathered informed individual Indians and tribal governments of the magnitude of the problem, and certainly during the 1980s the issue has not been settled. In fact, in 1987 the *Legal Review*, a publication of the Native American Rights Fund, focused its main article on federal burial policy. Contrasting the reverential treatment and reburial of physical remains of a British soldier who died near Philadelphia during the American Revolution with treatment accorded the remains of Indian dead, the article castigated government policy and the selfish attitudes of archaeologists and museum curators for their cavalier treatment of Indian remains.

The author traces actions toward Indian dead as based on the 1906 idea that the federal government "owned" the unearthed bones and artifacts, and denounced subsequent laws for perpetuating this idea. He attacks guidelines used by several federal departments because the agencies routinely interpret them as calling for placing a higher educational and scientific value on cultural sites and human remains than religious or cultural values. Thus, a frequent interpretation of the guidelines is that they prohibit reburial of Indian skeletons , but rather call for careful storage of such items in qualified institutions. This usually has meant university or public museums and historical societies. Calling the guidelines a cruel joke because they specify that the collections of such materials are supposed to be maintained "with the dignity and respect to be accorded all human remains," the report's author asked for an example of another ethnic group in the country that had the graves of its dead treated in a similar fashion.

Not all is lost on this issue, however, as museums and tribal representatives continue to discuss the matter. In fact, the item just cited concludes with the news that federal policies do seem to be changing, if only gradually. Several regional offices of the United States Forest Service have developed a new policy draft on the treatment of human remains that differs sharply with the long-standing Interior Department regulations. The draft calls for rapid reburial of human remains, but continues to accept the assumption that the federal government, not the tribes, holds ownership of these items. Even Robert McC. Adams, the present Secretary of the Smithsonian Institution, commented on this issue within the past year, when he wrote that museum curators, anthropologists, and archaeologists "have an obligation to return the Indian skeletal remains in our collections to tribal descendants." Nevertheless, as Indians continue to point out, this only refers to particular skeletons that have been identified as belonging to the ancestors of individual Indians living today. Under this call there is no perceived need to return such items to the particular tribes from which they were taken. Clearly this issue will continue to excite and anger Indian rights groups while educational and scientific institutions will be under heavy pressure to empty their collections of bones and skeletons for reburial.

In addition to religious freedom, voting privileges remain a continuing source of friction between Indians and the rest of society. Despite receiving full citizenship in 1924, reservation dwellers in particular encounter frequent discrimination over both registration and actual voting in state and local elections. Responding to tribal complaints about such problems, in 1968 Congress passed the American Indian Civil Rights Act, a law aimed at correcting future abuses. Lax enforcement and a waning of public support for social reform meant that Indian complaints received little attention. Continuing pressure from tribal leaders, however, persuaded Congress that further action was needed, and in 1975 an amendment to the Voting Rights Act called for registration facilities to be made available in Indian communities and on reservations. It calls for bilingual registration materials and personnel in areas where minority people—Indians and others—are unable to complete the required paperwork in English.

By the 1970s and 1980s Indian people became increasingly active in securing their rights, much to the dismay of local non-Indian politicians and many other citizens. As the numbers of registered Indians increased, so did a variety of moves to dilute the voting power of tribal people. At least one state, Arizona, considered establishing new counties, limited almost entirely to regions inhabited by Indians. In Montana, on the other hand, using countywide elections rather than the more common districtwide elections meant that Native Americans rarely had a major impact on the results. Occasionally, however, Indian voters strongly supported a single group of candidates, as in a 1982 primary election campaign in Big Horn County, Montana. There the slate tribal people supported gained control of the Democratic party and their victory brought forth an immediate opposition group, the Bipartisan Campaign Committee, that campaigned vigorously against the Indian candidates. The Indian-backed candidates won, but not without engendering strong anti-Indian feelings among a large portion of the voting public in the county.

These harsh, even racist feelings existed for generations and perhaps may be summarized by a 1979 letter written to one of the members of the United States Senate Committee on Indian Affairs. In it one of the Sanders County, Montana Board of Commissioners wrote to Senator John Melcher to complain of special treatment for the tribal people. He suggested that the federal government do away with all Western reservations because the government had "been taking care of RED MEN long enough" and had done an injustice to the Indians by "giving them everything." The letter did not complain about voting rights but about perceived unequal treatment, with the reservation people being seen as treated more favorably than the general population in the West. As he concluded his letter, the disgruntled county official asked rhetorically, "if it was not for the dumb white man paying taxes to take care of them [the Indians] what would they do?" The implication seems clear—Indians were less competent than other Americans, and they needed special help to survive.

The opinion that Indians were getting special treatment, something more than they deserved, remains strong in American public opinion. A 1986 incident in Arizona provides some insight into how widespread anti-Indian feelings continue to be in the American West. In January 1986 the Mobil Oil Corporation announced that it had removed the Custom Clearing Services Company from its list of potential subcontractors eligible to do contract work on the Navajo Reservation for Mobil. The stated reason for this action was a letter from Ronald Vertrees, president of Custom Clearing Services, in which Mr. Vertrees objected to a Navajo requirement that tribal members be given preference for jobs being done on the reservation by outside companies. Writing to the Office of Navajo Labor Relations, he said, "We hereby inform you that we do not recognize the legal existence of the so-called Navajo Preference in Employment Act of 1985 or any other part of the so-called Navajo Tribal Code." Characterizing the Indians as "members of the vanquished and inferior race," Vertrees refused to comply with the established tribal regulations. If a corporate executive can express such sentiments in his correspondence with tribal officials and with officers of a major corporation such as Mobil, this would seem to indicate the widespread nature of anti-Indian ideas and feelings still existing.

Such ideas and actions have not been limited to the western portions of the country, either, as recent scholarship has indicated. In New England and parts of the Southeast, tribal groups have struggled with discrimination for generations. In fact, the pervasiveness of anti-Indian attitudes throughout those regions caused native peoples to withdraw from all but the most basic contacts with the white population. The result of that action was that often the general population forgot that they had Indian neighbors, as tribal identity dimmed and in some cases disappeared. Then, to the surprise of many, during the ethnic and cultural awakening taking place during the 1960s and 1970s, these long-forgotten people appeared, claiming to be Indians. Even the scholarly community raised some doubts about the validity of claims to tribal identity and labeled such groups as tri-racial isolates. In regions where substantial numbers of blacks lived, tribal people struggled to avoid being classed as people of color. In their efforts to maintain a distinct cultural identity some tribal people resorted to funding their own schools so that their children would not have to attend racially segregated schools with blacks in the South. Even as far north as Long Island, New York, such people had some trouble maintaining their cultural identity. For example, the Poospatuck of Long Island outwardly resemble American blacks more than Indians, and while they have retained a presence in their ancestral homeland, the Poospatuck themselves are not entirely certain just who is and who is not a tribal member. The result is that although these people retain a slight Indian identity because of their long-time residence and their cultural survivals, to outsiders they appear most often as blacks rather than Native Americans.

There are many reasons why particular Indian groups lost their tribal identity, at least as far as the rest of American society was concerned. Of major significance, however, is the fact that despite the legal significance of tribal status, the federal government never established any clear definition of what constitutes a tribe. Indian groups include a broad range of size, degree of acculturation, and political and social organization, and these variants made it difficult, if not impossible, for bureaucrats to define a tribal unit. Not only have tribes had no recognized definition beyond the fact that they had dealt with the government in the past, but neither the government nor even the tribes themselves had an always agreed-on definition of what it took for an individual American citizen to be considered legally as an Indian.

In 1971 President Nixon repeated the long-standing view that the federal government had no responsibility for nonrecognized tribes. This being the case, such groups had no claim for help through the existing system. Only a year later, however, a federal Court of Appeals ruled otherwise. That year the Passamaquoddy Indians of Maine sued the United States, hoping to force the federal government to side with them in a legal action against the State of Maine seeking compensation for a 1794 loss of some twelve million acres of land that the Indians claimed had been illegal at the time. The Department of the Interior declined to support the Passamaquoddy because those people had no existing treaties with the government, and it told the Indians to seek redress from the State of Maine, not the federal authorities. Despite this stand, in 1972 the Court of Appeals decided against the Interior Department and in favor of the Indians by noting that "the absence of specific federal recognition in and of itself provides little basis for concluding that the Passamaquoddies are not a 'tribe' within the Act." This allowed the Indians to continue their suit against Maine, now with federal support, and in 1980, after repeated negotiations among the three parties, President Carter signed the final settlement agreement.

For the Passamaquoddy the legal victory brought funds for a land base and eligibility for existing federal programs. More importantly, however, the precedent set in this case opened the door to further gains by other Native American groups. When later court decisions ruled that the Department of the Interior had to respond within a month to tribal petitions seeking legal recognition, a new day dawned in federal-Indian relations. Despite BIA reluctance to initiate numerous hearings and to expand its authority to deal with formerly unrecognized tribes, there was no stopping the tide of change then underway. In an extended 1976 report, the American Indian Policy Review Commission focused new attention on the plight of the more than one hundred groups of Indians that still lacked official tribal recognition by the federal government. This report, coupled with the court decisions mentioned, prodded the bureaucrats into reluctant action, and in 1978 the BIA started the Federal Acknowledgement Project. Once it became apparent how complicated and slow the process was likely to be and how many tribal groups would seek recognition through this process, the government changed the project into the Branch of Acknowledgement and Research within the BIA. This federal office now deals with the ongoing process of dealing with Indian groups and is to receive, evaluate, and either accept or reject claims for tribal status from those who now lack such recognition by the government.

The prospect of gaining formal status as a tribe was not entirely new, because between the 1934 passage of the Indian Reorganization Act and World War II at least twenty-one tribes had achieved such a position through either legislative enactment or executive decision. A few others achieved the same end through private legislation prior to or despite the 1978 establishment of the present acknowledgment program. For example, in 1980 the Houlton Band of Maliseets in Maine, a group numbering only 350 people, received legislative recognition as a tribe. That gave them a chance to share in the Maine Indian Land Claim and provided the newly reconstituted tribe with nearly a million dollars. This money enabled them to buy some land and through that to reestablish their tribal presence in the state. Probably of more long-range significance, however, is the fact that with tribal status came eligibility for services and federal contracts with both the BIA and the Indian Health Service. With their new funds and the availability of existing federal services, the Maliseets gained both legal status and economic opportunities never before open to them.

Clearly, whether through congressional action or the 1978 acknowledgment actions of the BIA, the chance to acquire formal tribal status is one that few Indians want to miss. During the first ten years of the acknowledgment program 111 separate groups have filed applications for federal acknowledgment or are in the process of doing so. This widespread interest and action by the Indians clearly exceeded the expectations of the bureaucrats, and thus far the acknowledgment process has moved at a snail's pace. The agonizing slowness in being able to complete the acknowledgment process has resulted almost entirely from the nature of the process and the data each Indian group is required to provide as a part of its case. The 1978 regulations include a list of seven criteria, all of which must be satisfied, for tribal recognition. These are evidence that the group:

1. had been identified continuously as American Indian or aboriginal;
2. lived in a specific area or in a community viewed as American Indian, and that its members descended from a tribe that historically inhabited a particular area;
3. had maintained a tribal influence or authority over its members throughout its history and to the present;
4. had provided a written governing document or a statement of membership criteria and present governing procedures;
5. had provided a list of all known current members who could provide evidence of having descended from historically identified tribes or combinations of tribes;
6. was composed of a majority not members of other North American tribes;
7. and its members have not been terminated by federal law.

The creation of the Federal Acknowledgement Project brought temporary excitement to many Indian groups hoping to gain tribal status, but its potential far outstripped its results, at least in the last ten years. Few of the groups seeking recognition have strong local organizations or the funds needed to gather the necessary documents to support their claims. They lack the research skills to present a case proving their continuous status as Indians, and rarely do they have a land base that can be readily identified as an Indian community. In fact, the very actions they took in the past to ensure their physical survival now make it difficult for them to provide the documentary evidence demanded by the government. Such problems arose almost immediately, and critics denounced the program angrily, one labeling it a "vicious myth." Despite what seem like obstacles built into the program just to deter Indian success in achieving tribal status, the process has moved ahead slowly. As of June 1988 the Acknowledgement Office reported that it had 111 petitions and that it had completed action on twenty-two of them. Just half of the actions resulted in an award of formal tribal status, so considerable disappointment and confusion about this program exist.

During the 1970s and 1980s, then, the face of Indian America has changed considerably. Substantial numbers of tribal people continue to leave the reservations for economic or educational opportunity more likely to be found in the major urban centers. Even for the nearly half of Native Americans still residing on the traditional reservations the changes have been varied and nearly continuous. A renewed cultural pride infused many tribes and reservation groups as they strove to obtain their civil rights, as well as control of local reservation education, economic, and political affairs. These changes have not benefited all Indian groups evenly or come without continuing or even new difficulties. Even when federal courts rule in their favor or Congress provides funds to carry out negotiated agreements, the tribes do not always get the money, land, or other rights without a struggle or frequent delays. For example, the Mashantucket Pequot Tribe in Connecticut were to have received some $900,000 in order to buy a plot of 800 acres on what had once been their reservation. When the spending bill reached the desk of President Reagan, he vetoed it despite the unanimous approval of both houses of Congress. He defended the action by saying that the land was too expensive and that the State of Connecticut should have contributed a larger share of land and funds. Thus, while nearly everyone agrees that these Indians should receive the money, events totally beyond their control prevented this from happening.

Despite the difficulties some tribes encountered, the past two decades have permanently altered the relationships between tribal people and the United States government. New laws and a continuing series of favorable federal court decisions clearly have improved the Indian situation within the general society. Tribal leaders now know how to apply for the federal grants they see as necessary for continued economic and educational progress on the reservations. Increasingly, young Indians turn to higher education to acquire the skills and certification needed to become lawyers, physicians, and engineers. Whether they return to the reservations or not, their success helps smooth the way for another generation of students. The existence of Indian-operated colleges and reservation school systems insures tribal supervision and participation in the education of their children. Yet these trends should not obscure the continuing difficulties Indians encounter. In fact, as recently as February 1989 the Select Committee on Indian Affairs of the United States Senate reported that the testimony they had heard in their current investigation of Indian affairs "raises significant concerns about whether the federal government is adequately" protecting tribal "rights to land, water, forest, hunting, fishing, and mineral resources." Thus, while the changes of the past two decades have created a more favorable situation for American Indians than they have experienced at any time during the past century, long-term issues remain unsettled.

READINGS

For people with even a casual interest in American Indians, this selection of readings is only a tiny part of the vast literature on the subject. To get a fuller understanding of any of the topics included here, the reader should check the original edition of each article and examine the footnotes or other bibliographical material. In addition, the following books are recommended as good places to get further information about the people, ideas, and events discussed in the readings. The books are listed under the authors whose articles they supplement. All titles currently available in paperback editions are indicated with an asterisk (*).

James Axtell, "Colonial America Without the Indians: Counterfactual Reflections," and Alfred W. Crosby, Jr., "Virgin Soil Epidemics as a Factor in the Aboriginal Depopulation in America."

For general ideas about Indians in colonial America, see James Axtell, *The European and the Indian: Essays in the Ethnohistory of Colonial North America** (New York: Oxford University Press, 1981). The best study of smallpox and the Indians is E. Wagner Stern and Allen E. Stern, *The Effects of Smallpox on the Destiny of the Amerindian* (Boston: B. Humphries, 1945). For a look at disease in the Western Hemisphere, see Alfred W. Crosby, Jr., *The Columbian Exchange: Biological and Cultural Consequences of 1492* (Westport, Conn.: Greenwood Press, 1972), and Henry F. Dobyns and William R. Swaggerty, *Their Numbers Become Thinned: Population Dynamics in Eastern North America* (Knoxville: University of Tennessee Press, 1983).

J. Frederick Fausz, "Opechancanough: Indian Resistance Leader."

Helen C. Rountree, *The Powhatan Indians of Virginia: Their Traditional Culture* (Norman: University of Oklahoma Press, 1989), and Peter H. Wood, Gregory A. Waselkov, and M. Thomas Hatley, eds., *Powhatan's Mantle: Indians in the Colonial Southeast* (Lincoln: University of Nebraska Press, 1989) offer the most recent data on the Virginia tribes. For a more general discussion, see James Axtell, *The Invasion Within: The Contest of Cultures in Colonial North America* (New York: Oxford University Press, 1986).

302

Lyle Koehler, "Red-White Power Relations and Justice in the Courts of Seventeenth-Century New England."

Neal Salisbury, *Manitou and Providence: Indians, Europeans, and the Making of New England, 1500–1643*★ (New York: Oxford University Press, 1982) deals with the issues of power and control. See also Francis Jennings, *The Invasion of America: Indians, Colonialism, and the Cant of Conquest*★ (Chapel Hill: University of North Carolina Press, 1975). When using Jennings, be aware of his forceful anti-Puritan bias. Alden T. Vaughan, *The New England Frontier: Puritans and Indians, 1620–1675*★, rev. ed. (New York: W. W. Norton, 1979) may be too easy on the Puritans.

James P. Ronda, "The Sillery Experiment: A Jesuit-Indian Village in New France, 1637–1663."

Bruce G. Trigger, *Natives and Newcomers: Canada's "Heroic Age" Reconsidered* (Kingston, Ontario: McGill-Queen's University Press, 1985); and James Axtell, *The Invasion Within: The Contest of Cultures in Colonial North America*★ (New York: Oxford University Press, 1985) are both good as background for the issues raised by this author.

James H. Merrell, "The Indians' New World: The Catawba Experience."

In his recent book *The Indians' New World: Catawbas and Their Neighbors from European Contact through the Era of Removal* (Chapel Hill: University of North Carolina Press, 1989), James H. Merrell gives an extended discussion of issues raised in this essay. Richard White, *The Roots of Dependency: Subsistence, Environment, and Social Change among the Choctaws, Pawnees, and Navajos*★ (Lincoln: University of Nebraska Press, 1983) considers similar issues.

Margaret Connell Szasz, " 'Poor Richard' Meets the Native American: Schooling for Young Indian Women in Eighteenth-Century Connecticut."

Margaret Connell Szasz, *Indian Education in the American Colonies, 1607–1783* (Albuquerque: University of New Mexico Press, 1988) considers education in a wider context. For general discussion of missionary and educational efforts among the tribes, see Henry Warner Bowden, *American Indians and Christians: Studies in Cultural Conflict* (Chicago: University of Chicago Press, 1981) and Henry W. Bowden and James P. Ronda, eds., *John Eliot's Indian Dialogues: A Study in Cultural Interaction* (Westport, Conn.: Greenwood Press, 1980).

Peter C. Mancall, "The Revolutionary War and the Indians of the Upper Susquehanna Valley."

Virtually nothing exists in book length that considers the Indian experience during the American Revolution. Even most histories of the war itself make only passing references to Native Americans. For some data, see Jack M. Sosin, *The Revolutionary Frontier, 1763–1783*★ (New York: Holt, Rinehart and Winston, 1967) offers some data. William Cronon, *Changes in the Land: Indians, Colonists, and the Ecology of New England*★ (New York: Hill and Wang, 1983) and Christopher Vecsey and Robert Venables, eds., *American Indian Environments: Ecological*

Issues in Native American History (Syracuse: Syracuse University Press, 1980) both deal with changing tribal environments, although not during the Revolution.

Mary C. Wright, "Economic Development and Native American Women in the Early Nineteenth Century."
Historians have written little about the tribes of the Pacific Northwest, although the fur trade continues to attract attention. For general treatments of women and interracial contacts, see Mona Etienne and Eleanor Leacock, eds., *Women and Colonization: Anthropological Perspectives* (New York: Praeger, 1980), Jennifer S. H. Brown, *Strangers in Blood: Fur Trade Families in Indian Country* (Vancouver: University of British Columbia Press, 1980), and Sylvia Van Kirk, *"Many Tender Ties": Women in Fur-Trade Society in Western Canada, 1670–1870* (Norman: University of Oklahoma Press, 1980).

John Sugden, "Early Pan-Indianism: Tecumseh's Tour of the Indian Country, 1811–1812."
Most work on pan-Indian movements considers the issue from the late nineteenth century to the present, but good work on some significant leaders of the earlier era may be found in R. David Edmunds, *The Shawnee Prophet* (Lincoln: University of Nebraska Press, 1983), R. David Edmunds, *Tecumseh and the Quest for Indian Leadership*★ (Boston: Little, Brown, 1984), and Anthony F. C. Wallace, *The Death and Rebirth of the Seneca* (New York: Knopf, 1970).

Roger L. Nichols, "Backdrop for Disaster: Causes of the Arikara War of 1823."
The Arikara story is told best in Roy W. Meyer, *The Village Indians of the Upper Missouri*★ (Lincoln: University of Nebraska Press, 1977). For the role of the fur traders in this incident, see Richard M. Clokey, *William H. Ashley: Enterprise and Politics in the Trans-Mississippi West* (Norman: University of Oklahoma Press, 1980).

Jeanne Kay, "Native Americans in the Fur Trade and Wildlife Depletion."
Christopher Vecsey and Robert Venables, eds., *American Indian Environments: Ecological Issues in Native American History* (Syracuse: Syracuse University Press, 1980), Gary C. Goodwin, *Cherokees in Transition: A Study in Changing Culture and Environment Prior to 1775* (Chicago: University of Chicago, Department of Geography, 1977), and Robert F. Heizer and Albert B. Elsasser, *The Natural World of the California Indians* (Berkeley and Los Angeles: University of California Press, 1980) all provide general studies of this issue.

Theda Perdue, "Cherokee Women and the Trail of Tears."
In her larger study, Theda Perdue, *Slavery and the Evolution of Cherokee Society, 1540–1866* (Knoxville: University of Tennessee Press, 1979) deals with aboriginal gender roles in some detail. See also William G. McLoughlin, *Cherokee Renascence in the New Republic* (Princeton: Princeton University Press, 1986).

George Harwood Phillips, "Indians in Los Angeles, 1781–1875: Economic Integration, Social Disintegration."

The author has two books that consider the issues raised in this reading: *Chiefs and Challengers: Indian Resistance and Cooperation in Southern California* (Berkeley and Los Angeles: University of California Press, 1975) and *The Enduring Struggle: Indians in California History*★ (San Francisco: Boyd & Fraser, 1981). See also Albert T. Hurtado, *Indian Survival on the California Frontier* (New Haven: Yale University Press, 1988).

Richard White, "Indian Land Use and Environmental Change in Island County, Washington: A Case Study."

The same author deals with these issues at length in *Land Use, Environment, and Social Change: The Shaping of Island County, Washington* (Seattle: University of Washington Press, 1980) and *Roots of Dependency: Subsistence, Environment, and Social Change among the Choctaws, Pawnees, and Navajos* (Lincoln: University of Nebraska Press, 1983).

Katherine Marie Birmingham Osburn, "The Navajo at the Bosque Redondo: Cooperation, Resistance, and Initiative, 1864–1868."

The most complete discussion of this topic is Gerald Thompson, *The Army and the Navajo: The Bosque Redondo Reservation Experiment 1863–1868*★ (Tucson: University of Arizona Press, 1976). See also Peter Iverson, *The Navajo Nation* (Westport, Conn.: Greenwood Press, 1981) and Donald J. Berthrong, *The Cheyenne and Arapaho Ordeal: Reservation and Agency Life in the Indian Territory, 1875–1907* (Norman: University of Oklahoma Press, 1976).

John L. Tobias, "Canada's Subjugation of the Plains Cree, 1879–1885."

Most Canadian scholarship on this topic remains in article form. The best books are George F. G. Stanley, *The Birth of Western Canada: A History of the Riel Rebellions*, 2nd ed. (Toronto: University of Toronto Press, 1960); and Hugh A. Dempsey, *Big Bear: The End of Freedom*★ (Lincoln: University of Nebraska Press, 1986).

Frederick E. Hoxie, "From Prison to Homeland: The Cheyenne River Indian Reservation Before World War I."

The author gives a fuller discussion of this topic in *A Final Promise: The Campaign to Assimilate the Indians, 1880–1920*★ (Lincoln: University of Nebraska Press, 1984). For the experience of another tribe during the same era, see William T. Hagan, *United States–Comanche Relations: The Reservation Years* (New Haven: Yale University Press, 1976).

Nancy Shoemaker, "Urban Indians and Ethnic Choices: American Indian Organizations in Minneapolis, 1920–1950" and Peter Iverson, "Building Toward Self-Determination: Plains and Southwestern Indians in the 1940s and 1950s."

An early study of pan-Indian movements is Hazel W. Hertzberg, *The Search for an American Indian Identity: Modern Pan-Indian Movements* (Syracuse: Syracuse University Press, 1971). See also Loretta Fowler, *Arapahoe Politics, 1851–1978: Symbols in Crises of Authority* (Lincoln: University of Nebraska Press, 1982).

Donald Parman, "Inconstant Advocacy: The Erosion of Indian Fishing Rights in the Pacific Northwest, 1933–1956."
    Robert Doherty, *Disputed Waters: Native Americans and the Great Lakes Fishery* (Lexington: University Press of Kentucky, 1990) examines fishing disputes in the Midwest. Discussions of other tribes and resources include Michael Lawson, *Damned Indians: The Pick-Sloan Plan and the Missouri River Sioux, 1944–1980* (Norman: University of Oklahoma Press, 1982) and Jerry Kammer, *The Second Long Walk: The Navajo-Hopi Land Dispute* (Albuquerque: University of New Mexico Press, 1980).

Arthur Margon, "Indians and Immigrants: A Comparison of Groups New to the City."
    Jack O. Waddell and O. Michael Watson, eds., *The American Indian in Urban Society* (Boston: Little, Brown, 1971) is a good starting place. For other comparisons, see Leonard Dinnerstein, Roger L. Nichols, and David M. Reimers, *Natives and Strangers: Blacks, Indians, and Immigrants in America*★, 2d ed. (New York: Oxford University Press, 1990) and Larry Krotz, *Urban Indians: The Strangers in Canada's Cities* (Edmondton, Canada: Hurtig Publishers, 1980).

Orlan J. Svingen, "Jim Crow, Indian Style."
    No books deal specifically with this issue, but for related topics see Vine Deloria, Jr., and Clifford M. Lytle, *American Indians, American Justice*★ (Austin: University of Texas Press, 1983) and Vine Deloria, Jr., *Behind the Trail of Broken Treaties: An Indian Declaration of Independence*★ (Austin: University of Texas Press, 1985). Charles F. Wilkinson, *American Indians, Time, and the Law: Native Societies in a Modern Constitutional Democracy* (New Haven: Yale University Press, 1987) addresses similar questions.

William T. Hagan, "Full Blood, Mixed Blood, Generic, and Ersatz: The Problem of Indian Identity" and Roger L. Nichols, "Indians in the Post-Termination Era."
    For a sampling of ideas about contemporary issues, see Alvin M. Josephy, Jr., *Now That the Buffalo's Gone: A Study of Today's American Indians* (New York: Knopf, 1982), Sar A. Levitan and William B. Johnson, *Indian Giving: Federal Problems for Native Americans* (Baltimore: Johns Hopkins University Press, 1975), and Phillip Reno, *Mother Earth, Father Sky, and Economic Development: Navajo Resources and their Use* (Albuquerque: University of New Mexico Press, 1981).

INDEX